# Structuring the Information Age

Studies in Industry and Society
Philip B. Scranton, Series Editor

*Published with the assistance of the Hagley Museum and Library*

Related titles in the series:

Amy Sue Bix, *Inventing Ourselves Out of Jobs?
America's Debate over Technological Unemployment, 1929–1981*

Clark Davis, *Company Men: White-Collar Life and Corporate
Cultures in Los Angeles, 1892–1941*

JoAnne Yates, *Control Through Communication: The Rise of
System in American Management*

# Structuring the Information Age

Life Insurance and Technology
in the Twentieth Century

JoAnne Yates

The Johns Hopkins University Press
Baltimore and London

The Johns Hopkins University Press
2715 North Charles Street
Baltimore, Maryland 21218-4363
www.press.jhu.edu

Library of Congress Cataloging-in-Publication Data

Yates, JoAnne, 1951–
    Structuring the information age : life insurance and
technology in the twentieth century / JoAnne Yates.
        p. cm.
Includes bibliographical references and index.
ISBN 0-8018-8086-6 (hardcover : alk. paper)
    1. Insurance, Life—United States—History. 2. Insurance,
Life—Technological innovations. 3. Information technology—
History. 4. Computers—History. I. Title.
HG8951.Y38 2005
368.32'00973—dc22        2004022319

A catalog record for this book is available from the British
Library.

# Contents

# Acknowledgments

I have been working on this book for more than a decade, slowed by my contemporary research on use of communication and information technology, family illnesses, and life in general. During this long process, I have accumulated many debts—to archivists (a historian's best friends), interviewees, student assistants, colleagues at MIT and elsewhere, and friends and family.

Let me begin with the many archivists at insurance company archives and other repositories who have aided me in my efforts, several of whom are no longer at the archives where I worked with them. The archives of two companies I studied, Metropolitan Life and New England Mutual Life (since 1996 New England Financial), originally entirely separate, are now converging. Daniel May, MetLife archivist throughout the period of my research, was very helpful in providing unfettered access to that venerable institution's records, as well as in assembling illustrations from that archive. Phyllis E. Steele, archivist at the New England Financial Archives, helped me get access to relevant documents and to Robert Shafto, then CEO of New England Mutual Life, to interview him. These archives were, sadly, closed after that firm became a wholly owned stock subsidiary of MetLife. The archival materials are now folded into the MetLife Archives. Both former New England Financial archivist Phyllis Steele, helping out of her own generosity and devotion to historical publication, and Daniel May at the MetLife Archive helped me assemble the final artwork and permissions to use material from the New England Financial Archives. I greatly appreciate the efforts both have made on my behalf.

In Hartford, Hal Keiner, who was archivist for CIGNA Corporation when I worked there, was very helpful in orienting me to the Hartford insurance community. I also thank Paul Lasewicz, Aetna archivist at the time of my research, for his help at that firm. He has now moved on to be archivist at IBM, where he recently aided me in assembling some of the artwork for the book. Frances M. Bertelli, law librarian, helped me secure the final permissions from Aetna.

I owe a great debt to the staffs at the archives and libraries that provided the bulk of the unpublished materials about tabulators and computers. The Charles Babbage Institute provided invaluable records of Edmund Berkeley when he was at Prudential. My work there in the mid-1990s was aided by Arthur Norberg, director; Bruce Bruemmer, archivist; and Kevin Corbitt, archival assistant. The Hagley Museum and Library was another source of documents about the early computer industry. Michael Nash, then archivist, was exceptionally helpful, even digging out relevant materials from uncataloged collections. My research there during the mid- to late 1990s was facilitated by director Glenn Porter; Jon Williams, head of the Pictorial Department; Marjorie McNinch, reference archivist; and Carol Lockman, coordinator of the Center for the History of Business, Technology, and Society. The staff at the Library of Congress facilitated my access to the Herman Hollerith papers there. The staff of the Insurance Library Association of Boston generously gave me access to unpublished proceedings of insurance associations. Finally, many other archivists aided me in this research through referrals and responses to queries. I thank all of them for their aid.

Several members of the insurance and computer industries during the events chronicled here consented to be interviewed and thus provided added perspective. I very much appreciate the time of the following individuals (listed with relevant association): Robert Shafto and Jim Zalinski, New England Mutual Life; Robert Volante, John Hancock Insurance Company; Malcolm MacKinnon, Prudential; Jake Stewart, CIGNA; and John Redfern and Ed Kelley, IBM.

A number of students assisted me on this project over the years. Cindy Collins, then a Wellesley student, spent weeks reading, analyzing, and cataloging relevant materials from Aetna's archival files for me. Only her incredibly meticulous organization and documentation made it possible for me to come back to those records years later to mine them for Chapter 8. Bob Hanke, an MIT doctoral student in political science at the time, was also very important to my work, accompanying me on many of the interviews and serving as a sounding board as I thought through the early stages of the project. In 1995, Tom Callahan helped me organize the voluminous materials I had gathered so I could begin writing the book. Five years later, Maya Fernandez gathered the data for the many graphs of ordinary renewal expense ratio from *Best's Insurance Reports—Life/Health* and performed various statistical tests on the data. MIT students Hans Gottfried and Howard Hecht were also able assistants in the research.

Several colleagues and friends helped me along the way. I learned about Anthony Giddens, whose structuration metatheory shaped my research process, my theoretical framework, and even my title, from MIT Sloan School of Management colleague Wanda Orlikowski, my frequent coauthor on nonhistorical studies of information technology use. I also appreciate her help in thinking through a problem that arose late in my work. Naomi Lamoreaux, at UCLA, gave me useful comments on an early paper based on this research, prompting me to assemble the data that I used for the graphs throughout the book. Throughout the writing of the manuscript, Martin Campbell-Kelly answered my questions about computer and tabulator developments and read and commented on two different chapters at different points. Alfred D. Chandler Jr. encouraged me in my work on this project. James Cortada helped me gain access to IBM archivists at several points to obtain photographs. More recently, my Sloan School colleague Pablo Boczkowski took time to read the manuscript from front to back and gave me valuable suggestions for linking it to various literatures. Sloan colleague Erik Brynjolfsson guided me to literature on, and read the book passages related to, the productivity paradox. I thank longtime friend and MIT colleague Harriet Ritvo for her support throughout the book-writing process, as well as for her comments on my introduction and conclusion.

I presented pieces of this research in various forums over the years, including the following: MIT's Center for Coordination Science; Ecole des Hautes Etudes en Science Sociales, Paris; Washington Area Economic History Seminar, Baltimore; several meetings of the Business History Conference; Hagley Museum and Library, Wilmington, Delaware; Society for the History of Technology; London School of Economics; Tulane Colloquium in Science, Technology and Society, New Orleans; meetings of the Organizational Communication and Information Systems (OCIS) division of the Academy of Management; and the Cultural Turn IV Conference on Institutions and Instituting at the University of California at Santa Barbara. I appreciate many insightful comments from members of these audiences.

I wish to thank several people who contributed to the final stages of book preparation. Series editor Phil Scranton generously spent many hours providing detailed comments throughout the manuscript to guide me in my final revisions. Likewise, I benefited from the comments of two anonymous reviewers. At the Johns Hopkins University Press, senior editor Robert J. Brugger and assistant Amy Zezula responded to my many queries and gave guidance on text and artwork preparations. I thank independent designer Todd Sullivan for his careful work, often under time pressure, in assembling artwork and converting it to the specific electronic formats required by the Hopkins Press. I also appreciate the careful copyediting of and pleasant interactions with Grace Carino.

Last, but certainly not least, I come to my most important supporter, my husband, Craig Murphy. When this book appears, we will be approaching our twenty-fifth anniversary. I have been blessed with a husband who provides intellectual, emotional, and practical support, as well as love. I could not ask for more. My deepest gratitude and love goes to Craig, without whom I could not have written this book.

# Structuring the Information Age

# Introduction

Today, we live and work in what is often called the "information age." In the popular conception, it emerged relatively recently, as a post–World War II phenomenon linked to the digital computer. Indeed, the information age and the computer age are often used synonymously. Yet the computer did not simply appear unheralded and full-blown at the war's end, magically transforming how businesses functioned. Technologies to help firms process and use information have played a central role in U.S. business from the nation's beginning clear through the twentieth century.[1] From the U.S. Postal Service to typewriters, vertical files, and adding machines, technologies and techniques of information gathering, storage, manipulation, and communication have figured prominently in the evolution of firms and business practices. Understanding how today's businesses adopt and use computers requires us first to understand how these businesses used yesterday's information technologies and with what effect. Indeed, beginning the tale with computers would necessarily ignore continuities and magnify discontinuities with use of pre-computer information technology, overlooking important lessons for today and tomorrow.

This book examines how firms in one information-intensive industry, life insurance, adopted and used technology through most of the twentieth century, beginning with the computer's immediate predecessor, tabulating technology, and continuing into the computer era and through the 1970s. It addresses several questions. Why did firms adopt various technologies when they did? How did they use them? With what consequences for the firms, the technology, and the vendors? In particular, I focus on two themes: first, how technology and its use by firms mutually shape each other through ongoing interaction over time, and second, how firms' use of pre-computer technology shaped their subsequent adoption and use of computer technology.

In studying technology from the perspective of user firms, I both follow and extend recent scholarly trends. The social constructionist perspective on technology has, since the late 1980s, examined how relevant social constituencies have shaped technology development.[2] This approach initially led to extensive research on the role of individuals and social movements. More recently, literature on the social shaping of technology has looked beyond technology *development* into its *appropriation* and *use,* demonstrating that users influence not just the technological artifact that vendors sell but also "technology-in-practice," or what users do with the technology.[3] Typically, however, those studying the social shaping of technology have focused on the "social appropriation of technologies" by *individual* consumers.[4] This literature has not examined how *firms* as users can influence and be influenced by a technology through means including and extending beyond that of market power alone.

Yet tabulators and early computers were large-scale technologies aimed at—and priced for—organizational, not individual, markets. Firms, not individual consumers, purchased information technology, in the context of considerable industry-level discourse about its nature and use. Thus I have extended the study of user shaping to the firm and industry level. Of course, individual actions, particularly those related to corporate decision making about technology acquisition and use, are still critical to my story, and where information on individual actors and actions is available, I have incorporated it. When possible, I have also attempted to illuminate how clerical workers reacted to computer acquisitions (or how managers responded to their anticipated reactions). I have not, however, attempted to look systematically at the broad occupational reconfigurations (for example, the emergence of computer programmers and operators) that occurred in the shift from pre-computer to computer technology.[5]

Business historians, historians of technology, and contemporary information technology and management scholars have concentrated, to differing extents, on firms and industries, but more often on the *vendor* than the *user* side. In some cases vendor studies seem to be extensions of traditional, inventor-oriented computer history, more interested in who achieved what first than in the interactions between vendors and users, technology and its use.[6] Other studies are concerned with competitive dynamics in the manufacturing industry.[7] When scholars studying early computerization have examined user organizations, they have typically focused either on government or on defense contractors.[8] More recently, however, some historians have become interested in commercial use of information technology.[9] Only a few such treatments have looked closely at specific user industries or companies.[10]

Focusing on a specific industry—life insurance—allows me to examine how information technology and its application shape and are shaped by users' institutional structures.[11] As part of the financial services sector, life insurance represents an immensely important segment of the economy, though one that has not received as much historical attention as its importance would warrant.[12] Moreover, it is a highly information-intensive industry—that is, one whose activity consists almost exclusively of collecting, processing, and communicating information. Throughout the twentieth century, U.S. life insurance firms have been major users of mechanical, electrical, and electronic information technologies. Indeed, insurance companies interacted directly with vendors, in the form of either individual organizations or industry associations, shaping the technological artifacts as well as the technology-in-practice.[13] Unlike banking, another information-intensive business, insurance did not require specialized hardware fitted solely to that business. As an archetypal information business, life insurance provides a particularly appropriate user industry through which to examine the structuring of the information age.

This industry study illuminates issues regarding technological innovation in general and the information economy more specifically. For example, it illustrates some mechanisms, such as trade associations, by which user firms can agree on industry needs and influence vendors to develop technology that responds to those needs. At the same time, it shows the dangers individual firms can encounter when they attempt to shape a technology only to their own needs, including overcustomizing it to the firm's processes at a particular time and thus eventually reaching a technological dead end. The study also suggests one answer to a key information age puzzle known as the "productivity paradox"—the apparent absence of any direct correlation between user spending on computer technology and realized productivity gains until the late 1990s.[14] Despite extensive interaction with computer vendors and within-industry knowledge sharing through associations, insurance firms adapted their structures and processes to take advantage of computer technology only very gradually, creating a long lag between the investment and its payoff. Eventually computers provided gains primarily through allowing new ways of organizing, rather than through simply speeding up old ways. Although the heavily regulated insurance environment may have allowed or even encouraged this industry to adapt more slowly than some others, this leisurely pace lets us view clearly the organizational hurdles faced by its firms during the extended progression.

Moreover, by beginning the study around 1900, rather than 1950, I can examine how use of pre-computer technology influenced subsequent computer adoption and application. Historians of technology have increasingly examined pre-computer information technologies—focusing particularly on punched-card tabulators but considering other business machines, as well—to shed light on more recent developments.[15] Recent histories of the computer have recognized its antecedents not just in Charles Babbage's early nineteenth-century analytical engine, which anticipated much of their logic, but also, more concretely and directly, in business machines of the late nineteenth century and early twentieth, particularly tabulators.[16] Still, very few detailed treatments have followed the transition across what is often assumed to be a great divide between pre-computer information technologies and the computer.[17]

Tracing how user firms in a single industry experienced the transition from one technology to the next can provide important insight into patterns of computer use not readily understood otherwise. Although others have noted the relationship between tabulating and computing hardware, for example, they have not focused on the continuity between specific tabulating and computing applications. The insurance industry case study, carried across this technology transition, shows us how strongly old operating methods influenced use of new technology. In the first and most influential study of potential insurance computer use, a special committee of the Society of Actuaries, as the American Society of Actuaries was renamed in 1949, recommended a computer application—the "consolidated functions approach"—that essentially extended the integration of operating processes that insurance firms were beginning to implement on tabulators in the 1940s. International Business Machines Corporation (IBM) further reinforced this approach when it created and distributed application software based on it. Thus an application that first emerged in the late tabulating era dominated insurance computing through the 1960s. Factors such as past use patterns, association recommendations, and vendor-provided application software all influenced the insurance industry's adoption and application of computers.

Such factors influence, but do not ultimately determine, insurers' adoption and application of information technology. As I have argued elsewhere, Anthony Giddens' structuration theory,[18] a sociological metatheory of human agency and social structure, can usefully inform business history and history of technology.[19] Because it has influenced my thinking and even the title of this book, it deserves a brief and necessarily incomplete synopsis here. Giddens argues that although social structures, or institutionalized patterns of behavior on any level, influence individuals' actions, these structures exist only as human agents enact them. Individuals and institutional structures have a recursive relationship that Giddens terms "the duality of structure": structures shape actions, which in turn constitute the structures, in an ongoing, contextualized process. This relationship means that "the structural properties of social systems are both medium and outcome of the practices they recursively organize."[20] This notion has been extended to technology use, which may also be viewed as a structure with its own "duality of technology."[21] Structures, whether an industry association or a particular work process in a firm, both enable and constrain, but do not determine, individual human action. Human actors can always choose to act differently, either intentionally or unintentionally, and by doing so may undercut the structures.[22] One such action by itself cannot change a well-institutionalized structure, but when other individuals repeatedly follow that lead, the structure necessarily changes. Thus an institutionalized work process is not changed simply because a top executive says so. That executive and many others throughout a specific unit and the entire firm must also change their actions.

Viewed through this theoretical lens, then, the structuring or shaping of the information age is a dynamic process necessarily involving individual actions as well as organizational and industrywide routines, practices, and policies. The influence of existing structures provides continuity, while individual actions leading to firm actions such as technology purchases and reorganizations may initiate change. This book traces how the life insurance business shaped information technologies and their use in that business before, during, and after the advent of the computer, highlighting often ignored continuities in form and application. The structurational lens focuses attention on how firms' past uses of technology shaped their adoption and use of a new technology.[23] At the same time, this lens also highlights the reciprocal influence of technology adoption and use on life insurance firms. That is, I look at how the context shapes information technology adoption and use over time and how adoption and use influence the technology and its vendors as well as the insurance firms and industry.

The narrative that follows demonstrates the two major themes noted above—the reciprocal shaping of technology and its use, and the influence of past technologies and processes on the adoption and application of new technology—as well as highlighting several other key factors. Understanding something about the industry and its structures is an important starting point. In the United States, life insurance was initially offered primarily by fraternal organizations, and the public did not entirely approve of private firms selling it as a profit-making business. Around 1900, the largest insurance firms reinforced the public's ambivalent attitude with extensive corruption, exposed and condemned in the 1905 Armstrong Hearings of the New York legislature. Subsequently, many insurance firms mutualized, so that all "profits" were redistributed to policyholders. An ideology of quasi-public service, rather than of profit, came to permeate the industry, and firms commonly cooperated on many topics through professional and trade associations. Also in the early twentieth century, insurance companies discovered systematic office management as a guide in seeking efficiency, frequently through mechanizing clerical work. These two ideologies shaped the industry's adoption and use of tabulating equipment.

Because the life insurance industry was a major user of tabulating equipment, its firms and associations interacted extensively with vendors to shape the technology, in particular seeking printing capability in addition to sorting, counting, and adding capability. For example, a few firms hired an inventor to create customized equipment; several firms and associations stated their needs directly to the two primary vendors (Herman Hollerith, whose firm became IBM, and James Powers, whose firm became Remington Rand); and some firms exerted market power by switching from one vendor to the other as each added new capabilities. The industry's public service ideology encouraged firms to share knowledge through associations and bilaterally, while the systematic management ideology encouraged them to adopt information technologies such as tabulating equipment. Early in the tabulator era, insurance firms used the equipment to continue their current practice of subdividing processes into smaller and smaller pieces. By the 1930s and 1940s, when tabulators had acquired greater card capacity and printing capability, some firms changed application directions, integrating rather than subdividing processes. Insurance associations helped disseminate technology experiences and applications widely among firms.

Life insurance firms showed immediate interest in computing after World War II ended. Again, existing institutions such as firms and industry associations organized interest in, interaction with, and influence on potential vendors of this new technology. Life insurance helped shape early commercial computing technology, especially in the input/output area. The firms' and associations' unwillingness to give up eighty-column cards in favor of invisible magnetic tape, for regulatory and other reasons, encouraged development of card-to-tape and tape-to-card converters. During the 1950s, firms struggled with conflicting desires for continuity with the past, on the one hand, and rapid transformation based on the new, on the other. Although some leaders in insurance computing stated clearly that only by "reengineering" their processes could firms fully benefit from computers, most companies in this conservative industry found embracing an abrupt transformation difficult. In acquiring equipment and applications, most firms preferred to make any necessary changes gradually, following an incremental migration path, rather than to transform themselves immediately and abruptly. On the hardware side, this preference for incrementalism initially favored IBM, with its installed base of tabulators and its small, card-based Model 650 computer, over the large, tape-based UNIVAC. Because Remington Rand, which provided the only (minor) U.S. competition to IBM's tabulating business, bought the small firm that developed the UNIVAC, insurance companies consistently considered it the other primary option, reproducing the tabulator era's vendor choices. From the insurance industry's perspective, turning to other computer manufacturers broke vendor continuity, and thus few firms chose to do so. After its initial influence on computer input/output capabilities, insurance turned to shaping the emerging software side of computer technology, joining in cross-industry development of the COBOL business computer language and working with vendors (especially IBM) to influence application software. Here, insurance firms followed the trajectory of process integration already visible late in the tabulator era and extended in the consolidated functions approach. IBM's insurance application software bundled with its 1401 computer, which was based on that approach, in turn shaped technology use and gradual evolution in midsized and smaller firms.

Overall, the industry chose not to transform itself overnight but to build on existing technologies and processes, changing only very gradually. Industry structures allowed and encouraged this gradual evolution. A growing market, regulation that minimized price competition, well-developed industry associations that facilitated information sharing, and a labor shortage that allowed automation without layoffs all limited the pressure on firms to transform their organization and processes overnight. Moreover, the public service ideology also reduced competitive pressure and supported incrementalism over rapid transformation. A paternalistic attitude toward employees plus a sense that insurance was special and could not easily be understood by outsiders also favored training existing employees to program and operate computers, rather than hiring scarce programmers from outside, further slowing progress in developing computer applications. The resulting incremental migration may help explain information technology's productivity paradox. This industry case study shows that firms took roughly two decades to achieve the initial computerization and process integration that the industry set as objectives in the 1950s. Insurance firms' costs, based on a standard industry ratio that is only indicative, at best, increased from the 1940s up to the mid-1970s before finally turning downward, suggesting that bottom-line results were similarly delayed until firms had transformed their structures and processes to realize gains from the technology.

What follows is divided into two sections: Part I looks at life insurance and its use of information technology during the tabulator era. Chapter 1 establishes the institutional context of life insurance at the turn of the twentieth century. Chapters 2 and 3 trace the interactions between life insurance firms and their industry associations, on the one hand, and the emerging tabulating technology and its producers, on the other, from 1890 through the 1920s. Chapter 4 focuses on two industry associations, the Life Office Management Association and, to a lesser extent, the Insurance Accounting and Statistical Association, as they institutionalized firm cooperation around office management generally and tabulator use specifically at that technology's height, the 1930s and 1940s. This era sets the stage for associations' increased role with regard to computers in the 1950s.

In Part II, the book moves into the computer era, examining both the mutual influences of the computer and life insurance industries and the tabulator era's influence on the early computer era. Chapter 5 examines the earliest interactions between the life insurance industry and the incipient computer industry. It establishes the central tension firms experienced in adopting this new technology—the conflicting desires to change gradually over time and to embrace abrupt discontinuity—setting the stage for Chapter 6, which traces the first computer adoptions among insurance firms. Here that tension between incremental migration and rapid transformation is played out, with incremental migration becoming the norm. Chapter 7 follows subsequent computer adoption and application from the late 1950s into the 1970s, showing how profoundly the tabulator era influenced the computer era in this industry. Despite these continuities, however, gradual change continued, and new capabilities such as online access and time sharing were introduced. Chapter 8 looks more closely at case studies of two firms, New England Mutual Life and Aetna Life, using them to illuminate additional dynamics of change around the new technology and its use. Finally, the conclusion highlights key themes and structuring factors explored throughout the book and suggests what we can learn about the information age from tracing one industry's experience with information technologies over an extended period.

# Part I / Life Insurance
# in the Tabulator Era

Life insurance companies were among the earliest commercial enterprises to consider adopting tabulating technology after Herman Hollerith first devised the punched-card-based sorting and counting equipment for the 1890 U.S. census, and they became one of the largest user segments of the tabulator market during the first half of the twentieth century. Why did this service industry, rather than the manufacturing industries that played such a large role in introducing scientific and systematic management, loom so large as a user of this obscure but powerful new information technology? Why did insurance firms adopt this technology? How did they use it and how did that use evolve over time? How did they influence the technology itself? What effect did that use have on the firms? These are some of the questions I attempt to answer in the next four chapters.

Understanding how insurance firms interacted with the technology requires knowledge of relevant industry structures, including its context and culture. In 1905 life insurance passed through a key inflection point in the New York legislature's Armstrong Commission Hearings. In their wake, regulation was tightened to prevent abuses, simultaneously curbing price competition, and insurance firms adopted a public service ideology that shaped many aspects of industry culture. Insurers now saw themselves as different from other profit-making enterprises and defined growth, rather than profit, as their central goal. Associations, previously rare, proliferated as insurance firms cooperated to serve the public interest.

Between 1890 and 1911, insurance firms and associations first came in contact with Herman Hollerith and his new punched-card tabulating concept. Initially, the relationship was shaky, with insurance firms and the Actuarial Society of America (ASA) finding the idea promising but the equipment too slow in the sorting stage. Prudential's actuary even developed his own sorter. Eventually, however, Hollerith responded to user pressure by improving his system's sorting speed, and insurance interest increased. During subsequent decades insurance firms interacted extensively with Hollerith and his newly emerged competitors to encourage the development of printing capability. Competition between Hollerith and rival James L. Powers produced a stream of innovations including numerical and then alphabetical printing from 1911 to 1931. Insurance firms, anxious for printing capability, played an important role in this contest. By 1931 the firm Hollerith founded, now IBM, had emerged as the dominant market force. Meanwhile, printing and other new capabilities expanded the technology's possible applications in insurance, though initially insurance firms did not take full advantage of them.

Insurance associations encouraged the flowering of tabulator use in the 1930s and 1940s. In the mid-1920s, insurers had founded a national trade association for improving life insurance home office operations. The Life Office Management Association (LOMA) became a forum within which different insurance firms shared information about office technology use and through which the insurance industry interacted with the tabulating industry. A few years later a group of small midwestern firms founded a regional association focused explicitly on tabulator use, the Insurance Accounting and Statistical Association (IASA). It would emerge into national importance just as the computer appeared on the scene. Meanwhile, in the mid-1930s, insurance companies first developed a tabulator application that integrated tasks, rather than subdividing them as in the past, and that more fully used the technology's printing capabilities. By the late 1940s, this premium billing and accounting application was becoming more widespread, though still far from universal. It was a harbinger of what was to come in the early computer era.

# CHAPTER 1

# Insurance at the Turn of the Twentieth Century

Understanding life insurance firms' adoption and use of pre-computer information-processing technology during the first half of the twentieth century first requires an understanding of the institutional context in which this technology took root, the subject of this chapter. In the nineteenth century, U.S. life insurance initially took the form of voluntary mutual aid associations, beginning to emerge as a significant *business* only in the 1840s as U.S. attitudes toward insuring lives changed.[1] During the first half of that century, Americans accepted life insurance solely as mutual aid intended for social benefit; by the second half, they increasingly accepted it as a business transaction, as well. Both of these views shaped public attitudes toward insurance well into the twentieth century. Indeed, a critical formative event for U.S. life insurance, the 1905 Armstrong Hearings, conducted by a committee of the New York legislature to expose and root out corruption in life insurance, reflected this ambivalence and shaped two ideologies central to the life insurance industry's cultural and business context throughout the first half of the twentieth century: first, a public service ideology, and second, a business ideology focused on efficiency and growth.

## Ideology and Organization in Nineteenth-Century Life Insurance

Although informal and association-based aid to widows and orphans had long existed in North America, attempts to form life insurance firms before the 1840s typically proved unsuccessful.[2] Cultural and ideological factors—changing attitudes toward life, death, and the relationship between moral and monetary values—significantly influenced this lack of success. After that time, however, life insurance firms took root and expanded rapidly. As one scholar notes, "Spontaneous help was bureaucratized by systematic and rational risk-bearing techniques."[3] At the same time, however, many citizens still saw spontaneous charitable aid as "morally superior" to insurance as a business.

Several factors in the rapid expansion after 1840 reflected the public's and even the industry's ambivalence about life insurance as a product.[4] One of these factors was the increasing adoption of the mutual form of organization beginning in the 1840s. Almost all pre-1840 firms were organized as stock companies in which initial funds were raised from investors, who became stockholders entitled to profits on their investment. Starting with New England Mutual Life Insurance Company and Mutual Life Insurance Company of New York, both of which began operations in the early 1840s, new firms increasingly organized as mutuals. Mutuals distributed to policyholders all profits beyond those put back into the business.[5] They did this by offering so-called participating policies, which entitled the holder to dividend distributions of the firm's profits. An insurance firm organized as a mutual claimed at least some of the moral superiority of mutual aid, a factor that undoubtedly made life insurance firms more acceptable to the public, thus encouraging the post-1840 growth. Many stock-based firms founded after midcentury also sought to balance business and mutual aid by placing strict limits on the maximum return to shareholders, thus creating a hybrid form more acceptable to the public.[6]

By the last three decades of the nineteenth century, established corporations increasingly used monetary arguments (e.g., life insurance is a good investment; a large corporation is a safe investment; corporate organization enables efficiency) in addition to moral ones.[7] Nevertheless, both the public and the firms themselves remained ambivalent about the role of life insurance companies. The industry suffered from "an inescapable dilemma: in order to survive as a business life insurance was compelled to maximize profits, but profits alone remained a justification too sordid for an institution of its kind."[8] This public and industry ambivalence regarding insurance survived into the early twentieth century, when a public service ideology coexisted with a business ideology of growth and efficiency. Both would shape the adoption and use of information technology.

Whatever its moral standing, insurance by 1900 had certainly become big business. The so-called Big Three firms in the industry—New York Life Insurance Company, Mutual Life Insurance Company of New York, and Equitable Life Assurance Society—each had written policies with a cumulative value exceeding $1 billion (referred to as $1 billion of insurance in force), three to four times the total in 1885.[9] By 1905, when the Armstrong Hearings were held, the largest firm had policies exceeding $2 billion, and two additional firms (Metropolitan Life Insurance Company and Prudential Life Insurance Company) had passed the $1 billion mark.[10] Of the five largest firms at this time, two (Mutual Life and New York Life) were organized as mutuals, while the other three (Equitable, Metropolitan Life, and Prudential) operated as stock companies. Thus mutuals shared the market with stock firms, although the latter often had charters restricting the amount of profit that could be distributed to stockholders. Equitable and Metropolitan Life, for example, both restricted their profits to no more than 7%, the legal interest rate in New York State, and Prudential restricted its to 10%.[11] These charter restrictions essentially inscribed the ideology of benevolence and public service alongside that of profits even in stock firms. In practice, these differences in organizational form were even less significant. Stock firms typically sought to make their policies more competitive by distributing most of their surplus to policyholders, rather than to stockholders.[12] In fact, dividends to stockholders for all stock-based life insurance companies never exceeded 1% in the period up to 1905.[13] Meanwhile, these immense firms, whether organized as stock or mutual companies, grew vigorously, competing with one another on the basis of growth rate and size (measured by assets and insurance in force), rather than of stock prices or profits. The taint of corruption, not excess profits, led to the Armstrong Hearings.[14]

Growth was not the sole business value held by insurance executives. During the 1880s and 1890s, a business ideology later labeled *systematic management* arose in the manufacturing sector in response to growth, diseconomies of scale, and loss of control by owners and upper management.[15] This set of beliefs, which emerged in the writings of contemporary engineers and spread in the early twentieth century through the work of consultants known as systematizers, was broader and less specific than Frederick Taylor's better-publicized shop floor management system, scientific management. Although systematic management took different forms in different settings, its advocates believed that only through system could they achieve order and efficiency.[16] Owners and managers who saw themselves as modern and progressive rejected their old-fashioned methods and focused on system and efficiency.[17] By the early twentieth century, systematic management had spread from manufacturing to the office, where office managers sought efficiency through division of labor, systematization and standardization of processes, and improved information-processing technology, from card-filing systems to typewriters and adding machines.[18]

At the end of the nineteenth century, the rhetoric of system and efficiency was just beginning to penetrate insurance firms.[19] As the largest firms continued to expand, they required a growing clerical workforce to handle the necessary paperwork, in turn encouraging demands for increased efficiency through manual or mechanical means.[20] Rising costs among large firms often triggered at least the rhetoric of systematization, as well as a search, more or less intense and successful depending on the company, for ways of achieving it. The Big Three and other large firms experienced diseconomies of scale akin to those suffered by some manufacturing firms.[21] By one measure, the expense ratio (or expense rate) of the top ten life insurance companies rose from around 12% of income in 1870 to 19% in 1903.[22] Starting in the 1890s, insurance firms desiring to cut costs turned to the rhetoric and practices of systematic management as applied to office work. The search for efficiency as well as growth became a hallmark of the insurance firms' business philosophy.

## Life Insurance Products

In 1900, life insurance firms offered two major classes of insurance: ordinary insurance for those of middle and upper incomes and industrial insurance for industrial workers with very low incomes.[23] Ordinary insurance, developed first, consisted of policies written for relatively large amounts of money (typically thousands or tens of thousands of dollars at this time), with annual premiums paid to the insurance office either by mail or in person. The Big Three firms, as well as many smaller firms, sold ordinary insurance exclusively, though they offered different types of ordinary insurance policies. The Big Three used the notorious deferred dividend policy, introduced by Equitable's Henry Hyde, in their intense competition. These policies paid no dividends to policyholders early in the policy life but promised to pay higher dividends later to surviving policyholders who maintained their policies without lapse over longer periods, thus delaying policyholder recognition of rising costs. They were essentially, if not legally, tontines, long outlawed in Britain and the United States.[24] Such policies were one of the factors leading to the Armstrong Hearings.

In contrast, industrial insurance, started in England by the Prudential Assurance Company and introduced into the United States during the 1870s, was marketed to the masses of industrial workers, generally to replace or supplement fraternal insurance.[25] It offered small policies (denominated in hundreds rather than thousands of dollars) that would cover burial costs but not much more. Every week an agent went door to door in his or her "debit" (assigned district), collecting premiums in nickels and dimes.[26] Metropolitan Life and Prudential Insurance Company (modeled after but unrelated to Britain's Prudential Assurance), the rising young firms that had joined the Big Three, had roots in fraternal organizations and focused primarily on industrial insurance.[27] Their rhetoric of missionary zeal to aid poor industrial workers helped launch this type of insurance, intensifying the public service ideology associated with such firms, though perhaps also obscuring other, less idealistic motives.[28]

Although industrial insurance depended on the same general actuarial principles as ordinary insurance, with specifics adjusted for the differing mortalities of its target population, it had very different operating characteristics and cost structures. Collecting and accounting for the tiny weekly premiums on industrial insurance policies obviously cost more per dollar of insurance in force than collecting large quarterly or yearly sums for ordinary insurance policies, a difference reflected in higher prices per dollar of coverage. Indeed, the ratio of operating expenses to money paid out to policyholders differed greatly for the two insurance types, with firms specializing in industrial insurance having ratios twice as high as those of the Big Three ordinary insurance firms.[29] U.S. firms marketing industrial insurance recognized that they had to manage such costs as closely as possible, both to provide industrial workers with a real service and to have a salable product. In general, however, it was not until the 1890s depression that operating costs became a major concern to all insurance firms.

## Industry Structures: Regulatory Commissions and Professional and Trade Associations

The Armstrong Hearings would influence regulation significantly from 1905 onward, but state regulation had emerged earlier, with the gradual establishment of laws and of state insurance commissions empowered to examine the companies' practices and to require reports.[30] Legislation differed from state to state, and commissions differed in structure, powers, and interests. The rapid growth during the 1840s and 1850s led to increased regulation by the late 1860s.[31] Significantly, life insurance firms did not object to regulation, since regulatory oversight could be seen as assuring their reliability when their status was still uncertain; at this time, however, many firms would have preferred regulation on the federal rather than state level to reduce variability.[32]

In 1871, the superintendent of insurance for New York organized the National Convention of Insurance Commissioners to promote communication and coordination among state commissioners.[33] The convention saw as its mandate "to afford the fullest possible protection to the public, with the least possible annoyance or expense to, or interference with, the companies."[34] In its first meetings, the commissioners discussed recommending a common mortality table; adopting uniform standards for figuring reserves, taxes, dividends, and assets; and establishing standardized forms for preparing reports to the states. Such standardization, adopted gradually over subsequent years, reduced the difficulties facing large firms that sold business in (and thus had to report to) many states. At this stage, regulation was friendly and lax, interfering with the companies as little as possible.[35]

Another important set of insurance industry structures began to emerge before 1900: the many professional and trade associations that provided sites for cross-firm cooperation. The first unsuccessful attempts to organize representatives of life insurance companies into organizations began in 1859, in part responding to increasing pressure to regulate or reform the growing companies.[36] Areas of potential cooperation included, for example, lobbying to influence state legislation (an issue on which the insurance companies certainly had incentive to cooperate) and compiling vital statistics.[37] The successful launch of several associations, including the Actuarial Society of America (ASA), the Association of Life Insurance Medical Directors (ALIMD), and the National Association of Life Underwriters (NALU), finally occurred in 1889–90.[38] In 1953, one historian observed, "There are some two dozen trade organizations of national scope in the field of life insurance alone, at least a half dozen of which are of major importance."[39] All these organizations involved cooperative attempts to address common issues and problems. Because the tendency to cooperate in associations would play an important role in spreading knowledge about information technology use in the twentieth century, the origins of these earliest associations are worth examining more closely.

Actuaries, the specialized statisticians who guided insurance firms in managing risk by determining who to insure, what products to offer, and what prices to charge for them, followed a relatively straightforward path to what was arguably professional status. Actuaries possessed the most commonly accepted traits of professionals: educational qualifications and certification, increased status, and allegiance to the profession itself, not just to a firm.[40] They successfully claimed both a body of professional knowledge—the mathematics of mortality and risk—and something resembling a service ideal.[41] Since 1948, actuaries in England had had a professional association, the Institute of Actuaries.[42] Thus American actuaries could follow a clear example of cooperation within a professional association. Although the ASA was not formed until 1889, actuaries had begun communicating and taking steps toward professionalization earlier.[43]

This preparation helped the ASA coalesce rapidly into a professional association. In reminiscences on its twentieth anniversary, one member commented on the importance of professionalism:

> It is well in an organization like this to remember that the admission of a member and his value are determined solely by his character and his professional qualifications; by nothing else. I dwell upon this point because in discussions during recent years I have sometimes heard a member speak of himself and be referred to by others as representing such and such a company. . . . When this Society was formed there was much competition among some companies in the rush for business, a competition which at times took the form of bitter rivalry. It was a matter of surprise in some quarters that the actuaries could come together in frank conference as professional men and students, without a vestige of that feeling. And I believe that the example was not without its beneficial effect, beyond the limits of our own membership.
>
> But if [the] intention and purpose that this Society should be strictly a professional association should be lost sight of, and the idea gain ground and prevail that it is an association of the representatives of insurance corporations, then the usefulness of the Actuarial Society of America will be ended.[44]

Although most actuaries understood the importance of professional status and behavior, practices of firms around 1900 reflected the industry's cutthroat competition and made it difficult for actuaries to treat their professional allegiance as more important than their allegiance to their firms. Because the professional ideal endorsed expertise and judgment over simple application of strict mathematical rules, it certainly did not exempt actuarial science from political, cultural, and organizational pressures.[45] "Even the seemingly abstract and objective area of actuarial computation reflected prevailing corporate values," historian Morton Keller notes, in that companies embraced conservative actuarial reserve valuation principles as a reason for amassing larger-than-necessary reserves and undistributed surpluses to be invested (sometimes corruptly) or spent on excessively high expenses.[46] Still, the construction of actuarial identity through a professional association generated a peer community in which actuaries could express their uneasiness over such policies and through which they could attempt to change them, as reflected in the following 1893 statement from a past ASA president: "Many have cherished great hopes that our organization may be the means of bringing about some beneficent changes. The need of some reforms is universally conceded and is known to us more fully, probably, than to any others—we alone fully understand how much expense the premiums were made to bear and how much has been forced upon them, and we should do our best, as far as opportunity allows, to make the truth known and appreciated by all who are responsible for the present state of affairs."[47] Although the Armstrong Hearings' revelations of corruption suggest that these hopes were not fully realized, during the early twentieth century the ASA organized cooperative, multifirm actuarial studies, both before and after the Armstrong Hearings. Good actuarial practice required data broader than those collected by any individual firm, giving actuaries professional grounds for sharing information—and, necessarily, the related technology—across firms.

The other two organizations founded around the same time do not fit the professional model, requiring that we consider the motives behind their formation and subsequent knowledge sharing. Although the Association of Life Insurance Medical Directors, founded in the same year as the ASA, included many medical doctors among its members, they attended meetings based not on their common medical profession but on their common occupation as medical directors of insurance firms.[48] Indeed, firms, not individuals, belonged to ALIMD and sent representatives to meetings based on position, not credentials. Thus ALIMD followed a trade association, more than a professional, model.[49]

Early on, these medical directors adopted technology-enabled information sharing for the common good. In this case the information technology was a card index system based on Melvil Dewey's library cataloging systems and marketed by the Library Bureau, a firm that had expanded from selling files, cards, and indexing systems to libraries into serving a broad business market.[50] In 1890, after setting up card-based systems for several insurance firms individually, the Library Bureau sold ALIMD a plan for information exchange among many insurance firms "concerning cooperative printing of the list of rejected risks."[51] Each company sent names of individuals they had rejected as poor insurance risks to the Library Bureau, which printed them on cards subsequently distributed to all subscribers. This system was widely adopted by insurance firms and clearly served as the basis for ALIMD's own Medical Impairment Bureau (MIB), founded ten years later.[52] ALIMD supported this long-running information-sharing venture in an area in which collective benefits were clear.

The National Association of Life Underwriters, founded in 1890, consisted of sales agents representing member firms. Through this organization, insurance agents unsuccessfully attempted to raise their status by professionalizing the occupation. Then, as later, life insurance agents had a bad reputation among the public, reflecting the society's ambivalence about insuring lives, exacerbated by the hard sales approach of many insurance agents, especially during this highly competitive period.[53] Although the organization did not convince the world that insurance sales agents deserved professional status, it established an arena for negotiating occupational rules and norms, curbed the worst excesses of insurance sales, and formed a social network. Thus it helped constitute not a profession but an occupation, although with a fraternal element akin to that of the Masons.[54] This "brotherhood of salesmen," according to one scholar, "mediated between the notion of sales as a humanistic calling and as a competitive, acquisitive 'business,'" exemplifying the attempt to reconcile visions of insurance as a public service and as a business.[55]

Whatever the specific motives for forming and methods of maintaining associations, the insurance industry spawned many of them, from professional associations conferring status, such as the ASA, to trade associations offering fellowship, such as ALIMD and NALU. All these associations, however, facilitated cross-firm information exchange. Information sharing about tabulating and computing technologies would continue this tradition. Moreover, both associations and state regulatory regimes and commissions provided industry-wide structures that would shape the adoption and use of these technologies.

## Insurance Firms: Processes and Technologies

In 1900, insurance firms did not yet use complex technologies to handle their basic but extensive information-processing tasks. Nevertheless, they managed an array of information about, and generated several document types relating to, the many policies in their headquarters, referred to in the industry as home offices.[56] For actuarial purposes, a firm's home office maintained information about the person insured (e.g., age, health, occupation), supported its extraction, calculated many statistics based on it, and developed or modified products in light of it. To meet differing state regulatory requirements, it computed and reported various statistics on all its policies (e.g., value of policies and associated reserve requirements by state) and its financial transactions (including investments). For internal management purposes it maintained a cost accounting system, personnel records, sales records, financial accounts, agency accounts, and so on.[57]

Different processes and documents were associated with the two classes of life insurance. For ordinary insurance, firms received and processed applications and their supporting documents (often including reports of medical examinations), decided whether applicants qualified for policies, and either rejected the application or prepared and transmitted written policies to new policyholders. Once firms issued the policy, a one-time process, they began the ongoing information and document processing associated with maintaining policies. The home office generated and mailed notices of premium payments due (generally once a year, but occasionally quarterly), processed and sent receipts for premium payments received, monitored missed payments to reduce policy lapses, and responded to policyholder inquiries, changes of address, and other correspondence. When policyholders died, the office received and processed claims and issued payments. For agents and district offices, the home office maintained accurate records of policies (by agent and by district), responded to inquiries, figured commissions, distributed pay, and maintained employment records.

For industrial insurance, with its door-to-door premium collection, the home office maintained and updated the necessary records to guide agents in their weekly rounds, handled their remittances of premiums to the firm, provided receipts for payments, and credited payments to the policyholder's account. It also monitored missed payments, which could occur fifty-two times a year rather than at most four times, to prevent policy lapses.[58] When policyholders died, the home office verified and paid the claims. Because the number of policies required to reach a given "insurance in force" figure was much larger for industrial than for ordinary insurance, information-handling processes were correspondingly greater for comparably sized industrial insurance firms.

This catalog of information- and document-related tasks in life insurance focuses only on the most basic processes involved in servicing policies, omitting many complicating factors such as loans on policies, changes to existing policies, and dividend distributions to policyholders in mutual firms. Nevertheless, it illustrates some key characteristics of the life insurance business. First, handling this business required firms to generate many types and enormous numbers of documents. Some, such as the records of policies serviced by a particular agent, were solely for internal use, supporting the agents' work and facilitating the home office's communication with district offices and agents. Other documents—such as policies, premium notices, and receipts—communicated with customers and thus shaped their image of and ongoing relationship to the firm. Such documents required great accuracy over a long time— the lifetime of a policy could easily exceed half a century—to avoid creating problems in customer relations. Finally, the description of basic processes reveals what one contemporary expert termed "the outstanding characteristic of the life insurance office; that is, the repetition of the same data and same transactions in the various records and statistics. From the very moment a policy is issued this repetition stays with it until the ultimate termination of the policy."[59] Despite this repetition of data, however, companies handled the various processes independently, typically assigning each to a different department or unit.

A brief look at the technology and systems used in a few firms' home office operations will make the processes more concrete. In 1893, Metropolitan Life, then the fourth largest U.S. insurance company, moved its home office into the first of several buildings around New York's Twenty-third Street and Madison Avenue that it would ultimately combine to house its rapid expansion into the twentieth century. At this time it already employed 650 clerks (400 of them women) in its Industrial and Ordinary departments.[60] Within a year, the firm had grown to more than 1,000 employees in its home office, interconnected

*Fig. 1.1.* Work in one of many filing areas at Metropolitan Life Insurance Company. Courtesy of Bass Business History Collection, University of Oklahoma.

by a telephone switchboard with 100 lines.[61] Metropolitan Life bought its first typewriter in 1877, only three years after the device was first mass-produced at the Remington factory, and accumulated more than 1,000 of them by 1915.[62] By the 1890s women were the primary typewriter operators, using them to produce correspondence and complete forms. The firm's industrial insurance business "require[d] in its office management some four hundred different forms and blanks."[63] Document files containing policy records took up considerable space, as well (fig. 1.1). The magnitude of the information tasks facing Metropolitan Life is suggested by this statistic: its actuarial filing section alone completed almost *83 million* operations during the year 1896.[64]

By comparison, Equitable Life Assurance Society, the largest insurance firm in the 1890s, had a lighter operational burden than Metropolitan Life, since it handled only ordinary insurance. That was surely fortunate, given the generally old-fashioned and chaotic methods it still employed at that time. President Henry B. Hyde espoused the rhetoric, at least, of systematization and efficiency, as evidenced by statements such as "Great is the power of system, order and discipline" and by his apparent attempts to improve efficiency in the office.[65] Nevertheless, his efforts were haphazard at best, and during this period the home office remained traditional and inefficient. Although Hyde had his own letters typed starting in 1882, many clerks worked with pen and ink at high desks, addressing premium notices and signing dividend notices by hand; the firm stored policy records in heavy bound volumes, rather than more flexible and modern box files. Equitable had an outside telephone installed in 1890 but set up a small (twenty-two-station) internal telephone exchange only in the mid-1890s. Although its operating expenses at this time were much lower than Metropolitan Life's, that difference reflected the gap in cost structure between ordinary and industrial insurance, not greater efficiency.

While policy-related record keeping, communication with customers (e.g., premium collection, claims processing), and accounting, central operations of insurance home offices, all involved transaction processing, the actuarial function depended more on extensive calculation. Actuaries adopted mechanical aids to calculation relatively early, spreading knowledge of devices such as the arithmometer through the professional network so that the actuarial offices of many nineteenth-century insurance firms, large and relatively small, had such devices before they had typewriters. These devices, related to slide rules, used moving cylinders and sliding scales to multiply and divide more rapidly than the actuary could do by hand.[66] One of the earliest and most famous American actuaries, Elizur Wright, invented his own version of such a device, which he called an Arithmeter (fig. 1.2), to aid in his own calculations; his son, New England Mutual Life's actuary, used it there and began marketing it in 1869, but he found that it did not compete very successfully with its primary English competitor, Tate's Arithmometer.[67] Still, actuaries at a few firms, including, for example, Equitable and Pacific Mutual, adopted Wright's device. Firm size was not, apparently, critical to the spread of this technology, since New England Mutual Life had only 12% of Equitable's insurance in force and Pacific Mutual was much smaller still.[68]

Insurance firms' espoused ideologies, product lines, industry structures, and firm processes all set the stage for events surrounding the 1905 Armstrong Hearings, a critical historical turning point for U.S. insurance.

*Fig. 1.2.* The Arithmeter, designed by Elizur Wright, was used in New England Mutual Life's Actuarial Department in the 1890s. Courtesy of New England Financial Archives.

## Armstrong Commission Hearings of 1905

The Armstrong Commission Hearings on insurance abuses, conducted by the New York legislature in 1905, profoundly influenced the life insurance industry. The hearings changed insurance regulation; discouraged corruption, financial manipulation, cutthroat competition, and spending excesses; and encouraged the public service and efficiency ideologies.[69] The factors leading to the investigation initially emerged in the 1880s and 1890s. Between 1885 and 1905, the total assets of life insurance firms increased more than five and a half times, with the top five companies accounting for two-thirds of the growth.[70] During the same period, the largest five firms increased their insurance in force sevenfold.[71] In 1886, Equitable's Henry Hyde led that firm's push to surpass Mutual Life as the largest company in the industry, based on his introduction of deferred dividend, tontine-like policies.[72] At the same time, however, stiff competition and dividend caps kept even investors in stock firms such as Equitable from profiting directly. With stock holdings shut off as a route to wealth and power, Hyde and other executives of the largest firms, including New York

Life's John McCall and Mutual Life's Richard McCurdy, looked for other ways to benefit from their positions. As one historian of these events observed, "These men shared a hearty enthusiasm for growth at almost any cost, an enthusiasm fed in part by prospects for pecuniary reward and, in the reluctant words of a competitor, 'more, perhaps, for the pride in doing it than otherwise.'"[73]

This powerful group of insurance executives fueled growth of surpluses with deferred dividend policies and turned to high salaries, collateral investments, syndicates, low-cost personal loans, and other such perquisites as sources of money and power.[74] The Big Three firms developed extensive relations with the investment banking community, which both invested their surpluses and provided various mechanisms such as syndicates and collateral investments for channeling monetary rewards to the executives while keeping them (and other questionable activities) off the company books examined by insurance commissioners.[75] At the same time, the firms spent heavily on lobbying to protect their positions and to seek national, rather than state, regulation so as to simplify and better control it.[76] Equitable was the most flagrant in its abuses. Indeed, as early as 1882, actuarial consultant and regulator Elizur Wright had written, "Some day there will be a terrible crash in the Equitable. Its disruption is only a matter of a few years."[77] After Henry Hyde died in 1899, James Alexander became president, but with the expectation that Henry's son James Hazen Hyde would take charge when he acquired full control of his inherited stock.[78] In early 1905, the young Hyde organized a lavish and flamboyant company-funded party, triggering an internal but very public power struggle between pro- and anti-Hyde factions of directors and executives.[79] This public airing of mismanagement and excess led to Equitable's reorganization under a new president.[80] Even that was not enough to stem the scandal, which dominated the business and popular press and expanded to include other firms, particularly New York Life and Mutual Life but also, to a lesser extent, Metropolitan Life and Prudential.[81]

A few months later, the widening scandal led the New York legislature to form the Insurance Investigation Committee of 1905, chaired by William W. Armstrong, which conducted what became known as the Armstrong Commission Hearings into life insurance firms operating in New York State.[82] The committee looked at financial, operational, and regulatory aspects of life insurance in both stock and mutual companies. Equitable's troubles became public in part because of open fighting among its major stockholders and executives, but mutuals, especially the two largest (Mutual Life and New York Life), were by no means immune from the same criticisms. In fact, the mutual companies' policyholders had no more power than small stockholders in stock firms. The executive teams in all three firms operated with inadequate or self-interested oversight from directors and state regulators.[83] The hearings revealed the large sums of money spent by the Big Three on legislative lobbying, executive use of syndicates and collateral loans for personal profit, and many other abuses by these three firms, whether mutual or stock.[84] Beyond corruption, the commission also looked at inefficient practices that led to high costs, especially for marketing and sales of new policies. All three companies were exposed as riddled with corruption and mismanagement.

The two next largest firms, Metropolitan Life and Prudential, specialized in industrial insurance, though they also had relatively small ordinary insurance departments. They survived the investigation in better shape than the Big Three.[85] Because they served poor industrial workers, they could appeal to the ideological, missionary element of their work with more sincerity. In addition, their lobbying was quite modest and targeted compared with that of the Big Three. Moreover, they had distributed dividends to industrial insurance holders even when not required to by charter or policy. Still, theirs was not a complete vindication, though both later tended to present it that way.[86] Metropolitan Life was involved in investment syndicates, and Prudential had developed a relationship with Fidelity Trust that raised questions. Prudential's ordinary insurance business issued deferred dividend, semi-tontine policies, though Metropolitan Life's did not. While neither issued such policies in industrial insurance, their voluntary dividends were intended to make their policies more attractive despite the firms' very high costs and lapse rates, perhaps the most important issues raised with regard to industrial insurance. Although the hearings allowed the two firms to explain why costs and the lapse rate were inherently higher for industrial than for ordinary insurance, the publicity still drew attention to them.

In general, the hearings raised public and legislative awareness of the insurance business and highlighted the ideological contradictions around it. Shared ideology was more important than organizational structure (stock versus mutual) in shaping company actions.[87] Perhaps the most famous statement from the hearings, made by Mutual Life's Richard McCurdy, illustrates the problem: "This is the view I take of a life insurance company . . . that the object of that company is to diffuse itself as largely as possible. Every person ought to understand when he takes a policy of life insurance that he is not doing it solely for his own benefit, but that he is participating in a great movement for the benefit of humanity at large, and for every other person who comes in and takes a policy in that company, and in that way joins the great brotherhood. . . . That the life insurance company is an eleemosynary institution, to a very large extent, I have always believed all my life, and I believe it to-day."[88] The press mocked this quote, and Armstrong himself replied, "Treating it as a missionary enterprise, Mr. McCurdy, the question goes back to the salaries of missionaries." Armstrong's reply points to the essential contradiction underlying the industry at this stage. McCurdy and other top executives both claimed special status based on the larger social role of insurance but refused to submit themselves and their firms to social controls commensurate to that role. This contradiction was central to the hearings, and it had consequences for both the new regulations and the changed attitudes that emerged from it.

## Consequences for Life Insurance

In the aftermath of the hearings and the committee's official report came increased regulation, both externally by state legislatures and internally by the firms themselves. The report's recommendations ranged from relatively general to quite specific. In general, the committee encouraged mutualization of stock companies to reduce the inherent contradiction between the public service provided by insuring lives and the profits expected by stockholders. Although the committee had pointed out many problems in both mutuals and stockholding companies, "the paradox of a stock company that paid no significant dividends remained."[89] Mutualization would both bring stock firms' images in line with the public service claim and allow the stockholders to cash in their securities. Indeed, Metropolitan Life was already moving toward mutualization, and Prudential, Equitable Life, and many smaller companies would follow.[90] Although mutualizing would not eliminate a wide range of potential abuses, in combination with further regulations it would reduce the contradictions these firms faced and strengthen the public service ideology. Other committee recommendations reduced other possibilities for abuse. For example, the report urged prohibiting deferred dividend policies, participation in syndicates, and investments in stocks; requiring annual distribution of dividends to avoid accumulated surpluses; limiting the amount of new business a firm could acquire in a year, since competition made expenses for acquiring new business much higher than those required to maintain it; creating standard policies; reporting much specified information to the New York State Insurance Department; and limiting costs and sales commissions. The New York State legislature adopted most of these recommendations; many, though not all, states followed New York's lead.[91]

The reforms reduced the strident public criticism, and the industry adopted a new tone that suited the Progressive Era. The hearings had taken seriously the industry's claim of quasi–public service status and had reinforced relevant behaviors while limiting other types. At the same time, the hearings reduced the Big Three's influence and ultimately their size. By 1910, Metropolitan Life was the largest insurance firm, and Prudential was third, while Equitable had fallen to fifth.[92] All five companies had instituted internal reforms, as well. The firms shifted their focus from power to conservative and efficient public service. Soon, according to Keller, new legislation and improved internal controls transformed the life insurance enterprise: "Growth and size now meant systematized bureaucratization, not systematized power; investment policies perhaps were unimaginative, but they were not reckless or irresponsible."[93] Indeed, in 1905 Equitable chose as its new president Paul Morton, whose previous career included railroad management as well as a term as secretary of the navy. Morton considered himself "an organizer, a systematizer and a master of men," bringing more systematic business methods into that firm.[94]

Post-Armstrong regulation, maintained and increased through the twentieth century, combined with the public service ideology to reduce competition in the industry. In particular, limiting and standardizing allowable policy types lessened price competition greatly. Competitive incentives were generally lower in this highly regulated, quasi-public sector than in many other businesses.[95] This factor surely encouraged industry cooperation through associations and lessened competitive pressure to change rapidly.

The shift in focus from "systematized power" to "systematized bureaucratization" set the stage for interest in information technology and techniques in the early twentieth century. The industry structures and ideologies that emerged would shape, though not determine, tabulating technology adoption and use. The next chapter backtracks to 1890 to illuminate the beginnings of a technology and a relationship that would become central to life insurance in the twentieth century.

# CHAPTER 2

# First Impressions of Tabulating, 1890–1910

In 1890 Herman Hollerith invited members of the Actuarial Society of America (ASA) to attend a demonstration of information-handling equipment he had recently developed for the U.S. census: the punched-card tabulator. Thirty-five life insurance actuaries attended because, according to a news account, "any labor-saving device that can be used in the preparation of tabular statements is of interest to actuaries."[1] This event initiated decades of interaction between the life insurance industry (both firms and associations) and the tabulating segment of the business machine, or office appliance, industry. Although life insurance (and other businesses) also used many other office machines for handling information—from typewriters and calculators to addressing machines—tabulating systems were the most direct predecessors of computers.[2] They became central to operations in this information-intensive business.

Clearly, insurance actuaries were intrigued with Hollerith's tabulating system from the beginning. During the 1890s, however, other issues preoccupied them. In addition, many insurance companies were just learning the power of manual card files for storing and retrieving records. Moreover, although Hollerith recognized that his system had potential for commercial customers and made a few limited contacts with prospects, during the 1890s he focused primarily on developing his equipment for census applications. Only after he lost his U.S. census business early in the twentieth century did he turn his attention seriously to developing a commercial market, and even then insurance was not the first industry he targeted.[3]

Thus interactions between insurance and tabulating were limited through 1910.[4] Yet during this period, insurance firms and managers developed their initial impressions of the technology. How did these impressions shape whether and how insurance firms might use the technology? What did insurance executives convey to Hollerith about his technology's suitability to their needs? With what results for the technology, if any? This chapter addresses these questions, first tracing the origins of tabulating technology and then examining the earliest interactions between tabulating and insurance.

## Hollerith and the Emergence of Punched-Card Tabulating

Hollerith devised his tabulating system of mechanical and electromechanical devices to process the data collected in the 1890 U.S. census, preparing them for tabular presentation (thus the "tabulating" designation) more rapidly than would be possible by hand. He first encountered the problems of processing census data in 1879 when, as a recent graduate of Columbia, he was employed by the census to do statistical work.[5] During the next three years, Hollerith observed the immense volume of clerical work necessary to process the raw data from the 1880 census. Without some change in methods, he realized, the 1890 census data were unlikely to be processed and tabulated before the 1900 census began. During this work, Hollerith conceived a way to achieve the necessary speedup: representing the data by a pattern of holes punched on tape or cards and using specially designed machines to process them. Scholars have variously traced his idea to Dr. J. S. Billings, a more senior census employee; to the Jacquard loom, which used punched holes to control patterns woven into fabric; and to railroad tickets, on which a description of the passenger was encoded in punched holes.[6] Whatever the source of the idea, Hollerith himself clearly developed the system of devices that bore his name.

Tabulating systems differed from adding machines or typewriters in that the component devices were not intended to operate independently but as an in-

*Fig. 2.1.* Hollerith's pantograph punch, tabulator, and sorting box used in the 1890 U.S. census. Reproduced courtesy of the Smithsonian Institution (Photo no. 64551 and 64563).

*Fig. 2.2 (clockwise from top)* Hollerith key punch, sorter, and tabulator, early decades of the twentieth century. Key punch reproduced courtesy of the Smithsonian Institution (Photo no. 64549); sorter and tabulator reproduced courtesy of the ICL Historical Collection, National Archive for the History of Computing at Manchester, England.

terlocking system.[7] Tabulating systems included the cards themselves, along with devices for recording, sorting, counting, and later adding the data.[8] The card punch in Hollerith's original system (fig. 2.1) was a pantograph punch with a swinging arm and a perforated metal plate to guide the pin into one of the predefined positions. Between 1899 and 1901, Hollerith replaced this punch with a key-operated one devised for him by a former typewriter designer (fig. 2.2). The initial census cards were divided into irregular fields with cus-tomized letter or number codes in each punching position. In the 1890s, Hol-lerith developed a multicolumn format in which each column had places for holes representing decimal digits.[9] A group of columns, or a field, represented a number with multiple digits. Early in the twentieth century card size was standardized and the number of columns was increased gradually to forty-five, which remained standard until the late 1920s (fig. 2.3).

The counting device, called the tabulator, produced the numbers entered into census tables. Hollerith's original electromechanical tabulator was a hand-fed press attached to counter wheels. It used metal pins and tiny cups of mer-cury to complete electrical circuits, counting all the cards with holes punched in the particular configuration set by wiring the device. When a run ended, the operator recorded the number shown on the counter wheels. During the 1890s, Hollerith developed accumulators for adding totals in predefined fields,

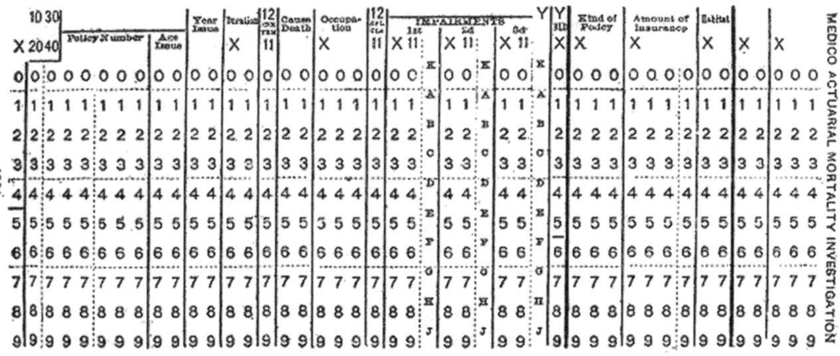

*Fig. 2.3.* Hollerith forty-five-column card designed for the 1910 Medico-Actuarial Mortality Investigation of the Actuarial Society of America. Reproduced from Arthur Hunter, "Method of Making Mortality Investigations by Means of Perforated Cards, Sorting and Tabulating Machines with Special Reference to the Medico-Actuarial Mor-tality Investigation," *Transactions of the Actuarial Society of America* 11 (1909–10): 254. Copyright 1910 by the Actuarial Society of America (Society of Actuaries). Reprinted with permission.

rather than simply counting cards. This added functionality greatly increased the device's potential uses. Early in the twentieth century he introduced tabulators that automatically fed the cards and used brushes to "read" them as they passed through the machine, thus speeding up the tabulating process.

During the 1890 census, the card sorting that logically preceded counting was handled as a by-product of that operation, using a primitive sorting box connected to the tabulator (see fig. 2.1). As the tabulator press "read" and counted the preset field on the card, holes punched in another preset field electrically opened one of two dozen lids on the sorting box; the operator placed the card into the box and closed the lid. This quasi-manual sorting prepared cards for the next tabulating run. Using the sorting box slowed the tabulating process so much that operators often sorted cards separately by pushing a knitting needle or similar implement through a specified hole. Early in the twentieth century, Hollerith introduced a separate sorting machine to sort cards into groups by the value in a given column.

Although primitive, Hollerith's original equipment processed data for the 1890 census faster than the former purely manual and clerical methods. It enabled the Census Bureau to handle the population increase since 1880 and to complete more varied and extensive tabular analyses than ever before.[10] It also started Hollerith out with a major, if highly episodic, customer for his machines. This periodic equipment use, along with the serious customer maintenance difficulties Hollerith encountered in a few instances, apparently encouraged him to initiate a practice that would later become key to the survival and success of the business: renting the equipment and selling the cards.[11] He sold only the card punch, the simplest device in the system.

Between decennial U.S. censuses, Hollerith initially rented the machines to the census organizations of other countries (e.g., Austria, Norway, and Canada) and to the U.S. Census Bureau for other enumerations, such as the 1900 agricultural census. Although he focused primarily on serving the census market and developing the improvements mentioned earlier, he also engaged in a few interactions with potential nongovernmental customers. These interactions with commercial firms became more sustained and central beginning in 1905, when the new census director, Simeon N. D. North, refused to award Hollerith the 1910 census contract, citing Hollerith's monopoly position and high rental prices. North then began hiring census staff to develop the Census Bureau's own tabulating equipment. Significantly, he hired James L. Powers, who would later leave the Census Bureau to start his own company, becoming Hollerith's primary U.S. competitor.[12] After North's decision, Hollerith's attention turned seriously to the commercial market.

Meanwhile, the commercial market for office appliances that processed information was beginning to develop. The systematic management ideology's emphasis on internal process and product documentation had greatly increased demand for devices and techniques to handle textual and numerical data.[13] The first typewriter that allowed a user to create text faster than with pen and paper went into production in 1874. During the 1880s and 1890s, other types of office equipment, from adding and calculating machines to filing equipment, were developed or improved, contributing to the burgeoning office appliance industry.[14] Tabulating systems would join this emerging market. Because only firms with a great amount of numerical data to be processed felt they needed these large and complex systems, their potential market was smaller, for example, than that for desktop adding machines. Information-intensive life insurance firms were obviously part of it.

## Early Insurance Challenges to Hollerith's Technology

According to a *New York Tribune* report of Hollerith's 1890 meeting with members of the ASA, guests included J. P. Lunger of Prudential of Newark, "whose company expects to use the machine."[15] At that time Prudential, which had already exceeded a million insurance policies, was second only to Metropolitan Life in number of policies handled, though both had less insurance in force than the Big Three.[16] Confirming the *Tribune*'s statement, Hollerith installed a primitive tabulating system at Prudential in 1891. Although he made several trips back to get it working, this first insurance customer—and first commercial customer—was evidently not satisfied, since the installation did not last. The aborted attempt epitomized the shaky relationship between Hollerith and the life insurance industry before 1910.

Prudential's unhappiness with the original Hollerith equipment centered on its sorting, which was too slow to handle the firm's large volume of industrial insurance records. Rather than waiting for Hollerith to improve the system's sorting capability, Prudential actuary John K. Gore took the unusual step of inventing a sorter himself and getting his brother-in-law to build it.[17] Gore installed it at Prudential by 1895, employing it to aid in performing valuations of industrial insurance policies, its initial and longest-sustained application, as well as for other statistical and operational purposes. His device, with its radial

*Fig. 2.4.* Gore sorters, designed by Prudential actuary John K. Gore, in use at the Prudential Insurance Company. Reproduced courtesy of the Prudential Insurance Company (CE207-1).

configuration (fig. 2.4) quite different from Hollerith's past or future designs, sorted cards mechanically, using pins and gravity, aided by electrically powered rotation. The device operated at up to 250 cards per minute, much faster than Hollerith's sorting box.[18]

In light of subsequent developments, however, Gore's approach had significant drawbacks that would ultimately pose problems for Prudential. First, although his system included a card punch and a sorter, it lacked any form of tabulator, thus requiring a manual or, much later, a mechanized process for counting cards or adding quantities.[19] Gore, an actuary rather than an inventor, showed no interest in creating a tabulating device himself. In fact, in 1901, only months before Hollerith's new sorter was first introduced, Gore wrote to Hollerith, "I have always had an idea that a combination of your system and my own would produce maximum results as to speed. In sorting vast numbers of cards, even including the counting, my system is much quicker than yours. When, however, by sorting, the numbers of cards in the various groups are reduced to the hundreds your system is the quicker."[20] This idea of combining the two systems was virtually impossible, however, because the Gore system used cards designed especially for it and incompatible with Hollerith's current or future cards.[21] The faster sorting initially made the lack of tabulating capability moot for Prudential, but when Hollerith introduced his new sorting device in late 1901, it was already as fast as the Gore sorter; subsequent improvements only made it more rapid while Gore's was not improved over the years.[22]

By the early twentieth century, Prudential had an installed base of Gore cards and a business process built around the device, showing the other side of the reciprocal interaction between technology and its use. Moreover, Prudential was proud of its sorter. Since Gore remained the company's actuary until 1934, there was also presumably some reluctance, whether his own or that of others, to dismantle his creation.[23] Thus the firm was long unwilling to abandon its investment of money, learning, and pride.[24] Not until the 1930s would the firm completely abandon its Gore equipment in favor of an extensive IBM setup.[25]

Although Gore's invention was soon outmoded, it should not be viewed as just a technological curiosity. From the insurance perspective, Prudential's rejection of the earliest Hollerith system and subsequent adoption of a sorter developed by its own actuary was the first of many examples in which insurance firms made adoption and use decisions based on their existing processes and perceived immediate needs. Moreover, Gore's development of his own new machinery to speed up the handling of Prudential's many policies was also the first of a few instances in which life insurance firms put efforts into in-house development of punched-card technology in order to create machines that would meet their current needs better than did commercially available equipment. Prudential's desire to speed up its processes is not surprising, given its huge number of policies. Moreover, the company was growing rapidly, doubling its insurance in force between 1890 and 1895, and again between 1895 and 1900, despite the Panic of 1893 and the ensuing depression.[26] In 1892 Prudential occupied its new corporate building, said to be "the biggest thing in New Jersey," filled with the latest technology, including telephones in every office.[27] Its home office labor force was growing by leaps and bounds, even though the sorter undoubtedly slowed this growth a bit when first adopted.

This path of *internal* technology development shaped specifically to its own needs, however, resulted in the company's commitment to an information technology that became increasingly outmoded and untenable over time, without offering an easy migration path to emerging opportunities. What economists and economic historians would call path dependence with a sub-optimal outcome began as Gore's—and Prudential's—path creation.[28] This single, albeit large, user firm initiated this technology path, but because it was an insurance firm, rather than an office machinery manufacturer, it did not follow up with further developments that could have created the increasing returns necessary to compete with Hollerith's technology. Thus, conditioned by the technical interrelatedness of the cards and equipment and the quasi irreversibility of investments in processes, Prudential became locked into a technological dead end.[29] Meanwhile, the rest of the insurance industry waited on the sidelines, initially falling behind Prudential in this area but ultimately benefiting from improvements in Hollerith's technology.

From the perspective of the commercial vendor, Prudential's rejection of Hollerith equipment because of its poor sorting capabilities proved to be the first of several instances in which insurance actors indirectly exerted market pressure on Hollerith's tabulating firm, encouraging the vendor to respond to their unmet needs. It was a signal to Hollerith that the insurance industry, a large and important segment of his potential commercial market, cared about slow sorting, identifying it as a critical problem, or what Thomas P. Hughes calls a "reverse salient," obstructing system development.[30] However, as another scholar has pointed out, "reverse salients [are not] given, independent of the actors involved. Most obviously, to agree on what constitutes a barrier to progress requires agreement on what one is trying to achieve. . . . That cannot be taken for granted."[31]

Hollerith's failure to respond immediately to this challenge suggests that he did not see the insurance perspective as primary at this point. The U.S. Census Bureau was still his principal customer. In addition, in 1895–96, he worked closely with a different commercial customer, the New York Central Railroad, to develop a system for processing the 4 million freight waybills it handled annually.[32] He adapted and installed machinery, first on a trial basis, then on a regular, long-term lease, for what became his first major commercial contract. On the basis of that contract he incorporated the Tabulating Machine Company (TMC), maintaining the previously established policy of renting the sorting and tabulating equipment while selling cards and card punches.[33] In addition to the other advantages offered by this business practice, it facilitated obtaining new business because the prospective customer did not need to purchase the equipment as a capital expense. His developments for the New York Central included redesigning the cards to arrange the holes in orderly rows representing digits and redesigning the tabulator that he was developing to enable it to add or accumulate quantities, rather than simply to count, thus improving parts of the system important to the railroad.[34] These improvements helped him finally secure the New York Central's business, a large contract for his fledgling firm. This breakthrough did not, however, enable him to capture more business from the railroad industry immediately, as he had hoped, since that industry, like life insurance, was conservative about adopting new equipment and changing business processes.[35] Nonetheless, the improvements helped in the next commercial markets Hollerith turned to, cost accounting in manufacturing firms and sales analysis and auditing for retailing. Hollerith did not yet see insurance as a key target and neglected faster sorting while developing other aspects of the system.

Although Hollerith's interaction with Prudential was unsuccessful, it was only the beginning of contact between Hollerith and the life insurance industry. During the 1890s, a few other insurance companies experimented with mechanized sorting and tabulating. Typically they contracted for specific studies with the "Improved Business Methods" department of the Library Bureau, the firm that had cooperated with the Association of Life Insurance Medical Directors (ALIMD) on a nonmechanized card system pooling firms' rejected applicants. The rental policy, although good for attracting and keeping customers, required Hollerith's company to make large capital investments in the machinery it rented.[36] Thus, beginning in 1896, cash-poor TMC contracted with the Library Bureau, already experienced with library and business card files, to manufacture and market equipment with TMC's patents internationally.[37] The Library Bureau's service arm also contracted with domestic customers other than the Census Bureau and railroads to provide services using this equipment.[38]

One of its earliest contracts was with Travelers Insurance Company, a moderate-sized firm dealing in ordinary insurance, to compile accident statistics for one year. In a 1901 letter to Hollerith, Travelers actuary Louis F. Butler described his firm's 1896 experience—and problems—with Hollerith equipment: "As I stated before, the original difficulty seemed to be that the subdivisions of our cards were so numerous that the time required to wire or set up a machine for the work was so great as to take away all advantage gained in the rapid tabulation after it was once set up."[39] Interestingly, Butler identified the slow rewiring process, rather than the slow sorting process, as the critical problem for Travelers, suggesting that Prudential's sorting complaints may have reflected in part its large industrial insurance business. In contrast, the problem of slow rewiring, which Hollerith would later improve by introducing an easy-to-use plugboard wiring system, was undoubtedly magnified by Travelers' smaller size and ordinary insurance business.[40] Despite this rewiring problem, Travelers found its experience with Hollerith equipment at Library Bureau not entirely useless, as Butler went on to explain: "We found, however, that the punch card served our purpose very much better than the written card previously used. We have therefore since that time used your punches in preparing the cards and have done our tabulating by means of knitting needles and comptometers. . . . The results have been so satisfactory that we shall continue to use the punch."

Apparently Travelers was not alone in this strategy, since Hollerith's correspondence with insurance company representatives around this time reveals that several wished to acquire cards and card punches, which could be purchased rather than rented, but not to rent other parts of the system.[41] At this time, manual files of tabbed, notched, or punched cards were just coming into common business use for storage and retrieval of structured data. Travelers and a few other insurance firms were improvising, using the Hollerith punch with knitting needles for sorting and retrieving data and comptometers for adding quantities.[42] Ironically, they were using part of what Hollerith had envisioned as a tightly linked technological system to perform the sorting function in another, less automated system. Nevertheless, Butler retained an interest in Hollerith's full configuration of equipment. In his 1901 letter, he both ordered more punches and inquired about whether improvements in the Hollerith equipment since 1896 would make it more useful to his firm than before. Subsequently, developments in the technological artifacts and in insurance use of them would lead to changes in both, so this use of the card punches in a different information-handling system never grew to challenge Hollerith's vision.

Meanwhile, in the late 1890s, Hollerith was so overwhelmed with his census and railroad business that he did not respond to the insurance firms' needs and failed to work with them. In a letter to his Library Bureau contact, H. E. Davidson, concerning Butler's inquiry, for example, Hollerith revealed that he wanted to retain this card punch customer but to delay any delivery of new equipment for at least one year until further improvements were made and more equipment manufactured.[43] Indeed, Hollerith was then designing improvements for the 1900 census, including a new key-operated punch and an automatic card feeder for the tabulator.[44] By failing to respond to Prudential's or Travelers' expressed needs, he was jeopardizing that market, a fact that he seemed to recognize but on which he had not yet acted. As he explained to Davidson in 1901, "I have at present appointments with several insurance actuaries, to which I have not been able to give attention on account of my rush here in Washington."[45] Nevertheless, in 1900 the U.S. Census Bureau, as well as insurance firms, often sorted cards manually with knitting needles, suggesting that the slowness of the sorting boxes was becoming more widely recognized. They were probably also incompatible with the tabulator's new automatic card feeder, though even the census was not yet using that feature very much.[46] By 1901, both the U.S. Census Bureau and insurance actuaries were indirectly and directly exerting pressure on Hollerith to speed up sorting.

Meanwhile, another challenge to Hollerith's equipment was emerging from the ASA. In response to a paper presented by Emory McClintock, Mutual Life actuary, at the fall 1900 ASA meeting, society members agreed to cooperate in a multicompany mortality study.[47] McClintock had argued that most publications concerning the general mortality experience of individual companies were useless and that "the same amount of effort might much better have been devoted to investigating special classes of business," so as "to learn how fishermen compare with farmers, how physicians compare with clergymen, and the like." To obtain adequate numbers for such comparisons, multiple companies would need to pool their statistics. This paper generated much spontaneous discussion and agreement in the eleven-year-old professional association, notwithstanding the fierce competition (and financial abuses) prevalent immediately preceding the 1905 Armstrong Hearings. As a result, the ASA cautiously but determinedly pursued this goal of amassing the data from which such comparisons could be made, first establishing a committee to examine the desirability and feasibility of such a project, then authorizing the committee to conduct the study it had designed.[48] Some actuaries clearly felt uneasy about what was happening in their companies and in the competitive life insurance marketplace at this time.[49] In undertaking this study they perhaps felt they were eschewing competition so as to build knowledge that would be useful to their firms and enhance the status of their profession. The committee members recognized that they could not handle so large a project manually. Thus, although the original committee members were all from firms focusing on ordinary, not industrial insurance, they added Prudential's Gore to the committee at the implementation stage because he had experience with both Hollerith's tabulating equipment and his own sorter.

Much of Hollerith's considerable correspondence with actuaries and insurance executives in 1900 and 1901 revolved around the ASA study, which was to be compiled in 1902.[50] Within weeks of the 1900 ASA meeting, an actuary informed Hollerith that a large, cooperative mortality study was likely, and soon committee members and other actuaries began to inquire about machine capabilities and ask to see the New York Central Railroad tabulating machinery.[51] His census work, however, preoccupied him, and he never connected with many of these actuaries. Ultimately he failed to secure an equipment contract for the ASA mortality study, despite last-minute correspondence with Prudential's Gore.[52] By late spring 1901, Hollerith's inability to respond rapidly to the ASA, combined with his system's limited sorting and rewiring capabilities, convinced the committee to adopt the Gore sorter for the study, perhaps the low point in Hollerith's early interaction with life insurance.

In late 1901, under pressure from the U.S. Census Bureau and the insurance industry, Hollerith finally introduced his own separate sorter.[53] The device initially processed 250 cards per minute, equivalent to the rate claimed for the Gore sorter; subsequent improvements would make it even faster.[54] Although it was too late for the 1902 ASA study, his new sorter would become a key part of his tabulating system, ultimately making it more attractive to insurance companies and other commercial firms, as well as to the Census Bureau.

## Increased Insurance Opportunities, 1905–1910

In 1905, when he lost the 1910 U.S. census contract, Hollerith turned to the commercial market in earnest. Perhaps reflecting his previous failure to obtain a contract for the 1902 ASA mortality study, the turmoil of the Armstrong Hearings, or simply his perception of greener pastures elsewhere, he did not initially target life insurance. Instead, he focused his sights on large railroad, utility, and retailing applications, including cost accounting for the Atchison, Topeka, and Santa Fe statistical offices, an application for the Denver Gas and Electric Company, and sales analysis for Marshall Field and Company.[55] His ongoing development of the equipment, however, continued to address common problems experienced by early insurance users. Between 1905 and 1907 Hollerith developed a plugboard system to replace the time-consuming rewiring system about which Travelers' actuary Butler had complained, speeding up changeovers in tasks.[56] This development, along with much-improved sorting capability, finally responded to the central needs expressed by the insurance firms initially interacting with Hollerith. Arthur Hunter, a New York Life actuary, apparently reflected a view common among actuaries when he noted at the 1910 ASA meetings that although elements of Hollerith's punched-card system had been around for twenty years, only recently had TMC finally developed the machines to a point that they were suitable for insurance use.[57] By 1911, when Hollerith's TMC merged with three other business machinery manufacturers to form the Computing-Tabulating-Recording Company (CTR) and Hollerith shifted from owner/manager to adviser, insurance firms and the ASA were providing significant business to TMC.[58]

By then, several life insurance companies had adopted Hollerith machinery for actuarial and occasionally for broader insurance purposes. In 1909 New York Life, then the second-largest insurance firm, converted its own manual actuarial mortality studies to a Hollerith system.[59] According to Hunter, the reasons for the conversion were clear: "While there is considerable expense involved in making a change from written to punched cards, the cost of installing the new system should be offset by the saving in clerk hire in from three to five years. In addition to the saving in money the saving in time and facility for making investigations in greater detail have induced many companies to look with favor on the new system."[60] He thus anticipated both monetary savings from reduced labor cost and increased investigatory capabilities, reasons shared by other insurance companies adopting the technology. Indeed, as early as 1901 the Library Bureau's Davidson had told Hollerith that the technology offered potential value to insurance companies by increasing analytic capabilities: "I am not sure that the knitting needle [and punched cards] would not do what they would want to do as well as your machine, but we may be able to induce them to attempt some things with your machine which they will not try to do with the knitting needle."[61]

Nevertheless, firms tended to identify gain from increased capabilities only after savings from simple labor costs. New York Life anticipated clear labor savings, even allowing for the extra precautions it had taken to assure accuracy. Accuracy, which most insurance firms saw as important for maintaining good relations with customers, was significant at several stages in insurance use of information-processing technology. In that firm's Hollerith system, operators independently punched two forty-five-column cards for each policy, on different colored cards, and then superimposed them and held them up to the light to visually check for errors. Although this method doubled card-punching time, Hunter argued that it constituted "one of the greatest advantages of the perforated card over the written card," since it resulted in two complete sets of cards, one of which could be kept in numerical order and the other in mortality investigation order.[62] Because the former set could be used to index the latter, this duplication saved time later in updating cards and in allowing subsequent investigations.

By this time, a few insurance firms were also using Hollerith machines for nonactuarial purposes—an early indicator of what lay ahead. At the same 1910 ASA meeting, Henry N. Kaufman, assistant actuary at the moderate-sized Phoenix Mutual Life Insurance Company of Hartford, described a fairly complicated system of Hollerith cards for ordinary insurance, probably but not explicitly that of Phoenix Mutual.[63] It included a new business card to record the details of new policies, a deferred premium card to "provide a method of obtaining the totals of the gross and net deferred premiums," a dividend card "to furnish an efficient means of transferring the dividends from the classification register or dividend sheets or from whatever records on which the dividends are first entered to the renewal cards," and several other types of cards with specific purposes. Obviously, in this case the Hollerith equipment was being used not just for actuarial investigations but for routine operating purposes such as tracking deferred premiums and sorting and adding loan amounts. Each card type was designed differently, some as combination cards with designated sections for handwritten entries alongside punched data. Labels printed over each set of columns allowed users to look up information on a specific card, just as they might have with pre-tabulator records. Like Hunter, Kaufman embraced duplicate card punching as the most economical way to ensure accuracy, arguing that it provided a useful additional set of cards.

Kaufman raised several issues that prefigured later uses of tabulating equipment in insurance. For example, he noted in regard to one application: "Although this Deferred Premium Card may not seem of sufficient importance to warrant installing the Hollerith machines for its use alone, yet I believe it will be found a very useful card where the tabulating machine is installed, as it is particularly well adapted for this kind of work, affording a very rapid means of ascertaining as soon as the books are closed the amount of the gross and net deferred premiums."[64] That is, even though particular applications were not necessarily anticipated or used to justify installation of Hollerith equipment, the new capabilities they provided—here allowing the firm to get data much more rapidly than in the past—were discovered to be very useful once the equipment was installed. Some innovative applications were thus emergent rather than planned.

Another prescient comment concerned the perceived need to have separate sets of cards for each separate application: "It may occur to some that as a good deal of this data is common to all the cards, one card could be planned that would cover everything, but of course the different uses to which these cards are put must be taken into consideration and also the manner of using."[65] For decades, insurance companies periodically noted the potential advantages of combining and consolidating their many sets of cards to create more efficient, integrated tabulating applications. However, the existing, functionally departmentalized structures and operating practices in insurance firms combined with the limited card size to constrain application of the new technology.[66] As a result, insurance firms typically used tabulating equipment and cards to handle one function at a time.

Finally, it is suggestive that New York Life, the second-largest firm in the industry by insurance in force, used the information-processing technology only for a straightforward actuarial application, whereas the moderate-sized Phoenix Life also used it for a wide array of operational applications, a pattern that would appear again in the early computer era. This difference probably reflected at least three factors: the relative size of the two firms, since in 1910 New York Life had more than fifteen times as much insurance in force as Phoenix Mutual; the larger firm's greater conservatism and difficulty in changing course; and its likely preoccupation with the Armstrong Hearings and their aftermath.[67]

Although the conference paper accounts of how these two firms used Hollerith equipment provide the most complete information on individual life insurance firm tabulating practices at this time, briefer mentions elsewhere indicate that these two companies were not alone. In a letter Kaufman sent to Hollerith on the latter's 1911 retirement from TMC's management, he mentioned that Hartford insurance firms already had seven or eight "machines" and several more were on order.[68] One such Hartford firm was undoubtedly Aetna Life and Affiliated Companies, which rented its first Hollerith equipment in 1910 to conduct a special compilation of mortality experience.[69] At around the time Hollerith received Kaufman's letter, he also received best wishes from a mathematician at Pennsylvania Mutual Life Insurance Company of Philadelphia who referred to that firm's pleasant relations with Hollerith and TMC.[70] TMC's 1911 annual report discusses insurance customers: "In insurance the Hollerith System is used for detailed records of every important feature in the business including classification of policies, and are [*sic*] in use by the Equitable, Mutual, New York Life, Penn Mutual and Home Life Insurance Companies, [and] the Hartford, Royal and Queen Fire Insurance Companies. Among the insurance companies which have recently adopted the Hollerith system are the Franklin, New Hampshire, National and Phoenix."[71] This list included the three largest ordinary insurance firms (New York Life, Mutual, and Equitable), as well as several smaller firms, some of which were based outside New York. Clearly Hollerith was making inroads into this market.

Perhaps the clearest signal of the life insurance industry's end-of-decade change in attitude toward Hollerith tabulators, as well as a mechanism reinforcing and expanding individual firm use of Hollerith equipment, was its use for the 1910 Medico-Actuarial Mortality Study undertaken jointly by the ASA and ALIMD. This multicompany study, which was conceived in 1909, undertaken between 1910 and 1912, and reported in five volumes between 1912 and 1914, covered more than 90% of all policies issued since 1885 in both the United States and Canada.[72] In describing how the joint committee adapted New York Life's tabulator-based method of undertaking actuarial studies to this multifirm study, Hunter noted that by this time, "the use of perforated cards [was] so well known that a lengthy explanation [was] not necessary."[73]

Insurance firms had submitted their data for the 1902 study written on tabular forms to be converted to the punched cards used in the Gore sorter. For the 1910 ASA study, however, the committee created and disseminated a set of codes for forty-five-column punched cards, allowing many firms to submit data already punched onto Hollerith cards: "There were so many companies who desired to use the Hollerith machines in supplying the data for the Committee that it was decided to prepare a standard card and standard codes which could be adopted by the companies if they wished to do so. By that means a great deal of labor is saved to the individual companies in addition to the advantage arising from a uniform code for the principal actuarial and medical data."[74] This new procedure for the 1910 study both reduced the committee's work and promised to make the companies' own subsequent analyses more efficient. The standard card had a few columns available for the firms to use as they wished, while the rest of the columns were devoted to the committee's codes. Firms supplying data in card form followed New York Life's system by punching two sets of cards to check for accuracy; after verification they submitted only one set to the committee, retaining the other for internal studies.

The adoption of Hollerith tabulating equipment for this Medico-Actuarial study revealed that life insurance actuarial departments now accepted this technology much more widely than they had in 1902. The new procedure of individual firms submitting one set of punched cards and retaining another furthered the network effect, introducing the machinery into other firms and creating further incentive for using it. As a result of this study, for example, Metropolitan Life's Ordinary Insurance Department adopted Hollerith equipment for its actuarial needs.[75]

By 1911, when TMC merged with two other firms to form CTR and when the Medico-Actuarial study had almost completed its data analysis, TMC had established a solid income stream from equipment rentals and card sales, primarily to commercial firms. In fact, its total income from those sources tripled between 1908 and 1910.[76] Yet TMC, still a small, inventor-dominated firm, struggled with product development and had not yet established the solid base of production, management, and marketing capabilities necessary to establish Chandler's first-mover advantage in its new industry.[77] Indeed, Hollerith apparently perceived marketing to be secondary at this stage, since he employed the Library Bureau as a marketing intermediary and failed to respond to actuaries at several points. The early publicity Hollerith received, combined with the strong insurance desire for better data-handling methods, made marketing unnecessary for this industry. Moreover, starting in 1907, TMC's weaknesses in manufacturing and management had created a backlog of unfilled orders that was not eliminated until 1909, a further disincentive to marketing.[78]

The insurance industry, as represented by both associations and individual firms, had just begun to realize the early promise of tabulating equipment suggested by Hollerith's 1890 demonstration and would soon become a more important user. However, TMC had yet to win the business of the two largest industrial insurance firms. Prudential was still using its Gore machines. Based on its participation in the Medico-Actuarial study, Metropolitan Life used Hollerith equipment for actuarial work only in its modest Ordinary Insurance Department: for its industrial insurance work, the company continued to use hand-sorted cards or bound registers.[79]

Insurance firms also tended to be fairly conservative, allowing their existing processes to shape their tabulating applications rather than exploring ways to reconfigure their processes to take advantage of the new technology. Actuarial uses were fairly direct translations from previous clerical processes. Nonactuarial uses, such as those Kaufman described, introduced only minor changes. For the most part, they simply continued the "systematic" approach then current among life insurance firms of dividing labor and processes very finely. They often simply translated nonpunched cards to punched cards and sometimes even created new, intermediate steps. Although the new technology sped up some of these processes, insurance firms did not use it to transform them.

At the same time, as insurance firms used this equipment more for operational purposes, they discovered that the equipment constrained, as well as enabled, certain uses at this stage. For example, Kaufman noted that the tabulating device had to "be ordered especially to meet the requirements of each particular office"; consequently, the office had to "carefully ascertain in advance" what fields it wanted to add because once the fields were established, they could not be changed.[80] Thus the tabulating machines themselves were not very flexible at this stage, although within two years CTR began to configure all equipment to allow accumulation on any column, thus greatly increasing flexibility.[81] Card capacity was also a constraint. As Kaufman explained, "It is necessary of course to have a number of different cards, as all the information cannot be punched on one card; and furthermore, it will facilitate matters if one card is not used for too many purposes, especially as the punching of the cards is a very small matter."[82] This capacity constraint reinforced life insurance firms' tendency to reproduce and reinforce the subdivision of processes into separate applications.

Broader insurance uses also highlighted the lack of any printing capability in the system. At this time, life insurance firms and associations used tabulating technology essentially as large and fast sorting, counting, and adding machines. An operator stood by the tabulator to record the number displayed on the dial each time it reached a total, an opportunity for inefficiency and inaccuracy. Moreover, any process that involved recording some quantity from each card, rather than just counting or aggregating large groups of cards, received only limited aid from the Hollerith equipment of this era. By contrast, many adding and calculating machines of this period, although they could not sort, could list (print) as well as add items and print a total, thus allowing visual verification for accuracy. Bookkeeping machines used with preprinted forms created permanent records as they listed, added, and subtracted. Insurance companies would be able to use the tabulating equipment for more and different types of processes when it acquired printing and document-handling capability.

Insurance and tabulating reciprocally shaped each other during the early years of interaction. Initially, the insurance industry saw Hollerith's equipment as promising but still limited, especially by slow sorting and rewiring. Gore's construction of an alternative sorting device for Prudential and the complaints of firms such as Travelers conveyed to Hollerith both insurance interest in sorting and tabulating functions and weaknesses these firms saw in the technology. The ASA's correspondence with Hollerith communicated industry needs more officially, and its choice of the Gore sorter for the 1902 mortality study conveyed his failure to meet those needs. In contrast, it approved and encouraged his subsequent developments by joining ALIMD to adopt Hollerith technology for the 1910 study, thereby providing many ASA members with their first substantive exposure to the technology and encouraging its wider use. The life insurance industry helped shape the early tabulating equipment Hollerith developed for the commercial market. Reciprocally, insurance processes took shape around the technology. At Prudential, such adaptation to the Gore sorter worked to its own eventual detriment. Most firms used Hollerith equipment to continue and extend existing patterns of functional subdivision, and the limited card size further reinforced this trend.

In subsequent decades, life insurance use of tabulating equipment grew. By 1913, insurance industry rental fees and card sales would account for nearly 15% of TMC's total revenues, giving the industry more market clout.[83] Tabulating's potential uses in the operational aspects of insurance soon made firms desire improved document-handling capabilities. In the next period the industry would exert its influence more deliberately toward that end.

# CHAPTER 3

# The Push toward Printing, 1910–1924

From 1910 through 1924, life insurance challenged the Tabulating Machine Company (TMC) and its successor both directly and indirectly to continue developing those aspects of the equipment that would make it more useful to insurance.[1] The life insurance industry encouraged the addition of printing capabilities—first numeric, then alphanumeric—to tabulating equipment, primarily by supporting Hollerith's newly emerging external competition: inventor J. Royden Peirce and competitor James L. Powers. Peirce posed an early threat to Hollerith's insurance business, but Powers, trained by the U.S. Census Bureau, was the more important challenger over time. Their threat gave TMC incentive to innovate, especially in printing. These episodes also demonstrate that insurance companies were becoming more interested in automating their processes, and consequently they were more active in shaping tabulating equipment and vendors to their perceived needs and in adapting their own processes as necessary. As the technology gained printing capabilities, they broadened their uses of it from primarily actuarial calculations to a range of operational applications. The continuing growth of the life insurance business and the growing importance of home office management set the context for changes in equipment and its use during this period.

## Life Insurance Growth and Interest in Home Office Management

After 1910, insurance companies grew rapidly and turned more seriously to streamlining their processes and cutting costs. A number of world events encouraged continuing growth in life insurance: the sinking of the *Titanic* in 1912 and the *Lusitania* in 1915, with their attendant loss of life and raised awareness of life insurance; World War I, with the establishment of the federal War Risk Insurance Bureau; and the influenza epidemic of 1918–19.[2] Many life insurance firms initially saw the War Risk Insurance Bureau as a serious threat, fearing that government would take over the business of insuring lives.[3] Ultimately, however, it benefited life insurance firms, as returning servicemen dropped their War Risk Insurance and bought private insurance when they married and settled down. As shown in figure 3.1, life insurance in force expanded rapidly after the war, at a rate exceeding that of national income and population.[4]

Not only were the major firms growing ever larger, but even moderate-sized firms now had $1 billion of insurance in force. In 1910, only six firms exceeded $1 billion; by 1930, seventeen companies did, and the largest twenty-five firms all had more insurance in force than 1910's seventh-ranked firm.[5] Although most firms no longer experienced the large diseconomies of scale common before the Armstrong Hearings, growth still required increases in their employment rolls, especially in home offices.[6] Increased demand led to rising wages and worker shortages in some areas and drew attention to rising office costs.[7] During the early decades of the century, insurance managers responded by adopting the systematic management techniques and technologies that were now moving from the manufacturing floor into the office. These centered around documenting all processes, orders, and results; analyzing results, typically quantitatively; and storing and handling all documentation and analysis to make this information readily available.[8] In insurance, these new approaches to management developed within the context of home office management, which was just emerging as an important concern in life insurance but would gain a more central role during the second quarter of the century.

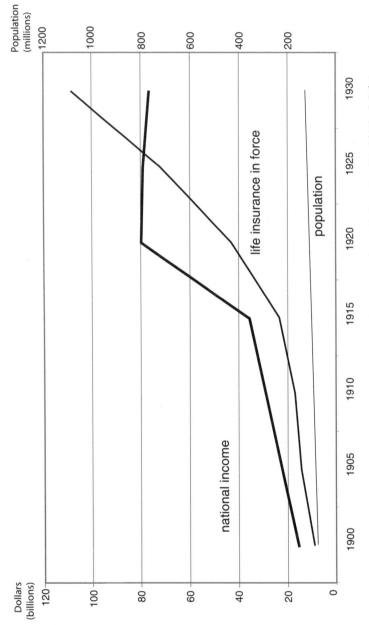

*Fig. 3.1.* U.S. life insurance in force grew faster than national income and population after World War I. Life insurance in force from Stalson, *Marketing Life Insurance,* app. 26; national income and population from U.S. Bureau of the Census, *Historical Statistics of the United States, Colonial Times to 1957* (Washington, D.C.: U.S. Department of Commerce, Bureau of the Census, 1960), ser. F 7, p. 139, and ser. A-2, p. 7.

The beginnings of this new managerial trend are evident in the chapters titled "Office Efficiency" and "Office Equipment" in a 1912 three-volume reference on insurance.[9] In the former, Melvil Dewey, founder of the Library Bureau, advocated the ideology of efficiency and system and delineated some of its current techniques. He mentioned the immense savings offered by "electric and other tabulating and computing machines" but primarily exhorted office managers and workers to set up and run an efficient office, especially as regards typewriting, duplicating, and filing of papers and cards.[10] In the subsequent chapter on "Office Equipment," Samuel F. Crowell discussed everything from desks to "Hollerith machines for statistical and accounting purposes."[11] Based on this reference work, neither the ideology nor the technology of systematic management was yet central to the insurance business, but both were beginning to gain attention.

The career of Harry A. Hopf in insurance and subsequently in office systematization also attests to the new interest in efficiently managing the home office. Hopf began at a moderate-sized and very conservative life insurance company, Germania Life, in 1902.[12] Around 1907 he began to suggest management innovations to Germania, including establishing an in-house magazine and providing lists of approved medical examiners to agents. In 1910, as head of the Medical Department, he first reorganized the Index Section, introducing a new system of file cards and establishing a systematic routine; he then proceeded to reorganize the entire Medical Department.[13] The conservative Germania did not receive his innovations well, even when they successfully reduced costs, but Hopf gained a reputation as an office systematizer externally.[14] While still at Germania, he directed the Rand Company's consulting service for life insurance companies. In 1914 he left Germania, taking a job at Phoenix Mutual, a company already making innovative use of the tabulator. In 1917, he gave a conference address on "Home Office Organization," describing a functional, line and staff organization for a life insurance firm.[15] In a section titled "Methods, Equipment and Standardization," he advocated both standardized procedures and extensive use of office equipment for recording, duplicating, and tabulating information related to operating as well as actuarial purposes. During the subsequent discussion, E. G. Simmons, a vice president of Pan-American Life Insurance Company, noted that when Hopf had consulted for his firm, the latter had instituted in that office a system of office management for handling the firm's business; Simmons added, "And we have never regretted it."[16] Simmons then stated the underlying premise beginning to gain currency in life insurance: "I believe that a life insurance company, to be successfully managed, must be systematically managed." Most insurance firms were more prepared than Germania to systematize routines and introduce technologies, if not to explore alternative organizational forms.[17] Meanwhile, by the late 1920s Hopf established his own consulting firm, H. A. Hopf and Company, Management Engineers, to devote full attention to systematic management in life insurance and more broadly.

Insurance interest in the tools and techniques of systematic management was clearly rising at this time and would encourage firms to adopt and use tabulating technology in various areas from actuarial to operational. It would also reinforce firms in their desire for printed documentation of tabulator results.

## The Emergence of Numerical Printing Capability

By 1910, many insurance firms were using Hollerith equipment to sort and tabulate cards, but at the end of each process, the operator had to record by hand the number shown on the dials. The machine's inability to list items being processed or to print the results of tabulation limited insurance uses of it. Although numerical printing capability was already available on adding and bookkeeping machines, Hollerith machines gained printing capability—first to print numbers, then to print alphabetical characters—only in response to significant competitive threats. In 1914 Gershom Smith, general manager of TMC, now a division of Computing-Tabulating-Recording (CTR), warned CTR's new president, Thomas J. Watson, that the insurance industry was threatening to defect from Hollerith machines: "There seems considerable to be feared from [the] Royden Peirce machine in connection with life insurance companies and the Powers Printing Tabulator in connection with other insurance companies."[18] He proceeded to cite rental fees and card sales for this segment of the market, which added up to almost $140,000 a year, nearly 15% of TMC's total 1913 revenues.[19] Insurance firms were involved in this competitive threat not just as customers but also, in a few cases, as sponsors and co-developers. The next stage of interaction between the tabulator and insurance industries centered around the emergence of printing capability in tabulators and the broadening of their operational uses in insurance companies.

### *The Initial Threat: Peirce Customized Printing Tabulators*

The first approach to printing capability in punched-card machinery came from J. Royden Peirce, an inventor who designed a few highly customized systems of punched-card equipment. His earliest related patent was awarded in 1907, though he emerged as a potential TMC competitor for life insurance business in the following decade.[20] Although some of his earliest work was specialized for electric utilities, by 1914 two life insurance companies had contracted with him to buy large installations of customized punched-card equipment that he would construct for them, jobs that by themselves clearly stretched the capabilities of his operation.[21] The first was Mutual Benefit Life Insurance Company, between Phoenix Mutual and Prudential in size.[22] In the late 1890s, Mutual Benefit had considered contracting with the Library Bureau to perform some actuarial work on Hollerith tabulating equipment, though whether it ever entered into such a contract remains unclear.[23] The firm subsequently developed an interest in Peirce and his equipment. At the 1914 Actuarial Society of America (ASA) meeting, Mutual Benefit actuary Percy Papps presented a paper describing the installation Peirce was developing for Mutual Benefit.[24] At the same time, discussion of Papps' paper revealed that Peirce was also under contract to develop an installation for Metropolitan Life, by then the largest U.S. insurance firm. Moreover, this ASA presentation guaranteed that actuaries at many other insurance firms also learned about this apparent alternative to Hollerith equipment.

Hollerith (and no doubt TMC general manager Gershom Smith) knew at least two years earlier that Peirce posed a competitive threat, based on a highly favorable 1912 report on Peirce's machinery to the President's Commission on Economy and Efficiency (PCEE).[25] A few months after the report had been presented to the commission, a friend forwarded it to Hollerith; with it, he sent a prospectus designed to raise funds for a proposed "Royden Company," based on Peirce's "entirely new system of perforated cards in conjunction with automatic selective machinery and adding machinery" and the related patents then held by the Peirce Patent Company.[26] According to the PCEE report, Peirce's system consisted of two devices: a "perforator" and a "distributing machine." The PCEE representatives saw a complete and functioning perforator, which looked like and in fact was a "combined typewriting and punching machine." This card-punching device differed from Hollerith's card punch in that the operator's keystroke simultaneously punched a hole and typed the corresponding number at the top of the card, making the card easily readable by humans as well as machines. In addition, the PCEE committee members observed an incomplete but highly promising example of a "distributing machine," which accumulated (added) totals, using a device based on expired adding machine patents, and then printed these totals out by categories on a paper tape. Thus both the card punch and the incomplete tabulating device included numerical printing capabilities. Although the report itself drew no comparisons between Peirce's and Hollerith's equipment, an accompanying letter from the PCEE chairman to a government official gave the advantage to Peirce: "From what we have seen of the Royden machines, completed and in the course of construction, they appear to contain features of distinct advantage over any of the Hollerith machines now on the market."[27]

Clearly such equipment, with its printing capabilities, would attract customers in insurance firms, railroads, and utilities, as well as accounting professionals, who felt that a written "audit trail" was necessary. The prospectus for the Royden Company listed individuals who had "expressed themselves ready to purchase and install the system as soon as put on the market," a list including the chairman and secretary of the PCEE, as well as comptrollers, auditors, and statisticians from a variety of businesses, including one life insurance firm.[28] The prospectus claimed, "Working models have been built and operated for three months without a hitch of any kind," and further, "Those who have made a thorough investigation believe that the proposition is as big a thing as the National Cash Register Company and a far bigger and more profitable venture than the Burroughs Adding Machine company." The Royden Company apparently never got off the ground, and Peirce himself never realized this business goal, though he would end up working for the highly successful IBM. The references to promising but only partially completed equipment would be a recurrent theme in Peirce's interactions with life insurance firms and others. His vision, which spurred further development from others, always outpaced his practical accomplishments.

By 1914, according to Papps' description, the Peirce system planned for Mutual Benefit included three machines, with a sorting machine added to the perforating and distributing machines. Such a system would, in theory, be able to perform all functions of the Hollerith card punch, sorting machine, and tabulator, but with the added benefit of printing, both at the punching and the tabulating stages. Although Peirce had built Mutual Benefit's card punches and sorters, he had not yet completed the distributing machine.

In describing the equipment and how Mutual Benefit planned to employ it, Papps suggested the directions of technology development and use his life insurance firm supported.[29] He pointed out that the Peirce cards increased potential capacity by representing the digits from one through nine using combinations of holes in four possible positions, rather than a single punch in one of twelve possible positions (fig. 3.2). This system allowed two rows of coding per card, thus potentially doubling the capacity of the forty-five-column Hollerith card, although Mutual Benefit had chosen to use only fifty columns of coded data, retaining space for additional handwritten data. These combination cards allowed both human and machine reading and could contain more total information, though some of it could not be read by machine. Moreover, a perforating machine operator could simultaneously punch the desired hole(s) in a column and type the corresponding number along the top of the card. Papps saw this feature as promoting more accurate punching as well as allowing users to read the figures. The sorter, which was a mechanical device based on pins, sorted only 180 cards per minute, compared with Hollerith's 250; Peirce had assured the firm, however, that later models would operate at 240 cards per minute. His tabulators, or "distributors," were custom made to

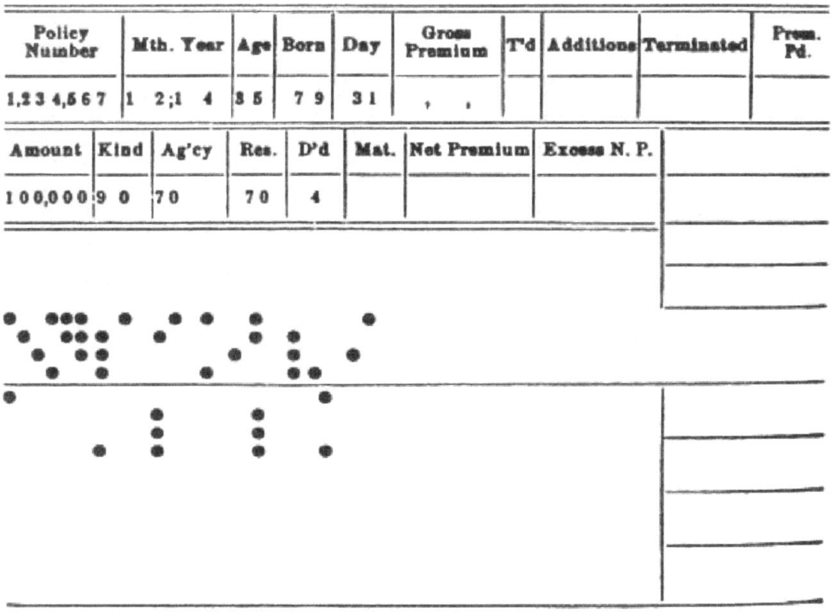

| Policy Number | Mth. Year | Age | Born | Day | Gross Premium | T'd | Additions | Terminated | Prem. Pd. |
|---|---|---|---|---|---|---|---|---|---|
| 1,234,567 | 1  2;1  4 | 3 5 | 7 9 | 3 1 | ,    . | | | | |

| Amount | Kind | Ag'cy | Res. | D'd | Mat. | Net Premium | Excess N. P. | |
|---|---|---|---|---|---|---|---|---|
| 100,000;9  0 | ;7 0 | | 7 0 | 4 | | | | |

*Fig. 3.2.* Peirce combination card designed for Mutual Benefit Life Insurance Company, showing two rows of numerical values and space for recording information by hand. Reproduced from Percy C. H. Papps, "The Installation of a Perforated Card System with a Description of the Peirce Machines," *Transactions of the Actuarial Society of America* 15 (1914): 50. Copyright 1914 by the Actuarial Society of America (Society of Actuaries). Reprinted with permission.

fit the user's needs. Indeed, Peirce himself used one that was connected to 100 adding machines and that printed out totals at the end. Mutual Benefit's customized tabulator would not need 100 adding machines, but it would be able to print out the designated data from each card on plain paper or preprinted forms, providing printed totals as needed.

Mutual Benefit planned two applications of the equipment, one actuarial and one operational. Each policy was to have two cards: a white individual valuation card, with the policy information used by the actuarial unit in calculating valuations and reserves; and a buff dividend card, used to transfer dividend information from renewal receipts. Both cards were combination cards with the first several punched fields on both cards designed to be identical so that the cards could be punched independently from different sources and then readily compared by aligning them and looking for buff through white holes and vice versa. Assuring the greatest possible accuracy was important to Mutual Benefit, as to other life insurance firms, and the human error rate for punching cards was unacceptably high. This partial duplication of data allowed a verifying step to catch errors yet avoided the excessive time required to punch complete duplicates that would only be discarded after verification. The last few punched fields on each card could be checked visually as needed, using the numbers typed at the top of the cards. The combination cards for operational use also accommodated the firm's existing practice "to show on the left-hand margin of the renewal receipt the entire account for the year of each policyholder with the company."[30] As Papps' description of the actuarial application makes clear, Peirce was going to design and build a tabulator highly customized to fit Mutual Benefit's existing processes:

> It is thought to be safer to have an independent valuation list in order that we
> may determine at any time the particulars of all policies in force, even if the cards
> are lost. For this reason we typewrite on loose sheets the number, age at issue, plan
> of insurance, and amount of each policy, grouped according to valuation order
> and then in numerical order. These loose sheets are then bound in book form and
> when a policy ceases to be in force, or is changed from one plan to another, the
> fact is entered in the valuation book. Mr. Peirce is prepared to build us a tabulat-
> ing machine which will be controlled by a counting device. Assuming that there
> are fifty lines on each page, we would set the counter at "50," place the page of
> the valuation book in the carriage, and the particulars of fifty cards previously
> sorted in valuation order would then be printed on the page. The machine would
> then stop of its own accord to allow the insertion of the next page of the valua-

tion register. As this machine will operate at the rate of about ninety cards a minute, it will readily be seen that the tabulating machine will not only avoid the chance of incorrect copying from the card to the list, but will add the totals and accomplish the work in a very small fraction of the time now required.[31]

The promised equipment would enable Mutual Benefit to continue many of its practices (including the bound book valuation list) without change while allowing verification for greater accuracy and less redundancy of effort than the Hollerith equipment.

The Hollerith equipment of that era, although immediately available for rental, did not offer many of these capabilities. In the discussion following Papps' presentation, he elaborated on why Mutual Benefit chose Peirce over Hollerith equipment, focusing on its operational use for dividend and renewal records:

I would like still further to emphasize the fact that the Pierce card is especially valuable to an office where the card is to be used as one of the permanent records. I do not want you to think I am opposed to the Hollerith machine or think the Pierce machine is better than the Hollerith for some purposes. There was no question in our office of using the Hollerith machine because it simply could not do the work. These records we have of our dividends, for example, and that is where we first wanted to use the Pierce machine, are permanent records. It was necessary for the mathematical department to enter the dividends on the cards and the renewal department to copy off the dividends onto the renewal cards. A flimsy card, which would be easily mussed up, and in that way made unavailable for the Hollerith machine, would not have been satisfactory at all. Furthermore there would not have been enough space on the Hollerith card for the necessary data.[32]

Thus Peirce proposed to build a customized system that would allow Mutual Benefit to maintain most aspects of its existing process while speeding up some. It offered many immediate benefits. Over time and without further development, however, the extremely customized system might have inhibited changes in process and upgrades to the technology. Such an outcome was ultimately preempted because Mutual Benefit was "forced to adopt the Hollerith card" when TMC bought out Peirce in 1922.[33]

Metropolitan Life assistant actuary J. D. Craig (son of actuary J. M. Craig) delivered the commentary on Papps' 1914 paper, in the process revealing that Metropolitan Life had also retained Peirce "to adapt his devices to the special requirements of the Actuarial Division."[34] Although Metropolitan Life's Ordinary Insurance Department continued to use the Hollerith equipment adopted for the 1910 Medico-Actuarial Study to perform its original actuarial task, the firm had not expanded its use either within the Actuarial Department or into operating areas, much less into the larger industrial insurance business area. Hollerith and his successors certainly could not ignore either their failure to expand their business within Metropolitan Life or that firm's retention of Peirce to build customized equipment for it.

After the Armstrong Hearings, Metropolitan Life had completed its conversion to a mutual company and increased its emphasis on the ideologies of public service and of business efficiency. It announced the public service ideology to policyholders as follows: "Insurance, not merely as a business proposition but as a social programme, will be the future policy of the Company."[35] It also argued that business efficiency was a necessary aspect of and precondition for true public service. A 1914 booklet describing its home office emphasized that "a constant effort is directed toward finding better methods and promoting efficiency."[36] Metropolitan Life's executives claimed that it had adopted the techniques and technologies of systematic office management for its own growth as well as for policyholder benefit. The company was already suffering from labor shortages, which would be a recurrent problem for life insurance firms during the twentieth century. Indeed, the booklet's description of the firm's ordinary insurance operation claimed, no doubt with some hyperbole, that "every labor-saving device or perfection in system that would operate to keep the clerical force within bounds has been inaugurated and successfully utilized in the Ordinary Department."[37] Problems of efficiency were even more salient in the labor-intensive industrial insurance business. Thus in June 1913, when J. M. Craig negotiated the firm's first contract with Peirce—for design and construction of a perforating machine, sorting machine, and listing-adding machine customized for the Actuarial Department—he was continuing Metropolitan Life's efforts to bring systematic and efficient methods to the firm.[38]

In his commentary on Papps' 1914 ASA paper, J. D. Craig mentioned several features of Peirce's equipment that he saw as particularly attractive. He, like Papps, found that both the printing punch and the combination cards made the equipment more versatile. In addition, he noted that once cards were sorted, the promised tabulating machine would automatically stop and total when a predefined code in some field changed, thus eliminating the need for the stop cards that had to be inserted manually in card stacks being tabulated using Hollerith equipment.[39] Finally, Craig cited the tabulator's printing feature as the major innovation Metropolitan Life expected to realize from the system: "The tabulating machine tabulates the number of policies, amount of insurance, annual premium, premium payable,—either annually, semi-annually or quarterly,—and deferred premium, according to the various subdivisions into which they are sorted; prints the detail of the classifications, as well as the totals, all the while recording restorations in red ink and cancellations in black ink. When the cards for one group are tabulated, the machine records the totals before proceeding to tabulate the next group."[40] The promised ability to list details from each card as it passed through the tabulator and to print out totals and subtotals—in two colors of ink—as it went, rather than to have the machine stop after each set of cards while operators recorded the numbers in the registers, would obviously improve efficiency and remove an opportunity for transcription error. Many internal reports, such as lists of policy numbers and amounts by location, could be created directly from cards. In describing its new system of accounting using the Peirce perforated cards then being installed, the 1914 Metropolitan Life pamphlet had boasted, "It is believed that these are the most complete machines for complex statistical purposes that have as yet been installed in any office."[41] The planned statistical applications, while primarily actuarial, had managerial uses, as well.

Although Peirce could conceptualize printing machinery that would fit into the existing or expanded processes of his clients, he had trouble delivering it. In his commentary on Papps' paper, J. D. Craig mentioned with regret, but not yet with serious concern, that sixteen months after the original order, Metropolitan Life had not yet received the equipment.[42] The equipment promised in 1913 was not completed until sometime between 1916 and 1918, and its key device, the listing-adding machine, cost double the original price, which had itself been questioned as potentially "prohibitive" in the first place, though the question had been brushed aside by J. M. Craig.[43] Peirce sold his equipment, rather than renting it, but the correspondence within the actuary's office does not reveal any strong reaction to this difference from Hollerith's policy. Nevertheless, although the final product of this first contract never lived up to all of Peirce's claims, it must have performed well enough to seem highly promising in comparison with the nonprinting Hollerith machines, for Metropolitan Life entered into another contract with him in 1918, based on an initial proposal first submitted in 1916.

This second contract involved a new twist on printing—the use of alpha-

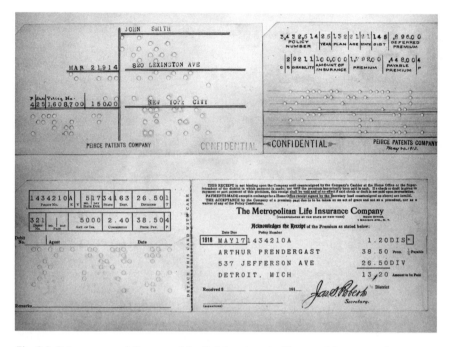

*Fig. 3.3.* Peirce prepared these confidential drawings to illustrate his proposed system of alphabetical tabulating cards for Metropolitan Life. The system he envisioned encoded all the alphabetical and numerical information needed to generate bills, receipts, and other operational documents. Reproduced courtesy of the MetLife Archives.

betical as well as numerical characters. The confidential drawings he prepared for Metropolitan Life in negotiating his contracts, some dated as early as 1913, showed Peirce's vision of a system that would use punched holes to encode the name and address of the insured, along with the relevant numerical information (fig. 3.3).[44] Although this vision was not part of the actuarial equipment made under the first Peirce–Metropolitan Life contract, it was integral to the 1916 proposal and subsequent 1918 contract. In 1916, Peirce proposed to construct customized punched-card machinery designed for the Ordinary Insurance Department's operational use. It would prepare and address premium notices, receipts, and stubs to be mailed to policyholders and would prepare various internal records, including a register of policies issued and an agent's list of notices.[45] The perforating machine, which resembled a typewriter (fig. 3.4), would punch numbers and letters into cards while simultaneously typing the corresponding letters and numbers along the top of the card. The promised system also included a listing machine and a machine for duplicating certain

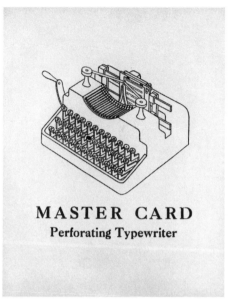

MASTER CARD
Perforating Typewriter

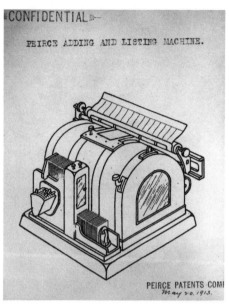

*Fig. 3.4.* Peirce prepared these confidential drawings to illustrate his proposed alphabetical perforating machine, which punched holes representing numbers and letters at the same time that it typed the corresponding letters and numbers along the top of the card, and his adding and listing machine. Reproduced courtesy of the MetLife Archives.

information onto another card for the Actuarial Department. Peirce's proposal laid out his vision for transforming Metropolitan Life's document creation processes through this system:

> By means of these machines all hand work in connection with the recording, notice sending and preparation of data for the Actuary's Office is entirely done away with. . . .
>
> I would point out, finally, what a great step in advance of anything which has heretofore been done in this line, these perforated card machines are. Once the primary card has been made[,] all the reports and notices from the beginning of the policy's career to its end will be made by machinery. *From the production of the card to the final reports in the Actuarial Division is one continuous automatic mechanical cycle.*[46]

In 1918, this proposal was converted into a contract, in which Metropolitan agreed to pay Peirce a salary and to establish within its home office "a factory for the development and manufacture, for its own uses," of sixteen different devices customized to specific operational and actuarial applications, from a notice and receipt machine to a state report tabulator.[47] The 1918 contract followed an internal recommendation responding in part to reports that Prudential's Gore and the International Banking Corporation were also interested in Peirce's device: "We believe the general plan is so broad in its scope and so important that we should not let this opportunity pass, particularly when we know that other people are interested."[48] Indeed, around that time Peirce also entered into two other major contracts for alphabetical punched-card systems for life insurance, one with the Insurance Division of the U.S. Veterans Bureau and one with Prudential.[49] In 1919 Peirce proposed that Metropolitan Life renegotiate its contract to share the development costs and outcomes with these two and potentially more organizations. Metropolitan Life turned down the opportunity, however, preferring to bear all the costs and to receive all the rewards of Peirce's customized developments, including the alphabetical capabilities.

Subsequently, some members of Metropolitan Life's Home Office Study Committee challenged the firm's strategy of supporting and waiting for Peirce's promised customized equipment, based on its high degree of specialization (and thus its inflexibility to changes in insurance processes, documents, or customer products) as well as on Peirce's seemingly infinite delays.[50] Nevertheless, committee advocates of Peirce's system continued to hold him to his contracts and to renew them until at least 1926, when an internal study revealed that the firm had already paid more than $1 million for Peirce's still incomplete development efforts. J. D. Craig, a prominent supporter of Peirce's efforts, stated an important underlying factor in this support: "Our fundamental proposition is that the Metropolitan is big enough, and its work important enough, so that we do not have to fit our system to existing machines; that time is not imperative; that the Metropolitan, rather than propose a plan to fit existing machines, can demand that machines be built to fit its system."[51] Clearly pride based on Metropolitan Life's size, importance, and consequent specialness was central to him.

The principal technical attraction of Peirce's system was its attempt to integrate all stages of information handling and document production, making it central to insurance operations, as well as to actuarial calculations. In this respect, Peirce anticipated applications of the late tabulator and early computer eras. Peirce's vision outpaced his mechanical and business abilities, however, and none of the three contracts for insurance tabulating systems was satisfactorily completed. The 1926 Metropolitan Life "Study of the Peirce Machines" assessed these efforts as follows: "In reviewing the other installations of Peirce machines one is impressed with the fact that in every case the installation has been practically a development and that a great deal of time has been consumed before machines have been delivered. On delivery considerable time has elapsed before the equipment is ready to use. In no one instance has there been a complete installation of equipment."[52] Ultimately, TMC would buy Peirce Patents Company for its alphabetical printing patents and hire Peirce himself to help TMC compete with its second external threat, Powers Accounting Machine Company.

## A More Serious Threat: Powers Accounting Machine Corporation

Gershom Smith's 1914 letter cited a second challenge to TMC: James Powers. This potentially more dangerous competitor was making inroads into the insurance market, again based on printing capabilities. The U.S. Census Bureau had opened the way for this competition when it hired Powers in 1907 to build its own equipment as an alternative to renting Hollerith's. The Census Bureau had equipment and expectations shaped by Hollerith. It still possessed Hollerith card punches and a set of old sorting machines from the 1900 agricultural census.[53] Thus Powers, unlike Peirce, designed devices to use cards compatible with Hollerith equipment, though his machines processed the punched cards mechanically rather than electrically.[54] In addition, when Powers left the Census Bureau in 1911 to form an independent firm, Powers Accounting Machine Corporation, he initially followed Hollerith's lead in establishing a business model based on rental rather than sale.[55] This approach made the machines accessible to more customers by eliminating a large initial investment, although it also created large capital requirements for Powers' firm. Technical compatibility and financial accessibility allowed and required him to compete directly with TMC for its existing customers while making it easier for first-time customers to try the equipment.[56]

Like Peirce, Powers recognized that a printing tabulator would open up more business applications. By 1913 Powers had developed working models of a numerical printing tabulator, and by 1915 he offered these tabulators for rental.[57] The Powers printing tabulator (fig. 3.5), as it was designated to emphasize this new capability, could both list selected data from each card processed and print totals.[58] A firm could use the Powers printing tabulator with customized forms that preprinted the necessary alphabetic information

*Fig. 3.5.* The Powers printing tabulator, available by 1915, could list numerical items and print totals. Photograph reproduced courtesy of the Smithsonian Institution, no. 93-13127.

to generate records and reports directly from cards. For example, insurance firms traditionally used pen or typewriter to create lists of each agent's policies for several operational purposes. Now, firms could use the Powers printing tabulator to sort cards by district and agent (both indicated by numerical codes); then, using appropriately designed forms with agents' names, they could create lists of numbered policies.[59] This device also offered another valuable feature, a "connection box" that could be changed to run another application.[60] Although the Powers printing tabulator did not have all the features promised by Peirce, it offered more than the Hollerith machines, and, unlike the Peirce machines, it was available immediately and at a known cost. A few medium-sized life insurance firms, such as Travelers and Phoenix Mutual, both Hartford firms that had already used Hollerith equipment, quickly adopted the Powers tabulator to gain printing capability.[61] The card compatibility and the rental basis of both Powers and Hollerith machines made such a switch relatively easy for them.[62]

While the largest industrial life insurance firms in the United States, Metropolitan Life and Prudential, were focusing on Peirce's promised equipment, the largest British industrial life insurance company, the venerable Prudential Assurance Company, was intrigued by the Powers printing tabulator. During the late nineteenth and early twentieth centuries Prudential Assurance, like other British insurance firms, had been reluctant to adopt any new office technologies, preferring to stick to its well-tested manual processing methods.[63] By 1910, however, Prudential Assurance actuary Joseph Burn was showing interest in office machinery in general and punched-card tabulating in particular, so when an opportunity arose to test the new technology, he seized it. In 1911, the Approved Societies Act legislated a new health insurance system for the working class in England, and the industrial assurance companies were asked to administer it. Burn decided to use this project, which was entirely independent of Prudential's regular insurance business, as an opportunity to test the new technology without risk. He set up a battery of machines from the British Powers agency, incorporated as the Accounting and Tabulating Machine Company, or the "Acc and Tab," to handle this work and immediately was impressed with the results.

Burn was so enthusiastic about the Powers equipment that by 1917 he wrote to the largest American industrial life insurance firm, Metropolitan Life, with a proposal concerning it.[64] He pointed out that the Powers tabulators, although they needed many further improvements, were "<u>much</u> better than Hollerith" machines and proposed the following plan:

> We have an idea that as the two biggest Industrial Insurance Companies who will probably be able to make the most effective use of such machines it might be to our mutual very great advantage if we could be in a position to control and if possible manufacture the machines which we decide are most useful.
>
> Although our primary object would be the insuring of our own supply at reasonable rates it is quite likely that not only this object might most easily be obtained in this way but a very remunerative investment as well.

His plan would have allowed the two firms to control future development of the Powers printing tabulators, pushing it in directions appropriate to their own needs as industrial insurance giants while assuring their own supplies at reasonable prices. He also proposed to share the initial costs as well as potential gains by promoting rental of the equipment to all interested commercial parties, including other insurance firms. Such a policy assured that the equipment would develop in ways useful to business in general, thus avoiding the technological dead-end fate of the Gore sorter. Moreover, the investment in Powers would likely be productive financially as well as operationally.

Metropolitan Life refused this proposal, with Vice President Hegemon writing, "Our experience convinces us that the Peirce machines are so superior to the Powers and Hollerith machines that they will eventually supplant both the latter, though now we are using all three."[65] Metropolitan Life, he added, preferred to remain the sole beneficiary of Peirce's development efforts sponsored by the company. Proceeding on its own, Prudential Assurance bought the Acc and Tab in 1919, thereby assuring its own supply and influence over further developments.[66] Prudential Assurance's approach to guiding development without attempting to monopolize its results turned out to be more successful than Metropolitan Life's proprietary approach. At this time, however, Metropolitan Life was focused on satisfying its own perceived needs as a large and important firm, including what some executives saw as its right to demand that technology be shaped to its processes, rather than vice versa.

### *TMC's Competitive Response:*
### *Delayed Catch-Up-and-Surpass Strategy*

TMC's loss of the two largest American industrial insurance companies (Metropolitan Life and Prudential) to Peirce and the largest British industrial insurance company (Prudential Assurance) to Powers, along with a few defections among the moderate-sized ordinary insurance companies in the United States, clearly threatened its domination of the insurance business.[67] At a time when TMC, under Thomas Watson's leadership, was investing in marketing, management, and manufacturing facilities to a much greater extent than Powers (and, of course, than Peirce), it still faced technical challenges, especially those related to printing capabilities. Shortly after recognizing the dual threat posed by Powers and Peirce, Watson had established an "Experimental," or research and development, Department to enable the vendor to better respond to such competition.[68]

Although this new department was charged with developing a printing tabulator with automatic control, a machine that Watson thought would be superior to the Powers printing tabulator, TMC offered no printing capability at all until 1921.[69] In 1914 Hollerith had filed his first patent for automatic control, which would eliminate the need for stop cards and constant operator oversight, and by 1917 the Experimental Department had constructed a prototype printing tabulator with automatic control. Nevertheless, TMC did not offer such a machine for rental until 1921. Most scholars attribute the delay to World War I, but at least one has argued that the long delay was intentional, so as to avoid making its nonprinting tabulators obsolete.[70] Whatever the reason for delay, TMC launched its first printing tabulator with automatic control in 1921.

Meanwhile, in 1917 TMC had introduced the verifier, responding to another need expressed by life insurance companies.[71] Insurance firms had consistently indicated that their business required great accuracy and that a normal level of input errors would be unacceptable. Previously, they had dealt with this problem primarily through punching duplicate sets of cards, to allow visual comparison. This new device allowed the firms to check the accuracy more efficiently. As the original cards were fed through the verifier, a second operator entered the same data, but without producing duplicate cards. The verifier locked up when the data did not match, forcing the operator to go back, check, and reenter. The new process saved time and cards, though it sacrificed the extra card set some companies had earlier seen as an advantage.

Insurance firms' continued interest in the Powers printing tabulator despite TMC's popular verifier suggests that only TMC's introduction of its own automatic printing tabulator in 1921 prevented continued erosion of its life insurance business. At that point, some life insurance firms that had previously changed to Powers, including Phoenix Mutual and Travelers, changed back to TMC's system (which they still referred to by the Hollerith name), based on the new model's combination of automatic control, printing capability, and greater reliability. A Travelers executive, for example, explained, "We did use Powers tabulating machines, until the Hollerith Automatic Control Printer came out, after which we shifted principally to that."[72] Similarly, a mid-1920s internal Metropolitan Life report compared Hollerith's printing tabulator favorably to Powers' for use in handling industrial insurance actuarial work, noting, "We use the Hollerith Printer Tabulator machines exclusively for all Classification work[;] the reason for this is, that 'Stop,' 'Space' and 'Total' cards are not required in the Hollerith Tabulators."[73] In addition to saving time, this feature also improved accuracy, since tabulators lacking automatic control would give the wrong total when the space card was not in place. Still, printing capability was essential for this shift back to TMC. The switch—and thus the industry's exercising of its market power—was eased by compatible cards and the rental policies.

## Initial Developments in Alphanumerical Tabulating and Printing

Although early in the century Peirce had seen the potential of alphabetical as well as numerical sorting, tabulating, and printing capability for insurance companies, he had been unable to realize it successfully in the highly customized and integrated installations he envisioned. As the first quarter of the twentieth century ended, Powers again seized the technological lead from TMC by creating the first workable version of alphabetical tabulating. This capability was essential before tabulators could be used for insurance operational applications, such as premium billing. Again life insurance—this time the British giant, Prudential Assurance—played a central role in this development. TMC would not introduce its version of this capability for a few more years, but it reached a milestone of its own. In 1924 its parent company, CTR, changed its name to International Business Machines Corporation (IBM), the name under which it would continue to fight off competition and grow in size and power for the rest of the century.

As early as 1915, the Prudential Assurance manager in charge of the company's Powers machine installation had seen the potential value of an alphabetical printing tabulator and begun working with the Acc and Tab to develop one.[74] Prudential Assurance later claimed that the innovation was directly related to operating its huge industrial insurance business, which at this time included 24 million industrial policies: "This development came about by the express desire of the Prudential Assurance Company, in order that the name of the assured might be printed mechanically in the Industrial Branch records."[75] After buying the Acc and Tab in 1919, Prudential Assurance funded and oversaw the final development of an alphabetical attachment to the regular Powers tabulator.[76] Reflecting its intended use for printing industrial registers, the attachment (available by 1920) printed alphabetical characters only in a specific cluster of columns set aside for that purpose. Prudential Assurance actuary Burn, like Metropolitan Life actuary Craig, had an ambitious vision for tabulating as part of insurance processes, but according to one historian, it had less to do with pride of size and more with reducing its expense ratio: "Joseph Burn saw this development as one which was crucial to his long-term plans to decentralize and reduce the cost of insurance policy administration. It would be a costly development, but one with vast potential for the Prudential business, allowing the complete accounting operation to be done by one system, and thus enabling them to dispense with their batteries of Addressograph and bookkeeping machines."[77]

By 1923, Prudential Assurance had the largest installation of such machinery in England and was using it to generate many of the lists and registers its industrial insurance business demanded (fig. 3.6), though it did not achieve full mechanization for another five years.[78] In 1924 an office machinery consultant described the installation and its results for company operations as follows:

> The most interesting and far-reaching installation of punch cards I have ever witnessed was at the Prudential Life Assurance Company of London, one of the largest industrial insurance organizations of the world. In their office the tabulating machines are a medium by which practically all of their office record work, whether actuarial, accounting, or statistical, is accomplished. Tabulators equipped with alphabetical units by which names of the insured and agents can be tabulated from the punched cards take the place of the typewriters. All agents' statements, and their life and lapse registers, are made directly from the cards punched for each policy in force. To complete this remarkable installation was a gigantic task extending over a number of years and entailing an immense amount of patient work, but the results in the actual savings accomplished, increase in effi-

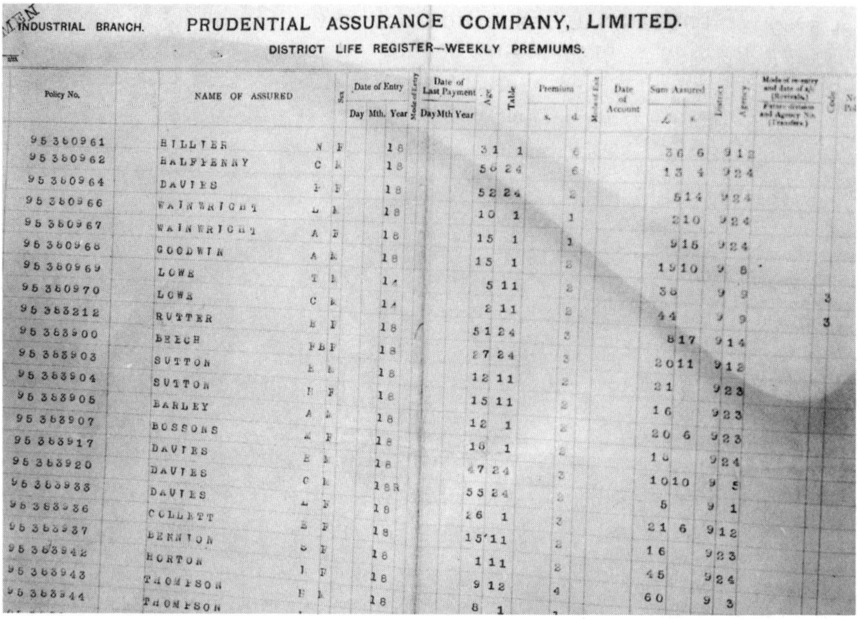

INDUSTRIAL BRANCH. PRUDENTIAL ASSURANCE COMPANY, LIMITED.

DISTRICT LIFE REGISTER—WEEKLY PREMIUMS.

| Policy No. | Name of Assured | | Sex | Date of Entry Year | Age | Table | Premium d. | Sum Assured £ s. | District | Agency | Code |
|---|---|---|---|---|---|---|---|---|---|---|---|
| 95360961 | HILLIER | N | F | 18 | 31 | 1 | 6 | 36 6 | 9 | 12 | |
| 95360962 | HALFPENNY | C | K | 18 | 56 | 24 | 6 | 13 4 | 9 | 24 | |
| 95360964 | DAVIES | F | F | 18 | 52 | 24 | 2 | 514 | 9 | 24 | |
| 95360966 | WAINWRIGHT | L | L | 18 | 10 | 1 | 1 | 210 | 9 | 24 | |
| 95360967 | WAINWRIGHT | A | F | 18 | 15 | 1 | 1 | 915 | 9 | 24 | |
| 95360968 | GOODWIN | A | L | 18 | 15 | 1 | 2 | 1910 | 9 | 8 | |
| 95360969 | LOWE | T | L | 1[illegible] | 5 | 11 | 2 | 36 | 9 | 9 | 3 |
| 95360970 | LOWE | C | L | 1[illegible] | 2 | 11 | 2 | 44 | 9 | 9 | 3 |
| 95363212 | RUTTER | E | I | 18 | 51 | 24 | 3 | 817 | 9 | 14 | |
| 95363900 | BEECH | F B | F | 18 | 27 | 24 | 3 | 2011 | 9 | 12 | |
| 95363903 | SUTTON | E | L | 18 | 12 | 11 | 2 | 21 | 9 | 23 | |
| 95363904 | SUTTON | H | F | 18 | 15 | 11 | 2 | 16 | 9 | 23 | |
| 95363905 | BARLEY | A | L | 18 | 12 | 1 | 2 | 20 6 | 9 | 23 | |
| 95363907 | BOSSONS | M | F | 18 | 16 | 1 | 2 | 16 | 9 | 24 | |
| 95363917 | DAVIES | E | L | 18 | 47 | 24 | 3 | 1010 | 9 | 5 | |
| 95363920 | DAVIES | C | K | 18R | 55 | 24 | 2 | 5 | 9 | 1 | |
| 95363933 | DAVIES | L | F | 18 | 26 | 1 | 2 | 21 6 | 9 | 12 | |
| 95363936 | COLLETT | E | F | 18 | 15′ | 11 | 2 | 16 | 9 | 23 | |
| 95363937 | BENNION | S | F | 18 | 1 | 11 | 2 | 45 | 9 | 24 | |
| 95363942 | HORTON | I | F | 18 | 9 | 12 | 4 | 60 | 9 | 3 | |
| 95363943 | THOMPSON | F | L | 18 | 8 | 1 | | | | | |
| 95363944 | THOMPSON | | | | | | | | | | |

*Fig. 3.6.* The British Prudential Assurance produced its District Life Register for 1923 using a Powers alphabetical tabulating machine. Reproduced from Metropolitan Life's "Report on Perforated Card Systems of English Companies," December 13, 1923, courtesy of the MetLife Archives.

> ciency of office operation, and elimination of peak loads exceeded the original expectations of the officers.[79]

Thus the British Powers agency, under Prudential Assurance's ownership, led the race for alphabetical tabulating.

Prudential Assurance did not follow Metropolitan Life's policy of attempting to retain all costs and benefits of development itself. Rather, it planned to direct the development and recoup its investment by supplying machines to other insurance companies. In fact Burn, a zealous missionary for office organization and mechanization, actively helped the Acc and Tab market the equipment to other British insurance companies.[80] Despite openly sharing the technology, Prudential Assurance cut its expense ratio almost in half between 1920 and 1939. Although other British insurance firms reduced their ratios, as well, Prudential Assurance consistently outperformed the others on this measure.[81] Until after World War II, the Acc and Tab continued to thrive as a well-funded subsidiary of Prudential Assurance, holding royalty agreements with U.S.-based Powers Accounting Machine Company and its subsequent acquirer, Remington Rand. This situation allowed the Acc and Tab to avoid the financial crises that weakened Powers during the 1920s and to compete on much more even terms with the British Hollerith agency than Powers did with TMC and later IBM.[82]

After Hegemon refused Burn's offer to collaborate in tabulator development efforts, Metropolitan Life began to add its weight to alphabetical developments in the original U.S. Powers firm, although the exact set of players and sequence of events are obscure. Sometime before 1924 Powers had apparently developed a machine with thirteen-letter alphabetical capability, a device that had only limited application (and not in insurance, where names were essential).[83] In late 1923, a committee of Metropolitan Life executives visited Prudential Assurance's offices in London to see its tabulators, which could handle twenty-four letters, a capability that they cited first among "the more important additions and improvements that have been made by the British Powers Company" and that made the machines clearly superior to the thirteen-letter tabulators offered by Powers in the United States.[84] Their report also outlined in great detail how Prudential Assurance applied this machinery in its industrial insurance operations. Starting in 1924, in parallel with its funding of Peirce's efforts in ordinary insurance operations, Metropolitan Life's Home Office Study Committee also began working with Powers and TMC (part of the newly named IBM) to develop ways of using and modifying their equipment to mechanize more of the insurance firm's operating processes, including those related to industrial insurance.[85] For these developmental efforts, unlike the efforts with Peirce, Metropolitan Life provided very little monetary support, since the two vendors were competing to acquire all of this huge firm's business.

Metropolitan Life obviously modeled its work with Powers on the achievements of Prudential Assurance and the Acc and Tab. A framed 1925 commemorative sample—listing names as well as numerical information of some industrial insurance policies—claims to be a "Sheet Run on the First Alphabetic Tabulator in the United States," which was "Constructed by the Powers Accounting Machine Company for the Home Office Study Committee of the Metropolitan Life Insurance Company."[86] The accompanying text states the application the committee had in mind: "The machine will now produce life and lapse register sheets from punched cards showing all the details necessary for Home Office and District Office purposes as well as subtotals for each class of transaction and a grand total for the week's business."[87] Although this application was not, apparently, implemented, the committee's interactions with Powers suggest that the largest American life insurance firm was shifting away from its early and expensive strategy of solely funding Peirce's developments and was now working closely with Powers, as well. The interactions also indicate that in the United States, as in England, a major industrial insurance company was actively pushing the development of alphabetical tabulating capability by working with a viable tabulating vendor. Indeed, Powers introduced the full alphabetical tabulator into the U.S. market around the time of this interaction.[88]

Thus in the mid-1920s, three years after finally introducing its first numerical printing tabulator in 1921, the Hollerith organization was again experiencing competition for insurance customers from Powers, this time over alphabetical tabulating. The threat was clear, of course, even before 1924, based on the Acc and Tab's developments in England. In 1922, as an initial step toward addressing it, Watson bought Peirce's main engineering shop, acquired the rights to his patents, and hired Peirce himself to help the firm develop its own alphabetical tabulating machine.[89] The essential incompatibility of Peirce's system with the Hollerith machinery, along with Peirce's continued work for Metropolitan Life, may help account for yet another long lag before IBM introduced its alphabetical tabulator in 1931.[90] Of course, industrial life insurance was not its only customer, nor was alphabetical printing the only tabulator development in which insurance was interested. The lag was filled with other new introductions, as discussed in the next chapter.

From 1910 through 1924, insurance users, along with other commercial customers such as utilities wanting to speed up billing and accountants desiring an audit trail, encouraged the development of printing capabilities. Given the industry's heavy dependence on documents in its operations, it supported developments that allowed it to combine data manipulation with document production, including first the printing tabulator and later the alphabetical tabulator. Firms such as Travelers, Phoenix Mutual, and Mutual Benefit signaled their needs through their market choices, adopting the first printing tabulators developed by Powers and Peirce, then trading them back in when TMC introduced its own, with additional features and better reliability. Meanwhile, lead users on each side of the Atlantic—industrial insurance giants Metropolitan Life and Prudential Assurance—deliberately invested in developing tabulating technology, though using different approaches.[91] Prudential Assurance bought the British Powers agency, enabling the insurance firm to fund and shape technology development directly, though without intending to be the sole funder or the sole beneficiary. Indeed, it allowed the firm to continue competing in the British market and helped it sell the new tabulator to other insurance firms. Metropolitan Life, on the other hand, initially contracted with Peirce to develop customized proprietary technology to support its existing processes. Then, when delays mounted, the Home Office Study Committee, established to improve processes and adopt technologies, sought competitive developments from Powers and even TMC. Meanwhile the American Prudential, in attempting to move on from the Gore sorters, also contracted with Peirce for custom equipment, again hitting a technological dead end.

While all these mechanisms encouraged tabulating vendors to develop printing capabilities, different approaches differentially affected the life insurance firms adopting them. Companies could shift back and forth between Powers and Hollerith technologies relatively easily, given the rental policies and card compatibility at this time. Prudential Assurance's approach seems to have worked well, both financially and strategically. Metropolitan Life's approach was much less successful; ultimately, the firm invested considerable money and time for a highly customized but inflexible proprietary system that was never successfully completed. A study of the British capital equipment industry similarly found that although user involvement in diffusion was important to innovation, "for the individual user-firm, exclusive reliance on the inventions of its own machine shop was a high-risk strategy. . . . If pursued dogmatically, it could lead to expensive mistakes, technological dead-ends, inefficient and even obsolete machinery."[92] Such a strategy was inherently even more risky when the user firm was overseeing innovation in an area requiring fundamentally different skills, as was the case with Metropolitan Life. Furthermore, its predisposition toward special-purpose machines designed around its existing processes built inflexibility into the system it was attempting to develop. One of the advantages of the evolving commercial devices, including those produced by the British Powers agency, was their ability to be reconfigured as well as combined with other components, thereby creating a much more flexible system.

These actions by the largest firms, along with the market-mediated shifts of the smaller firms and the role of industry associations such as the ASA in setting technology standards for cooperative studies and facilitating information exchange, certainly influenced technological developments in directions that the life insurance industry as a whole saw as desirable. The added printing and alphabetical capabilities eliminated many opportunities for transcription errors and opened up operational applications by allowing document creation. Speaking at the first annual conference of the Life Office Management Association in 1924, B. F. Dvorak, an independent consultant, noted the increasing insurance use of tabulating and summarized the reciprocal influence of printing capabilities on insurance practices as follows:

> [The use of punch cards] is so general that every life insurance executive is more or less familiar with them, and it suffices to say that the cards once correctly punched are a permanent record and may be rapidly sorted into any desired order or classification and then used as an actuating medium in a tabulator for the purpose of preparing the required statements.
>
> Because the original Hollerith tabulator was a non-listing machine, the punched cards were seldom used for direct preparation of records and their use was more or less limited to the various analysis work.
>
> This condition was changed when the Powers, and a few years later the Hollerith printing tabulator, made their appearance on the market. These tabulators opened a new field for the use of punch cards.
>
> The practice of tabulating original records directly from punch cards is gradually becoming more common and is taking the place of former analysis of records after they were made by hand.[93]

Thus firms could now use printing tabulators to make insurance operating processes, as well as actuarial analysis, more efficient and accurate by creating internal reports and records directly from cards.

In the tabulating industry itself, technological advance was often driven by competition. The rental business model may have created pressure on vendors to delay introducing new innovations so as to avoid making existing equipment obsolete. Consequently, development came in part through two challenges to Hollerith's market domination, both based on expanding the equipment's capabilities and both encouraged by the insurance industry. The competition from the Powers company, in particular, pushed TMC and later IBM to develop new technical and organizational capabilities, including establishing research and development capabilities and learning to work more closely with major user industries such as life insurance. This competition would continue in the second quarter of the twentieth century.

# CHAPTER 4

# Insurance Associations and the Flowering of the Tabulator Era

The second quarter of the twentieth century was the height of the tabulator era, when tabulating installations became entrenched in insurance companies and both the technology and its use continued to evolve. Life insurance firms institutionalized interest in and cooperation regarding office management in a new national insurance organization—the Life Office Management Association (LOMA). It provided a forum within which managers and executives discussed, shared, and encouraged ongoing evolution of tabulating technology and its use within home office management. A few years later the Insurance Accounting and Statistical Association (IASA) emerged in the Midwest, focused specifically on insurance use of tabulating technology, but it would attain national stature only during World War II. As the technology's document-handling capabilities continued to develop—rapidly through 1931, more incrementally during the Great Depression and World War II, then rapidly again in the postwar period—insurance firms used this technology for more processes, while IBM solidified its ascendancy as the dominant vendor.

During this period, insurance firms and organizations played a less aggressive role in shaping the technology artifacts than they had in the preceding quarter century. Nevertheless, the associations, typically working through member committees, actively shaped insurance use of technology by sharing knowledge of current office practices (including tabulating) and recommending those they judged to be appropriate and effective. Technology committees also invited vendor representatives to attend and contribute to technology-related sessions. Finally, the associations sponsored well-attended equipment exhibits at which vendors displayed new devices and their potential applications to insurance processes. Although they did not play an aggressive role in shaping technology artifacts during this period, insurance associations visibly influenced insurance use of technology. They would subsequently play an even more prominent role in shaping insurance adoption and use of computers.

The proceedings of those associations also provide a window onto insurance applications of tabulating technology, revealing one continuing and one new trend. Following a path established earlier, insurance companies increasingly used tabulating equipment not just in actuarial calculations but in operational processes such as billing and accounting. This focus on the operational would continue into the early computer era. Moreover, an earlier trend reversed itself, and a movement from individual and compartmentalized to integrated insurance applications began to emerge. Although most tabulating processes were still single, freestanding operations, in a few cases firms adopted more integrated premium billing and accounting processes, establishing the initial trajectory that most insurance firms would follow during the early computer era.

## LOMA and the Development of Life Office Management

Although insurance companies devoted only limited efforts to improving office management in the early twentieth century, by 1924 home office management had grown important enough to become the focus of a new life insurance trade association—the Life Office Management Association.[1] This organization coordinated firms' efforts to adopt systematic office management, including the use of office appliances such as tabulating equipment. In its early years LOMA established a norm of sharing knowledge about office practices and technologies in the name of efficiency and public service. This focus continued through the 1930s and 1940s but was augmented and reshaped by depression, war, and postwar concerns. LOMA shaped the insurance context within which tabulating technology adoption and use occurred.

## *Sharing Knowledge in the Name of Efficiency and Public Service*

In his opening remarks as the "temporary" chairman at LOMA's organizing meeting, Franklin Mead, secretary and actuary of Lincoln National Life Insurance Company, noted that the presence of 143 delegates from 87 life insurance companies "seemed to be sufficient proof of the need for a permanent association to study and develop problems concerning Home Office Administration."[2] The original delegates represented small and large firms from all regions of the United States as well as Canada, with both stock and mutual organization. Corporate membership would grow rapidly over the next few years, reaching 153 firms by 1931.[3] In 1930, 18 of the 25 largest firms sent contingents to the conference, including Metropolitan Life, and by 1950 all of the largest 25 firms had joined.[4] The original delegates occupied various positions within their firms, with secretary and actuary the most common, followed closely by assistant secretary.[5] The high representation of the corporate secretary's office clearly reflected the typical firm organization, in which the secretary was responsible for office organization. By 1930, assistant secretaries outnumbered secretaries, with vice presidents and actuaries following, and middle-level managers with titles such as "Manager, Policy Department" were becoming more numerous. The meeting attendees were a mix of company officers and managers in subsequent years, but the emphasis was clearly more operational than policy-oriented.

Mead summarized the new association's purpose as "constructive work in the field of Home Office organization and management." In his welcoming address, Arthur F. Hall, president of host company Lincoln Life, described the organization's founding as an expression of "the fine spirit of helpfulness and the willingness to discuss and exchange ideas concerning mutual problems which has existed in the life insurance business in recent years"—a tangible embodiment of the public service ideology.[6] He connected cooperative public service with business efficiency in the new association's mission:

It is the opinion of many life insurance executives that one of the greatest problems which confronts us in the future is the problem of reduction in costs. Every improvement in service and every decrease in the cost of operations will permit lower rates, thus widening the market for insurance and increasing its opportunities to serve.

More significant even than this is the recognition of the idealism of our profession as embodied in the purpose of this gathering. Behind it is a well-defined appreciation of the premise that the public service fostered by life insurance is our mutual responsibility to mankind, and the support of any agency aiming to promote the general welfare and advancement of the business is both a duty and a privilege which we all share.[7]

In this formulation, a cooperative approach to office management would reduce costs, making insurance more accessible to the public and simultaneously encouraging continued market growth. Moreover, Mead noted that existing insurance industry organizations had not paid adequate attention to these issues.[8]

Talks at the ensuing LOMA meetings underscored how important a cooperative approach was to the officers and members. E. E. Reid, general manager of London Life and acting LOMA president in 1927, argued that the rapid growth of clerical positions in the life insurance business gave firms strong incentives to cooperate in this area, in which LOMA could serve as "a Clearing House of inestimable value."[9] Although he anticipated more intense competition and closer margins in the industry, he implicitly assumed that the competition would occur in the sales arena, not in office management. Reid's 1928 presidential speech noted that although individual firms would do their own research in some areas of home office management, on some occasions "group experience [was] necessary to guide our judgment," and some types of research carried costs too high to "be borne solely by one Organization."[10]

Further, as Henry Holt, assistant actuary of National Life Insurance Company and chairman of the committee studying office appliances, suggested at the 1927 conference, cooperation through an association would give the industry more leverage in its relations with office appliance manufacturers.[11] After urging members to fill out and update questionnaire cards about office appliances, he added: "The dissemination of such information should create a demand sufficient to enable the manufacturers to co-operate with us in bringing out the now seemingly impossible in mechanical devices." This potential market power would not be actively pursued until the late 1930s, when the Committee on Office Equipment began explicitly inviting equipment manufacturers to attend and exhibit their equipment at LOMA meetings, partly to instill "greater interest on the part of these companies in the development of their products for the particular needs of the life insurance business."[12] In the organization's earliest years, however, the primary argument for collaborating on the questionnaire was that all would benefit from mutual information sharing. Based on reported questionnaire return rates and continued organizational growth, the majority of member firms not only espoused cooperation to improve business efficiency and serve the public but actively cooperated, as well.

The ideology of business efficiency evident in LOMA rhetoric was increasingly tied to the systematic or scientific office management movement. Life insurance came late to systematic office management, lagging behind some other industries that had studied it intensely for more than a decade, "very probably," as one LOMA member put it, because "insurance officers have not felt this data to be quite so essential for their purpose as it [was] in the case of commercial institutions."[13] This wording, which does not classify insurance as a commercial institution, suggests that executives may have seen their public service ideology and the wave of mutualization following the Armstrong Hearings as making insurance special and shielding it from the need for greater efficiency. In forming LOMA, however, they expressed increased urgency about pursuing business efficiency through improved office management.

At LOMA's first meeting, papers and "Roundtables" or "Discussional Conferences" covered home office organization and structure, policy records, procedures for establishing and documenting standard practices, and the use of office machinery—all standard aspects of systematic office management as already popularized by such magazines as *System* and *Industrial Management*.[14] One roundtable conference, for example, advocated establishing written instructions for all aspects of clerical operations in order to standardize the work and to allow a managerial review of tasks so that "useless operations" might be eliminated.[15] Indeed, Continental Life Insurance Company's Adolph Rydgren, roundtable chairman, noted that the "greatest advantage [of standard practice written instruction] is that it defines the manner in which the work should be done to conform to a practice which is known by experience to be the best"—a nod to scientific management's notion of "the one best way." At a later conference, B. J. Perry of Massachusetts Mutual Life Insurance Company, head of a LOMA committee on standardizing equipment, stated another basic tenet of systematic management: "Standardization is the modern way of making permanent each advance."[16] Indeed, such a committee's existence publicized the issue and encouraged member firms to standardize their office machinery and furnishings. William Henry Leffingwell, one of the best-known consultants in systematic office management, was invited to address the association's third annual conference, and others from this movement also addressed the organization during its first decade of existence.[17]

At the same time that LOMA embraced efficiency through system and standards, it also demonstrated interest in a contrasting but complementary managerial movement: the multistranded ideology variously referred to as human relations, industrial relations, or personnel management. Initially, industrial welfare emerged around 1900 to advance the Progressive movement's humanitarian goal of bettering workers' lives.[18] Employee social clubs, in-house publications, and shop conferences were all techniques to forward this agenda. As applied by managers, this ideology also had a more instrumental side, helping to address labor problems and "personalizing" increasingly large and impersonal firms. The personnel management function emerged as another key strand, with the individuals in these positions seeking system and efficiency among the human, as well as nonhuman, elements of work.[19] For the insurance companies, this philosophy not only complemented systematic management but also aligned with the public service ideology. Thus it is not surprising that by 1930 a handful of LOMA conference attendees were members of personnel departments, and that number would keep increasing.

In the 1926 conference, LOMA president Henry Wireman Cook, of Northwestern National Life Insurance Company, identified the association's domain, as revealed in contributions to its first two meetings, as consisting of personnel, mechanical equipment, and planning.[20] "Personnel" encompassed the many human relations issues that home offices faced; "mechanical equipment" included efficient use of all office technology from desks and card files to tabulators; and "planning" covered systematic business management for efficiency. Thus office equipment, including tabulating technology, was seen as necessarily accompanying the two ideologies, human relations and systematic management, though it was typically more closely associated with the latter. At the first conference B. F. Dvorak, a Chicago-based accountant and systematizer, discussed tabulator applications to actuarial and operational work in home offices.[21] In his 1928 presidential address, Reid highlighted the coexistence of efficiency and human relations in a formulation in which office technology typified systematization: "Mechanizing the work and humanizing the relations."[22] The formation and rapid growth of LOMA demonstrate that, starting in the mid-1920s, insurance firms were ready and willing to take a more active approach to improving office management. This role would shape insurance use of tabulating technology.

## Continued Emphasis on Cooperation and Efficiency during Depression and Wartime

In the 1930s and 1940s, life insurance continued to share information on office management through LOMA. The Great Depression posed economic and regulatory challenges but was not as hard on life insurance as on many other industries.[23] Life insurance in force grew through 1930, dipped slightly, though less than national income, and then began rising again (fig. 4.1). Unlike the banks, most insurance firms remained solvent, and the policies of those few that went under were reinsured by other firms. Insurance was not federally regulated, but state regulators intervened in two significant yet rela-

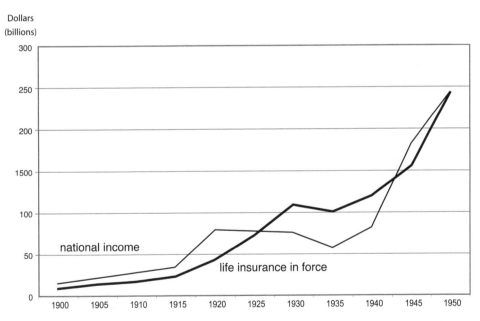

*Fig. 4.1.* Life insurance in force in U.S. insurance companies dipped less than national income during the Great Depression and then continued to grow with national income. Life insurance in force figures from American Council of Life Insurance, *1992 Life Insurance Fact Book,* 24; national income figures from U.S. Bureau of the Census, *Historical Statistics of the United States, Colonial Times to 1957* (Washington, D.C.: U.S. Department of Commerce, Bureau of the Census, 1960), ser. F 7, p. 139.

tively limited ways. First, at the end of 1931 and 1932, when plummeting stock prices threatened to make insurance reserves inadequate, the National Convention of Insurance Commissioners announced that insurance firms could, for purposes of computing year-end reserves, value their securities at the higher market prices of June 30, 1931.[24] After the banks and stock exchanges were closed, state insurance regulators intervened a second time, limiting policy loans and cash surrenders to prevent a similar crisis in insurance. Within a few months, however, these regulations were eased or removed on a state-by-state basis.[25] Indeed, some firms did not feel the need even for this brief moratorium.[26]

Potentially more threatening to life insurance enterprises than these supportive state regulatory actions was the 1938–40 Temporary National Economic Committee (TNEC) investigation of economic power concentration. They feared a repeat of the Armstrong Hearings, possibly leading toward federal, rather than state, insurance regulation. Despite some aggressive questioning and the Securities and Exchange Commission staff's critical report to TNEC, however, the ultimate outcome seemed relatively innocuous to the industry, and the threat of federal regulation evaporated.[27]

While the industry survived the Great Depression in relatively good shape, issues related to economic and social conditions (e.g., the decreasing value of assets, the increasing demand for policy loans, and an epidemic of suicides among holders of large policies) dominated discussions in both general life insurance associations such as the American Life Convention and more topically or occupationally focused ones such as the Actuarial Society of America and LOMA.[28] LOMA considered depression-related issues relevant to its charter, since the adverse business conditions only made improving office processes and cutting costs more important. Depression conditions gave member firms more common interests, such as recalibrating clerical salaries and conserving existing policies, rather than spurring interfirm competition in this area.[29] In his 1934 presidential address G. W. Skilton of Connecticut General Life Insurance Company stated that the organization would continue its cooperative activities during troubled times: "The numerous new operating problems and frequent and rapid changes which characterize our economic and political transition should stimulate co-operative effort. True, we could all progress slowly, each company using the experimental method (or as I call it, the 'trial and error' method), but it is economically and socially sound that we should pool our efforts and share the advantages of research to the benefit of our respective companies and the life insurance industry."[30] Thus the impetus behind LOMA's cooperative mission was still strong.

The balance within LOMA's own conference programs shifted somewhat during the depression decade, with personnel and cost-control issues taking up an increasing proportion of attention, while insurance use of mechanical equipment took up less. Still, equipment exhibits continued, and special reports and conferences focused specifically on equipment use in particular applications. Moreover, the depression drew firms' attention to business methods such as cost accounting in which life insurance still lagged behind manufacturing.[31] Insurance bookkeeping operations were organized around the annual statement, the form and content of which were determined by the state insurance commissioners, Prudential's L. R. Menagh Jr. explained. Thus these operations differed from what the firms might have instituted if they had organized their bookkeeping departments primarily to obtain expense information and secondarily to furnish figures for the Annual Statement. Menagh's LOMA Committee on Departmental and Functional Costs worked hard to develop standard measures for life insurance, seeing these as a way to improve efficiency by allowing comparisons over time and across companies.

In addition to its existing activities, during the 1930s LOMA initiated some new cooperative programs, the most important of which was an educational institute that offered certificate or degree programs to members' nonprofessional office employees. Nevertheless, one of the TNEC board's few criticisms of life insurance was that the industry needed to expand its programs to better educate employees interacting with policyholders and the public.[32] By 1942, LOMA Institute was planning changes, recognizing "that a positive program for building up an understanding on the part of policyholders and the public at large of the place, purpose, record and contribution of life insurance to the social and economic life of America, [was] a major responsibility of the business."[33] Thus the public service ideology continued to serve as a rhetorical touchstone for its efforts.

The 1940s would present many new challenges to insurance. In fall 1941, even before the United States entered the war, LOMA presentations acknowledged the new conditions firms faced: "greater employee turnover, higher operating costs, scarcities of basic materials for some office equipment and greater emphasis upon the time element of work schedules."[34] A year later, conditions had changed more radically. Indeed, LOMA officially canceled the 1942 conference to save transportation costs, although an annual proceedings volume with the submitted papers was still published.[35] At wartime meetings, as during the depression, LOMA programs reflected problems peculiar to the era, such as handling premiums for members of the armed forces and dealing with labor and equipment shortages, as well as anticipating and planning for the adjustments that would be needed after the war.[36]

Moreover, by this time fourteen states had passed Guertin laws, requiring that by 1948 firms abandon the badly out-of-date American Experience Table used since 1868 and adopt a new standard mortality table.[37] Although this new table better reflected actual mortality, it left companies with tighter safety margins and required more careful calculation of interest rates used in their various formulas. The shift would also temporarily increase their immediate needs for employees and for calculating technology. In the face of such problems, however, LOMA officers maintained their cooperative rhetoric and activity. In his 1943 presidential address James B. Slimmon, vice president and secretary of Aetna Life Insurance Company, stressed the value of continued cooperation: "During the past twenty years our business has been required to adjust itself to an era of 'boom' prosperity, a serious depression and a World War. We have passed through a period of rapid change which has brought forth new problems in the field of organization, methods, and procedures. We have come not only to recognize the possibilities but also to acknowledge the value of cooperative research in our specialized field of management."[38]

In 1944 LOMA president Edmund Fitzgerald of Northwestern Mutual Life Insurance Company identified the major postwar challenge to member firms as "the adoption and effective use of the management techniques developed under the exigencies of war."[39] By 1946 and 1947, however, another, even more urgent problem had emerged: the end of the war did not bring the anticipated easing of labor shortages. In a 1946 special conference on personnel issues, Helen L. Washburn, personnel manager of Home Life Insurance Company, described the situation: "The problem of securing new employees has been a difficult one since the beginning of the War, and has grown only a little better since its end last year. It is a pressing problem, not only for the personnel staff, but for managers who must face the difficulties of reorganization and peace-time expansion with a staff which is not only inadequate in numbers but in some cases inadequate as to qualifications."[40] In her subsequent analysis, she identified several problems: relatively low salary levels (though many firms had raised them to be competitive locally), the repetitive and boring aspect of the work, limited opportunities for advancement, the gender definition of jobs that limited employment of untrained men returning from the war, and limited training of entry-level workers on the "why," not just the "how," of insurance work.[41] In the following year, E. L. Baldwin, assistant personnel director of State Farm Life Insurance Company, observed that recruiting was only half the battle and that retention was critical, citing turnover figures in his firm that had skyrocketed from 16% in 1936, to 21% in 1941, to 62% in 1946, despite various efforts including creating smaller work units, reducing working hours, changing job classifications, adding training, and establishing an activities association and a housing bureau.[42] Others also lamented the difficulties and elaborated on what steps their companies had taken to deal with hiring and turnover. Nevertheless, most speakers claimed that their firm's salaries were in line with the local market, often providing figures to support the claim.

Papers and special conferences demonstrated that the industry was attempting to address this problem cooperatively. Still, the persistent shortage of workers, especially in light of the postwar life insurance boom (see fig. 4.1), would become an important backdrop for computer adoptions beginning in the 1950s. Meanwhile, another association, founded earlier with a more circumscribed mandate and geographical scope, emerged on the national insurance scene during the war years, just in time to play a major role in educating insurance firms about new developments in computing technology during the postwar era.

## The Emergence of IASA

In 1928, shortly after LOMA's founding, the Peoria, Illinois, representative of the Tabulating Machine Company (still referred to as TMC even though it was now part of IBM) brought together a group representing all his insurance customers.[43] He believed, according to founding member George Westermann, statistician of Peoria Life Insurance Company, "that he, as well as his customers, could learn a great deal from meetings of this type and also that he would be able to sell more tabulating equipment as a result."[44] The group that gathered represented eight Illinois and Iowa insurance firms as well as the Illinois Insurance Division and TMC. By title, the attendees ranged from actuary and secretary to auditor and statistician—a composition similar to LOMA's. Although it originated as a local group, this gathering would ultimately grow into a national insurance association focusing on information technology use.

The organization quickly established its identity as an insurance association focused on tabulating methods, rather than a tabulating user group. The group's first constitution stated its intent "to promote the discussion of office methods and practices as applied to life insurance companies, particularly with reference to punched cards," and limited its active membership to "life insurance organizations and associations and State Insurance Departments," thus barring tabulating vendors from full membership.[45] By 1930, the organization invited the Powers Division of Remington Rand to exhibit equipment as well, ending the exclusive relationship with IBM.[46] In seeking a name, the participants initially chose Life Office Methods Association over Punched Card Accounting Association to make clear its primary affiliation with life insurance.[47] In 1933 the members changed that to the Insurance Accounting and Statistical Association.[48] The new name omitted reference to *life* insurance, since this trade association, unlike LOMA, welcomed members from all insurance branches.

IASA maintained its small size and regional nature for its first decade, since those characteristics made it attractive to its earliest members. Conference attendees represented fewer than twenty firms until the late 1930s. As business conditions improved, however, the association began to grow rapidly. In 1940, IASA's membership exceeded 100 firms, including representatives from both coasts and Canada.[49] To accommodate its membership, the organization created separate tracks for life insurance and for fire and casualty insurance. By 1948 IASA had 380 member companies (more than LOMA's 207), including Metropolitan Life and Prudential, and a permanent secretary.[50] Even then, midwestern firms dominated the association, which met outside that region only once before 1950.[51]

During the 1940s, the organization matured in other ways, as well. In 1941, the president of IASA drafted a mission statement for inclusion on current and future programs:

> Impelled by the increasing demands of management and supervisory officials for information regarding the affairs of our companies, and impressed by the potentialities of modern automatic electrical and mechanical equipment to the compilation, classification, summarization and presentation of the mass of data inherent to the business of insurance, the INSURANCE ACCOUNTING AND STATISTICAL ASSOCIATION is an organization of office technicians devoted to the study, research, development and exchange of ideas on the use of punched card and other office equipment as applied to insurance routines to the end that we may employ the

most efficient, practical and economical methods in our accounting and statistical procedures for the benefit of our respective companies.[52]

This statement established the members as office technicians in the insurance business, differentiating them from LOMA's broader methods specialists. IASA also amended its constitution and by-laws to state that it was a nonprofit organization that did not use funds for lobbying purposes, thus rejecting one function generally attributed to trade associations.[53] A director of research was also created to manage the research files with results of member surveys.

By the 1940s, then, IASA was transformed from a local users group to a national insurance association focused on tabulating. The organization played a secondary role to LOMA in shaping tabulator use in the 1930s and 1940s, but in the 1950s it would emerge into a leading role with computers.

## Increasing Tabulating Capabilities and New Insurance Uses

From the founding of LOMA and IASA to the introduction of IBM's alphabetical tabulator in 1931, IBM gradually gained ground over Powers' firm, in the insurance industry as well as the U.S. market.[54] IBM's move to the eighty-column card in 1928 ended the card compatibility that, together with the rental model, had enabled insurance firms to change between the two vendors with minimal technical and financial difficulty, though such changes would disrupt their relations with vendor sales and maintenance personnel. By 1931 IBM had assured its ascendancy. In subsequent years, changes continued, though they were less dramatic than before. During this period the insurance firms did not aggressively drive technology changes as they did before 1924, but they continued to influence developments to a more limited extent. In addition, insurance applications of tabulating systems began to evolve in a new direction, shaped by technical capabilities, existing insurance processes, and new models shared through associations such as LOMA and IASA. By midcentury, accumulating changes had set the stage for insurance adoption of the first commercial computers in the 1950s.

### Rapid Developments and IBM Ascendancy

By the mid-1920s many American life insurance firms had established extensive tabulating machine installations, the majority with IBM equipment. A 1925 office machinery survey conducted by Henry Holt, actuary of the National Life Insurance Company, indicated that 47% of the responding companies used tabulating systems, respectable but still considerably below the 87% that reported using addressing machines.[55] At this time, Holt noted, Peirce equipment could no longer be obtained, and the competition was solely between Hollerith and Powers equipment: "The people putting out the Hollerith and Powers equipment are actively competing for the American market and are endeavoring to improve and enlarge their service. The enthusiastic salesmen of either line may make extravagant claims of superiority for his equipment. However, our experience with each leads me to believe that neither has a monopoly on the desirable features."[56] Although Holt endorsed neither type, other speakers at the late 1920s conferences more often referred to Hollerith than to Powers equipment. In a 1926 panel on using office machinery, for example, all three who mentioned punched-card tabulation referred to Hollerith equipment.[57]

Industrial insurance firms were the principal insurance users of Powers tabulating machinery.[58] Industrial insurance operations depended heavily on lists and account registers with policyholder names followed by numerical information, exactly the task the Powers alphabetical printing tabulator was designed to perform. Still, many fewer firms offered industrial than offered ordinary insurance, limiting business from this segment. Moreover, the two largest industrial insurance companies, Metropolitan Life and Prudential, were behind in mechanizing their processes, having wasted time working with Peirce. In a 1929 LOMA session on industrial insurance, Otis Grant, actuary of Life and Casualty Insurance Company of Tennessee, noted that his moderate-sized firm had the largest installation of tabulating machines in any industrial insurance firm in the United States.[59] Grant demonstrated how his company used the Powers alphabetical tabulator to print register pages and even to print the variable portion on the insurance policy's first page.

Although industrial insurance and a few ordinary insurance firms had adopted Powers equipment for its alphabetical capabilities, references to Hollerith equipment predominated in the LOMA proceedings, suggesting that proportionately fewer insurance firms shifted from Hollerith to Powers equipment after the latter's introduction of alphabetical printing than after the earlier introduction of its numerical printing tabulator. The demand for limited alphabetical tabulating and printing was lower among the many ordinary insurance firms because they depended on bills and receipts rather than lists and registers, and these required three-line addresses that could not be handled by the Powers machine. Thus the addresses had to be printed by Addressographs.

Moreover, Powers lacked the solid financial footing and the managerial expertise necessary to overcome Hollerith's lead. For example, in 1924 when the head of Metropolitan Life's Home Office Study Committee met with Mr. Pritchard, president of Powers, to discuss their joint development efforts concerning alphabetical tabulating, Pritchard noted that his firm's financial problems limited how much it could experiment without compensation.[60] This financial weakness, with its accompanying weakness in marketing and service, was a significant factor in Powers' failure to capitalize on its mid-1920s technological lead. In November 1927, Powers merged with several other office machine companies into Remington Rand, shoring up its financial situation.[61] The tabulating business, however, was never the central component of that larger firm as it was of IBM. In fact, initially the merger seems to have reduced the visibility of Powers tabulating equipment to the insurance industry. Representatives from IBM, Powers, and Remington Rand all attended the 1927 LOMA conference, a month before the merger.[62] In 1928, the IBM contingent increased from one person to four, including the manager of its new Insurance Department. At the same time, Powers disappeared from the conference attendance list entirely, and none of the ten Remington Rand representatives was affiliated with the new tabulating division.[63] Only in the following year did Remington Rand list two people from the "Powers Accounting Machine Division."[64] Between 1924 and 1931, Powers continued to introduce new tabulating products, but one historian has assessed these innovations as more technology-driven than market-driven and thus not valuable enough to the market to cause users to switch vendors.[65]

Meanwhile, in 1928 IBM introduced a key innovation for insurance users: the eighty-column card that remained its standard well into the computer era (fig. 4.2).[66] In doing so, IBM addressed a major limitation of existing tabulating systems—limited card capacity. At that year's LOMA conference, Norman O. Mick, a consultant and systematizer from the System Company, spoke about recent developments in office equipment, enthusiastically praising the new card: "The extra columns are useful in a variety of ways to life insurance companies. For instance, one insurance company punches the amount of accidental death benefit and disability income in addition to the face amount of the policy, and is thus able to value all three in one operation."[67] Before 1928,

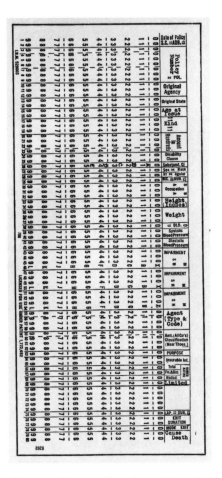

*Fig. 4.2.* IBM's eighty-column card increased card capacity and would last as a storage medium into the early computer era. From Charles E. West, "Some New Uses for Modern Punched Card Equipment," *Transactions of the Actuarial Society of America* 35 (1934): 271. Copyright 1934 by the Actuarial Society of America (Society of Actuaries), Schaumburg, Illinois. Reprinted with permission. Reproduced courtesy of Baker Historical Collections, Harvard Business School.

Powers and IBM both used a standard forty-five-column card; this card had low enough capacity that some insurance applications already required multiple cards per policy or many separate sets of cards for different processes. This capacity constraint would only grow worse with alphabetical tabulating, since alphabetical fields for names typically required twelve to eighteen of those columns, restricting the number available for numerical fields and often requiring multiple cards for even the most basic data on a single policy. When the eighty-column card was used with the alphabetical tabulator IBM finally introduced three years later, it had room for a substantial alphabetical field as well as multiple numerical fields.[68] Moreover, IBM could, if a customer desired, modify its tabulating equipment to use both the new eighty-column cards and the old forty-five-column cards, thus offering a new feature without making existing cards obsolete.[69] This backward compatibility, welcomed by all existing customers, was especially valuable to insurance firms, since they retained and used cards for the lifetime of the policyholder.

The new cards were not, however, compatible with Powers equipment because the narrow slotted holes of the IBM eighty-column card did not fit the mechanical pins of the Powers tabulators.[70] In addition, this new card configuration, which proved to be stronger than the old cards, was patented.[71] In its desire to remain competitive Remington Rand introduced its own high-density format two years later—a ninety-column card that used two rows of short columns per card, with multiple holes punched in the same column to represent characters.[72] The vendor also offered redesigned machinery to use the cards, but the new devices were not initially backward compatible, a factor that made them much less attractive to insurance firms. Moreover, incompatibility between the two vendors would henceforth discourage switching from one to the other. Interestingly, Metropolitan Life knew three years before the official announcement that Hollerith and Powers cards were likely to become incompatible, suggesting that someone at IBM leaked the information in an attempt to gain a competitive advantage.[73]

Although insurance firms welcomed the eighty-column card's expanded capacity and IBM's other innovations, they moved cautiously to avoid disrupting their existing tabulating applications. Despite Mick's—and IBM's—hard sell, a LOMA study presented at the 1931 conference showed that adoption of the eighty-column card was proceeding relatively slowly: "There are only six of the sixty-eight companies that are using the eighty column card, and three of these are using both the eighty and forty-five. Twenty companies indicate that they are considering a change-over from the forty-five to the eighty, because of the greater capacity thereof. In a good many cases, the work in connection with the changeover has delayed the move. There seems to be no fear as to the reliability of the new equipment."[74]

The firms trusted IBM's reliability, but taking advantage of the new capacity obviously required changing their current processes, by combining existing cards or adding new data to cards. Moreover, converting millions of cards was a large task. Prefiguring events in the transition to computers, insurance firms played a role, though a minor one, in encouraging IBM to develop aids to simplify conversion. At the 1931 LOMA session on punched-card use, panelist H. W. Rhodes, assistant mathematician at Mutual Benefit, described his firm's experience working with IBM (still referred to as Tabulating Machine Company) on an experimental machine that could aid conversion:

> Something over a year ago, I was talking to Mr. Jones, of the Tabulating Machine Company [who was present at the panel], about the installation of a mortality card on the Hollerith System, but that we would need an eighty point card to cover the data we would require. He than spoke to me about a reproducing machine, which had not at that time been perfected. I learned that we could transfer some of the data now appearing on our forty-five point card which would be necessary for the mortality card.
>
> We drafted an eighty point card to fit our needs and the Tabulating Machine Company installed their machine in our office. We have now transferred about twenty points from the forty-five point card to the eighty point card, and have perforated about 400,000 cards.
>
> . . . The Tabulating Company not only furnished the machine for this work, but also furnished one of their own men to handle it.[75]

IBM was willing to work with an existing customer to make the transition, probably planning to gain insurance company feedback on the experimental machine as well as to keep a customer happy. By the 1932 conference both vendors had added conversion devices to their lines.[76] Although insurance was undoubtedly not the only user industry requesting conversion devices, IBM clearly heard and responded to the demand.

The proceedings of LOMA's 1930 conference shed considerable light on insurance attitudes toward and use of tabulating technology. First, Franklin Life Insurance Company's statistician R. W. Leib, chairman of a committee on punched-card use, reported on the state of the art in insurance tabulation.[77] Of the eighty companies responding to his committee's questionnaire, 85% reported using punched-card equipment, up from 47% in the similar 1925 study.[78] He described the competitive situation as follows:

> The majority of the companies are using the Hollerith equipment of the International Business Machines Corporation. The others are using the Powers equip-

ment. Three are using both. General comments on the serviceability and adapt-ability of both types of equipment are favorable. The Powers machine, where in use, seems to have been chosen in many cases for its alphabetical feature and the possibility of the use of the eleventh and twelfth positions on the card. It also has been particularly recommended by some for adaptability in connection with ac-counting work. Most of the users give as their reason for the selection of the Hol-lerith equipment its greater flexibility and speed.

In addition to noting the slow changeover to the eighty-column cards, he men-tioned some other new additions to the Hollerith line that had become im-portant in insurance use, including the verifier, the fully automatic key punch, and the interpreter, which made permanent card files more useful by typing the punched numbers at the top of the card.[79]

Leib also identified some trends in insurance applications of tabulating technology. He commented on the typical progress from early actuarial uses to more operational ones: "It seems to have been developed at the outset for han-dling valuation and insurance account records, and gradually has been ex-tended until at the present time it takes care of many tasks of an accounting and statistical nature."[80] Leib's committee also attempted to determine the size at which a firm should adopt such equipment, tentatively concluding that "there seems to be no definite time when it is most desirable." Company ex-ecutives surveyed had placed the adoption point between $50 million and $100 million of insurance in force, but Leib observed that "quite a few of the companies using cards report under fifty millions of insurance in force." Fi-nally, he mentioned another factor affecting the timing of punched-card adop-tion: "Frequently a company doing a health and accident or an industrial [in-surance] business finds it to their advantage to use punched cards therewith, and frequently extend their system to their ordinary [insurance] business, al-though they have only a small volume of it." Leib ended by reminding the au-dience that all punched-card applications described in the report were being used by some LOMA member, so LOMA headquarters could put interested par-ties in touch with the relevant firms. Thus he highlighted LOMA's function as a clearinghouse and coordinator for information sharing related to tabulating.

Another session in the 1930 LOMA conference focused on premium billing and accounting and related activities, an application area that would become the primary focus of tabulating innovation by the 1940s.[81] Panelists spoke about eight firms, all of which used Hollerith punched cards in some aspect of premium collection and accounting, though all still used Addressographs to address premium bills. Phoenix Mutual's Frank E. Fricke, field auditor, described the most extensive and significant of the applications.[82] This firm had adopted Hollerith equipment early and switched to the Powers printing tabulator shortly after it arrived on the market.[83] When the Hollerith machine added numerical printing and automatic control, Phoenix Mutual returned to its original vendor in 1924 and, like most ordinary insurance firms, remained with Hollerith even when Powers introduced alphabetical printing. In 1930, Phoenix Mutual was centralizing detail work and encouraging home office departments to cooperate closely in eliminating as many duplicate records as possible. According to Fricke, "The whole scheme of the system centers on punched cards."[84]

Phoenix Mutual built its new system around the eighty-column card, "allowing greater analysis and elimination of some cards."[85] Moreover, it "planned to use the punched card for the imprinting of premium, dividend, loan interest and total due on receipts in addition to the various functions, and to maintain control accounts of our premium operations." Thus the company was using the equipment's numerical printing capability to create customer documents, as well as to combine aspects of premium billing and accounting. As the lengthy discussion after this talk demonstrated, other firms were quite interested in Phoenix Mutual's system.[86] Six years later, D. N. Clark, comptroller of Phoenix Mutual, described the completed installation as successful, resulting in direct yearly savings of $30,000 and, importantly, improving the control (accounting) system. Implementing the eighty-column–card system guarded against errors, made subsequent changes easier, smoothed the work flow, simplified the Accounting Department's organization, and even improved morale of some personnel, who learned new jobs as a by-product of this change.[87] Phoenix Mutual's ordinary renewal expense ratio (ordinary RER), an imperfect cost measure that nevertheless gives some sense of change over time, shows that costs began dropping steeply in 1930 (fig. 4.3), consistent with Clark's claims of cost saving. Indeed, at its lowest point, the firm's ordinary RER fell well below the thirty-firm average. Only in 1946 did expenses return to their previous level, suggesting either that the system was no longer adequate for Phoenix Mutual's volume or that other factors such as labor costs were increasing its ordinary RER.

In 1931 IBM's announcement of its delayed but superior alphabetical tabulating product removed the advantage that Powers had claimed since 1924. At

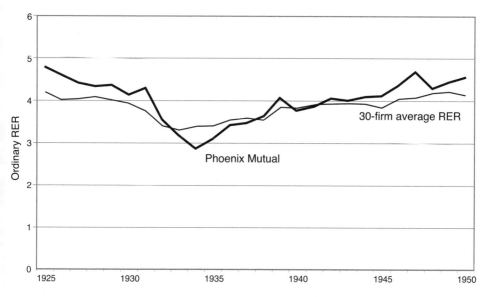

*Fig. 4.3.* Phoenix Mutual's ordinary RER began dropping steeply around the time that the new premium billing and accounting system was installed. Based on figures from *Best's,* 1925–50.

that year's LOMA conference, Franklin Life statistician Leib once again led discussion on punched-card use.[88] During the discussion, W. L. Schwenker of Remington Rand reminded attendees that the new Powers machine, which could now tabulate a ninety- or forty-five-column card, alphabetically or numerically, was on display with the other office equipment. T. R. Jones of IBM's newly established Insurance Department dominated the discussion, however, and stole Schwenker's thunder by preannouncing IBM's own soon-to-be-released alphabetical tabulating machine. Jones was clearly on the offensive, touting the firm's new card-duplicating machine and its electric verifying machine and signaling that IBM intended to lead rather than follow in subsequent rounds of innovation. He even asked LOMA members whether they were interested in an alternative verifying machine that IBM could manufacture if there was adequate demand, suggesting that IBM welcomed insurance industry input. Finally, he suggested that he could add to the discussion on several issues, since IBM's Insurance Department was amassing considerable information about such uses. This episode demonstrated the strength of IBM's legendary marketing prowess, as well as IBM's recognition of the insurance market's importance. Moreover, it suggests that IBM, like the LOMA committees and meetings, spread information about use of tabulating among insurance companies.

The IBM Type 405 alphabetical tabulator—or "electrical accounting machine," as IBM, but not most insurance users, now termed it—was an immediate and profitable success, notwithstanding economic conditions.[89] Although some industrial insurance firms and a few ordinary ones would continue to use Remington Rand's Powers tabulating equipment, by 1931 IBM had established an eight-to-one advantage in the overall tabulating market, an advantage that seems to have held for insurance, as well. Reliability and good service, added to its strong and targeted marketing, provided insurance users with good reasons to choose IBM. It would retain its dominant position for the rest of the tabulator era.

## Continued Adaptation through the Depression

As the depression settled in, incremental developments in tabulating technology and in insurance use of it continued, though during this period insurance was less active in shaping the technology artifacts and more concerned with developing its own use of the technology. The steep downturn of the 1930s revealed the brilliance of Hollerith's original rental strategy, along with the capabilities of IBM's management. Although acquiring new customers was more difficult, user firms typically kept rental installations already in place, since tabulating technology was seen as improving efficiency. Consequently, rental revenues as well as the profitable sale of cards continued. Clearly, the structure of IBM's business was well suited to smoothing the impact of economic ups and downs.[90] Its revenues continued to climb through 1931. Although they dropped slightly in 1932 and 1933, by 1934 they exceeded the 1931 level.[91] Thereafter, the information-processing demands of New Deal agencies and programs such as the National Recovery Administration and the Social Security Administration added to the demand for tabulating technology, and revenues continued to rise. Throughout the depression, IBM paid dividends to its stockholders.[92] In contrast, Remington Rand, though larger than IBM throughout this period because of its nontabulator revenues, weakened during the decade, in part because it never succeeded in fully integrating its diverse pieces into one well-run management structure.[93] Its total 1939 revenues were well below their predepression level and only 10% above those of IBM, rather than 200% as they had been in 1928.[94] IBM's advantage over Remington Rand in the tabulating business exceeded ten to one by 1940.[95]

In the mid-1930s, both manufacturers continued to introduce new devices and features attractive to insurance companies.[96] Now, however, Remington Rand was more often the follower than the leader in introducing new machines such as the direct subtraction tabulator, automatic verifying machine, and alphanumeric interpreter.[97] In some years Remington Rand's LOMA exhibit subordinated its Powers tabulating systems to other office appliances and supplies, such as typewriters and Kardex Visible Files, whereas in other years the Powers Division took the lead.[98] In IBM exhibits, tabulating equipment was always the primary product family on display. Perhaps most indicative of the future was IBM's 1935 exhibit, in which it demonstrated an integrated premium billing and accounting system. IBM's description of the exhibit was printed in the LOMA proceedings:

> The International Business Machines Corporation chose the subject of Premium Accounting and Premium Notice and Receipt Writing to demonstrate their automatic electric bookkeeping and accounting machines, and electric writing machines.
>
> Featured in the demonstration was the alphabetic electric bookkeeping and accounting machine, with compensating carriage, arranged for writing premium notices and receipts. This machine produces complete the premium notice, receipt and as many additional stubs, such as the second notice, home office stub, etc., as may be required. Its compensating carriage will handle any of the standard continuous form paper as supplied by the various paper companies.
>
> It can also be equipped to handle individual notice and receipt forms rather than continuous forms. When so equipped it will automatically feed blank notice forms and eject them completed with the name and address of insured and all necessary policy data. Both continuous form and individual form machines will produce notices and receipts complete, showing name and address of insured, premium and loan interest due, dividend credit and the net amount due. Either form of machine will also perform all the functions of a standard alphabetic printer.
>
> The International Automatic Multiplier was also demonstrated as it plays an important part in premium accounting. The multiplier was demonstrating the automatic extension and punching of commission on premium cards.[99]

This hypothetical premium billing and accounting application went a step further than Phoenix Mutual's application by printing addresses onto the bills and receipts. It pointed the way for insurance to eliminate Addressographs, directly generating customer documents such as the premium notice and receipt, as well as related internal accounting documents or stubs. It also made use of another IBM innovation, the Type 601 automatic multiplying punch, which multiplied two numbers from a card and punched the product into a blank field on the same card. Around the same time, *Business Week,* which cited IBM as one of the office appliance firms aggressively innovating in their offerings, described 601s as "machines designed for issuing utility bills to customers or premium notices to insurance policyholders."[100] Such machines were part of multidevice tabulating systems that demonstrated the capabilities offered by the accumulated innovations of the previous decade. The demonstration system shows that IBM was aggressively marketing to insurance customers at this time. Indeed, in this case IBM was attempting to influence insurance use.

At the next year's LOMA conference, Phoenix Mutual and Oregon Mutual Life Insurance Company both described their state-of-the-art premium billing and accounting systems, with the former company focused on accounting and the latter on billing. Phoenix Mutual's Clark described the completed system he had previewed in 1930.[101] He said that the company viewed this process as a great improvement over its former system, particularly extolling its premium accounting component. Nevertheless, as his description made clear, the new process still required close synchronization of the tabulating process with the Addressograph-based printing process. Oregon Mutual had just established a process that imprinted name and address information onto the bills directly from cards, similar to IBM's 1935 demonstration. Indeed, G. E. Cannon, assistant actuary, acknowledged IBM personnel for "their able assistance" in establishing this new system.[102] Oregon Mutual adopted this change as part of a wider plan intended to simplify its accounting work and "to expand the uses of the machines to more readily obtain valuable information for statement and statistical purposes"; starting from this revised process, the company "merely added one more set of cards—that is, the name and address cards—to obtain the premium notice."[103] The process still required using three to five cards per premium notice, each generating a separate line of the name and address. In 1941 IBM would introduce a tabulating machine that allowed multiple-line addresses to be printed from a single card, but not until after the war ended would that device be available for commercial firms.[104] Still, Oregon Mutual had succeeded in eliminating the use of the Addressograph and the typewriter so that its entire process of premium billing required only tabulating equipment.

Phoenix Mutual and Oregon Mutual pointed the way forward with these integrated applications, but others would follow only gradually. A 1938 LOMA study of how member life insurance companies handled premium billing for ordinary insurance revealed that only two out of the ninety-five companies making up the stratified sample used a tabulator to imprint "identifying data" onto forms, while seventy-nine used Addressographs, and fourteen used typewriters.[105] Meanwhile, companies were learning to use tabulating equipment to integrate multiple steps in other applications, as well. For example, in the 1937 LOMA conference Lester H. Van Ness of Acacia Mutual Life Insurance Company described that firm's proposed process for calculating new premium rates and producing new rate books.[106] In analyzing the most common methods for performing this task, which were designed around using calculating rather than tabulating machines to perform the calculations, this firm discovered that only about one-quarter of the operations involved actual calculations, whereas three-quarters involved recording figures, by handwriting or typing. The speaker noted that the newly designed, tabulator-based process would integrate and speed up both types of processes, estimating that it would complete the job in one-quarter the time and at a 40% reduction in cost while also producing cards that could be used to obtain many useful by-products.

LOMA also encouraged firms to introduce tabulator-based systems for cost accounting, particularly functional rather than department-based cost accounting.[107] Insurance firms were late in adopting cost-accounting systems, but in 1937 a new LOMA Home Office Departmental and Functional Costs Committee developed a standardized functional accounting system to allow firms to monitor their costs and compare them with those of other firms. Cost savings from the tabulator application were expected not from replacing labor, since the cost-accounting system itself was new, but from using the data it provided to reduce costs elsewhere. During the prepared discussion of the committee's work, M. H. LeVita, statistician for Fidelity Mutual Life Insurance Company, listed eleven additional uses for the cards prepared for cost accounting, from auditing expense account totals on the ledger to obtaining total investment expense.[108] So tabulator-based cost-accounting systems could be integrated into additional information processes within the firms.

By the mid-1930s, even many industrial insurance firms, the earliest and strongest supporters of the Powers alphabetical tabulator, were switching to IBM. In a 1937 session on using punched-card machinery and procedures to generate industrial insurance registers and policies, several firms mentioned using IBM equipment, and some specifically noted that they chose it over Powers.[109] In 1935, having given up on Peirce and retired its old Gore sorters, Prudential had finally begun the long process of switching its major industrial insurance records and accounting processes over to IBM tabulating equipment, previously used only for a few minor processes.[110] In the 1947 LOMA conference, Frank Beebe, general manager at Prudential, would describe the fully realized system, completed in time to allow Prudential to use it for a few years before beginning its gradual conversion to computers.[111] The persistence of Powers punched-card devices in the conference exhibits through the 1930s and 1940s suggests that some life insurance firms continued to use them. Nevertheless, presentations, discussions, and exhibits indicate that most firms active in LOMA used IBM equipment by this time.

By the end of the depression decade, life insurance accepted tabulating equipment as a business necessity. In outlining the developmental stages of life insurance firms, Ralph W. Beeson, secretary of Liberty National, claimed that a tabulating department was absolutely essential to every insurance company that had reached $10 million of insurance in force and could usefully be adopted piece by piece from a new firm's founding.[112] In his 1940 LOMA presidential address, William P. Barber Jr. of Connecticut Mutual Life Insurance Company noted, "The developments of the decade in reproducing printing and multiplying through perforated cards have revolutionized this field. A great many clerks have been made available for other work in the home offices through the extensions of this phase of our business."[113] Thus depression-era developments in insurance tabulating use, though less dramatic than those before 1931, proved significant. Insurance firms did not exert pressure on the two vendors' product development as aggressively as before, but the experiences of Phoenix Mutual and Oregon Mutual suggest that joint work—and at least some reciprocal influence—between the insurance and tabulating industries continued.

### The Forties: Gradually Increasing Sophistication of Technology and Use

During the 1940s, developments in tabulating technology continued, though the evolution of insurance use was slowed by wartime equipment and labor shortages. Gradually, however, companies began to combine more operating processes in a single run. In 1944, Milton Effros, Supervisor of Metropolitan Life's Standardization Bureau, summarized developments in punched card machinery that were not yet available commercially: "The new machines will increase the speed and flexibility of punch card equipment. In some cases they will combine within a single unit, functions which heretofore were performed by several different machines. For example, it may be possible to run tabulating cards through a machine which will simultaneously reproduce data from other cards, perform a multiplying operation, and interpret the tabulating cards, all in one run through the machine."[114] This description hints at further integration to come. The developments in insurance use of tabulating technology during this decade would set the stage for, and establish trends extending into, the early computer era.

A key development for expanding potential insurance uses of tabulating—automatic carriage control that allowed tabulators to print up to three lines from a single card—was not available for commercial rental until 1946.[115] LOMA's 1941 Exhibit guide included what may have been an initial description of this feature and its potential use: "Of outstanding interest was the demonstration of the Alphabetical Punched Card Accounting Machine, equipped with automatic carriage for the speedy preparation of premium notices and receipts, checks, and other documents and statements."[116] This passage does not clearly indicate whether the automatic carriage described could actually print multiline addresses from a single card, and for the next four years wartime austerity precluded equipment exhibits at the LOMA conferences and delayed availability of new equipment. Nevertheless, some insurance firms seem to have kept informed about technological developments. By the 1944 conference Metropolitan Life's Effros revealed knowledge of several machine developments, including those allowing three-line printing from a single card, that were on the horizon: "Several new machines and devices were about to be released shortly before Pearl Harbor. Others have since been developed for use by the armed forces. . . . Alphabetic tabulators can be equipped with an additional set of reading brushes. The additional set of brushes makes it possible to list as many as three lines of alphabetical printing from a single card, such as a name and address. It may be possible, therefore, to use this machine to write checks and to prepare such forms as premium notices and receipts from a single tabulating card."[117]

In 1946, when equipment exhibits resumed, both IBM and Remington Rand demonstrated machines with this valuable capability. As the report of LOMA's Office Planning and Equipment Committee indicated, "Undoubtedly these machines will have application for writing premium notices, for addressing commission statements and for other combination addressing and tabulating jobs."[118] In an era of growth and labor shortages, this new feature might allow companies to simplify and integrate several elements of the insurance premium billing and accounting process, using a single set of machinery rather than two (tabulating system and Addressographs). The trend toward increased integration of multiple steps was also evident in the Addressograph-Multigraph Corporation's development of addressing machines with rudimentary tabulating functions, as described for the 1946 LOMA exhibits: "Combine punched hole accounting functions with the usual writing of names, addresses, and descriptive data embossed on Addressograph metal plates. These accounting functions include automatic figure-writing, adding subtracting, multiplying, as well as the automatic punching of fixed statistical data into tabulating cards."[119] The large potential insurance and utility demand for integrating tabulating and address-printing functions is reflected in this convergence from two different technological angles.

In the next several years, the tabulator's new printing capability seems to have gained popularity in insurance much faster than the Addressograph's new and limited tabulator capability, reflecting good marketing and trust particularly in IBM's reliability and field maintenance. In 1946, the same year that IBM and Remington Rand first made this three-line printing feature available, a LOMA survey reported on how thirty-five firms of various sizes prepared and mailed premium bills. Of the twenty-two firms that mailed notices from home rather than branch offices, seventeen used Addressographs to produce the notices, whereas only two used the tabulator with multiple cards and preprinted forms, indicating that such an application was possible but not popular before the new introductions.[120] In the next few years, however, LOMA and IASA publications included multiple accounts of firms converting the premium billing and sometimes accounting functions fully to tabulating equipment.[121] Most tellingly, a 1952 regional IASA survey of premium billing and accounting methods found that more than 40% of the Dallas-area firms surveyed used tabulating equipment for the entire premium billing and accounting process.[122] A trend toward using tabulating equipment for an integrated premium billing and accounting process had clearly been established. It would continue in the early computer era.

After the war, several other improvements in tabulating technology also set the stage for the computer era. As Roland Mangini, Planning Department manager at John Hancock Insurance Company and chairman of LOMA's Eastern Office Planning and Equipment Committee, explained in his 1947 LOMA presentation that IBM's new 600 line of tabulating equipment involved several innovations.[123] The first, referred to as a "programming device," was apparently a primitive method for controlling a sequence of steps: "The Type 602 Calculating Punch employs for the first time what I.B.M. calls a Programming Device. This permits the introduction of extra cycles or the repeating of an entire basic series of cycles. This means that simultaneous or successive use of all four basic mathematical processes—addition, subtraction, multiplication and division[—]may be scheduled (or programmed) for calculating and punching results into each card as it passes once through the machine." Still far from the notion of programming that would soon emerge, this device prefigured what was to come. Indeed, as Mangini commented, "I think we may expect to see wide use of this programming principle as I.B.M. develops new machines—a number of which are now in the field on test." Mangini also noted the importance of the "extensive use of electronics" in the Type 603 multiplier.[124] Although IBM had used electronics in an auxiliary capacity in a few other machines released earlier in the 1940s, the 603 was the first to use electronics centrally, thereby gaining in speed and accuracy. A third innovation was the "first notable effort by I.B.M. to streamline and sound proof its tabulating machines."[125] The streamlined look evident in the 604 (fig. 4.4), introduced in 1948, provided a model for IBM's early punched-card computers, as well.[126]

*Fig. 4.4.* The IBM 604 electronic calculator, the high point of tabulating technology, was introduced shortly before the appearance of early commercial computers. Photograph courtesy of IBM Archives.

A final development noted by Mangini both reflected IBM's increasing standardization and had significance for the future. He noted that IBM's new S series (e.g., S-405, S-416) devices were to be supplied in standard capacities, "practically for stock, rather than being tailor-made for each individual customer or job as has been done in the past."[127] Such standard machines would be delivered more rapidly—in five months rather than nine for the S-405, for example, given the postwar backlog. Previously, tabulating equipment had included both standard pieces such as the card punch and somewhat customized pieces such as a tabulator configured to the user organization's needs. Now insurance firms and other users would be able to trade off delivery speed against customization. This shift suggested that the insurance industry's role in shaping this relatively mature technology would decline even further.

Alongside continued evolution of, and insurance enthusiasm for, tabulating technology, however, appeared evidence of parallel developments in, and emerging insurance excitement about, computing. In the same 1947 LOMA conference at which Mangini talked about new tabulating devices, for example, the Prudential's Edmund Berkeley, soon to become a major figure in the new field of computers, spoke on the early stages of that technology.[128]

From IBM's point of view, "insurance companies were among the largest and most sophisticated business users of punched-card machines in the late 1940s and 1950s."[129] In the early decades of the tabulator era, these large and information-intensive firms and their associations had played an important and sometimes quite active role in shaping not just their own use of the technology but also tabulating technology itself and even the competitive landscape in the tabulating industry.[130] In the final decades of the tabulator era, insurance played a more limited role in technology development. Insurance processes built around this technology, however, continued to evolve gradually, shaped by the actions of insurance firms and trade associations, as well as by the available devices. Within these associations, companies shared their experiences in using such systems, leading to the spread of certain integrated operating applications, such as functional cost accounting and especially premium billing and accounting. For the most part, however, companies adopted new applications slowly and carefully. Ralph J. Hasbrouck, a Prudential supervisor speaking at a LOMA seminar on industrial insurance, described the typical process as follows: "When a new system, such as the punched card accounting system, is put into effect, it is usually designed to fit in with the former methods and at its inception cause as little upheaval as possible. However, once operating smoothly, investigation may reveal that economies or improvements can be effected by a close scrutiny of the remnants of the former system."[131] The desire for efficiency, although universally espoused, was often paired with a desire for continuity. The result was gradual, incremental change in which insurance actors developing new systems were strongly influenced by institutionalized structures such as existing departmental structure and processes.[132]

# Part II / Life Insurance Enters the Computer Era

Part I traced the reciprocal influence between life insurance and tabulating technology as insurance firms adopted and used this equipment. Now we turn to the computer era. Computers are commonly seen as producing an abrupt discontinuity with the past. How did insurance firms experience the transition to computers? How did their experience with tabulating technology influence their attitude toward and adoption of computers? What influence did the installed base of tabulating equipment and existing applications have on the adoption and use of new computers? Did insurance companies attempt to shape the new technology as they did the old? This part addresses such questions.

The reciprocal influences between tabulating technology and life insurance adoption and use of it continued into the early computer era, structuring the insurance industry's adoption and use of computing technology. As this new technology began to emerge, a few insurance companies again exerted direct and aggressive pressure like that demonstrated in the early tabulator era to shape the hardware's development for commercial uses. Industry associations played an increasingly important role in spreading knowledge about new technology and shaping how insurance firms might use it. Committees within the Society of Actuaries (previously the Actuarial Society of America), Life Office Management Association (LOMA), and Insurance Accounting and Statistical Association (IASA) played extremely influential roles in shaping how insurance companies thought about computers and their uses. They also interacted extensively with the vendors, shaping their understanding of the insurance market and, ultimately, the application software some vendors created.

A central feature of early insurance adoption and use of computers was the tension between two conflicting desires: on the one hand, a conservative preference for a very gradual transformation of processes, always maintaining some continuity with past equipment and processes; on the other hand, a desire for rapid transformation and discontinuity with the past to gain more benefit from the technology. This tension initially played out during the 1950s, with results remaining in evidence much longer. Some of the individuals and groups leading insurance interactions with computing saw the potential for rapid transformation—or "reengineering"—of insurance processes to take advantage of the new computers. Despite this vision, however, most firms initially followed an incremental migration path that would transform their structures and processes only over decades, not months or even years.

Consequently, insurance companies typically moved gradually as they adopted and used computers. Their preference for incremental migration favored IBM, since most had large IBM tabulating installations in place. Even more important, most had millions of eighty-column cards that they were loath to exchange for the UNIVAC's magnetic tapes with invisible data. For most insurance companies, IBM's ability to combine stored-program electronic computing with reliable card handling and conversion was very attractive, allowing them to migrate gradually from tabulator-based processes to computerized ones that took full advantage of the technology's new capabilities. Thus the small, primarily card-based IBM 650 and 1401 computers were enormously successful in insurance.

Throughout the 1960s and 1970s, this preference for incremental migration was evident in application software as well as hardware. IBM developed a bundle of programs designed specifically for insurance, based on earlier work done by a committee of the Society of Actuaries. This software package institutionalized the combined premium billing and accounting application, providing further continuity between the two eras. Many insurance firms remained IBM customers all the way to the more advanced IBM 360 and 370 computer lines. Whatever vendor they chose, however, they adopted new applications and changes in processes slowly. Established industry and regulatory structures played a role in this, as did culture and ideology. A closer look at two firms' evolving computer use demonstrates these factors in greater detail, illustrating the important role that key individuals, as well as structures, may play in shaping a firm's evolving use of this technology.

# CHAPTER 5

# Early Engagement between Insurance and Computing

The final years of the tabulator era overlapped with the initial years of the computer era. As prewar and wartime developments in stored-program electronic computing proceeded, insurance as a major user of existing information technology began to follow these developments with interest.[1] A few individuals, such as Prudential's Edmund C. Berkeley and Metropolitan Life's John J. Finelli, interacted with emerging computer vendors on behalf of their companies, influencing the development of input and output devices for commercial computers. Representatives of insurance firms also worked cooperatively within several associations—the Society of Actuaries, Insurance Accounting and Statistical Association (IASA), and Life Office Management Association (LOMA)—to learn about this new technology and to build visions of how insurance might use it. The most widely disseminated vision for applying computers in insurance extended the premium billing and accounting application just emerging in insurance tabulating.

## Advances in Computing

According to most historical accounts, the digital computer emerged during World War II, though certainly developments in analog computing and even forerunners of digital computing had preceded it.[2] In most traditional accounts, scientists, the military, and military contractors loom large, as do arguments over the primacy of various technical developments and of different countries. The focus here on a single commercial user industry, life insurance, does not require detailed history of all these technical developments; nor does it entail entering into the debates over technical primacy. What follows summarizes only a few key technical developments with some relevance to the insurance story.

General Electric (GE) and Bell Laboratories, among the leading centers for electrical engineering, both initiated computer-related developments in the interwar period.[3] GE, which needed such analog computers for designing electrical power networks, built a differential analyzer during the 1930s.[4] At around the same time, but working on a digital rather than analog model, Bell Labs mathematician George Stibitz developed a way to use telephone relay switches for binary calculation, using the principles of Boolean algebra.[5] By 1939, he and his colleagues had developed the complex number calculator, later to be called the Bell Labs relay computer, which he demonstrated at the American Mathematical Society's 1940 meeting. During the war, he built such relay-operated calculators for the U.S. Armed Forces. Although the Bell Labs relay computer was neither very rapid nor particularly versatile, in the 1940s Stibitz and his Bell Labs team conceived several notions that would be important to later computers.[6] Neither line of interwar development proved central to the model of commercial computing that emerged in the 1950s, but a few members of the insurance industry would notice even these precursors.

Another set of technical developments extended punched-card tabulating techniques in the direction of digital computing. IBM's Wallace Eckert developed a switch connecting various devices in a tabulating installation (multiplier, tabulator, summary punch) to allow them to carry out up to twelve operations on a single card without human intervention.[7] This switch was used in specially built machines, initially known as the Aberdeen relay calculators and later as pluggable sequence relay calculators (PSRCs), designed to speed up ballistics computations at the U.S. Army's Ballistic Research Laboratory in Aberdeen, Maryland. One computer historian views these machines, installed in 1940, as "the missing link between punched card equipment and the stored program digital computer."[8] A similar commercial adaptation of punched-card tabulating equipment to handle sequences of operations occurred initially at Northrop Aircraft, a major IBM customer.[9] In 1946 IBM introduced an up-graded Type 603 multiplying punch with vacuum tubes to replace the Type 601. Northrop connected this device to a tabulator and tied in a bank of relays to store numbers, resulting in an assemblage that could carry out short sequences of calculations without human intervention. When IBM upgraded the Type 603 to the Type 604 in 1948, the new machine included the 603's vacuum tubes plus sequencing capabilities like those developed for the Aberdeen relay calculators, allowing the 604 to handle up to sixty sequential operations.[10] Seeing that Northrop's adaptation could offer value to its other customers, IBM incorporated this new Type 604 into an ensemble of machines similar to Northrop's and marketed it as the Card-Programmed Calculator (CPC).[11] In the late 1940s and early 1950s, IBM installed several hundred CPCs in commercial firms. This extension of tabulating capabilities to incorporate vacuum tubes and allow limited sequencing of operations approached computing from the tabulating side.

Another development extending tabulating capabilities even further into the realm of computing—the Automatic Sequence Controlled Calculator (ASCC), or the Harvard Mark I—would figure in the insurance and computing story. Harvard mathematician Howard Aiken conceived this system's general outline.[12] In 1936, Aiken, then a physics graduate student, began seeking a company to make a large-scale digital calculator that would enable him to solve equations for his dissertation work. By 1938, he persuaded James Bryce, IBM's chief engineer, to back the proposal to build such a calculator, and Thomas J. Watson, IBM's president, agreed to fund its development. With funding of $100,000, Bryce put Claire D. Lake, the developer of IBM's first printing tabulator, in charge of the project and a team of engineers. Aiken initially sat down with Lake to explain his requirements, including fully automatic operation for extended periods of time. Although Aiken suggested what might later have been called the system's architecture, Lake and his team of IBM engineers worked out the detailed system design and developed the necessary equipment, all within IBM. Most components in this fifty-one-foot by two-foot electromechanical system derived from tabulating technology (fig. 5.1). Punched tape, often in loops that repeated instruction sets again and

*Fig. 5.1.* The Harvard-IBM Mark 1, or the Automatic Sequence Controlled Calculator, was initially conceived in outline by Howard Aiken and realized by IBM. Courtesy of the IBM Archives.

again, controlled the sequence of operations. This system's speed was slow even by tabulator standards, but it could operate for hours at a time controlled only by the tape.

By the time the ASCC was completed and installed at Harvard in 1944, the war was in progress, and Aiken had become a commander in the U.S. Naval Reserves. In preparation for its dedication, Watson insisted on having industrial designer Norman Bel Geddes design a modern, stainless steel and glass face for it. Moreover, he added a $100,000 endowment for operating expenses to the money spent developing the machine, which already exceeded the original $100,000 commitment. Given the time, money, and creativity IBM had put into the system, Watson was shocked when Aiken and the navy issued a press release naming Aiken as the sole inventor of what came to be called the "Harvard Mark I," not even acknowledging that IBM had fully funded the machine's development and operating expenses. Watson was furious, and the announcement created a serious rift between IBM and Aiken's Harvard lab. By some accounts, however, his outrage spurred Watson on to further efforts in computing.[13] Meanwhile, by producing subsequent systems named Harvard Mark II, III, and IV, Aiken reinforced the notion that he had invented the Mark I. Like the other early "computers" coming out of the tabulating side of computing, Mark I did not ultimately establish the operating model for the first commercial computers. Nevertheless, this electronic calculator and the ill will it generated would influence a key player in the insurance industry's early interaction with computing.

Another key line of development, this time growing out of the electronic side of computing, was the construction of the ENIAC (Electronic Numerical Integrator and Computer) at the Moore School of Electrical Engineering, University of Pennsylvania (fig. 5.2).[14] Between 1943 and 1945, John W. Mauchly, a physics professor, and J. Presper Eckert Jr., an electronic engineer, developed and constructed this electronic calculator to compute ballistic tables for the U.S. Army.[15] With its 18,000 vacuum tubes, it could calculate much more rapidly than the tabulator extensions discussed earlier in this chapter, but it was highly vulnerable to tube failure. It also required long and complex setups of switches and plugged wires, more time consuming and complicated than setting up tabulator plug boards or the loops of punched paper tape used by the Mark I. In addition, it could store only twenty numbers. Even as the ENIAC was still being built, Eckert and Mauchly teamed up with brilliant mathematician John von Neumann, who had learned of the ENIAC relatively accidentally, to develop a new concept for the ENIAC's successor: the EDVAC (Electronic Discrete Variable Automatic Computer). The plan for EDVAC included the notion of the stored program, which became a defining characteristic of computers. In this machine, mercury delay lines would hold instructions as well as numbers, both stored on paper tape or cards until they were fed into the computer in advance. In June 1945, von Neumann wrote up the ideas behind this newly conceived machine in what was intended to be a draft for internal circulation.

This document, "A First Draft of a Report on the EDVAC," received much wider and more public circulation than originally expected, thus preempting any patent application and contributing to the ultimate breakup of the Moore School team.[16] In 1946, Eckert and Mauchly left the Moore School to start their own company, initially called the Electronic Control Company (ECC), to exploit this new computing concept commercially. It signed its first contract with

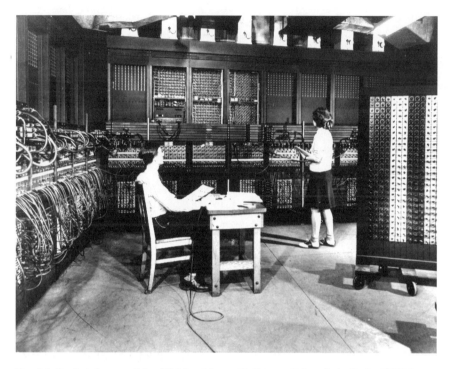

*Fig. 5.2.* During the war, John W. Mauchly and J. Presper Eckert Jr. built the ENIAC, based on vacuum tube technology, at the Moore School of Electrical Engineering, University of Pennsylvania, to compute ballistic tables for the U.S. Army. Reproduced courtesy of the IBM Archives.

the Bureau of the Census in that same year, promising an EDVAC-type computer, soon renamed the UNIVAC (Universal Automatic Computer). As Eckert and Mauchly developed plans for the UNIVAC, they decided to replace punched cards or paper tape with magnetic tape for storage. The magnetic tape would distinguish the UNIVAC from other early computers available to commercial firms such as life insurance companies. It was, according to one computer history, "both the most ambitious and the least successful aspect of the project."[17] Meanwhile, within a year EEC needed more cash to keep the company afloat, so it contracted with Northrop Aircraft Corporation to build a small computer to guide missiles—the BINAC (Binary Automatic Computer). This peripheral project would slow its development of UNIVAC, the machine that was central to its business plan of providing computers to commercial businesses.

# Initial Insurance Interest in and Interactions with Computing

These developments in computing and the nascent computer industry during the war and in the immediate postwar period drew insurance industry attention. In part, this notice demonstrated ongoing actuarial interest in all issues related to numerical calculation.[18] Although actuaries played an important role in the interaction, however, the most common early computer applications in insurance would not be actuarial but operational. In addition, this early engagement reflected the industry's continuing focus on improving insurance office methods, as demonstrated in LOMA's activities. Moreover, insurance office managers and efficiency experts were struggling with the problems caused by clerical labor shortages that developed during the war and continued after it, exacerbated by a life insurance boom.[19] Life insurance in force grew by 51% from 1948 to 1953, at the same time that the total number of insurance policies (a better indicator of work volume) rose by more than 24%.[20] During this period, total employment in the life insurance industry grew 14%, greater than the 12% increase in total nonfarm employment in the United States but not enough to keep up with the increased data-processing load. Thus compelling practical reasons accounted for high levels of insurance industry interest in any new computing machinery that might reduce the growing demand for clerical labor. A few insurance figures would take a more aggressive interest in influencing, not just following, the developments. Of greatest importance were the interactions between Prudential's Berkeley and various potential vendors. His contacts with Eckert and Mauchly's company, in particular, influenced the development of commercial computing equipment.

## *Insurance Interest in Computing Developments before and during the War*

Life insurance was alert to computing's potential even before the war, both within and outside the United States. As early as 1936, E. William Phillips, a British actuary and the general manager for Great Britain of Manufacturers Life Insurance Company, argued that actuaries should switch from a base-ten system to octal or binary notation to allow them to use electronics in their calculations.[21] The paper containing this argument, presented to the British Institute of Actuaries and printed in the British *Journal of the Institute of Actuaries*, gained Phillips some followers who shared his interest in electronic insurance computation, including John J. Finelli, a Metropolitan Life actuary who would play an important role in the insurance and computing events of the late 1940s and early 1950s.[22]

Edmund Callis Berkeley, a mathematician and actuary who worked for Prudential first in its Actuarial Department and then in its Methods Department, explored issues related to computing in the early 1940s.[23] In memorandums and reports written throughout 1941 and 1942, Berkeley explored possible applications of symbolic logic (particularly Boolean algebra) to Prudential's work, including to wiring tabulator plug boards—an application now recognizable as a predecessor of computer programming. Berkeley also translated perspectives, needs, and preferences between the insurance industry and potential computing vendors.

Berkeley first emerged as a go-between in the early 1940s, when he began talking to firms developing new computational devices, with an eye toward Prudential's possible use of them for insurance work. He visited General Electric's laboratories to learn about GE's differential analyzer and Bell Labs to discuss that company's electrical relay computing machine. Although neither machine was well suited to insurance uses, his reports indicate that even this early he was both learning about the technology and conveying information about the insurance market to these potential vendors. His memo reporting on a November 1941 visit to Bell Labs to see George Stibitz's electrical relay computing machine revealed a two-way exchange of insurance market information between Berkeley and his Prudential colleague E. F. Cooley, on the one hand, and the men they met at Bell Labs, on the other:

> Dr. Fry pointed out that a good deal of development work would be required before the principles now used in the Complex Computer could be applied and a computing machine adapted to our uses could be developed. As a rough estimate he mentioned $250,000 as the possible cost of such development work. He inquired if the Prudential might be interested to that extent in financing such development. Mr. Cooley replied that it is quite conceivable that the Prudential would be so interested, if there appeared to be a possible saving in clerical salaries to equal a reasonable annual "write-off" of the development costs plus cost of maintenance.[24]

Similarly, his report on his visit to GE's labs early in 1942 records the following exchange:

These men first wanted to know how we thought their machines might solve problems for us. I explained that my present purpose was to search out the correspondence between mechanical operations, abstract operations, and the operations taking place in an insurance company, with a view to a variety of applications of machines and abstract systems to insurance company problems. . . . Mr. Kuehni inquired if we would be willing to pay from $100,000 to $250,000 for the development and production of a new machine. I said that, depending on clerical and other savings computed on reasonable assumptions, we would be willing, and that we were now paying an amount of that order in each year for punch card machines and equipment.[25]

So even as the United States entered World War II, a dialogue had begun between a representative of a major life insurance firm and the early experimenters with new computing technologies.[26]

Broader as well as more intense insurance interest in new modes of computing developed during and after the war. The armed forces and government agencies recruited many mathematically trained actuaries and other insurance employees to work on military projects involving statistics and operations research.[27] In conducting such work they helped improve the accuracy of bombsights; worked with army statistics on casualty rates, personnel structure, and retirement benefits; helped create a strategy for antisubmarine warfare; and took part in code-breaking activities.[28] Almost a quarter of the scientists involved in Philip Morse's Anti-Submarine Warfare Operations Research Unit (ASWORG) in 1942, for example, were actuaries.[29] Franklin D'Olier, Prudential president during the war, was appointed chairman of the Strategic Bombing Survey Commission designed to indicate how effective Allied bombing had been.[30] Under the direct supervision of Harry J. Volk, a Prudential officer in the methods area, and using a huge punched-card installation, this commission gathered and analyzed voluminous statistics on bombing raids. Work on such projects typically involved large-scale IBM tabulating installations, but a few actuaries worked directly with the new computing technology being developed during the war. While serving in the U.S. Naval Reserves, Berkeley was stationed at Harvard, where he observed operations of the Mark I and worked with Aiken on constructing the Mark II.[31] Whether insurance actuaries worked with tabulators or with the early quasi-computers, their wartime experience, according to a historian of the actuarial profession, gave them "prompt appreciation of the potential in electronic computers" after 1945.[32]

## Berkeley and the UNIVAC

Prudential's Berkeley was clearly a leader in the initial interaction between insurance and computing, and both Berkeley and Prudential would play an even more important role immediately after the war in shaping computing technology to commercial, as opposed to military or scientific, needs. During this important period, Berkeley continued to act as a mediator and translator between the two industries, interpreting the desires of each to the other as he sought to acquire the new technology for Prudential.[33] Berkeley would influence the UNIVAC's development significantly in input, output, and verification, all critical areas for commercial computer users.

In 1946, when Berkeley returned to the Prudential after his war work, he pursued contacts with potential vendors of new computing machinery with even greater intensity than before. Within weeks of returning, he met with representatives of IBM, Bell Labs, and Radio Corporation of America (RCA) and wrote his first draft specifications for "sequence controlled calculators" for Prudential.[34] He held two meetings with IBM. First, he visited the Watson Laboratory at Columbia University, where he met with his prewar acquaintance Dr. Wallace Eckert and "learned about the program of the laboratory, saw its IBM machines, and two novel relay multipliers." Subsequently, he invited IBM's R. R. Seeber Jr. to discuss "requirements of the Company in regard to sequence controlled and other new types of calculators."[35] Both Eckert and Seeber were then working on the Selective Sequence Electronic Calculator (SSEC), the powerful, one-of-a-kind machine that was to be Watson's triumph over Aiken, but they apparently did not mention it to Berkeley.[36]

Berkeley did not view these meetings as very fruitful. Berkeley's displeasure with IBM may indicate that he believed the Mark I was primarily the product of Aiken's invention rather than of IBM's research and development efforts. Possibly influenced by this perspective and the related ill will between the two organizations, as well as by IBM secrecy about the new work, Berkeley reported that IBM was not actively working on new computing technologies. He subsequently asserted, "It seems clear that International Business Machines, Endicott, N.Y., is not to be included in this list [of potential vendors] at the present time, because of their paramount investment and interest in punch card accounting machines, and the great backlog of demand for such machines."[37] In the following year, he gave Prudential upper management three reasons not to contract with IBM to construct a sequence-controlled calculator for Pruden-tial: IBM's financial interest in punched-card tabulating equipment, Aiken's view that IBM was not good enough to engineer such a machine, and Berke-ley's opinion that IBM was too secretive about its product development to al-low Prudential to be involved.[38] Berkeley clearly perceived this third criterion as quite important. Although he understood that the in-house development approach followed by Gore a half century earlier was not feasible with this new technology, he sought a real maker-user collaboration. He also predicted, "There is no prospect of modern electronic machinery from IBM before the next four or five years elapse and probably much longer," a prediction that turned out to be fairly accurate for IBM but also for the makers of UNIVAC, which would become his preferred option.

Although he rejected IBM, Berkeley was intensifying his contacts with other organizations, such as Bell Labs and RCA, that he considered to be potential vendors so as to learn about the latest technological developments and simul-taneously to communicate Prudential's requirements. In early 1947, Berkeley reported that during the last five months of 1946 he had initiated sixty visits with individuals or groups to discuss potential insurance applications of the new computing technologies.[39] In reporting on these visits, he attempted to educate Prudential's upper management about how valuable these new computing technologies might be to its business and to advocate direct in-volvement with technology developers. In a late September 1946 memo, for example, he identified three currently operating sequence-controlled calcula-tors—IBM's ASCC, or Mark I, at Harvard; the ENIAC at the Moore School; and Bell Labs' relay calculator built for the army—and described some of their ca-pabilities and current shortcomings for business uses, such as inadequate stor-age.[40] He then listed twenty different Prudential departments that could po-tentially use such "calculators" and justified further investigation: "Because of the possibility of material saving, it is in the interest of the Company that a study should be made of the places in the Company where sequence controlled calculators could be applied and of the specifications which such calculators should meet for Company problems." Cost savings would be the principal—and almost exclusive—argument for adopting computers in the early decades. Finally, he requested additional personnel to help him identify such uses and prepare to run an insurance problem on Bell Labs' general-purpose relay cal-culator.[41]

Most notably, in late 1946 Berkeley generated the first draft of a document

entitled "Sequence Controlled Calculators for the Prudential-Specifications"—
his first attempt to formulate and communicate Prudential's perceived needs
to the nascent computer industry.[42] This document demonstrates clearly that
Berkeley was attempting to shape the technology to meet Prudential's desires
and those of insurance more generally, just as insurance firms had done in the
early tabulator era. Although the specifications reflected insurance applications Berkeley envisioned, they were not stated in insurance-specific terms.[43]
They included minimum form standards for numbers to be manipulated;
amount of, and speed of access to, memory; speed of various mathematical
and logical operations such as addition, multiplication, and determining the
greater of two numbers; ability to follow a sequence of operations and perform
varied routines; existence of auxiliary machines to convert tables, instructions,
and routines into and out of machine language rapidly; reliability; and ability
to run unattended. In addition, he included some nontechnical requirements
such as availability by purchase (not rent), cost, service availability, and "engineering cooperation" with Prudential in the "design and development of the
machine and other features."[44] In this last specification, Berkeley revealed that
he was not simply waiting for a commercial product to appear—he intended
for Prudential to shape product development to insurers' needs.

During early 1947, Berkeley continued to report to his superiors about the
rapidly evolving technology and its potential applications to insurance.[45] He
listed potential insurance applications ranging from complex actuarial calculations with limited outputs to routine operations with little calculation
but considerable input and output, such as the premium billing process.[46] At
the same time, Berkeley's discussions with potential vendors such as Engineering Research Associates (ERA) and Raytheon about developing a sequence-
controlled calculator for Prudential became more serious. He solicited and received several proposals responding both to his initial draft specifications and
to conversations.[47] ERA's and Raytheon's proposals received relatively little
subsequent consideration, in part because he seems to have been much more
interested in the proposal from ECC, Eckert and Mauchly's partnership, later
to be incorporated as Eckert-Mauchly Computer Company (EMCC).

Berkeley talked with John Mauchly in January 1947 at the Symposium on
Large Scale Digital Calculating Machinery at the Harvard Computational Laboratory.[48] After that, the two men corresponded extensively about a potential
development contract between Prudential and ECC.[49] At this point Eckert and
Mauchly had two confirmed customers—the Census Bureau and Northrop

Aircraft—and a pending contract with a third customer, A. C. Nielsen Company.[50] While the contract with Northrop was for the more specialized, defense-related BINAC machine, the contracts for the other two specified a general-purpose machine to be called the UNIVAC. By mid-February, Mauchly had submitted an initial proposal built around ECC's detailed response to Berkeley's preliminary specifications.[51] A comparison of the two documents reveals some areas in which Prudential's requirements would influence development of what would become the first commercially available stored-program computer in the United States.

On most internal computational issues, ECC could easily equal or surpass the standards Berkeley set.[52] For example, ECC could promise to add two numbers in two milliseconds, much faster than Berkeley's stated requirement of twenty milliseconds). Only in the area of rapid random access to stored tables did Mauchly express concern about delivering what Berkeley wanted, since magnetic tape could provide "unlimited memory" but had to be searched sequentially. Mauchly argued, however, that the proposed machine's storage capacity and the ability to calculate rapidly would help compensate for slower table lookup.

Berkeley's criteria for input, verification, and output caused the most serious difficulties for ECC, highlighting what became key issues in the early development of commercial computers. Berkeley had required an auxiliary machine for translating data and instructions into some medium that was readable by both humans and machines, such as punched paper tape or cards, to allow checking of input. Because Eckert and Mauchly envisioned magnetic tape as the sole entry and storage medium, Mauchly proposed that magnetic tape could be sent through a printer and printed out for checking. In general, however, he felt that verification should be done automatically, not by human readers: "Proof-reading by visual methods and other methods which involve human scanning of the entire data for detection of errors are not in general to be recommended. More efficient methods of detecting and correcting errors can be devised for use with this equipment." This response reflected Mauchly's notion of how the technology should be used. Berkeley, drawing on his long experience with tabulating technology, was not ready to accept this aspect of Mauchly's vision, and he subsequently maintained his belief that conversion equipment was needed to provide a humanly readable medium.[53] Over the next decade and beyond, almost all the insurance firms would echo the requirement for a humanly readable input and storage medium. Output speed posed another difficulty. The ECC proposal was vague but optimistic about output speed. Berkeley had stipulated, "If the machine is very rapid, it should be equipped with multiple output units." In response, Mauchly stated that multiple automatic typewriters could be used to print final results from magnetic tape, though he erroneously attributed this output demand primarily to Berkeley's desire to check the accuracy of inputs by printing out and proofreading them. Mauchly apparently did not yet fully understand the huge input-output needs of insurance and many other commercial applications.

The ECC proposal also addressed additional requirements that Berkeley had enumerated. Mauchly claimed, for example, that ECC could provide adequate reliability to meet Prudential's standards, but he evaded Berkeley's stated stipulation of unattended overnight operation by explaining that the speed of the machine would make such use infrequent. Moreover, he argued, "The large output of which such a machine is capable in a given time is certainly ample justification for providing an operator who will see to it that the machine is kept busy." The proposal responded to most of Berkeley's remaining criteria, including making clear that ECC planned to cooperate with Prudential (and other firms) in developing the machines. Mauchly quoted a purchase price of $150,000 for the first computer, decreasing to $40,000 for the sixth through tenth computers. This price far exceeded Berkeley's suggested $10,000 to $20,000 per computer, but Mauchly pointed out that this price reflected development, not mass production. Indeed, he could point to his previous exchanges with Berkeley concerning the potential value of acquiring such a machine at an early stage: "The economic value of these machines to insurance companies has already been estimated by Mr. Berkeley and it is evident from his estimate that it is sound economics to obtain machines at an early date even though their costs may include part of the development expense rather than to postpone the acquisition of such machines until a somewhat indefinite future time when the development costs will have been paid by others." Eckert and Mauchly had been collecting pricing and market information, as well as performance desires, from Berkeley.

Berkeley's specifications clearly influenced ECC's proposal. Moreover, since ECC did not propose to develop a custom machine for Prudential but rather a general-purpose machine for the broad commercial market, Berkeley and Prudential were helping to shape the emerging configuration of the UNIVAC, particularly with regard to peripherals.[54] As one computer historian noted in relation to ECC's Prudential proposal, "The role of the customer in helping to set objectives [was] fairly explicit."[55] During the subsequent three months, informal correspondence and negotiation between Mauchly and Berkeley shaped a more detailed ECC proposal to Prudential, dated May 16, 1947.[56] In it, ECC discussed potential insurance applications, including premium billing, mortality studies, and group insurance. ECC also proposed that it would develop some sort of card reader to convert punched cards to tape. Indeed, Mauchly even recommended that Prudential convert its premium billing processes for ordinary insurance to tabulating equipment and punched cards so that when the new computer was ready, Prudential could run those cards through a reader to convert them to magnetic tape, rather than entering them directly onto tape. This negotiation with Berkeley and Prudential demonstrated to Eckert and Mauchly that even an insurance executive like Berkeley, who was very open to new technology, proved unwilling to give up the security of humanly readable, as well as machine-readable, punched cards.

A few days after receiving this second proposal, Berkeley recommended that Prudential accept it and sign a contract for such a machine. In making the case to his superiors, he commented that "they alone of our prospective suppliers wished to come and survey in a day or two our typical problems at no cost to us" and that Raytheon, ERA, and the Moore School "have hardly begun to investigate thoroughly input and output devices, large automatic files, etc. for business applications."[57] Although Berkeley had recommended going full speed ahead, Prudential executives proceeded more cautiously, deciding to sign only a developmental contract, with the option to convert it to a purchase contract once specific milestones had been met.[58] Although many of these milestones would be missed and renegotiated, in late 1948 (around the time that ECC was incorporated as Eckert-Mauchly Computer Corporation) Prudential converted it to a purchase contract for a UNIVAC computer.[59] By then, however, Berkeley had left Prudential.[60]

Berkeley's aggressive involvement in the UNIVAC's development was unusual for the insurance industry during this era. Moreover, neither Berkeley nor Prudential remained in center stage by 1954 when the first few UNIVAC computers were delivered to insurance customers. After Remington Rand purchased EMCC, the office machines firm realized that the contract purchase price, variously reported at $150,000–$300,000, was much too low.[61] It succeeded in canceling Prudential's UNIVAC contract and then offering Prudential an option to buy the computer at a much higher price—an option that Prudential did not exercise.[62] Nevertheless, Berkeley's interaction with vendors in the emerging computer industry, especially his exchanges and negotiations with Mauchly over verification and the inclusion of tape-to-card and card-to-tape peripherals with the UNIVAC, helped mold the initial configuration of commercial computers. Indeed, in 1954 a Remington Rand UNIVAC executive acknowledged this influence to an insurance audience: "Almost from its inception in 1947, UNIVAC has been associated closely with insurance. Specifications from one large life company [Prudential], one other commercial company [A. C. Nielsen], and the Bureau of the Census, determined the completion of its design in 1949."[63] Another UNIVAC official discussed more specifically what that computer's design owed to studies conducted for these three organizations:

> The results of these studies showed that while the arithmetic units which were common in the many different computer developments at that time were quite adequate to do the commercial processes needed, the primary requirement was to get data into the computer's internal memory and arithmetic system rapidly, and get the computed results out rapidly; that the computer mustn't be tied . . . to the slowest speeds of keyboard input devices, or output printing devices; that these must be separate units and, furthermore, for commercial work, that the equipment must be completely self checking.[64]

As in the tabulator period, life insurance was a significant potential customer for the new machines. Although military and government influence on computer technology was enormous, life insurance (in the form of Edmund Berkeley and Prudential) also influenced its adaptation to commercial needs.

## An Industry Educates Itself about the Computer

Although Berkeley apparently led the industry in interacting directly with potential computer vendors during the late 1940s, Prudential was not the only insurance firm desiring to educate itself about the new technological developments. In 1946, for example, Berkeley accepted an invitation to visit Metropolitan Life, where (with Prudential's approval) he "talked to thirty actuarial men on sequence controlled computing machinery, and discussed applications in insurance."[65] The two largest insurance firms were both watching developments closely. Broad insurance interest in this topic revealed itself in activities of at least three different insurance associations: LOMA, IASA, and the Society of Actuaries (called the ASA until 1949).[66] LOMA had long followed the evolution of information-processing techniques and technologies, among other home office management issues. IASA, with its focus specifically on punched-card use, had become a national player in this arena more recently, and by the mid-1950s it would emerge as a key insurance forum dealing with computer use. The Society of Actuaries, however, started its activities concerning computing first and documented them the best of the three. Moreover, the committee established within this organization most visibly represented the insurance industry to the emerging computer industry. This committee's reports would significantly shape insurance executives' views of how the new computers might best be used in their firms.

## Early Interest in Computing at LOMA and IASA

Many insurance executives were interested in new computing technology but recognized that they needed to collaborate with others to investigate how best to take advantage of it. At LOMA's 1946 conference, technology reports focused on developments continuing from before the war.[67] By the following year, however, LOMA members were acknowledging wartime innovations in computing, including sequence-controlled calculators. In detailing the new offerings from IBM at the September 1947 conference, John Hancock's Mangini reported on new developments in IBM tabulating equipment, discussing the Type 602 calculating punch, with its programming device, and the Type 603 electronic multiplier, with its extensive use of electronics.[68] Mangini chaired LOMA's Eastern Office Planning and Equipment Committee, which saw such tabulating-based moves toward computing as clearly within its purview. The same report briefly mentioned the sequence-controlled calculator but for more information referred his audience to Berkeley's subsequent talk titled "Electronic Sequence Controlled Calculating Machinery, and Applications in Insurance."[69] In this paper, one of three that Berkeley presented at insurance associations this year, Berkeley reported on the activities of a recently formed LOMA committee, the Electronic Sequence Controlled Calculator Committee.[70] This seven-person committee, led by Berkeley, had already met four times and visited the existing experimental computers at Harvard and the Moore School. LOMA's committee did not ultimately generate influential reports such as those created by the Society of Actuaries, in great part because Berkeley left the insurance industry, and consequently LOMA, in 1948.

In his 1947 LOMA paper, Berkeley undertook to educate that association's members, as he had his Prudential colleagues. He described how electronic sequence-controlled calculators worked and briefly listed existing machines, including the ENIAC, the Mark I, and the Bell Labs relay computer. He then explained the principles behind two critical new components: electronic vacuum tubes and magnetic recording. Next he enumerated several new types of peripheral devices that he felt insurance offices would need along with the sequence-controlled calculator itself: a translator to convert between magnetic tape and other media such as punched cards, a verifier to compare information on one magnetic tape to that on another, and a selector to allow rapid selection of information on a magnetic tape. In describing these as-yet-nonexistent devices to this large insurance audience, he was indirectly pressuring vendors such as ECC to develop them. Finally, he spoke about insurance applications, listing them as shown in table 5.1 and describing the medical index application in more detail. One listed area, premium billing, would turn out to be the most popular early application, since the difficulties of random access lookup using magnetic tape would make the medical index less attractive to firms. In this meeting, then, Berkeley introduced LOMA members to some of the possibilities of computers.

During the next few years, sequence-controlled calculators received relatively little attention at regular LOMA conferences, though the Type 604 electronic calculating punch was introduced, and IBM exhibit personnel welcomed discussion of the Card-Programmed Calculator that incorporated it.[71] In 1950 a representative of the Planning and Equipment Committee men-

Table 5.1. *Some Possible Insurance Applications of Computer Equipment*

| Accounting | Procedures | Actuarial Calculations |
| --- | --- | --- |
| Payroll | Cash surrenders | Premiums |
| Commissions | Extended insurance | Reserves |
| Premiums | Claims | Dividend scales |
| Loans | Issue records | Expense analysis |
| Investments | Policy writing | |
| Dividends | Premium billing | |
| General ledger | Life registers | |
| Bank balances | Lapse registers | |
| | Production records | |
| | Medical index | |

*Source:* Adapted from Exhibit 6, Edmund C. Berkeley, "Electronic Sequence Controlled Calculating Machinery, and Applications in Insurance," *Proceedings of the Life Office Management Association* (1947): 126.

tioned the trend toward electronics before reviewing more prosaic development:

> The consensus of opinion about the recent developments is, in a few words: "the big news is electronics." . . . Most of you are gradually becoming familiar with some of the progress in the field. You have read or will read the fine exposition by Edmund C. Berkeley in his new book *Machines that Think;* you know of the recent acquisition by Remington Rand of the Eckert-Mauchly Computer Corporation . . . ; you have seen or will see soon the new IBM-card-programmed electronic calculator . . . ; and as a result you are becoming increasingly aware that these electronic machines will gradually result in obsolescence of older types of office equipment and increased mechanization of office procedures. There seems to be no doubt but that the trend in this direction will result in displacement of clerical workers . . . and slow down the uninterrupted increase in the proportion of clerical workers which has been going on during the last three decades. . . . This would open up a real field for savings in over-all costs.[72]

This passage gives a sense of what most members knew and from what sources, including Berkeley's popular book on computers, published within a year after he left Prudential and building on talks such as the ones he gave at the three associations.[73] It suggests that the average life insurance office manager was following developments in this area, at least, and saw electronic computers as potentially helpful in dealing with labor shortages.

In 1947, the peripatetic Berkeley presented another paper on this subject at the IASA annual meeting, continuing his campaign to educate the insurance industry on this subject.[74] In this paper, he included more technical details than he had in the LOMA one. To demonstrate the trade-offs among storage media, for example, he illustrated the cost and speed required for changing a digit from 0 to 1 for relays, electronic tubes, magnetic tape, and photo film (table 5.2). On the basis of this comparison, he argued that "the new types of machines that are going to come along will be based on magnetic tape and electronic tubes."[75] He ended with a much briefer review of potential applications than in the LOMA talk. This time, however, he highlighted the premium billing application: "Certainly, at the same time that the machine prepares the premium notice, it could calculate the dividend, calculate the loan interest, total them and put them down."[76] At the 1950 IASA conference, H. T. Engstrom, vice president of Engineering Research Associates (one of the small firms competing to build computers), gave a talk on the future of computation.[77] The

*Table 5.2. Comparison of Media Storage by Cost and Speed*

| Storage | Unit Cost | Change Speed |
| --- | --- | --- |
| Relay | $10 | 1/100 second |
| Electronic tube | 50¢ | 1/1,000,000 second |
| Magnetic spot | 1/100,000¢ | 1/10,000 second |
| Film | Small | Zero |

*Source:* Adapted from Edmund C. Berkeley, "Sequence Controlled Calculators," *Proceedings of the Insurance Accounting and Statistical Association* (1947): 43.

audience's questions and Engstrom's answers revealed a range of interests and knowledge among audience members. Other than these two papers, however, IASA's proceedings remained focused on punched-card tabulating applications until 1950.

In 1950 LOMA and IASA were two of the four insurance associations that cooperated with Remington Rand (which had by then acquired EMCC and the UNIVAC) in creating the "Remington Rand Forum on the Use of Electronics in the Insurance Industry."[78] According to one attendee,

> It was at this forum meeting that the Univac computer system was first introduced and its operations explained to representatives of the insurance industry and the leaders of the various industry associations had an opportunity to outline their ideas on data processing applications for the electronic computer in the life, casualty, and fire segments of the insurance business. The results of this meeting made the industry well aware of things to come and many of the larger companies organized staff committees to make feasibility studies with respect to the desirability of using a computer system for their data processing work.[79]

A highlighted panel of insurance representatives included speakers from Prudential, Metropolitan Life (both representing LOMA), and Phoenix Mutual (representing IASA), all discussing their investigations of potential computer use within their own firms and its application to life insurance more broadly.[80] Thus it is clear that by 1950 at least a few individuals within member companies in both LOMA and IASA were educating themselves about developments in this new technology, and in a handful of cases they were well into investigations of its potential for their firms.

## The Society of Actuaries Study

Despite the LOMA and IASA activity, the association most visibly representing the insurance industry to vendors up to 1952 was the Society of Actuaries. Actuaries used complex calculations in their work and had been highly involved with wartime computational activities. Their organization became the primary site for insurance activity, influencing both vendors and insurance firms. These actuaries, many of whom held high executive positions in their firms, had in mind the interests not just of the actuarial departments but of the entire enterprise. Indeed, they quickly concluded that computers would ultimately need to be applied to routine operations outside the actuarial area to justify their cost. At the Society of Actuaries' May 1947 meeting, two important events initiated its involvement in computing: Berkeley gave his first major talk on computing to insurance industry members, and the association formed the Committee on New Recording Means and Computing Devices to study the potential of the electronic calculating equipment on the horizon.

As he would in his LOMA and IASA presentations, Berkeley described the new technology and discussed its cost and potential uses in insurance.[81] In this talk, Berkeley explained the new electronic computing machines by analogy to calculators and punched-card tabulators connected in series. He argued that the cost of such computing machines, quoted by vendors as in the range of $100,000–$125,000, was considerably lower than the cost of a comparable tabulating installation and its operators, and he described the range of possible insurance applications. Finally, he cited two major motivations behind insurance adoption of electronic computers: reductions in clerical labor and the ability to undertake calculations not feasible in the past.

Three other members of the Society of Actuaries delivered formal comments on the paper, revealing considerable interest in computers and varied visions of what they could accomplish for the insurance industry.[82] William P. Barber Jr. and Edward A. Rieder emphasized Berkeley's argument that such machinery would not simply enable firms to process the same information more rapidly but would allow and encourage firms to rethink what information was processed and how. Rieder extended Berkeley's observation that nineteenth-century actuarial formulas were devised for easy manual computation, noting, "If this thought is carried far enough, we arrive at the surprising conclusion that the whole structure of life insurance as we know it to-day can, in large measure, be traced to computation limitations," and speculating about possible changes in insurance practices when this new electronic computational machinery became available.

Even more important than Berkeley's paper at the 1947 Society of Actuaries meeting was the association's founding of the Committee on New Recording Means and Computing Devices.[83] This committee's work on potential insurance use of computing was widely viewed as the most significant before the first computers were delivered in 1954.[84] Metropolitan Life's Malvin Davis chaired the committee through 1955, succeeded by the same company's John J. Finelli, an important committee member from the start.[85] Other members included Barber of Connecticut Mutual Life Insurance Company and Walter Klem of Equitable Life Assurance Society, the fourteenth- and third-largest life insurance firms, respectively.[86] By 1948, the committee was already busy: "Mr. M.E. Davis, Chairman, submitted a written report . . . in which he . . . stated that the Society's Committee is in the process of developing a model office setup . . . built around the latest developments of new equipment, with a view to aiding both insurance personnel and the scientists engaged in the development of such equipment in a better understanding of: (a) the usefulness of these developments to life insurance companies and (b) the specific problems that still must be solved to make such equipment practicable for use by life insurance companies."[87] Davis clearly intended the committee to educate both life insurance firms and potential computer vendors on each other's perspectives as well as to form the life insurance industry's views of how it might use that technology.

The committee worked hard over the next four years, presenting its work in 1952, first to the Society of Actuaries membership in its April meeting, then, in response to great interest, in a special September meeting open to nonactuarial insurance personnel and representatives of potential vendor firms (e.g., IBM and Remington Rand).[88] The committee's initial and most important written report was based on the September meeting and was distributed to member companies and meeting attendees. It reveals frequent and significant interactions between the life insurance industry and the emerging computer industry well before 1954, when the first computers were delivered to firms. The committee conveyed perceived insurance industry needs to vendor firms such as Remington Rand's UNIVAC Division and IBM and worked closely with them on responses to those needs.[89] Within the insurance industry, it also served as a major information source about computers and their potential application to insurance work. The report traced how visions of computer use developed and spread within the industry, and it presented a detailed description of its sample (recommended) insurance application, the "consolidated functions approach," which would shape insurance adoption and use of computers for almost two decades. Its importance justifies a close look.

Davis's opening overview claimed early insurance and particularly actuarial interest in applying the wartime developments in machine computation: "It is not surprising that at the end of the war some of us began to feel that machinery of this kind might be very useful in the business world." He went on to articulate the essential problem faced by the committee: "that life insurance people and electronic engineers were two groups who did not speak each other's language. . . . It became apparent that some medium was necessary to bridge the gap between the two."[90] Actuaries, he stated, chose to do so jointly, through the existing Society of Actuaries structure, to save each firm from having to do it separately. In thus cooperating with regard to technology and its use in insurance, these firms and individuals were continuing a tradition clearly observable in insurance associations during the tabulator era. The committee saw its purpose not as endorsing particular equipment but as reporting to member firms what it had learned.

Davis provided some background on the new computing technology itself to help in understanding its capabilities, describing it in terms of existing tabulating technology. He focused primarily on magnetic tape, explaining it by analogy to the familiar punched cards. Although he presented magnetic tape as the inevitable processing medium, he noted that sorting data sequentially recorded on magnetic tape posed problems. For feeding data into computers, the committee, like Berkeley, preferred running punched cards through card-to-tape converters, rather than directly entering data onto magnetic tape, which was "slower and somewhat more difficult to check and control" visually.[91] For output, Davis noted that existing tabulator-based printing technology was better than any currently available method of printing directly from tape but that higher-speed tape printers were being developed. Programming, Davis explained, was like wiring tabulator plugboards, noting that it was "a laborious job" and that "libraries of standard routines" similar to standard plugboard wirings were not yet available to facilitate it.[92] Consequently, the committee recommended using computers for standard rather than special jobs.

Davis also sketched the process of elimination by which the committee arrived at the consolidated functions approach, Finelli's influential sample application occupying the middle section of the report. Although the committee members began by considering actuarial uses such as mortality studies and financial analyses, computation-intensive applications that fit contemporary portrayals of computers as complex calculators, they quickly became convinced that this work was rarely extensive enough to keep a computer busy and allow it to pay for itself. Next the committee turned to a storage and retrieval application. Because accessible file storage of paper policies and records occupied considerable space in most firms, the notion of replacing paper with a compact, updatable electronic file for use in looking up policy information seemed very attractive. Still, this application faced two difficulties—sequential search and legal standing—that were insuperable at this time. Because magnetic tape did not support random access to policy information, retrieval was actually very slow. Moreover, committee members feared that legal and regulatory acceptance of magnetic records as the primary policy records would be slow in coming. "We concluded, therefore, that . . . we would probably need a visual record . . . which would be generally accepted by the courts and regulatory bodies—at least until wide use of tape has become commonplace."[93] Thus the committee rejected this application, as well.

Ultimately, the Society of Actuaries committee concluded that the real gains to be made with electronic computers would be found in what it called "regular policy service," an operational application:

> This is the work which is necessary to tell the policyholder about his premium due and, on participating business [in which policyholders also share the profits], to develop the annual dividend payable, the additional insurance that dividend would purchase if it is to be so applied, the interest which would be due on a policy loan if any exists and the like. This area involves regularly sending out premium notices and statements to the policyholder, involves a fair amount of computation and the handling of large numbers of policy records and seemed to be a place in which electronic information processing equipment might be able to do a substantial amount of good.[94]

In particular, the committee focused on the integrated premium billing and accounting application that many firms were gradually implementing on tabulating technology. In determining how to use both punched-card and magnetic-tape computers for such an application while taking advantage of their new capabilities, the committee established several principles, or "guide posts," for insurance computer applications:

1. An electronic computer should be applied to the whole job, not to some separately departmentalized piece of it. . . .
2. Small jobs should be combined with others. . . .
3. Source records should be consolidated. . . .
4. Make all calculation [*sic*] at one time. . . .
5. Use a self-checking machine.[95]

The first four principles stand in contrast with early insurance applications, both clerical and automated, which tended to be finely subdivided; they were, however, an extension of the newer tabulator-based integrated premium billing and accounting application that was just gaining popularity at this time. The fifth principle is a partial response to the verification problem that had concerned Berkeley. The problem of input verification remained, but a self-checking machine (such as the UNIVAC) was intended to control and check its own internal operations as it functioned.

Finelli presented the heart of the committee's work, the consolidated functions approach, a general plan applicable to both card- and tape-based computers. Finelli stated that the committee's objective was "to produce a workable system, not the best possible system," to be used "as a take-off point" in each firm's own deliberation.[96] He explained the committee's thinking as follows: "To illustrate the ideas involved in concrete form, we took the procedures of one particular company and worked out, in considerable detail, a way in which they could be accommodated by an electronic computer which had already been marketed. The plan which resulted from this effort is what we call the Consolidated Functions Approach."[97] Finelli and the committee had tested the plan only on the IBM card-based SSEC, but they included procedures for a tape-based computer, based on the UNIVAC's specifications. For both card- and tape-based computers, however, they assumed punched cards as input, since Finelli saw cards as necessary: "To avoid to the degree possible a complete dependence on the operating effectiveness of such complicated equipment, complete compatibility with punched card systems seems to be an almost essential requirement."[98] For the tape-based computer, these cards would be converted to magnetic tape with a card-to-tape converter. Thus continuity with existing media was built into the plan. The output procedures were also independent of the computer, using tabulator-based high-speed printers and assuming that high-speed printers for computers would soon be available. Thus the committee reinforced Berkeley's message to vendors that potential insurance cus-

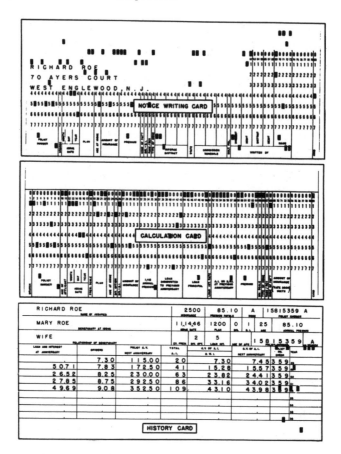

*Fig. 5.3.* Three cards per policy—a punched notice-writing card and calculation card, and a typed or handwritten history card—formed the heart of the consolidated functions approach. From M. E. Davis, W. P. Barber Jr., J. J. Finelli, and W. Klem, "Report of the Committee on New Recording Means and Computing Devices," Society of Actuaries, September 1952, 28–29. Copyright 1952 by the Society of Actuaries, Schaumburg, Illinois. Reprinted with permission.

tomers would need visible input and rapid output and consequently card-to-tape and tape-to-card converters as well as high-speed printers.

The consolidated functions plan balanced current and future needs. It integrated the tasks typically involved in tabulator-based billing and accounting applications, as well as several other related functions, using three cards per policy (fig. 5.3)—two punched cards and one printed history card on which premium payments and other facts were typed or handwritten. The history card was included, after some debate, "based on the belief that such a readable record would be essential in any conversion to the more highly mechanized operating systems to be expected in the future."[99] These three cards consolidated all the information that had previously been stored on approximately ten different cards or files in the firm modeled. Other cards were created and used during the annual processing, but they were discarded afterward.[100]

Because the committee wanted an application that would work with already existing equipment, not one depending on future developments, it limited the use of the new computing equipment. A diagram of annual policy service, reproduced in figure 5.4, shows that "the job of the electronic computer is limited to the one box—the making of figures. The other operations involved are manageable with the standard lines of equipment which have been available for some time."[101] The plan clustered all the computing tasks into one annual servicing of the cards, producing punched cards then used with tabulating or other equipment to fulfill other necessary processes. For the magnetic-tape

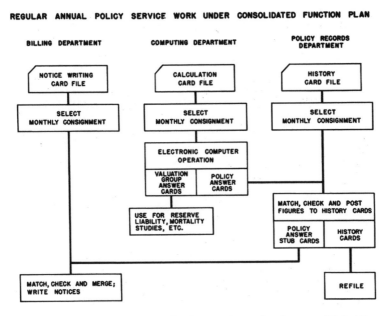

*Fig. 5.4.* The computer's work in annual policy service under the consolidated functions approach was restricted to calculation. From M. E. Davis, W. P. Barber Jr., J. J. Finelli, and W. Klem, "Report of the Committee on New Recording Means and Computing Devices," Society of Actuaries, September 1952, plate 12, p. 31. Copyright 1952 by the Society of Actuaries, Schaumburg, Illinois. Reprinted with permission.

computer, this stage involved converting the cards into tape and answers on tape back into cards, using magnetic tape as the medium for calculation but not for the records themselves or their subsequent uses. Although the committee did not report expected overall savings from the consolidated functions plan, it noted specific gains from two sources. The first was the consolidation of ten files into three and the consequent savings in noncomputerized operations. "The work reduction which results from such a consolidation is very substantial," Finelli observed, reducing clerical effort by about one-fifth for various policy transactions.[102] Indeed, most of the savings could be accomplished by consolidating the files while still using tabulating equipment only. Second, in the computer operation itself much policy and general statistical information could be obtained at a low cost of about three-quarters of a cent per policy. Finelli pointed out, "Even if the work has to be done in duplicate to make absolutely sure that it is right, this looks like a very inexpensive way of producing that much information."[103]

Committee member Klem, in his "Summation" of the report, focused on this new technology as a way to curb rising costs. Klem suggested that magnetic-tape computers would clearly benefit the very large firms but that firms with moderate volumes would benefit from the smaller, punched-card electronic computers, and even smaller firms might consider buying time on another firm's computer. Klem emphasized continuity as well as change. He recommended that companies interested in acquiring the new technology designate a group of high-level executives familiar with all aspects of the firm to "act as the integrating group" and to deal with any necessary reorganization.[104] He also recommended that firms train their own insurance employees to run the computers, since only homegrown staff would be able to "judge the kind of answer which would be acceptable, . . . the degree to which traditional approaches may be modified, and other such matters."[105] Computers could generate substantial savings if they were accompanied by consolidating functions and reorganizing units in firms. Such changes, he suggested, would have to come incrementally: "Realization of their full potential will lead us to the consolidation of many different kinds of work which now are departmentally separated. This, however, is not necessarily a matter of sudden, drastic reorganization. The program indicated is more likely to be the introduction of an electronic computer for one related series of procedures, and the gradual step-by-step adaptation of other routines as we learn at first hand the machine's capabilities and limitation."[106] According to Klem, the computer need not be a disruptive technology that would immediately sweep out all the old ways of conducting business. He ended by urging companies to begin making preparations for using computers.

This committee presentation was widely attended, which attests to the insurance community's interest in the new technology. It had an educational, even evangelical tone.[107] The firms represented on the committee, as well as a few others, had already started internal investigations of how they might use a computer and what kind of computer they should purchase.[108] The report urged other firms to do likewise. Committee members clearly hoped that the consolidated functions plan would serve as a starting point for insurance computer use. The report also reveals tension between desire for a rapid transformation that immediately realized the potential implications of the technology, on the one hand, and a pragmatic focus on achieving such extensive change gradually, through an incremental change process, on the other. In a paper presented in the following year at a broader computer conference, Davis would state that insurance had learned from this study that firms would ultimately need "a basic reengineering of present procedures" to gain the most out of computers.[109] Even in emphasizing the potential to reorganize firms around computerized processes, however, he advocated not an overnight transformation but an incremental, experimental approach to getting there: "It is hardly likely that a company would embark on such an undertaking without acquiring some first-hand experience in operating a data processing system." The punched cards and the clerically maintained history cards of the consolidated functions approach established a clear connection with pre-computer operations—as well as less risky operation and legal standing than magnetic tape.

## The 1953 IASA Conference

Roughly a year after the Society of Actuaries committee presented its initial report, IASA sponsored a two-day conference entitled "Electronics and Its Future in the Insurance Industry," which "mark[ed] the inauguration of an educational program whereby IASA members could learn more about the new electronic machines that may revolutionize many insurance procedures."[110] Although IASA had 575 member companies representing all types of insurance, the committee that ran the conference, as well as the conference program itself, was dominated by life insurance firms.[111] The IASA committee organized the two days around Remington Rand and IBM, respectively, as "the companies that had had the most contact with the insurance industry and had equipment most nearly ready and adapted for insurance use at this time."[112] In addition to more general talks, each day included a panel discussion in which representatives of life insurance firms discussed their plans for using the technology.

By now, Remington Rand had an Insurance Records Department like IBM's. On the first day, its manager spoke about the scope of that company's offerings, including its high-speed electronic tabulating equipment; the UNIVAC, acquired in 1950; and the scientific and engineering computing equipment of ERA, even more recently acquired by Remington Rand. Most of the discussion, however, focused on the UNIVAC's adaptations to insurance. The director of Remington Rand's Applications Research and Engineering Department, Herbert F. Mitchell, emphasized the UNIVAC's connections to the insurance industry by pointing out that "the specifications for it were governed by one large insurance company [Prudential], one other commercial company and the Bureau of the Census, which is a semi-commercial application."[113] From studies done with these three organizations, he said, they had learned important lessons:

> While the arithmetic units which were common in the many different computer developments at that time were quite adequate to do the commercial processes needed, the primary requirement was to get data into the computer's internal memory and arithmetic system rapidly, and get the computed results out rapidly; that the computer mustn't be tied up to the slowest speeds of keyboard input devices, or output printing devices; that these must be separate units and, furthermore, for commercial work, that the equipment must be completely self checking. The equipment must not allow any error of any kind to get into the data being processed.

Clearly, the message from Berkeley and the insurance associations had gotten through.

Mitchell also noted that of the "fifty man-years [that] have been spent in the preparation of routines or programs for commercial applications . . . two-thirds—at least two-thirds—of this work has been done in the insurance industry."[114] Although he included all insurance in this estimate, of the five major applications, four were for life insurance and one for fire insurance, demonstrating that life insurance dominated the UNIVAC application work done so far. The four life insurance applications included "the preparation of premium notices and the allied dividend and commission calculations," insurance valuation (an actuarial application), "the preparation of the consolidated function plan in connection with the work of the Society of Actuaries," and "another combined policy run."[115] Each of these applications except the original consolidated functions approach was programmed in conjunction with a specific insurance company. The companies that had developed UNIVAC applications so far had heeded the Society of Actuaries committee's advice to train insurance people to do the work: "In one of the cases all of the programming was done by personnel of the company concerned. In several of the others, a great deal of the programming was done by their personnel and our personnel working along with them in obtaining these results."[116] These examples illustrate, Mitchell argued, "that we have actually proven UNIVAC in its applicability to the insurance industry."

In summarizing this UNIVAC session at the 1953 IASA annual meeting less than two months later, George Runyan of American United Life Insurance Company highlighted what had been said about the insurance industry's favorable position in this early stage of commercial computing development: "Thanks to the machine companies and a few men in the insurance industry we now stand in a more favorable position than other industries. Of course, most of the time on UNIVAC has been spent on government operations. However, some of this work parallels our work to some extent. Furthermore, two-thirds of the non-government work which has been done by these machines has been in the insurance fraternity."[117] More concretely, Runyan explained the "rule of thumb" he had learned for how large an insurance firm should be to consider purchasing a UNIVAC: "50 million dollars fire or casualty premiums or one billion dollars life insurance in force." Finally, he recommended that firms consider moving to a higher level of tabulator mechanization before adopting a computer: "Because of high speed card to tape converters and the better organization of procedures in highly mechanized companies, it would appear simpler to install electronic data processing machines where punched cards are presently in use, than where manual methods predominate."[118]

The second day of the IASA-sponsored Electronics Conference was devoted to IBM. The proceedings reflect the fact that IBM was then lagging behind Remington Rand in addressing the emergent business computer market.[119] In a general session presenting what it had to offer to insurance, IBM did not focus on existing, punched-card offerings such as the SSEC or the CPC. T. V. Learson, sales manager of IBM's Electric Accounting Machine Division, suggested why as he attempted to counter the criticism initially voiced more than five years earlier by Berkeley and apparently still current in the insurance industry: "I believe some skeptics have expressed the thought that IBM is so wedded to the punched card, industry should look elsewhere for a solution."[120] He denied that, claiming that "IBM has continually obsoleted its huge inventory of punched card equipment with improved models at a constant and fast pace."

This defensiveness about cards probably accounts for Learson's subsequent focus entirely on the new IBM 701 computer, publicly announced only two weeks previously, with its auxiliary tape storage and processing capabilities.[121] This computer was known within IBM as the "Defense Calculator" and was actually aimed at the scientific and defense market; the first model had begun operations at Los Alamos Scientific Laboratory only days earlier.[122] It suffered from the same problem that the UNIVAC had faced early on and was now addressing with some success—slow input/output. Several months later IBM would announce another large-scale, magnetic-tape-based computer, the 702, aimed at the business market.[123] Meanwhile, it had only the 701 to present and could offer none of the concrete insurance examples that Remington Rand had delivered. Although IBM had outpaced Remington Rand in the insurance tabulator market for more than two decades, at this stage the situation was reversed. The IBM team, drawn predominantly from the Product Planning Department and the Applied Science Division, could conduct only very general discussions.[124] Nevertheless, members of the IBM team were able to highlight some issues insurance firms would have to deal with as they contemplated the move to computers, including input/output and standardization and consolidation of steps on existing punched-card equipment before moving to tape computers.

E. C. Carlson, representing the very large Mutual Life Insurance Company, reviewed the IBM presentations for the IASA meeting two months later.[125] In addition to repeating Learson's assertion that IBM was "not wedded to the punched card completely," Carlson talked about the IBM recommendation that functions should be centralized and consolidated in order "to accomplish everything possible in one pass through the machine."[126] He also summarized what insurance firms should do to get ready for electronic computers: consolidating records into a single punched-card file, training employees in programming, and standardizing routines that would eventually be put on tape, perhaps using smaller, card-based machines such as the 604 electronic calculator or the CPC. Finally, Carlson noted IBM's closing message: "Smith Homan closed the meeting for IBM, suggesting that we go back to our respective companies and get ready to use these new electronic techniques. IBM will now go forward, using the hardware and components of the 701, to furnish our industry with a workable tool. He offered the 701 as the means of trying out segments of new procedures, thereby testing the feasibility of their new techniques.[127] IBM was doing its best to maintain a presence in this emerging market as it rushed to catch up, but Remington Rand's UNIVAC Division was clearly leading.

The Electronics Conference spawned some controversy among insurance firms. At the 1953 IASA meetings, Kermit Lang, of Equitable Life Insurance of Iowa, responded to the session summaries, discussing what he saw as limitations of computers for life insurance at that time.[128] After noting that the meeting should have been entitled "A CONFERENCE ON MAGNETIC TAPE OR TAPE PROCESSING MACHINES," he asserted that tape, though it was a compact storage medium, posed major challenges:

> Also we must remember that magnetic tape equipment is still "around the corner"—for business and industry, at least—for two very practical reasons:
>
> 1. Because there is no really efficient electronic sorter-collator for magnetic tape.
> 2. Because there is no random access to the information stored in magnetic tape.[129]

Lang also observed that using a magnetic-tape computer required centralization and consolidation of operations, "whereas the trend in some large life insurance companies is in the opposite direction—toward decentralization—in order to achieve faster and better service to policyholders."[130] A later speaker from Prudential reinforced this concern, saying that the improvements in policyholder service from decentralization were more important than savings in accounting costs.[131] Ultimately, Lang questioned whether moving to magnetic-tape computers really made sense in comparison with "the tried and tested electronic machines" already available, arguing, "In any event, punched cards and punched card machines will have their place in the tabulating room for a long time to come." His presentation reflected the industry's ambivalence toward trading its cards for magnetic tape.

This special IASA conference and the summary report during the annual IASA conference, along with earlier efforts in the various associations, demonstrated the life insurance industry's sustained interest in educating itself about electronic computers, as well as its ambivalence about magnetic tape. As the

Remington Rand/UNIVAC presentation made clear, life insurance was at the forefront of interest in non-defense-related commercial computing. The conference proceedings also revealed that in early 1953 insurance companies viewed Remington Rand and IBM as the two primary vendors, just as they were in the tabulating market. At this point, Remington Rand's UNIVAC Division was working more visibly to attract insurance customers.

In the immediate postwar years, then, firms and individuals in the insurance industry had worked independently and through associations to educate themselves about potential uses of electronic computers for insurance work. Driven by rising costs and clerical labor shortages in a time of rapid industry growth, as well as by a felt need to maintain familiar and reliable operating methods, especially as they touched customers, insurance firms were eager to try the new technology but remained wary about its risks for a business heavily dependent on accurate long-term record keeping. Even the most extensive and influential study of potential insurance use of computers, conducted by the Society of Actuaries committee, revealed a tension between the desire for immediate transformation, on the one hand, and belief in incremental change, on the other. This tension would characterize the era of early computer adoptions, as well.

# CHAPTER 6

# Insurance Adoption and Use of Early Computers

Until the early 1950s insurance firms had studied and experimented with computers, but none were yet commercially available. In 1952 and 1953, as vendors announced the imminent arrival of the first commercial products, pioneering firms began to place orders, and in 1954 they received their first electronic stored-program computers. Although most computer adopters understood that they would need to change their processes to take advantage of the technology, they differed in their visions of how to achieve that change. The tension between desire for an immediate radical break with the past, on the one hand, and a preference for achieving change incrementally, on the other, played itself out in firm after firm during the mid-1950s.[1] Only a few companies ultimately ordered the UNIVAC, its magnetic tape a visible symbol of the break with the past. Even among those, the tension between rapid transformation and incremental migration was evident in their choices of insurance applications. The 1952 Society of Actuaries report had rejected applying computers to single functions such as actuarial work, instead developing and presenting the consolidated functions approach, which required organizational restructuring and integration of insurance processes to achieve efficiency. The first four firms choosing the UNIVAC split in approaches to using it, with two simply computerizing existing tabulator applications, an initial step on an incremental path, and the other two adopting integrated applications that required more radical reengineering of processes.

As more insurance firms adopted the computer, a technology popularly viewed as a radical technological innovation, the vast majority chose to transform their processes gradually, by incremental migration, rather than to attempt an immediate and disruptive transformation.[2] This cautious approach applied to both hardware and applications. Thus these companies typically began with IBM's card-based 650 computer, transferring an application from tabulation equipment with only minimal change. This choice reflected a broader market movement in computer adoptions, as well. Ultimately, only 46 UNIVAC I computers were installed, compared with more than 2,000 IBM 650s.[3] A few firms choose an intermediate route, adopting the IBM tape-based 702 and 705 computers when they became available.[4]

## Early Adoptions of the UNIVAC

After Remington Rand acquired Eckert-Mauchly Computer Corporation— along with the UNIVAC—in 1950, the new management canceled existing contracts for the UNIVAC and raised its price to more than $1,250,000. Prudential took its canceled 1948 contract and the enormous price hike as an opportunity to rethink its earlier decision. It continued to work with the UNIVAC Division of Remington Rand, developing a 1951 test application including premium billing and dividend and commission calculations, a subset of the processes integrated in the committee's consolidated functions plan.[5] The vendor saw the trial as successful, stating in a printed pamphlet: "The material presented here, together with the information that has already been sent to the Methods Division of Prudential, should provide a reasonable basis for a comparative cost study of the proposed system and the present system. It is our considered opinion that appreciable savings will result from this electronic installation."[6] The Prudential management, however, concluded, "Although the demonstration was successful, it was decided that the UNIVAC would not be economical for our use."[7] Prudential's decision not to renew its order "allowed Remington Rand to sell the computer earmarked for Prudential to the Metropolitan Life Insurance Company."[8]

In the spring of 1954 Metropolitan Life was consequently the first insurance company to take delivery of a UNIVAC (fig. 6.1), the ninth one built and only

*Fig. 6.1.* Metropolitan Life was the first firm to take delivery of a UNIVAC. Because the components were so large, they had to be hauled up the side of the building. "A Genius of Sorts," *Home Office,* June 1954. Courtesy of MetLife Archives.

the second to go to a commercial company.[9] Late that year Franklin Life Insurance Company received its UNIVAC, and two more insurance firms, John Hancock Mutual Life and Pacific Mutual Life Insurance, acquired theirs in 1955. Insurance firms accounted for a quarter of the sixteen UNIVACs delivered in 1954 and 1955, reflecting both their importance as a user market and the attention Eckert and Mauchly and Remington Rand had paid to the industry. These four companies fell into two groups by their sizes, their chosen applications, and the amount of reengineering undertaken: large firms that computerized existing tabulator operations, and smaller firms that consolidated and integrated multiple existing operations.

## Large Firms/Existing Applications: Metropolitan Life and John Hancock

Early in 1953, Malvin Davis, vice president and actuary of Metropolitan Life as well as chairman of the Society of Actuaries committee, recommended purchasing the firm's first UNIVAC.[10] Metropolitan Life had plenty of reasons to buy a computer. Because it was chronically short staffed owing to the labor shortages that had plagued it since before the war, it was interested in any office automation that would slow its ever rising demand for clerical labor.[11] Furthermore, as the world's largest life insurance enterprise, with 44.5 million policies and 1952 assets of $11.6 billion, it certainly had the volume of clerical work necessary to make such equipment pay, if any insurance company did.[12] Moreover, Davis and Finelli had been active on both the Society of Actuaries committee and a similar internal committee, attesting to their own and the firm's interest in the new technology.

Beyond these general reasons, however, a paper Davis wrote for the Eastern Joint Computer Conference in late 1953, after the order and before the arrival of the firm's first UNIVAC, gives an unusually detailed and relatively contemporaneous account of how Metropolitan Life decided when and what to order and how to use it. Davis framed the decision to buy a UNIVAC in terms of three alternatives: "[The prospective user] may choose a system designed to operate from punched hole devices (punched cards or punched tape) thus limiting the speed and the degree of automation possible while keeping the price low. He may choose instead a system designed to operate from magnetic tape, thus reaping the advantages of greatly increased speed of operation. His other choice is to sit out the developments a little longer . . . with the expectation that future equipment will permit more automatic processes than now possible."[13] Clearly Davis viewed the tape approach as promising greater speed gains than a card-based system. Although the Society of Actuaries committee had concluded that the UNIVAC had a slight cost advantage over the card-based computer, the differential was not large, and Metropolitan Life executives and directors wanted to know how the computer would be used before signing off on this large technology expense. The paper discussed some of the factors considered and the decision made:

> These studies [by the Society of Actuaries committee] made the consolidation idea appear very attractive, not only as a means of reducing operating costs but also as a means of streamlining the organization along workable lines. However, on the other side of the ledger, there were a number of deterring factors. Such a program would take a long time to install. The gains would appear only after a fairly extensive conversion had been made. The conversion would require producing punched card records for several million life insurance policies now recorded in typewritten card form. The loss of a very substantial investment in an existing recordkeeping system had to be taken into account. In addition, the capacity of the company to make the required changes was being taxed to a considerable extent by the several conversions to punched card [tabulator] systems currently being made. To these deterrents must be added the element of risk which exists in introducing equipment as yet untried on any commercial application. The company, therefore, although inclined to accept the idea that some sort of consolidated operation was indicated as a long-range objective, still felt that a system should be applied to a localized area as a means of getting started.[14]

Company executives thus tied the purchase decision to finding a suitable application with a lower risk than the consolidated functions plan. In the spirit of this mandate, Davis recommended a more conservative beginning—computerizing an existing actuarial application that developed "insurance statistics needed for the company's financial statement and for various experience analyses."[15] Finelli would later refer to this initial application as intended "to prove out the equipment."[16]

Consequently, even though Davis and Finelli had been centrally involved in developing the consolidated functions plan, Metropolitan Life did not initially adopt it, turning instead to an application area that the Society of Actuaries committee eliminated early in its deliberations as too small to pay off for most firms. Although Metropolitan Life's sheer size made installing the consolidated functions vision daunting, it guaranteed a large enough actuarial application to realize savings while giving the firm experience with the UNIVAC. With tabulators, this work demanded "an assembly of more than 100 separate punched card machines (involving a yearly rental of about $225,000)."[17] Even with the added cost involved in initially operating the old and the new systems side by side, Davis calculated that savings in equipment and operator costs would allow the company to recover its purchase price in less than four years, making the new system an attractive investment. Indeed, this favorable anticipated payback in great part drove the decision to proceed with the UNIVAC rather than to await future developments. Another factor was Davis's calculation for the Society of Actuaries report that the consolidated functions approach implemented on the current (UNIVAC) technology provided 90% of the gains that could be expected from a future scenario that included hoped-for improvements, so delaying the acquisition in anticipation of such improvements did not pay.

Metropolitan Life's size figured significantly in its decision to move ahead with the actuarial application, but perceptions of risk also played a role. The application calculated figures for financial statements and for the mortality experience analyses based on which the company would develop new products and determine new premium rates.[18] Although errors in such calculations could presumably involve substantial financial risk, Davis's account suggests that Metropolitan Life executives did not view this application as risky. As Davis wrote, "This area of work is of such a nature that it permits the introduction of an electronic processing system with a minimum of disturbance and risk." Of course, the fact that the old and new systems would initially run side by side partially mitigated the risk by allowing staff to check the figures. But Davis seemed more concerned with a different point: "The system could be gainfully introduced into this particular area without requiring a major reorganization elsewhere as a condition precedent. This provided the facility for a first-hand understanding of its capabilities and limitations through actual use, without risking the entire recordkeeping system of the company on its success."[19] Endangering the records system central to any insurance company seemed the greater risk.

Three organizations that were focused more on computing technology than its use—the Institute of Radio Engineers, the American Institute of Electrical Engineers, and the Association for Computing Machinery—sponsored the 1953 Eastern Joint Computer Conference, at which Finelli presented Davis's paper.[20] After acknowledging the "very remarkable amount of progress [that] has been made in the 10 years or so since the laboratory prototypes of current data processing systems were developed," Davis's paper concluded by calling on the audience to shift from emphasizing technology to emphasizing its use:

> Some of us believe that by far the major portion of the ultimate potential can be achieved with systems that already exist. We are therefore inclined to the view expressed by Professor P. M. S. Blackett when he said:
>
>> ". . . relatively too much scientific effort has been expended hitherto in the production of new devices and too little in the proper use of what we have got. . . ."
>
> Parallel with your development of new and improved components for data processing systems, extensive investigations into the manner in which they can be used should be conducted by potential users.[21]

Although he was wrong about how much potential remained to be realized on the technology side, Davis correctly stressed the need for more work on use.

Most relevant here, he also stated that such studies "must, of course, take into consideration the necessary gradual manner in which radical changes should be introduced,"[22] expressing a common attitude toward the introduction and use of computers in the life insurance industry. Davis thus made explicit Metropolitan Life's strategy in choosing its initial application. By 1956, after it had gained experience with the first computer, Metropolitan Life acquired two more UNIVACs, installing various other unintegrated applications, including payroll, premium billing, and claims distribution.[23] In viewing its first computer and application as an initial step in an incremental process, Metropolitan Life ultimately chose the more conservative strategy.

John Hancock Mutual Life Insurance Company was the other large firm to adopt a UNIVAC in the first two years. The fifth-largest life insurance firm by assets, though still less than a third the size of Metropolitan Life, it had recently grown rapidly and faced increasing labor shortages.[24] Like Metropolitan Life, it had initially focused on industrial insurance but now also had a growing ordinary insurance business of roughly 2 million policies.[25] Its large size made John Hancock another good candidate for the UNIVAC, permitting it to achieve economies without extensive organizational change.

John Hancock did not decide to buy a UNIVAC until 1955, but its management had been following developments before that. In the late 1940s, Roland Mangini, the company's Planning Department manager, was the chairman of LOMA's Eastern Office Planning and Equipment Committee, which was following developments in sequence-controlled calculators. Around this time, a group of company executives looked into the emerging computer field but decided that neither the magnetic-tape-based technology, which they saw as essential to true computers, nor the company's own insurance processes were ready.[26] Instead, the firm devoted the next several years to integrating and mechanizing its ordinary premium billing system on punched-card tabulating equipment, an increasingly common conversion during that period.

After that conversion was completed in 1954, John Hancock's top management established an internal committee to reconsider acquiring a magnetic-tape computer.[27] It used the premium billing application that it had just installed on tabulating equipment as the basis for comparing four vendors' available tape-based computers: IBM's 702 and successor 705 models, Remington Rand's UNIVAC, RCA's Bismac, and Raytheon's Datamatic.[28] A year later, the firm ordered a UNIVAC under the now available rental-with-option-to-purchase plan, and it was delivered by late 1955.[29] The decision, according to Harold F. Hatch, associate controller in charge of installing the computer and application, "was based on four major factors, (1) availability of the computer (2) metal tape (3) field tested in our own industry (Metropolitan) (4) the option to purchase, if we desired to do so."[30] John Hancock chose to rent initially because it planned to upgrade to a UNIVAC II system as soon as it was available. The committee decided relatively rapidly, although the company had continued to think about computers since its earlier look at them. Because it considered only magnetic-tape computers, it chose the one machine available and already tested at another (very similar) insurance company.

John Hancock's initial application was the same recently mechanized premium billing operation that it used to evaluate the alternative computer systems.[31] The company explicitly decided to proceed one step at a time, rather than to attempt a complete integrated system, such as that envisioned by the Society of Actuaries committee:

> Rather than await the "machine of the future" and approach conversion with a sweeping over-all plan, the decision was made to begin immediately in a more limited way to develop experience and train a staff on an available and time-tested computer. . . .

> The "application by application approach" was therefore selected:

> 1. To give the Company a chance to evaluate results without committing the entire organization to the electronic program.

2. To develop gradually a climate of acceptance.

3. To minimize at the outset the problems of retraining and relocating personnel.

4. To enable the experience gained in one application to speed successive operations.

5. To minimize the organizational and communication problems which so complicate very involved projects.[32]

Anticipating many potential organizational problems as a result of this dramatically new technology, John Hancock executives chose to implement it gradually. Given this approach, premium billing was chosen as the first application because it could be isolated from other insurance operations and because it "was already fully mechanized on standard punched card machines and offered an opportunity for relatively easy conversion."[33] John Hancock mailed out the first UNIVAC-created premium bills in June 1956, only eleven months after it ordered the computer.

Although premium billing, unlike Metropolitan Life's actuarial task, affected customers, in other respects it represented an easy and direct conversion from tabulators to computers, gaining economies by speeding up the process, not by the extensive organizational consolidation discussed in the Society of Actuaries plan. Like Metropolitan Life, then, John Hancock chose a relatively incremental initial application, even though both had adopted the tape-based technology. Because of their size, both firms could gain efficiencies even from directly converting existing processes, without major restructuring.[34]

## Smaller Firms/Consolidated Applications: Franklin Life and Pacific Mutual

The other two firms that adopted UNIVACs in the first two years—Franklin Life and Pacific Mutual—were much smaller than Metropolitan Life and John Hancock and chose very different application strategies. Both midsized companies reached or exceeded $1 billion insurance in force, the rule of thumb for what size firms should consider acquiring a UNIVAC.[35] In an IASA presentation about his firm's first computer application, Pacific Mutual's D. K. Swinnerton explained the role of size in shaping the choice:

Obviously, a large volume work load is essential if you are to have an economically sound application for a large scale data processing device. Accordingly, it appeared to us that there were two broad general approaches to installing this type of equipment. The size of the company pretty much dictates which of the two approaches would be followed.

First, in a very large company, it is practical to convert the work of one department or one function—the work of a single department having sufficient volume.

Second, in a medium or smaller sized company, the work volume of one department is not adequate. It, therefore, becomes necessary to use a consolidated or combined functions approach. In this manner, sufficient work volume can be achieved by combining a number of related operations.[36]

These two midsized firms could, of course, have waited and chosen the card-based 650 for an incremental approach to change, but both adopted the magnetic-tape UNIVAC. Given their size, they also chose integrated applications that involved much more internal reengineering than those of Metropolitan Life and John Hancock. That is, they chose abrupt over gradual transformation. In both cases, particular internal factors seemed to encourage firm executives toward this less typical path.

Franklin Life, a stock company headquartered in Springfield, Illinois, and holding roughly 1% the number of Metropolitan Life's policies, prided itself on being the first life insurance firm to order a UNIVAC, back in June 1952, though it received its computer after the larger company did, in early 1955.[37] A. C. Vanselow, Franklin Life's administrative vice president, who took the lead in introducing the computer, had learned about the Mark I during World War II and had followed developments since then.[38] He would champion the technology. The driving force in the firm's early adoption of the UNIVAC, however, was a space crisis brought on by its incredible growth during the 1940s and 1950s. By 1954, according to President Charles E. Becker, it had "scored more than an 850% increase in volume of insurance in force since 1940."[39] With sales growing at more than five times the industry rate, by 1954 the company had leaped to a rank of eighteenth in total ordinary insurance in force.[40] This rapid growth precipitated a space crisis. The company had expanded its building from four stories to twelve and ultimately to twenty-four in 1953, and more growth in employment and records storage would require building another building.[41] Consequently, the top management was open to Vanselow's proposal that the firm order a UNIVAC.

Vanselow worked with Remington Rand to survey possible applications for the computer, determining that "for a medium size Company such as ours with approximately 400,000 policies and one billion [dollars] of ordinary insurance in force it was necessary for such electronic equipment to embrace all functions involving highly repetitive tasks such as Premium Billing, Premium Accounting, Agency Commission Accounting, and Valuations, if it was to be economically sound."[42] Thus the proposal he took to the board of directors in late 1951, which promised the same four-year payback period that Metropolitan Life's committee had predicted from its UNIVAC, involved applying the computer to a range of operations similar to that of the not-yet-publicized consolidated functions approach. Using the computer, Franklin Life ultimately consolidated twelve separate files of documents and punched cards into one 240-character master file and one address file for each policy. These files were maintained on magnetic tape, without the punched-card backups that most other insurance firms were initially unwilling to relinquish, allowing the company to use a single master file that would have required three eighty-column cards.[43] Franklin Life clearly choose the path of immediate transformation over that of incremental migration.

None of the accounts of this implementation state unequivocally whether the firm actually realized the four-year payback promised. Still, in early 1957, before completing the conversion, Vanselow cited many benefits the firm had gained from the computer; it had absorbed a doubling of policies with no personnel increase, reduced space for record-keeping storage and staff, performed new operations previously impossible for the company (e.g., calculations, report generation), reduced errors, and reduced payroll cost per amount of insurance during a decade when the salary scale almost doubled.[44] Franklin Life itself must have been convinced of the benefits, since it installed a second UNIVAC in 1959.[45] In 1961, Vanselow claimed that the second UNIVAC would pay for itself by 1962.[46]

In 1962, Franklin Life's Paul McAnarney provided a little more insight but still no definitive payback analysis.[47] He noted that early in the firm's conversion to the UNIVAC, some termed it a success and others a failure, but by 1962 key home office personnel agreed fairly unanimously that it was a success. He estimated the purchase and installation costs ($1.3 million) as well as the conversion costs ($0.8 million) for the first UNIVAC—for a total initial outlay of just over $2 million.

> Although the above expenditures are quite substantial, we feel this initial one-time expense was money well spent. Our rapid growth would have necessitated the building of a large addition to our present home office facilities and we have deferred that building for seven years as a result of converting to EDP. In that same

period of time our number of employees has increased 18 per cent whereas the number of policies in force has increased 43 per cent and the volume of insurance in force has risen 124 per cent. Another basis which can be used for comparison is the ratio of the number of items billed to the number of home office employees (see Exhibit No. 1) The number of items billed per employee increased 57 per cent from 1954 to 1962.[48]

The exhibit he referred to (fig. 6.2) was dramatic. It showed items billed and number of home office employees rising sharply in fairly parallel lines from

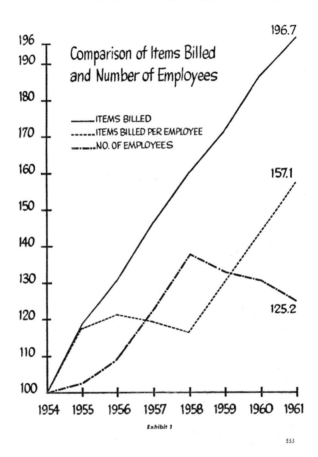

Fig. 6.2. Franklin Life's Paul McAnarney presented this "Comparison of Items Billed and Number of Employees" at the 1962 IASA meeting as evidence that the company had successfully reduced the growth and even absolute number of clerical employees per items billed. Paul McAnarney, "The Successes and Failures of EDP to Date," *Proceedings of the Insurance Accounting and Statistical Association* (1962): 553.

1956 to 1958, when number of employees began to drop continuously, though gently, from 1958 to 1961. In tandem, items billed per employee, after a dip between 1956 and 1958, began to rise sharply and steadily. In addition, McAnarney summarized some figures that Executive Vice President George Hatmaker had reported to the Boston Society of Security Analysts:

1. Insurance in force per employee has increased from $1,574,000 to $4,044,000 in the past ten years.
2. Payroll costs per $1,000 of insurance have been reduced from $1.84 to $1.13 despite a 58 per cent increase in salary per employee during the same period.
3. In 1961 general insurance expenses actually decreased $151,000 despite a gain of $382 million of outstanding insurance.[49]

These statistics suggest that Franklin Life's top managers considered the installation successful, though they could not (or would not) present a precise payback analysis.

The last life insurance firm to install a UNIVAC in the initial two years was Pacific Mutual, another midsized firm. In operation since 1868, the company had suffered a financial crisis that led to its reorganization by the California State Insurance commissioner starting in 1936.[50] When it ordered its UNIVAC in the early 1950s, Pacific Mutual had emerged from the depths of the crisis and was growing relatively rapidly, though not as rapidly as Franklin Life. It was in the process of mutualizing what had previously been a stock company.[51] As a result of its reorganization, top management had already taken stringent measures to cut operating costs, using tabulating and other non-computer technology, and wanted to take more. The firm's interest in acquiring a computer dated from the September 1952 presentation of the Society of Actuaries committee report.[52] According to R. D. Dotts, "As a result of this meeting our Administrative Vice President asked Remington Rand to make a presentation outlining their suggestions for approaching such a step."[53] Pacific Mutual approached the decision very methodically, training two men in programming, visiting various computer installations, and establishing an internal committee to evaluate whether such machines were practical for the company's use, to decide which equipment would best fit its needs, and to "be prepared . . . to guide necessary organizational and systems changes if such recommendations were approved."[54]

Having decided that the key question for a middle-sized life insurance company such as Pacific Mutual was not "which device was most efficient" for its use but rather "whether any large scale device was economically sound for installation," Pacific Mutual investigated applications before equipment.[55] Early on, based on the Society of Actuaries report, the internal committee had concluded that "for a company [Pacific Mutual's] size ($1 billion ordinary insurance in force, $½ billion group insurance in force, 350,000 ordinary policies) the best approach was based on the 'consolidated functions approach' for handling the ordinary insurance record keeping." To determine whether such an approach would pay, the committee undertook a detailed time study of existing work and compared it with test results from computer manufacturers. Dotts summarized the results: "The studies in all took nearly a year and just under 10,000 man hours to complete but they resulted in information indicating that Pacific Mutual did indeed have an application that was economically sound, utilizing a large scale electronic data processing device."[56] Indeed, by the spring of 1954 the committee had determined that "a total outlay of $2 million for a large-scale system would pay its way fully in five or six years on this one ordinary insurance operations application alone."[57]

Although based on the consolidated functions vision, this application in one respect was even more complex and integrated. It was designed as a daily cycle system—that is, it processed all records on a daily basis, making any updates on a first run and then producing updated status information, on a high-speed printer, for all policies.[58] This approach reflected a difference between Pacific Mutual and many other firms in handling policyholder service. Most insurers handled policyholder service through branch offices. The home office records were the basis for routine servicing such as premium billing but did not constitute the record of daily changes. In the contrasting general agency system that Pacific Mutual used, the home office handled all policyholder records and services. In this case, the record had to be updated promptly because it was used daily "to supply policy status information for use in completing service transactions."[59] Having chosen a consolidated functions approach with daily cycle processing, the committee also determined through its studies that the company would achieve major savings by eliminating all visual records—both punched cards and typed history cards—and depending entirely on the tape record and the printed output.[60] Thus the plan for using the UNIVAC would require complex changes in all aspects of insurance processes: "It is not merely a means of doing with electronic data processing devices the same work that was formerly done on electric and electronic accounting machines. It is a sweeping new approach to the problem. Its economies come not so much from a faster, higher powered machine as from the single file concept processed daily to meet the relatively random reference needs of service to our policyowners. Thus, the new type giant electronic data processing machines are the first machines that offered this potential."[61] Pacific Mutual thus chose immediate reengineering of its processes, with its end point even beyond what the Society of Actuaries committee had suggested.

After determining the application, the internal committee decided which equipment to adopt by process of elimination. Early on, it rejected the IBM 701, as well as binary and non-alphanumeric machines such as the CADAC 102-A, made by Computer Research Corporation.[62] It asked IBM to decide whether the 702 (a more business-oriented successor to the 701) or the card-based 650 better fit Pacific Mutual's needs, and IBM recommended the 702. The committee's detailed studies then focused on the IBM 702, the UNIVAC, and the ElectroData Model 204 computer.[63] Soon, the committee rejected the ElectroData computer as requiring more manual processing than was desirable. IBM, as much as Pacific Mutual, ultimately eliminated the 702: "IBM 702 was rejected for our purposes only after determinations by their own representatives had indicated that it was not competitive with the Univac on our work unless it were to be provided with buffers to enable it to read, write and compute relatively simultaneously. Subsequently the IBM 702 was withdrawn from further order taking and it was announced that the machines that were to be built would, in general, be built without buffers."[64] At that point, the committee had to decide whether to wait for new developments such as the IBM 705 or the not-yet-available RCA computer or to "satisfy [itself] with the older design but more proven data processing system—the Univac of Remington Rand." It chose the latter course, ordering a UNIVAC that would be installed in August 1955.[65]

## Personnel Issues

Giddens' structuration theory suggests that a single individual cannot change a social structure, including a technology-use structure.[66] Others must also enact the changed structure. Thus it is important to look at how people lower, as well as higher, in the hierarchy responded to change someone has initiated. These four early adopter firms had to face personnel problems, including choosing and training programmers and dealing with employee fears or resistance. The latter issue received more public attention. In his *Giant Brains; or, Machines That Think*, Edmund Berkeley had flagged unemployment as a potential consequence of using "giant brains" or "robot machines," especially if they were not controlled by society.[67] Similarly, a 1952 *Fortune* magazine article titled "Office Robots" noted, "There are two extreme views—both probably wrong—about what all this will mean to society. One holds that it will mean decimation of office staffs and technological unemployment on a scale heretofore unseen. The other holds that everything will work itself out fine, as in the past, without human intervention."[68] During the 1930s, many felt that machine-age manufacturing mechanization had led to unemployment, and these fears appeared again, although not quite so powerfully as during the depression, with respect to computer-based office automation in the 1950s and 1960.[69]

Aware of the specter of technology-driven unemployment, insurance firms adopting computers typically attempted to defuse this issue. In the 1955 LOMA conference, IBM's J. A. Dollard devoted considerable time to implementation problems concerning people. In explaining why pre-computerization application surveys took so long, he noted

> the passive resistance which you meet within the organization—the fact that people object to change. . . . You cannot issue a directive because it doesn't work. You must break them in and tell them what you propose to do.

> They are afraid of their jobs—afraid of losing control of paperwork—afraid of losing control over people, and there are a hundred and one reasons why they think this way and it is human nature—there is nothing wrong with it—it is something that you must overcome in some kind of selling program.[70]

Although fears of job loss were widespread in insurance, they seemed to be exaggerated. Because insurance companies had faced increasingly severe labor shortages since the beginning of World War II, they would have little need to displace workers during this initial decade of computerization. Nevertheless, employees worried about such displacement, so many firms attempted to address their fears.

The two large companies had somewhat different approaches: John Hancock apparently imposed change on its workforce by fiat, whereas Metropolitan Life devoted great care to such personnel issues. Available accounts suggest that John Hancock's Hatch was autocratic and relatively unconcerned about employees' fears but took great care with personnel issues related to choosing and training programmers.[71] He was a firm believer in training programmers from within the firm: "We have hired some outside people, but there is no substitute for your own people who are acquainted with your business. It is much easier to teach your own people the Computer than it is to teach outsiders the business."[72] Deciding *which* people to train, in his view, was the challenge. In response to initial failures in such choices, Hatch and his colleagues developed an aptitude test focusing on logical reasoning, which Hatch felt worked well to screen potential programmers. They also arranged for beginning and advanced programming courses, a course to educate management about computers, and an operators' course. Unfortunately, no available records reveal how employees responded to Hatch's method of handling the change, but this approach and labor market conditions make it likely that John Hancock, too, avoided any technological displacement.

Metropolitan Life, in contrast, displayed a very paternalistic attitude toward its huge staff. Moreover, its long-running shortage of clerical labor made it possible and desirable for the firm to deal with the 133 workers displaced by its first computer application through reassignment and attrition rather than through layoffs.[73] According to a 1955 U.S. Labor Department study, Metropolitan Life "planned most carefully for the computer, not only in the technical aspects, but in the sensitive field of human adjustment to change."[74] While Metropolitan Life publicized its computer installation both internally and externally, it also communicated clearly to its employees that the computer would not cause layoffs.[75] In addition, getting the application up and running and closing down the old operation was a two-year process, allowing the company plenty of time to inform the 133 persons to be replaced, to interview them about their job replacement preferences, and to get them placed elsewhere. Indeed, the Department of Labor stated that "the mechanics of introducing the change was [*sic*] exemplary."[76] In 1956, as Metropolitan Life awaited the arrival of its next two UNIVACs, it displayed a model UNIVAC in the lobby for all employees to examine (fig. 6.3).[77] It also conducted an internal publicity campaign emphasizing its very real ongoing labor shortages and the fact that layoffs would not be needed (fig. 6.4), thus attempting to reduce fears of job loss and possible resistance to the new computers. By 1956, the company standardized the careful procedures it had developed for reassigning employees displaced by computers.[78]

The two smaller firms also present a contrast in methods of dealing with personnel issues, but perhaps a less stark one than that between John Hancock and Metropolitan Life. The evidence about Franklin Life's treatment of these

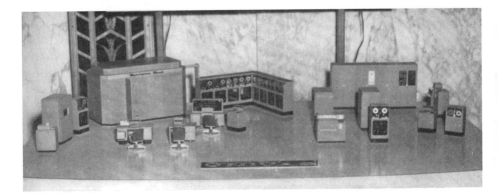

*Fig. 6.3.* Metropolitan Life set up this model UNIVAC in its lobby so employees would become familiar with it. "Two More Univacs, but There's Still a Need for Additional Clerks," *Home Office,* June 1956, 9. Courtesy of MetLife Archives.

*Fig. 6.4.* Metropolitan Life conducted a concerted campaign to show employees that UNIVACs would not eliminate employment demand. "Two More Univacs, but There's Still a Need for Additional Clerks," *Home Office,* June 1956, 7. Courtesy of MetLife Archives.

issues is scanty and somewhat contradictory. One piece of anecdotal evidence suggests that some employees were skeptical about the computer's potential usefulness.[79] After the contract was signed in 1952, Frances E. Holberton of Remington Rand's UNIVAC Division visited the company, and her account is consistent with this view. She later claimed that management had not told the clerical workers that the company had bought a UNIVAC and that her efforts to study the work and help design the new computer application were made difficult by clerical workers being secretive about what they actually did because "they were afraid they were going to lose their jobs."[80] Vanselow, who championed Franklin Life's UNIVAC, gave a different account in 1954. He noted that after signing the UNIVAC contract, the firm had chosen five members of the Planning Department to take a "familiarization course at Remington Rand."[81] No general communication with the workforce had taken place up to this point, but some followed it: "Upon [the five employees'] return a general announcement was sent to all employees explaining the application of our procedures to Univac, stressing the fact that such a decision had the full support of management in an effort to provide a better method of processing repetitive and monotonous daily tasks, thus permitting our continued expansion without increasing the number of employees. Further assurance was given that all employees doing a good job would not be released and that normal attrition, reduced hiring, reassignments and increase in business will accomplish the transition to magnetic tape equipment."[82] Subsequent accounts were consistent with this plan, referring to growth in policies handled by the same number of personnel, not to cuts in personnel, as the source of the UNIVAC's benefits. Given the firm's stunning growth rate, acquiring the computer almost surely produced no serious layoffs and incurred only limited passive resistance. In fact, given the scant attention the computer drew even in the official company history, it seems to have been overshadowed by sales growth.[83]

McAnarney's 1962 IASA talk sheds additional light on employee reactions. Having interviewed "key personnel" in the home office for their reactions to the "EDP conversion," he reported that "the once caustic comments had turned into glowing phrases of praise."[84] His view somewhat reconciles the conflicting reports of how the system was received, suggesting that many grumbled early in the process but within ten years changed their tune. Moreover, he noted that the field sales force, initially apprehensive about the conversion, even though it would affect their work only indirectly, "will be the first to admit our system is much more efficient and current than the old—complaints are indeed rare today."[85] The UNIVAC generated commission checks and statements every other week, rather than once a month, a change that undoubtedly made sales agents happier. In addition, among the new reports made possible by the system was "a new statement of paid and terminated business . . . which gives the writing agent (copies are also sent to the general agent and regional manager) a complete record of net paid business for renewal commission qualifications, additional first year commissions, persistency, and production bonus. This consolidated report has been received most enthusiastically." Giving this information to the sales agents, as well as those above them, assured better reactions from these key players in the sales-oriented firm.[86]

In contrast to Franklin Life's apparent initial secrecy about acquiring a computer, Pacific Mutual began to plan its organizational and personnel approach to the sweeping changes three years before the machine was installed. As a UNIVAC salesman noted much later,

> Almost immediately they set up a program through their house organ where they would have an article once a month talking about electronics and how it was going to impact the company, and how it would impact the employees. They had a wonderful program where they would let everybody in the company know what the machines were going to be doing, when they were coming in, and all about them, and the fact that [reductions] would be through attrition. They assured their people that they were planning this whole operation and that they were thinking of the people first.[87]

In his 1954 article, Dotts noted that executives felt such a program of information and education was necessary:

> It was our belief that neither time study nor any other steps in this direction would be successful to the degree hoped for unless employee information and education backed it up. To this end a meeting was held of all personnel from the ordinary insurance and related processing areas for the purpose of advising them that the study was being undertaken. It was explained that it had the full support of management, that its objectives were such that the end result hoped for would be a savings in expense through a reduction in staff and that the nature of the work done by the computer, if one were installed, would be such that the highly repetitive and perhaps equally monotonous tasks would be the ones that would disappear. . . . Coupled with this was the assurance that no employee doing his job competently would find himself a sacrifice on the altar of machine efficiency.[88]

This final assurance probably helped secure employee cooperation during the ensuing study and eventual acquisition of a computer. At the same time, Pacific Mutual also began choosing and training programmers, two-thirds of whom came from within the firm; analyzing all proposed changes in nonelectronic processes to make sure they were compatible with electronic processes; and considering "employees in jobs likely to be displaced whenever openings appeared in nonaffected departments."[89] In this last move, company executives were attempting "to solve some of [the company's] more troublesome personnel relocations in the two years prior to actual dependence on electronics, substituting new and less-skilled hires in the jobs which will be eliminated." They felt that the overall personnel implications of these process changes would be to raise "the average job 'level' of our personnel. . . . The monotonous repetitive operations will have been reduced or eliminated."[90]

In the final stages of the move to the UNIVAC, Pacific Mutual took a highly unusual approach. Because many of the people working on the old system with its "dull, repetitive tasks," both manual and tabulator-based, were trained to staff the new, computer-based system and others had already been moved into new jobs, the company faced a staffing problem during the several-month-long changeover period during which both systems would operate side by side. In the words of the company history, "A solution was found—one fully in keeping with Pacific Mutual Life's traditional ingenuity: the wives of the executives and management personnel entered the company's employ! And it worked. Dubbed 'Project Helpmate,' enthusiastic wives learned their tasks promptly and discharged their duties with aplomb. Morale throughout the company was never higher. That timely service to Pacific Mutual Life—and to their husbands—is worthy of special praise. Their duty done, the wives had speeded the day for the company's change-over to the electronics age."[91] Although this solution is rife with ironies, the description also suggests that management had successfully socially constructed the new, computer-centered work as more interesting than the old, aiding the changeover from one system to the other.

Thus, while employee fears of technological displacement played a role in this story, the effects of any displacement were mitigated by the labor shortages endemic to the growing postwar insurance industry and were carefully managed by some firms. Indeed, the monotonous clerical jobs most likely to disappear were also those hardest to fill in the tight market. Consequently, although two of these firms devoted more resources to this issue than the other two, none of them faced labor disruptions serious enough to have drawn publicity.

## Business Results

All four of these firms publicly claimed that their computer systems were quite successful, and two claimed that the equipment would pay off within four years; nevertheless, gauging the actual impact of the early computers on outcomes in these four insurance firms is extremely difficult. Although Metropolitan Life never performed a detailed post hoc analysis, Finelli later claimed that the payback on Metropolitan Life's three UNIVACs—figured as "yearly saving before amortization with the investment required to achieve that saving"—was around 35% per year, a very healthy return on investment if accurate.[92]

Unfortunately, a common and appropriate outcome measure across all the firms is very difficult, if not impossible, to find. Stock price, for example, cannot be used because most of the largest firms were mutuals.[93] In addition, stock price includes factors, such as sales growth and investment results, that are not affected by computers. In these early years, computers were more likely to have affected expenses than revenues, so a publicly reported expense ratio, ordinary renewal expense ratio (ordinary RER), can serve as a very rough proxy.[94] It reports the ratio of costs related to ongoing ordinary insurance operations to total ordinary insurance in force.[95]

This expense ratio does not show a clear and consistent relationship between acquiring a UNIVAC and lowering costs for these four firms. Neither Metropolitan Life nor John Hancock achieved long-term cost reduction until the second half of the 1970s, mirroring the trend in the largest thirty firms as a whole.[96] Metropolitan Life's ordinary expense ratio started out below the average trend line, indicating lower-than-average costs, but then rose toward it (fig. 6.5). That firm acquired its first UNIVAC in 1954, a second and third UNIVAC in 1956, and upgrades from UNIVAC I to UNIVAC II starting in 1957; nevertheless, its expense ratio rose until 1976, with just a brief dip from 1962 to 1968.[97] John Hancock's expense ratio (fig. 6.6) remained below or at the thirty-firm trend line until 1961, when it began to climb above that line, indicating higher-than-average costs. Only in 1978 did the company's costs turn downward again.[98]

The Society of Actuaries committee argued that the real gains would come from reengineering rather than from automating, suggesting that the computer's influence on costs should be more positive for the two medium-size firms that more thoroughly overhauled their processes. Their results were a little better, but the differences are not clearly tied to computerization. At Franklin Life, growth, rather than acquiring a computer, seems to have driven long-term reduction in costs, but the computer apparently reinforced rather than reversed this trend. Franklin Life's expenses (fig. 6.7) had started downward in the late 1940s, and they continued downward after the firm adopted its UNIVAC, crossing to below the thirty-firm average in the year after the UNIVAC was installed and continuing downward into the early 1960s. The costs then stabilized, remaining below the trend line into the 1980s. Although the

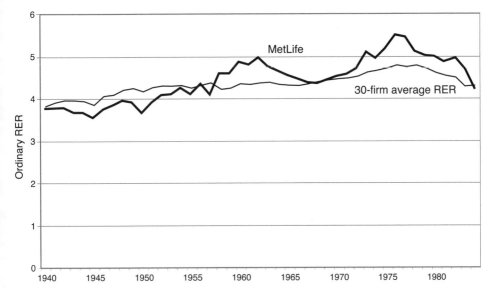

*Fig. 6.5.* Up to 1962, Metropolitan Life's ordinary renewal expense ratio (ordinary RER) rose in relation to the average ordinary RER for the largest thirty firms. After a dip back toward the average from 1962 to 1968, it continued to rise until 1976, when it started falling again into the 1980s. *Best's,* 1940–85.

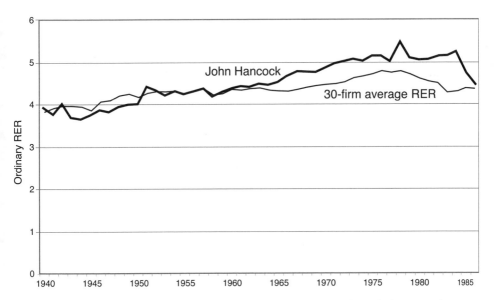

*Fig. 6.6.* Average ordinary renewal expense ratio for John Hancock was below or at the thirty-firm average until 1961 and then began to climb until 1978, when it finally began to decline into the 1980s. *Best's,* 1940–85.

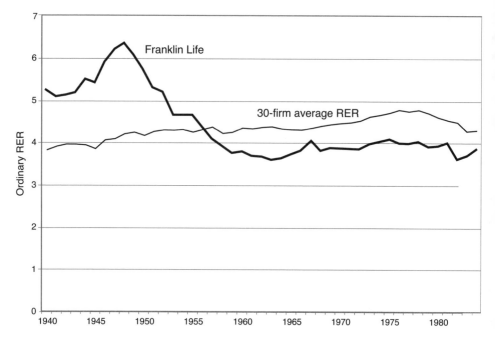

*Fig. 6.7*. Franklin Life's ordinary renewal expense ratio fell from 1948 to 1963 and then stayed below the thirty-firm average at roughly the same level on into the 1980s. *Best's*, 1940–85.

computer clearly did not initiate the downward trend in costs, which began well before its adoption, it may have reinforced it. At Pacific Mutual, costs had risen much higher than the thirty-firm average before they turned down in the early 1960s and followed an uneven but long-term downward trend (see fig. 6.8). Only in the late 1970s did the downward trend become more consistent. Its postbankruptcy reorganization is as likely to have helped the company cut costs as its acquisition and use of a UNIVAC. Still, the downward trend began around 1960, as opposed to 1975 for the thirty-firm average, an improvement that could have resulted in part from the advanced application Pacific Mutual undertook. Thus the picture looks slightly better for these two firms but certainly does not allow us to draw any definitive conclusions.

Of course, focusing on cost reduction may ignore hard-to-measure gains from better customer service, availability of statistics not previously practical to compute, and more rapid production of managerial reports. Pacific Mutual, in particular, felt that it gained many such advantages from its conversion. At

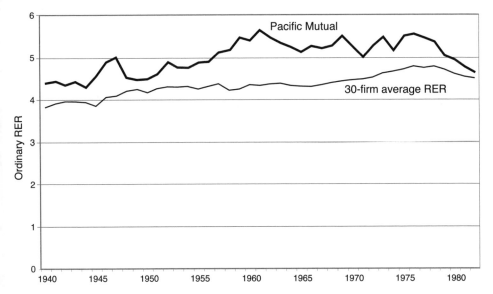

*Fig. 6.8.* Pacific Mutual's ordinary renewal expense ratio was above the thirty-firm average and rising until 1961, when it started an uneven downward trend that gained steam in the late 1970s and into the 1980s. This drop might reflect the delayed effect of its computer acquisition. *Best's*, 1940–85.

a 1955 LOMA panel discussion, when Dotts was asked whether cost savings were the sole justification for introducing an electronic data-processing system, his reply was revealing: "Susceptibility of a master file maintained on magnetic tape to analyses never before attempted provides advantages, including competitive advantages. Earlier availability of certain data is also important."[99] Such advantages, as well as the new reports cited by Franklin Life, could not be realized in the applications first computerized by Metropolitan Life or John Hancock, since they were simply faster versions of processes that could be done using punched cards. But Franklin Life and Pacific Mutual, given their internal changes, stood to gain more in a form that would not be captured by ordinary renewal expense ratio analysis. Still, contrary to the rhetoric of that era, none of the four firms showed dramatic improvements in costs that may be linked directly to acquisition of computers. Perhaps even firms choosing rapid and radical transformation could not immediately realize the benefits.

The UNIVACs acquired by these four firms were not the last to be adopted, by insurance firms or others. Indeed, at the 1957 IASA conference, Quentin Lane, of Life and Casualty Insurance Company, described his firm's recent acquisition of a UNIVAC and its current attempts to implement what it termed a "combined functions" approach that would integrate premium billing and accounting, policy loan billing and accounting, and payment of policy dividends.[100] So Remington Rand continued to gain occasional new UNIVAC sales to insurance firms, as well as selling additional UNIVACs to firms that already possessed one. But production of UNIVACs was still slow, and competition had already appeared.

## Incremental Migration via the IBM 650

Although Remington Rand's UNIVAC Division and its successors continued to cultivate insurance firms over subsequent years and generations of computers, UNIVAC had achieved its highest share of the insurance market in 1954. The Bureau of Labor study of all computers in the insurance industry counted two, both UNIVACs, installed in 1954 but more than twenty, of which only two were UNIVACs, installed in 1955.[101] One was the IBM 702 that Prudential ultimately chose over the UNIVAC.[102] Many others were IBM 650s, a smaller card-and-magnetic-drum-based machine—a more advanced version of IBM's Card-Programmed Calculator tested by the Society of Actuaries committee—that fit handily into existing tabulator installations, as well as insurance procedures. By 1956, IBM led in computer sales to the entire commercial market.[103] In a pattern recognizable from the tabulating era, Remington Rand (which became Sperry Rand in 1955) had initially moved ahead technologically with the UNIVAC, but IBM rapidly overtook it in sales and ultimately in technology, as well.

### The Rapid Ascendancy of the 650

In 1954, the LOMA and IASA annual meetings featured papers and sessions on traditional punched-card tabulating equipment and applications as well as large magnetic-tape computers (especially the UNIVAC).[104] The IBM 650, which had been announced in the previous year but was not yet commercially available, did not appear on LOMA's program but received some attention at IASA meetings, particularly in a session describing it and in a panel organized to examine possible application for it.[105] In introducing the 650 session, panel chair George Hamilton of Phoenix Life noted, "Although this session is billed as a panel discussion, I think it should be called a study shop because we're all groping around in this area of electronics and can do a little groping together this morning."[106] In describing the 650, Paul Knaplund, an IBM field technical representative, pitched the new machine as an intermediate step between tabulating technology and the large tape-based computers:

> Although the best known representatives of this class of equipment [computers] are large systems including many functional units, such as the IBM Type 701 and 702 machines, it has been found possible to incorporate many of the advantages of the giant systems into a smaller unit, the IBM Type 650 Magnetic Drum Processing Machine.
>
> The Type 650, using a compact, high-speed magnetic drum for information storage, combines the advantages of large storage, rapid calculation, "stored-program" control, and synchronized card input and output in a single functional unit. With this machine it is possible to simplify existing punched card procedures and also to extend mechanization into new areas. . . . As in the use of the giant data processing systems, the 650 performs in a single automatic procedural step work that would require several machine operations using previous punched card equipment.[107]

He demonstrated considerable knowledge of existing punched-card applications and how the 650 could be used to improve them. Merl Hague, the IBM representative on the panel discussion, provided a useful table comparing features of recently introduced IBM equipment, from the 604 electronic tabulator to the large-scale 702 magnetic-tape machine, with the 650 just past the middle (table 6.1), closer to the computers than to the tabulators. Then three life insurance speakers outlined the applications they were planning to implement on the new machines, including, for example, reserve and dividend calculation. The proposed applications were all limited and tentative.

Only two years later, however, the popularity of the IBM 650 was overwhelming. The electronics session of IASA's 1956 meeting provides a snapshot of the computer industry from the perspective of the insurance industry.[108] It included three papers on possible or existing UNIVAC applications (by Phoenix Mutual, John Hancock, and Pacific Mutual), one on Prudential's use of the IBM 702, and *eighteen* on IBM 650 applications.[109] The chair of one panel discussion, Equitable Life's Kermit Lang, commented on how rapidly the 650 was bursting onto the scene, comparing it with the 604 electronic tabulator

Table 6.1. *Comparative Features of IBM Electronic Data-Processing Machines*

|  | 604 | 607 | CPC | 650 | 701 | 702 |
|---|---|---|---|---|---|---|
| Announcement date | 1948 | 1953 | 1949 | 1953 | 1953 | 1953 |
| Storage (number of decimal digits) | 50 | 66–162 | 290–930 | 10,000–20,000 | 20,000–8,000,000 | 2,000,000–575,000,000 |
| Card input/output | 100/100 | 100/50 | 100–150/35 | 200/100 | 150/100 | 250/100 |
| Magnetic tape | No | No | No | No | Yes | Yes |
| Page printer | No | No | Yes | No | Yes | Yes |
| Program control | Wired | Wired | Wired/stored | Stored | Stored | Stored |
| Monthly rental | $550 up | $800 up | $1,775 up | $3,250–3,750 | $11,900–15,000 | $20,000 up |

*Source:* Adapted from table presented by Merl Hague at the 1954 *IASA* conference, "Panel Discussion of Life Insurance Applications of the IBM Magnetic Drum Calculator Type 650," *Proceedings of the Insurance Accounting and Statistical Association* (1954): 463.

only four years earlier: "At the IASA meeting in Cincinnati in 1952, as I recall, we had a big workshop on the 604, and of the 50 people in the room only two represented companies which had a 604 installed. Think of the contrast now! Today there are at least a dozen life insurance companies with 650s installed. I am sorry that we couldn't have all these companies represented here on these two panels but the 650s delivered in the last few months have been so numerous that we just were not quite able to keep up with all of them."[110] Papers on 650 applications covered topics from expense accounting to loss reserve file updating.[111] The 650 dominated the electronics sessions, absorbing far more time and attention than the UNIVAC or the IBM 702.

By 1957, the final report of the Society of Actuaries committee noted that nine U.S. life insurance firms had installed twelve large-scale computers with magnetic-tape input and output and that forty companies were using one or more card-based machines—mostly IBM 650s.[112] Moreover, large companies that bought UNIVACs or IBM 700 series computers often bought IBM 650s, as well. For example, in December 1954 John Hancock became the first company to take delivery of an IBM 650, before it acquired its UNIVAC in 1955, and by 1956 it had four 650s.[113] Prudential, which had been the earliest supporter of UNIVAC development during Berkeley's days, installed an IBM 650 before it acquired the larger IBM 702.[114] It continued to use 650s in addition to more powerful IBM computers well into the 1960s.[115]

In the mid-1950s, many insurance companies found adoption of the UNI-VAC or other tape-based computers difficult for several reasons that did not apply to the IBM 650 alternative. Insurance firms were typically suspicious of magnetic tape and reluctant to abandon cards. Indeed, the Society of Actuaries committee revealed in its 1955 report that no user of tape-based computers had yet totally replaced cards, and the legal status of magnetic tape was still unsettled.[116] Moreover, insurance companies had to have a long time horizon in their business, and they were reluctant to endanger major processes that worked to move to an untried and legally questionable medium such as magnetic tape.

Insurance firms that had IBM tabulating installations immediately faced another major change if they chose to acquire a UNIVAC or another non-IBM product. IBM had a longstanding vendor relationship with most insurance firms based on huge tabulating installations. These relationships—a form of lock-in encompassing the sales force's contact with decision makers, the familiar rental model of equipment acquisition, and the customer engineering service force's contact with tabulator operators—would be disrupted if firms chose alternative vendors. No matter how rapidly firms made the transition to a new computer, most would need to rent tabulating equipment for many more years and might be wary of upsetting good existing relations. Moreover, any that wanted to use IBM peripherals to bridge the card-tape divide would face different problems. In a late 1940s memo, Berkeley noted that Prudential's current tabulating equipment contract with IBM allowed it to use rented IBM equipment for experimental work or connected to machines made by other firms *only* when it had IBM's explicit permission.[117] This situation presumably persisted into the 1950s, so IBM could potentially cancel tabulating rental contracts, thus jeopardizing an insurance firm's ability to do business, for actions such as attaching an IBM high-speed printer to other vendors' equipment without approval.[118]

In 1954, then, most life insurance firms were not yet ready to adopt the tape-based UNIVAC or even to order the IBM 702 tape-based computer, which had been announced in 1953 for shipment in 1955.[119] At just this time, IBM offered them its card-based 650 computer, the first step of an easy and incremental migration path from the present, tabulator-based processes to processes transformed to take advantage of computing technology. In the late 1940s the UNIVAC had posed an active threat to IBM's commercial business, one that IBM executives felt they must counter to keep their customers.[120] The IBM 701/702 and 705 computers were their direct response. The card-based 650

*Fig. 6.9.* The IBM 650 card-and-drum-based computer, which physically resembled the 604 electronic calculator, fit smoothly into existing tabulator installations, allowing companies to take a small first step on an incremental path toward full computerization and integration of processes. Courtesy of IBM Archives.

with its magnetic-drum memory (fig. 6.9), however, was the more effective immediate response.

Later, historians of IBM's early computers explained why the 650 was so successful: "It was very competitive, not only in performance and price, but also in its concept as a small, reliable machine offering the versatility of a stored-program computer in a punched-card environment. This last consideration was important to prospective customers whose data processing requirements were not large enough to justify trading the convenience of the familiar punched card for the vagaries of magnetic tape."[121] The IBM 650, with monthly rental just over $3,200, posed a less formidable hurdle than the UNIVAC, with a $1.25 million initial purchase price. Moreover, its rental model was a familiar one. When a questioner at a LOMA panel discussion raised the issue of whether to rent or buy, especially given the possibility of rapid obsolescence, panelist Charles G. Groeschell from Northwestern Mutual Life Insurance Company responded:

> If a machine is eventually used for five years or longer on a one-shift operation, or two and one half years or longer on a three-shift operation, it will probably cost less to purchase the machine. Since any company which goes through the huge conversion problem to prepare for one of these machines will probably keep and use the machine a good deal longer than that, it seems wise to buy from a pure cost angle. However, there are other intangibles to be considered in each individual case and they are difficult to evaluate. As a result, many companies are compromising by renting with an option to buy.[122]

Many potential insurance computer users were initially reluctant to commit themselves totally to the new machines, preferring the safety net of the rental relationship to which they were already accustomed.[123] The 650 could be rented only until IBM's 1956 consent decree, in which it agreed to offer all its equipment for sale as well as rental.[124]

Insurance firms flocked to the IBM 650. At the 1955 IASA conference, Glenn O. Head of United States Life Insurance Company described his firm's easy decision to rent a 650: "In November, 1953, it appeared to us that we could use the recently announced IBM Type 650. Our investigation before ordering the machine was not extensive. We felt that our job was big enough to use a machine of this size, and we had confidence that IBM would build one that would be workable and well serviced."[125] The firm's existing relationship with IBM and confidence in its service made the decision simple. An automation consultant described the similar ease with which Equitable Life Insurance Company of Iowa selected an IBM 650: "The data processing equipment of different manufacturers was not compared because it is company policy to use only one make of equipment, such as one make of typewriter, one make of adding machine, one make of punched card equipment. The selection of the IBM 650 was justified on the basis that it would replace IBM punched card equipment, either installed or on order, with an approximately equivalent monthly rental."[126] In this case, pricing comparable to that of tabulators combined with a practice of standardizing office equipment, a common business policy, decided the matter. Even when firms undertook more detailed analysis, the decision seemed relatively easy. For example, Carl O. Orkild, manager of a casualty insurance company's Methods Research Department, analyzed a particular application on three computers available for rental, determining that "a 2%

saving would justify consideration of an IBM 650; 5%, an ElectroData computer; 12%, an IBM 702; and 17%, an IBM 705."[127]

The IBM 650 thus provided an easy beginning of a migration path from the tabulator era into the computer era. Adopting it speeded up processes and reduced growth in clerical staff, without yet requiring a firm to reconfigure its processes or its vendor relations. In a 1956 IASA presentation, Blackburn H. Hazlehurst of Connecticut General focused directly on the 650's role as a stepping-stone to larger computers. He assessed his firm's pilot projects as follows: "The pilot approach to mechanization is perhaps a little slow, but it does give us an opportunity to thoroughly test some rather radical new ways of servicing our business before we make any very large commitments."[128] The 650 offered the first stage of a gradual and incremental path eventually leading toward more radical changes in business methods.

Finally, as a comparison of figures 6.9 and 4.4 shows, the 650 computer even physically resembled the 604 electronic calculator already offered in IBM's tabulating lineup. Although this visual relationship was probably less a conscious decision than a default design allowing IBM to bring the 650 to market rapidly, it nevertheless encoded the 650, both symbolically and functionally, as similar to the familiar 604.[129] Its relatively small size and wheels made it more mobile than the huge UNIVAC, which was typically hoisted up buildings in crates. Its styling made it fit in with the most recently manufactured tabulating equipment, and it required little alteration to the environment. It could even use the same peripherals. Hazlehurst noted that the 650 "had to occupy the same physical space previously occupied by [his company's] 607."[130] As Paul Chinitz, a UNIVAC sales manager, later put it, the 650 "slipped right in to the existing punched card processing scheme. It was punched cards in, it was punched cards out, and it was just like it was a bigger calculator for them."[131] Insurance firms enthusiastically embraced this familiar-looking and -acting machine.

IBM succeeded in retaining conservative insurance customers by offering them the tabulator-like 650 as a first step on an incremental path toward eventual transformation of organizational structure and business processes. Moreover, adopting the 650 allowed firms to maintain vendor relations established with IBM during the tabulator era. As the common saying went, no one ever got fired for deciding to go with IBM. IBM's card-based 650, along with its business approach and existing relationships, allowed insurance executives to maintain considerable continuity with the tabulator era as they began their long journey into the computer era.

## 650 Applications

Insurance executives also tended to choose 650 applications based on familiar, bread-and-butter tasks. Although some started with single, actuarial applications such as valuation, many began with premium billing operations, often consolidated with closely related functions such as premium and loan accounting operations. In many cases firms directly transferred existing punched-card applications to the 650 computer. For example, at the 1957 IASA conference Phoenix Mutual's G. J. Williams stated, "We have used this equipment, so far as our punched card system output is concerned, to duplicate our present output."[132] Connecticut General's Hazlehurst noted that the 650 displaced a 607 tabulator and that, since his firm's payroll was on the 607, the first job it moved to the 650 was its payroll.[133] As these direct transfers showed, adopting the 650 as a firm's first stored-program computer allowed insurance companies to avoid large discontinuities in user processes, as well.

Other applications were relatively small but allowed some rethinking of existing functions. For example, Aetna Life's Nathan D. O'Neil described using the 650, combined with traditional tabulating equipment, to maintain a mortgage loan due file for Federal Housing Administration (FHA) and Veterans Administration (VA) mortgage loans, eliminating the need for a ledger history card.[134] Some firms initially designed relatively simple applications that they intended to consolidate with other functions in the future, when they moved to larger equipment. According to Walter DeVries, Equitable Life used a "block" approach to conversion, with each functional block developed and converted individually but designed ultimately to fit into a consolidated functions plan.[135] As he explained, "The Equitable's plan is to use 650 machines as an intermediate step to a full 705 installation, by programming, testing and setting up operating procedures for dividends, commissions and several related projects, first for the 650 and then translating these programs to 705 programs." The operations would ultimately be consolidated on the larger, 705 computer. A. L Wright of Manufacturers Life Insurance Company of Toronto stated that his firm was not likely to achieve a full-scale consolidated functions plan on a large computer soon, for reasons including the magnitude of the change, "a reluctance in certain parts of the company to accelerate the trend to mechanization," and worries about personnel displacement problems.[136] Given this reluctance, "a more logical approach, from [his firm's] point of view, was to proceed more slowly, obtain a medium-size computer and deal with functions separately. Ultimately the aim would be the consolidation of the various functions into an operation which could utilize a large computer." His company acquired a 650, and "the first major application planned for the machine was a combination of valuation and dividend procedures," a small initial consolidation that would point toward later, more extensive ones.

A few firms went further than this, consolidating or reengineering multiple functions. Equitable Life's Kermit Lang commented, "Of the ten companies participating in the panel discussions on the 650 yesterday and today, it is interesting to note that eight are adopting, or have so far followed, a functional approach to the use of the 650. That is, they have used it for particular applications such as commission accounting, dividend accounting or premium accounting. On the other hand, two of the smaller companies, in order to justify the 650, have felt they needed to consolidate their punched card files and put practically all of their machine work on the 650."[137] The two firms adopting a consolidated functions–like approach from the start were United States Life and Pan-American Life. At a 1955 IASA electronics session, United States Life's Glenn Head noted that his company was planning for a 650 and that the consolidated file approach was "one of the fundamental features" of its plan.[138] The next year, he reported that the firm had consolidated five punched-card files (valuation, master premium, master dividend, advance premium deposits, and loan master) into a single card file, a serious but not yet comprehensive consolidation of the functions related to ordinary life.[139] Waid J. Davidson explained that Pan-American took the consolidated file approach even further:

> The consolidated file is the closest approach to the use of magnetic tape and can be transferred easily to magnetic tape. By using the file as we have it set up, our people will become used to working with a file similar to tape. . . . Thus we can go to tapes in two small steps rather than one large one. . . . The cost of maintaining one file is considerably less than maintaining many separate files. . . . Back in the early days, a Company had all information pertaining to a given policy in one location. As the complexity of the business increased, it became necessary to scatter this information throughout many departments; however, with the advent of data processing equipment it has now become possible to again consolidate the records in one place.[140]

He viewed the 650 application as an incremental step toward such a consolidated function application on a larger tape-based computer.

These two firms represented the vanguard of 650 applications, however, and most insurers adopting 650s in the 1950s used them in much more prosaic applications only incrementally different from tabulator applications. As late as 1964, LOMA's industrywide survey of insurance data-processing applications indicated that the most common application was still premium notice billing, by this time almost always combined with premium accounting and often with commission calculation and accounting.[141] The basic billing and accounting operations, which some companies began to automate in the late tabulator era, were still central to computer applications fifteen years later. In the early years, 650 applications were almost always either direct conversions of existing tabulator operations or a combination of two or three such operations, in some cases already partially consolidated on tabulating equipment. A consolidated functions plan of the sort the Society of Actuaries committee envisioned was initially rare, though firms often saw it as a desired end point of the transformation involving computers. The approach to 650 applications, then, also tended to be explicitly incremental.

## Personnel Issues

Although adopting an IBM 650 did not require the scale of personnel considerations faced by those installing a UNIVAC computer, companies installing the 650 were at least introduced to the same concerns: training computer programmers and dealing with fear of technological displacement. In introducing Aetna Life's O'Neil at a 1957 IASA session, Chair Kermit Lang noted that the panelist had "gained experience on the IBM 604, the Card programmed Calculator and the 650 and gradually worked into the electronic data processing field. He is now in charge of the Aetna's Central Data Processing Development Department and is currently studying the programming for an ElectroData now on order for the Aetna."[142] In his training, the 650 clearly provided a bridge between the 604 electronic calculator at the top of the tabulating line and a computer such as ElectroData's.[143] R. Walden of Mutual Benefit Life claimed that in developing some small applications for its 650, "we have used the 650 as a source of education for many of our key people." Moreover, he continued, "As we gain more experience and get involved in larger capacity equipment with Magnetic Tapes, we will have to break the operation into specific functions."[144] Thus, many firms and individuals saw the 650 as a stepping-stone in developing expertise and organizational capacity in programming and operating computers.

Pan-American Life's Lloyd Gross had to deal with the same set of personnel issues that firms installing larger machines faced. To prepare for its 650, Gross sent an assorted group—"two methods analysts, one actuarial student, three department heads, and one vice-president"—to a one-week programming course conducted by IBM.[145] Subsequently, this group met several times to develop the firm's first application, settling on a single-record integrated system. The group members also decided to combine methods analysis and programming, making the two methods analysts who had attended the program into "methods analyst programmers," then training two additional people to work with them—an accounting student and another actuarial student. As an aside, Gross noted that these four methods analyst programmers included two men and two women.[146]

Although Gross did not indicate whether he faced much resistance in creating the Data Processing Department, he noted some issues that arose around the specter of technological displacement. He expected the new system to eliminate about forty clerical jobs, which he planned to handle gradually by transfers and normal turnover. Some resistance emerged at early stages: "We made the mistake at first of not informing everyone in the company of our plans for automation and some of the fears and misconceptions that our employees had were fantastic. We are doing everything in our power to overcome this now and by the end of the year our communications should be such that we will have a good understanding among the personnel."[147] Gross learned that extensive employee communication about computer acquisition was desirable even on a small-scale machine like the 650. Thus, in personnel issues as well as in other areas, the 650 provided an incremental advance beyond existing tabulating technology and toward organizational transformation based on large-scale data-processing equipment.

### Results

Because these 650s became so ubiquitous in the early years of computing and were used in so many different ways, it is difficult to gauge their effect on firm outcomes. The average expense ratio for the largest thirty firms rose gradually until 1975, suggesting that these early machines probably did not significantly reduce costs. Contemporary evidence suggests that the incremental approach offered by the 650s was significant primarily in easing the transition to the next-generation computers. A mid-1960s academic study of the impact of computers on life insurance companies found that firms replacing manual or tabulator systems with more advanced computers took more than 40% longer from feasibility study to computer installation than those replacing IBM 650s.[148] The authors interpreted these findings as an indication "that a high level of confidence and a willingness to move ahead fast existed among those companies whose previous technical experience had brought them close to the level of the modern computer."[149] On the other hand, the study found no significant difference in the time firms took from installation through programming and debugging to first online use, suggesting that the experience provided by the 650 did not go very far in preparing firms to program the next generation of computers.

## A Compromise Choice: The IBM 702 and 705

Although most insurance companies chose either the UNIVAC or the IBM 650, a few large firms took a path that IBM and particularly Thomas J. Watson Jr., soon to take leadership of IBM from his father, saw as critical to IBM's own transition into the computer era—by adopting IBM 700 series tape-based machines.[150] IBM announced the 702, its first business-oriented data-processing computer, in 1953, but it did not become available until early 1955, a year after Metropolitan Life and Franklin Life acquired their UNIVACs. IBM made the tape-based 702s compatible with earlier tabulating systems by providing tape-to-card and card-to-tape converters and by combining the new computers with its familiar, fast, and effective punched-card peripherals. As IBM historians later noted, the 702 "was convincing and congenial to users of punched-card machines, and the problems of training and familiarization were minimized."[151] IBM described its 700 series computers as "a combination of existing functional abilities in a single machine," with greater speed and flexibility.[152] This choice also allowed insurance firms with IBM tabulating installations to retain their existing vendor relations. Thus the 702 was an attractive alternative for larger firms that wanted high-capacity, tape-based computers but still wanted a gradual, not an overnight, transformation.

Although the 702 had some advantages over the UNIVAC, including superior tape handling and modular construction in units that looked familiar and fit in an elevator, it was not as reliable as IBM had hoped.[153] But the 705, announced in 1954 and available by 1956, replaced the 702's erratic tubes with newly developed core memory, thus providing improved processing speed and reliability while maintaining compatibility with conversion equipment. These qualities attracted business customers, including insurance firms, that IBM cultivated.[154] In January 1957, it conducted a seminar on life insurance and data processing that drew attendance from thirteen life insurance firms, as well as a representative each from LOMA and IASA.[155] IBM speakers presented information directly but also encouraged attendees to share industry-specific user information such as their current or future plans and each company's master record tape file.[156] Equitable and Prudential adopted the IBM 702 and 705 computers, along with 650 computers, attempting to balance old and new ways of doing business while still maintaining vendor continuity. In choosing applications to computerize, Equitable chose an explicitly incremental migration path, whereas Prudential attempted a rapid transformation. Their business results, however, were similarly discouraging.

## Equitable Life Assurance Society: Gradual Migration

At this time, Equitable was the third-largest insurance firm, after Metropolitan Life and Prudential.[157] It did not carry out any "elaborate 'feasibility study'" to decide whether to computerize; rather, it felt that its size alone was a clear indicator that the firm could gainfully use a computer.[158] Equitable began gradually, acquiring three IBM 650s in 1955 and 1956. Because it adopted its first 700 series computer only in 1957, it skipped the less reliable 702 for the 705. As the company acquired the higher-capacity 705s, it transferred applications originally programmed for the 650 directly onto them, in simulated 650 mode. Office automation expert R. Hunt Brown described the advantage of the approach: "Using this method, it was possible to bring onto the 705 some tested systems within a fairly short time. In general, this approach made it possible to start in a limited area with a small staff and gradually increase the effort by bringing in more systems as experience developed in planning, programming and operation functions."[159] Emulating the 650 on the 705 thus eased the transition, but it omitted reprogramming that would have allowed the firm to take advantage of the 705's increased capabilities.

Equitable followed an equally incremental plan in choosing applications. It adopted a "functional block approach," in which pieces of its operations were computerized one at a time. This approach maintained the existing functional organization until "at some future time these blocks would be integrated into a single system, having as its heart a master tape file."[160] Thus Equitable computerized functions such as computing ordinary insurance dividends, figuring agents' commissions, preparing new policies, and billing for premiums, each individually. The first three were initially programmed on the 650 and then moved onto the 705; the fourth function, premium and policy loan interest billing, was developed directly on the 705. By 1962, Equitable had integrated only premium billing and accounting.[161] In general, the conversions "brought onto the 705 many EAM [electronic accounting machine, or tabulator] procedures previously associated with 650 operations."[162] Thus, while this procedure made the incremental migration relatively painless, it preserved many aspects of the old system, from functional divisions to eighty-column records. Although the functional block approach enabled the large company to realize some cost savings, such as eliminating seventy-five clerical jobs by converting the dividend block, it deferred the potentially greater advantages of integration and transformation.[163] Essentially, the system operated as a faster tabulator installation during the 1950s and into the early 1960s.

Even with this incremental approach, Brown noted, "Equitable reports that conversion planning and implementation have proved to be difficult."[164] Indeed, the firm discovered that additional training was needed as each conversion approached. On the positive side, it had needed to initiate no technology-driven layoffs: "Equitable has encountered no difficulty as far as relocating displaced personnel is concerned. As in most insurance companies, Equitable has considerable turnover every year, and the company feels that the computer will not replace employees so fast as to exceed the needs arising from growth and turnover. In any event, the Society has promised that no person will be discharged because of the introduction of these new systems."[165] Presumably Equitable had discovered the need for considerable employee communication during this process.

Thus Equitable migrated from its old, tabulator-based methods to new ones gradually, moving data onto the IBM 705 while continuing to follow existing, functionally distinct procedures. In 1962 the firm finally initiated a more extensive change involving new IBM computers and a Cashier's Automatic Processing System (CAPS), which tied the 100 cashier's offices (later called general services offices) to the home office.[166] This system went into full operation in 1972, finally breaking down some of the barriers between functional "fiefdoms."[167]

## Prudential: Troubled Attempt at Rapid Transformation of Operations

Prudential's continuing growth, rising costs, and labor shortages strongly motivated it to adopt electronic data processing.[168] After it rejected the second, more expensive UNIVAC contract in 1952, Prudential made several false starts before settling on IBM. According to James A. Daley, manager of the Electronic Service Division at Prudential during the late 1950s, the company "briefly considered designing [its] own data processing system," a move that would have echoed its ultimately counterproductive development of the Gore sorter more than fifty years earlier.[169] In early 1953, it decided instead to lease Control Research Corporation's CRC-102A, a smaller computer that used both magnetic tape and card input, reversing that decision when IBM announced the 702 in 1953. After Prudential confirmed that the new system should be able to do the firm's ordinary insurance premium billing and accounting, it ordered a 702, for delivery in 1955. Before the 702 arrived, however, IBM announced the 705, and Prudential decided to start on the 702 but shift to multiple 705s as soon as the newer model was available.

Once it had made the equipment decisions, it was just beginning the hard part of its computerization. IBM delivered the first 702 in September 1955, but despite a growing staff, the 702 Ordinary Project team under Daley began limited operations on it only in early 1957.[170] The team planned to convert the ordinary insurance records to tape and to create a unified application with "premium billing and accounting, commission calculation and accounting, preparation of agents' production records, and the preparation of many annual statement figures."[171] As Daley explained Prudential's approach in 1957, "The Prudential chose to take full advantage of the abilities of this new equipment and did not pursue the course of minimum systems changes—using the 702 or 705 as a type of 'electronic tabulator' where the conventional plugboard is the computer program. Our basic approach has been to take full advantage of the essential operating characteristics of the equipment."[172] Prudential was clearly attempting a rapid reengineering of its insurance processes, rather than Equitable's gradual migration. Daley further noted that his team chose the applications with the goal of integrating "'functionally fractured' clerical and punch card systems" and that "electronic computers have offered a chance to halt the trend to greater subdivision of home office operations."[173]

Daley admitted, however, that the company had consistently underestimated the time necessary to make an application operational; a much later account clarified the difficulties.[174] Given Prudential's enormous size, a test conversion of 6 districts (out of 252) required Daley's team to convert more than 13 million punched cards to tape, a feat that took four weeks. Merging the files into a single master record took much longer and programming the application longer yet. The first 705 to arrive at the Newark home office in September 1956 was immediately devoted to the same application, though the next three 705s went to other regional home offices (RHOs).[175] By late 1957, Prudential upgraded the older 702 to a second 705 for the Newark office. Even with this added power, the project team had to divide the application into two phases, completing Phase 1, including the premium billing itself along with two related functions, for twelve pilot districts during 1957 and for the rest of the districts in 1959. By 1960, the team finally completed the second phase. Ultimately, and contrary to management's intentions, Prudential's path probably ended up resembling Equitable's incremental block approach more than the rapid transformation Daley sought, though Prudential still followed a somewhat more aggressive schedule. Even with the largest computers then available, a familiar vendor, and a goal of transforming its processes, a very large firm such as Prudential faced enormous challenges in achieving an integrated application.

Along with the greater power and capacity of the 700 series computers came greater difficulty in programming such large applications. In general, Daley noted, Prudential had problems choosing programmers. Unlike John Hancock's confident Hatch, Daley did not believe that a simple test could select appropriate personnel to be trained to program computers.[176] Instead, Daley's team selected programmers based on their performance in programming school, though that required investing much more in each candidate. No off-the-shelf computer applications yet existed, and Prudential, like most life insurance firms, preferred to train its own employees to program rather than attempt to hire scarce programmers from outside and teach them about insurance. In addition, Daley stressed an area of personnel planning that appeared "to be obscured many times in electronics installations by the expectation of personnel displacement[:] adequately training the line personnel required under the electronic system." All these factors undoubtedly contributed to Prudential's problems.

Meanwhile, Prudential was also using several 650 computers, an interesting source of internal comparison. The main Newark office acquired the first 650 in 1955, putting it to work quickly and profitably on such discrete applications as the "Group Annuity Year-End Valuation."[177] Top management at Newark also determined that the Canadian RHO was not large enough to warrant a 705, sending it a 650 instead. Working with fewer policies and the simpler 650, the Canadian RHO found that its programming went more smoothly than Newark's on the 702s. When problems with programming the ordinary insurance application on the 702s continued and expanded, Thomas Allsopp, second vice president in charge of the Planning and Development Department (within whose domain Daley's ordinary project team fell), requested a cost study of Prudential's computerization efforts.[178] The ten-year projection looked terrible, with only the Canadian 650 ordinary system recapturing its development and installation costs. Even after changing assumptions and adding new information, "the 650's still looked better than the 705's, particularly in the smaller offices."[179] As a result, late in 1956, "Mr. Allsopp and Comptroller Wendel Drobroyk agreed that the proper path would be for the larger offices [in Los Angeles, Jacksonville, and Newark] to have 705's and the smaller ("Mid-Continent") offices [in Minneapolis, Philadelphia, and Houston], 650's."

This decision reduced projected operating costs, but even in 1978, according to an internal report on computerization, "the Mid-Continent Decision [was] still occasionally debated."[180] Fortunately, this report provides a rare after-the-fact assessment of costs and paybacks: "Viewed narrowly in terms of the operating costs of existing processes, [the decision] seemed to be sound. According to the published cost reports, the 650 systems were profitable. Although most 702 system operating costs eventually were below the pre-computer cost levels at the end of 1964[,] nearly $2,000,000 of pre-installation costs had not yet been offset by operating savings. A whole generation of computers had been passed by and the 705's were fully amortized. By then, the Mid-Continent RHO's had been replaced by 1401's [*sic*], which also operated profitably."[181] In the long run, then, the 700 series computers were not profitable for Prudential, even though the firm had purchased, rather than rented, them, based on an expected five-year payback. Judged as investments, the 702 and 705 computers were an expensive experiment, while the 650s, with their more limited applications, proved sound.

Given the cost analysis, Allsopp's decision to use 650s in the smaller offices made sense. Although initially disappointed not to receive 705s, executives at the Mid-Continent RHOs put smaller, less integrated systems into place quickly and successfully, and these systems were profitable. But as early as

1958, the problems of mixing machines and applications at the various offices were emerging:

> There have been many complaints by the Regional Home Offices with regard to the great volume of instructional material received from Newark. . . .
>
> Getting at the heart of the problem is difficult. The great amount of instructions is one aspect; another is the complexities introduced by different RHO systems and organizations.
>
> For example, there are five different systems now employed in the Company for Ordinary issue. In what terms should the Corporate office write instructions pertaining to Ordinary issue? Should Newark write a special set of instructions for each of the five different systems? The problem with this course of action is that Newark would have to maintain experts in each of the five different systems. This would not only be expensive, but the experts, removed from the actual scene of operation, would soon develop ivory-tower qualities.[182]

In 1963, when Executive Vice President Robert W. Harvey announced a new strategic direction to "Advance and Unify" the many systems into a single improved one, none of the offices wanted to change. Thus, although using 650s in the smaller RHOs paid off for Prudential in the short term, the decision to use different computers (and applications) in them than in larger offices created long-term problems. Its experience underlines the problematic nature of programming software applications, especially integrative ones, in huge firms.[183]

## Results

Both Prudential and Equitable adopted IBM 650 and 700 series computers, a seeming compromise between the UNIVAC and the IBM 650. Prudential attempted to transform its insurance processes immediately and radically, while Equitable follow a very slow and incremental change path that it hoped would take it to a similar end point. Prudential, however, encountered obstacles that slowed its change process to a pace not much faster than Equitable's. Interestingly, despite their different application strategies, Prudential's and Equitable's costs for handling ordinary insurance were quite similar from the late 1940s into the 1970s, both rising slightly over time (fig. 6.10).

The Bureau of Labor study of insurance computerization credited the industry with having "pioneered in the application of office automation," not-

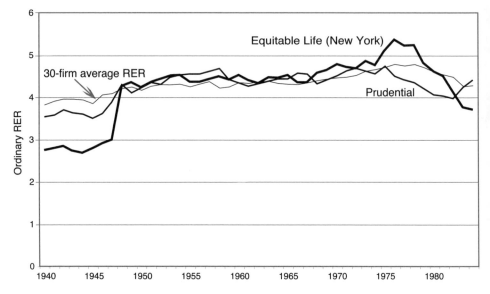

*Fig. 6.10.* Prudential and Equitable had similar, gradually rising ordinary renewal expense ratios (ordinary RERs) until the early 1970s, when Prudential pulled ahead. Equitable's ordinary RER continued to rise into the mid-1970s, when it began falling rapidly, catching up with and surpassing Prudential's ordinary RER in the early 1980s. *Best's,* 1940–85.

ing that "insurance companies were among the first business firms to use electronic computers."[184] Their early experiences with computers, however, illustrate how powerfully existing methods and practices shape the adoption and use of new technology. Insurance firms initially chose between adopting the large tape-based UNIVAC, which only the largest firms could adopt without attempting a rapid transformation of processes, and adopting the familiar-seeming card-based IBM 650, which allowed firms to change their processes only incrementally as they moved them to these small computers.[185] In some cases, big firms adopted both, using the 650 for smaller jobs and a UNIVAC for larger ones. Some firms, like Equitable and Prudential, chose IBM tape-based 702 and 705 computers over UNIVACs, at least assuring continuity in vendor relations and in card-based peripherals. By the later 1950s, a few ordered large- and medium-scale computers from other vendors. At the 1958 IASA conference, for example, A. E. DuPlessis of Travelers Insurance Company spoke about his firm's decision to order four RCA Bizmac II computers, large-scale, tape-based systems.[186]

In addition to choosing which type of equipment to adopt, companies had to decide how to begin using it, choosing between applications that required firms to reengineer insurance processes immediately to take advantage of the new technology and applications that allowed incremental migration toward a distant, but perhaps similar, end point. Metropolitan Life and John Hancock adopted UNIVACs, more clearly breaking with the tabulator past, but chose a gradual approach to computerizing insurance processes, reducing their risk in this arena. In 1955, Howard J. Ditman, New York Life's vice president, argued, "The best approach is to accept the premise that an electronic data processing system in insurance is a truly revolutionary development."[187] Even though an integrated application poses challenges, "to treat such a radical innovation as merely an adjunct to the traditional division of administrative responsibilities, to consider it as merely a glorified punch card or addressograph system, is to underestimate grossly what may be accomplished." Consistent with this perspective, middle-sized Pacific Mutual and Franklin Life chose to adopt both a UNIVAC and a new, integrated system that broke with their previous, finely subdivided processes. Based on public accounts, these transformations seem to have been fairly successful, though firm cost results were only mildly better than those for Metropolitan Life and John Hancock. Large firms attempting to adopt an integrated approach immediately encountered additional problems, as Prudential's experience illustrated. Most firms chose a gradual migration path, moving from tabulators to IBM 650s and adopting applications that built on existing tabulator applications. Only in the mid-1970s would many of them achieve the transformation of insurance processes that the Society of Actuaries committee articulated in 1952.

The incremental migration path also aided IBM's successful repositioning from the tabulator to the computer business. Market figures suggest that insurance firms were far from alone in taking this more cautious path, and IBM benefited from and took advantage of this tendency. As one computer history points out, "it was not the large-scale 700 series that secured IBM's leadership of the industry, but the low-cost Magnetic Drum Computer."[188] IBM sold more than 2,000 card-based 650s, which Thomas J. Watson Jr. called "computing's 'Model T,'" and life insurance bought many of them.[189]

# CHAPTER 7

# Incremental Migration during the 1960s and 1970s

Rapid postwar insurance growth continued into the 1980s, exceeding the growth rate for national income considerably (fig. 7.1). Although more than 1,000 life insurance companies, most of them stock firms, were established between 1945 and 1964, at the end of that period large mutuals still dominated the industry, with 10% of the firms holding 60% of insurance in force and 70% of assets.[1] Between 1955 and 1965, ordinary insurance in force increased by 130% and the number of policies—a better indicator of data-processing demand—by 34%.[2] Group insurance, a new and important area for many insurers, recorded 205% growth in insurance in force. Although industrial insurance business remained flat, total life insurance in force increased by 142% and total life insurance policies by 35%. Around the same time, insurance employment grew by 32%, a rise that was, according to the U.S. Bureau of Labor Statistics (BLS), "significantly greater than employment gains in the nonfarm sector as a whole."[3] Still, that increase did not quite keep pace with the growth in number of policies, thus exacerbating the wartime labor shortages without improved productivity. Growth continued during the subsequent decade, with total life insurance in force increasing by 138% and number of policies by 19%.

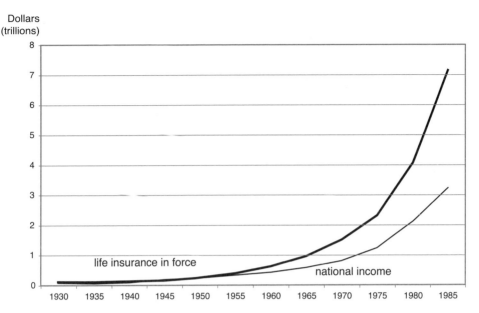

*Fig. 7.1.* Life insurance in force continued to grow rapidly from 1950 into the 1980s, considerably outpacing national income. Insurance in force from American Council of Life Insurance, *1992 Life Insurance Fact Book,* 24; national income from U.S. Bureau of the Census, *Statistical Abstract of the United States: 1987,* 107th ed. (Washington, D.C.: U.S. Department of Commerce, Bureau of the Census, 1986).

Other changes were adding to the variety as well as volume of data that insurance firms handled and thus to the demand for computers. In 1965, the BLS described these changes:

> Fundamental changes in industry organization have taken place since 1945. Less than 20 years ago, State regulations strictly limited the types of insurance a single company could sell. Now, all types of nonlife insurance can be sold by one carrier, which may affiliate with a life carrier to sell "all lines." When State regulations were changed a decade ago, consolidations and mergers [of life firms with other types of insurance firms] followed and former single line companies diversified.

> Marketing of insurance has also been modified. For example, packaging and simplification of coverages (risks) into a single comprehensive policy, such as the fast-growing "homeowners" policy, eliminates coverage overlap for consumers, increases selling efficiency, and reduces office servicing costs. In addition, a wide

variety of new coverages—from dental care to nuclear accident—are being introduced. A variety of advertising media are now used to reach a mass market and direct selling to consumers is done by some carriers. Finally, sales on a standardized
group contract basis have added millions of policy certificates without the necessity to "sell" each individual covered.[4]

As firms increased their range of insurance offerings, they needed to manage
more different types of information. The growth in size and variety of data-
processing needs combined to influence demand for computers, as noted in a
1972 LOMA publication:

> The arrival of computers could hardly have been more fortuitous for life compa-
> nies. In 1954, life companies employed over 350,000 workers with nearly three-
> fourths of them engaged in office operations. The demand for insurance was in-
> creasing yearly, fostered by a growing population and by rising personal incomes.
> In addition, the industry was undergoing major organizational changes. Change
> in state laws permitted more multiple-line operations. Many single-line compa-
> nies diversified, while others merged. The combined effect of these factors was a
> steep rise in life company data volumes and in the variety of processing that was
> required.[5]

These combined factors helped explain continuing insurance interest in computing, despite the difficulties encountered in the conversion to and ongoing
operation of computers. The BLS report, based on a large-scale study, revealed
that in 1963 firms accounting for 80% of all insurance employees already had
computers installed, and those accounting for 5% more had computers on order.[6] Computers were thus approaching universality in all but the smallest
firms. BLS researchers estimated that 800 computers were operating in about
300 firms industrywide that year. Insurance firms would continue to increase
their computer use during the following decade, as well as to adopt new types
of related equipment, such as telecommunications connections, that vendors
made available.

By 1975, consulting firm Booz, Allen and Hamilton estimated that data-
processing costs (including computer hardware, software, and operating costs)
constituted 20% of total expenses in insurance, placing the industry second in
information technology investment only to the securities industry and ahead
of banking, the airlines, retailing, manufacturing, and utilities.[7] The IBM 1401
followed by the IBM System 360/370 lines dominated insurance hardware, and

the consolidated functions approach shaped the most popular application software.[8] Only during the second half of the 1970s did insurance finally move on from its original computerization goals to entirely new issues.

## Developments in Hardware Adopted by Insurance Firms

As the major vendors developed their hardware offerings, insurance firms chose which to adopt, generally favoring equipment supporting incremental changes to, rather than rapid transformation of, existing processes. For most of this period, insurance did not intervene directly to shape computer hardware developments, but as a significant part of the commercial market it shaped them indirectly. In general, firm choices favored IBM, which dominated the insurance market as it did the commercial market as a whole. Sperry Rand's UNIVAC maintained a significant presence in this market, however, based on both that machine's early technical edge and the installed base of Remington Rand's Powers tabulator. Several other vendors appeared less frequently.

Most life insurance firms found the IBM 1401, available in 1960, an excellent addition to the IBM line. Successor to the 650, the 1401 was a small-scale, low-cost computer system with transistors and core memory. It was inexpensive, fast, and much more reliable than the vacuum tube–based 650, though without the optional magnetic-tape drives it still resembled that computer externally (fig. 7.2). It took card input and output and could be used with or without magnetic tape. IBM had added the tape units, even though doing so delayed the system's initial announcement by a month, for several reasons: "For one thing, it made possible a larger market forecast for the 1401 system, including now not only steadfast punched-card users but also those interested in acquiring small tape processing systems. Second, the existence of tape in the system would greatly ease the upward movement of 1401 users to larger computers as their data processing needs expanded. Finally, the availability of a tape-connected 1401 eliminated entirely the need for a control unit that had been planned for the chain printer."[9]

As the tape unit highlights, IBM planned the 1401 not just as a central processor but as a system with three or four components, thus distinguishing it from many of its competitors' products. One computer history traces this approach to IBM's "marketing managers, who recognized that customers were

*Fig. 7.2.* Without the optional tape drives on the right, the IBM 1401 still bore some resemblance to the 604 and 650. By adding the tape drives, an insurance firm could advance on its incremental path toward comprehensive computerization. Courtesy of the IBM Archives.

more interested in the solution to business problems than in the technical merits of competing computer designs. As a result, IBM engineers were forced into taking a total-system view of computers—that is, a holistic approach that required them to 'take into account programming, customer transition, field service, training, spare parts, logistics, etc.' This was the philosophy that brought success to the IBM 650 in the 1950s and that would soon bring it to the model 1401."[10] This description highlights the extent to which the 1401 continued and extended the notion of incremental migration started with the 650. A customer could remain with its familiar vendor, IBM, for the total package. IBM found this approach even more successful with the 1401 than with the 650, delivering a total of 12,000 systems.[11] The 1401 completed IBM's successful transition from a tabulating vendor to a computer vendor, with its computer revenues finally equal to those of its tabulators in 1962.

The 1401 was extremely popular with life insurance firms. A 1964 LOMA study of electronic data-processing (EDP) use reported on ninety-one companies with computers that LOMA classified as medium scale and fifty-six with computers classified as large scale.[12] IBM's 1400 series dominated the medium-scale category, accounting for just over three-quarters of the machines reported. Of the remaining twenty machines, five were another small IBM model, the 305 RAMAC (Random Access Memory Accounting Machine), with vacuum tubes and magnetic-disk storage, and another was the IBM 1620, a small scientific computer, giving IBM 83% of this selected piece of the insurance market, close to the 89% of total market revenues it captured that year.[13]

A few insurance firms had adopted medium-range machines from vendors competing with IBM's 650 and 1401. The LOMA list included, for example, three small UNIVAC 1004s, four UNIVAC Solid State 80s and 90s, two RCA models (301 and 304M), two NCR 315s, one Burroughs 220, and one Honeywell 200.[14] Sperry Rand introduced the UNIVAC Solid State 80s and 90s, the former using eighty-column and the latter ninety-column cards, in late 1958 to compete directly with the 650, offering a lower price and faster speed.[15] UNIVAC even provided "an IBM 650 emulator program to ease conversion" from the 650, but after an initially successful sales period, IBM's announcement of the 1401—at the same price and a much faster speed—drastically slowed demand for the UNIVAC Solid State 80 and 90. The year of LOMA's study, Honeywell introduced its 200 model as compatible with the 1401 but faster and less expensive; an accompanying program called "Liberator" translated software written for the 1401 to work on it.[16] Honeywell's announcement triggered a flurry of orders for the 200 and a corresponding slowdown in orders for the IBM 1401, prompting IBM to accelerate its announcement of the System/360 line to stem the losses.[17] As in the tabulator era, some life insurance firms were ready to switch to a competitor when the transition looked easy and the option better, but IBM responded to such competition by introducing further improvements that brought customers back to it.

On the large-systems front IBM also dominated the market. Beginning in 1959 IBM offered the transistor-based 7090, 7080, and eventually the 7070 as successors to the 700 series computers.[18] Although the 1963 LOMA study did not list what computers the larger firms used, other studies shed light on this area. In 1967 Thomas L. Whisler and Harald Meyer conducted a LOMA-sponsored study that looked in detail at twenty firms weighted toward the larger end of the spectrum.[19] Half of these firms used IBM 705s or 7000 series computers. Another six firms had IBM 1400 series computers or IBM 305 RAMACs. Of the remaining four companies, three had UNIVAC I or II computers, and one firm had an RCA Bizmac, a small and relatively unsuccessful early RCA computer.[20] In a 1977 LOMA-sponsored book on insurance data-processing systems, Charles H. Cissley provided snapshots of three large companies' computer systems at several different times.[21] In 1964, Company A had three different IBM models, including one 705, one 7074, and eight 1401s; Company B had one RCA 501 and one RCA 301; and Company C had one IBM 705 and three computers from the IBM 1400 series. Here, although IBM claimed most of the market, RCA had a foothold. Three years later, Kenneth Hills, former IASA vice president, considered Honeywell's IBM-compatible computers as the third option for insurance firms, after IBM and UNIVAC.[22]

Despite these alternatives, however, life insurance favored IBM through the early 1960s, with UNIVAC a distant second and other vendors even farther behind. In the mid-1960s, Robert C. Goshay, an academic scholar of insurance and computing, described the basis of this relationship: "Product loyalty, and hence the influence of the supplier, is apparent in EDP adaptations in the insurance industry. Undoubtedly the established supplier has had the edge over would-be competitors by virtue of his knowledge of management's personality, philosophy, and uses and needs of equipment (whether leased or purchased)."[23] In addition to loyalty, the installed base provided an indirect form of lock-in. In this case, the established vendor was overwhelmingly IBM, since it dominated the tabulator era and had introduced many insurance firms to computers via the 650 or, for a few larger firms, the 702 or 705. Still, Remington Rand also had a (much smaller) installed base of tabulators and early UNIVACs, giving it an advantage, albeit a more limited one, as well. The external similarities between IBM's tabulators and smaller computers reinforced its installed-base advantage. The 1401 computer system was particularly popular among insurance firms, as shown by the many early 1960s IASA proceedings papers about 1401 applications.[24] Moreover, although the 1401 system could stand on its own, it could also be connected to a larger IBM computer such as the 7070.[25] Another major cause of the 1401's popularity with insurance companies was undoubtedly the '62 CFO (Consolidated Functions Ordinary, 1962) software IBM created for insurance firms using the 1400 series computers, discussed in the next section. Overall, IBM made it easy for insurance companies to remain its customers.

Although initially when firms chose between IBM and UNIVAC they also necessarily chose between leasing and buying, the two decisions were uncoupled relatively early. In accordance with its 1956 tabulator-based antitrust consent decree, IBM offered its tabulators and computers (both 650s and 700 series models) for rental or purchase; in parallel, other vendors offered the option of leasing rather than buying.[26] The trade-off between leasing and buying computers, a general problem that Martin Amlung, a representative of Ernst and Ernst, identified as "relatively new in the business world," became the subject of considerable discussion.[27] As early as January 1957, Aetna's Nathan O'Neil reported on such discussions at the IBM-sponsored Life Insurance Data Processing Seminar: "The topic appearing frequently in after-hours conversation was the possibility of purchasing EDP systems. IBM personnel usually were not in evidence when this was discussed. It seemed reasonable to many that the cost of the system could be written off in 7 years and that others should follow the lead of at least two companies represented and take advantage of the lease-purchase plan. The fact that purchase price would affect current year's surplus was recognized as a problem but no solution was suggested."[28] Insurance users were interested in buying as soon as the option was offered, although they often hesitated before making what they perceived as a greater commitment to a particular technology.

By the 1960s, the debate continued more publicly. As Goshay noted in 1964, two factors not directly related to financial terms tended to drive insurance firms' decisions about whether to lease or buy: the relationship between the insurance firm and its existing vendor (the loyalty and lock-in factors), and "the outlook of management concerning technological obsolescence."[29] Although remaining with an existing vendor had mixed advantages and disadvantages, the obsolescence factor drew Goshay's ire. He directly opposed the often stated assumption that "greater 'flexibility' and obsolescence protection [may be had] in leasing since the insurer can always terminate the lease agreement when technological opportunities present themselves in the form of new equipment." As he put it,

This statement, however, is rather naïve for two reasons. One is that it premises a pricing process in the market place for computers which has not equated and will not equate such flexibility and protection differences in the costs of leasing vs. purchasing. Equipment lessors, of course, will reflect the cost of obsolescence in their leasing price mechanism.

The second reason is that the statement ignores the significant developmental costs in EDP which tend to "lock-in" the insurer (or any other firm) to a particular type and use of equipment, regardless of whether it is leased or purchased. Technological advance must proceed considerably before these developmental costs can be overcome. Moreover, considerable time elapses before any given system reaches a level of maturity sufficient to permit determination of whether or not more technologically advanced equipment is desirable.[30]

His first argument derived from neoclassical economics and certainly reflected the *perceived* cost of obsolescence, since the actual life of a given technology generation was not initially clear to observers. The "lock-in" argument—here in a very direct form—reflected experience of the time, effort, and cost required to develop a new system. Software development was a large component of these costs, but even with vendor-provided software, installing a new system was expensive and time consuming, making this argument very vivid for insurance firms. Insurance firms were also extremely wary of disrupting their relationships with their customers, reinforcing this argument. Some saw lock-in as applying primarily to buying equipment. For example, Franklin Life's James Cranwill noted in an IASA presentation that one of the potential disadvantages of purchasing is that "you may want to change hardware before it is fully depreciated. You may lock yourself in because you purchased."[31] As Goshay pointed out, however, it applied equally to a firm leasing the equipment.

Beyond these two factors, purely financial analyses of the trade-off also received attention. Ernst and Ernst's Amlung, presenting at the 1969 IASA conference, listed several issues for firms to consider in evaluating the alternatives:

— Determination of the minimum period of use,
— Definition of the financing alternatives,
— Calculation of cash flows under the alternatives,
— Determination of the rate of return or earnings rates to be used,
— Will earnings rates change during the period under review,
— How will the liquidity of the company be affected,
— Factors of obsolescence, residual values, and price level changes,
— Effects on total and price level changes,
— Effects on the financial statements of the company,
— Income tax considerations.[32]

He particularly stressed how the cost of capital, a factor he felt was being ignored by many firms, influenced each alternative's net present value.[33] Cranwill pointed out that life insurance firms differed from most other types of firms in one relevant respect: "We in the life insurance industry are also in the investment business and therefore are normally in a better position to purchase than a company required to borrow such funds."[34] With plenty of funds to invest, life insurance firms did not need to factor in any additional costs of borrowing beyond opportunity costs when deciding whether to purchase or lease.

Another important factor in computing the value of buying versus leasing was the rate of planned computer use.[35] Rental plans, like today's automobile leasing plans, charged extra for use beyond a base level. Thus one advantage of buying over leasing was that "You may use the hardware as much as you like without running into added rental costs."[36] Further complicating the analysis, firms often underestimated in advance how much they would need to use the computer: "The experience of insurers leasing equipment seems to be that additional time is needed (beyond that originally planned) in order to satisfy new demands induced by management's new-found familiarity with and appreciation for the technology—as well as to solve unanticipated operational problems, such as re-runs, testing, and operator inefficiency."[37] The structure of such leasing agreements tended either to increase costs or to discourage new technology uses. Thus, according to Goshay, "There appear to be greater and better opportunities for planning with purchased equipment."[38] The industry discussion of buying versus renting pointed to a complex decision, but one that was now separable from the choice of vendors.

For most life insurance firms, the next major hardware change after the 1401 (or, less frequently, the 7070) was the third-generation IBM System/360, announced in early 1964 for delivery starting in 1965.[39] With this system, IBM was offering the first range of different-sized computers that were all upwardly compatible, allowing relatively easy upward migration *within* the range. However, the System/360, which used a combination of transistors and early integrated circuits, was *much* faster and more powerful than previous computers. It was intended to make IBM's and other manufacturers' existing computers obsolete. This system offered insurance firms a large performance gain but also a significant discontinuity with previous hardware and software. The new system ultimately reinforced IBM's overwhelming domination, which would continue with the 1970 announcement of the 370 range, the 360's more incremental successor. Shortly after IBM announced the System/360, UNIVAC followed with its 1108. Like the 360, it incorporated integrated circuits as well as transistors; moreover, it exceeded the 360's capabilities in supporting multiprocessing, or the linking of multiple processing units.[40] UNIVAC ultimately sold almost 300 of the 1108 systems, a success in UNIVAC's terms but not close to the 3,800 System/360 models of different sizes shipped in 1965 and 1966 alone.[41]

Despite the System/360's apparent leap in technology, with its partial use of integrated circuits and its (not fully realized) potential for time-sharing, most insurance firms adopting it still attempted to migrate processes onto it gradually without immediately transforming them. In part, this reflected IBM's failure to complete the new operating system on time, as discussed in the next section. Indeed, 360s were initially shipped with 1401 emulators, encouraging firms to shift their existing applications onto the 360 without reprogramming—and perhaps changing—them to take advantage of the technology's capabilities beyond increased speed.[42] The snapshots provided in the 1977 LOMA study revealed the progression for just three firms, though Cissley claimed that "the general trends revealed are typical of most companies in the insurance industry."[43] Company A had two 360s by 1967 but still used other models including a 705, a 7074, and several 1400 models. By 1970, that firm had thirteen 360 models of various sizes, and by 1973 it had added some 370s to its 360s. Still, in 1976 it also continued to use a 1401 and a 7074, indicating that it had not yet converted all applications to the new hardware. During the same period, Company B expanded its use of RCA computers but also added its first IBM machines, a 7074 and a 360 model, in 1970. After UNIVAC took over RCA's computer business in 1971, Company B continued to hedge its bets, maintaining both the RCA/UNIVAC machines and a few IBM machines. By 1973 it had added two IBM 370 machines but still operated the RCA computers beside them. Company C, like Company A, used solely IBM machines. Although it was clearly a somewhat smaller firm and had fewer machines, it had added 360s by 1967 and 370s by 1973. As late as 1976, it, like Company A, still had working 1401 machines as well as 360s and 370s. Thus insurance firms moved their processes onto the new 360s gradually (and with the further aid of emulation), smoothing their transition.

The 370 range, announced in 1970, brought further incremental technology advances, with true integrated circuits and semiconductor memory.[44] It also expanded the 360's quite limited time-sharing capabilities. Development of technology for true time-sharing, in which multiple terminals had direct access to the computer and each person could use a terminal as if it were a single computer, was initially encouraged by educational and government users more than by insurance and other commercial users. IBM offered this capability only with the 370, though preliminary versions were available on some later 360 models.[45] This configuration allowed access to data and computations directly, rather than requiring the home or field office employee to send a request to the home office and then wait for it to be batch processed and to receive a response in return, as was typical of most early telecommunications and computer networks in insurance.[46] In late 1970 UNIVAC introduced a computer with similar claims, the 1110, an improvement on the 1108.[47]

This ability to combine a central computer with telecommunications equipment to allow remote access (even if not full time-sharing) proved to be an important advance for insurance. From early on, insurance firms had liked the idea of linking home offices with regional offices or agencies. As early as 1955, Nationwide Insurance acquired a 650 computer and an IBM transceiver that it hoped to use for a premium billing application. "The transmitting and receiving device duplicates sets of punched cards at remote points by means of telephone, telegraph or radio circuit."[48] Through this primitive telecommunications device, Nationwide intended to coordinate the billing process with its fourteen regional offices, rather than to centralize it. This vision apparently took some time to realize, since five years later Nationwide's Robert Kissinger explained at an IASA conference that the company was just then preparing to install a "Data Transceiver system" to link its main and regional offices.[49]

He also described some of the available telecommunications hardware insurance firms could use in following this new trend.[50] He gave the most attention to the Kineplex card and magnetic-tape transmission systems, made by Collins Radio, and to IBM Teleprocessing's equipment, including magnetic-tape terminals and data transceivers, but he also mentioned equipment made by Friden, RCA, and others. Data transmission offered greatly increased speed, the option to transmit data via one medium (punched card or punched paper tape) and receive it on another (magnetic tape), and the ability to use regular toll lines rather than private leased lines. Moreover, Kissinger suggested applications for which data transmission might be useful, including policy rating, billing, file reference, and immediate recording of data from remote locations. The 1963 BLS study also noted this trend toward connecting field offices with home offices using data transmission networks over telephone and telegraph lines.[51] Agents and office employees at peripheral locations could thus transmit queries to the main computer, with responses to queries transmitted back.[52] In the early 1970s, Cissley and colleague Jean Barnes commented that the new minicomputers could also be used as satellite systems at agencies, connected to the large home office computer by a telecommunications network.[53]

Metropolitan Life, with more than 800 district offices in addition to its huge home office, adopted an extensive data communications network. During the early 1960s, it replaced its UNIVACs with large Honeywell computers (800 and 1800 models).[54] In 1963, Metropolitan Life and Honeywell jointly announced the development of a network based on its Honeywell 1800 computer:

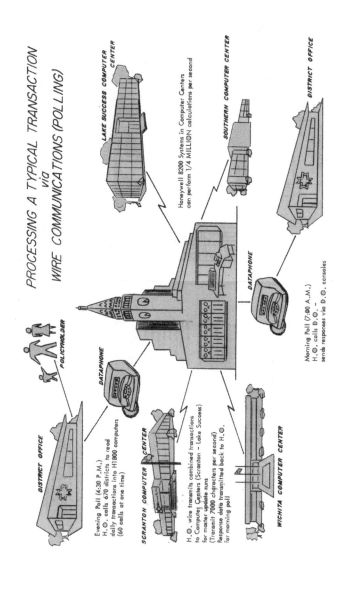

## PROCESSING A TYPICAL TRANSACTION
### *via*
## WIRE COMMUNICATIONS (POLLING)

**DISTRICT OFFICE**

**POLICYHOLDER**

**DATAPHONE**

**LAKE SUCCESS COMPUTER CENTER**

Honeywell 8200 Systems in Computer Centers can perform 1/4 MILLION calculations per second

**SOUTHERN COMPUTER CENTER**

**DISTRICT OFFICE**

**DATAPHONE**

Morning Poll (7:30 A.M.)
H.O. calls D.O. –
sends responses via D.O. consoles

**DISTRICT OFFICE**

Evening Poll (4:30 P.M.)
H.O. calls 670 districts to read daily transactions into H1800 computers (60 calls at one time)

**SCRANTON COMPUTER CENTER**

H.O. wire transmits combined transactions to Computer Centers (Scranton – Lake Success) for master update runs
(Transmit 7000 characters per second)
Response data transmitted back to H.O. for morning poll

**WICHITA COMPUTER CENTER**

*Fig. 7.3.* Metropolitan Life's telecommunications network, built around Honeywell computers linked to the central and district offices by data transmission, integrated field office and headquarters. Pamphlet, ca. 1970, in MetLife Archives, box 19 03 02, folder: Electronics Installations 1970–1986, box 1: 1970+. Reproduced courtesy of MetLife Archives.

The system—which it is believed would be the largest commercial data commu-
nications network in history—will consist of a Honeywell 1800 computer in the
Home Office and a communications console in each of the Company's District
Offices. . . .

Key element [*sic*] in the advanced system will be the data communications console located in each District Office. It will be equipped with an optical scanning
unit capable of reading premium notices and automatically transmitting the data
over long distance telephone lines to the central Honeywell 1800 system.[55]

This scanning unit would read a special bar code imprinted on premium notices before they were mailed out from the home office. Using this system, Metropolitan Life would be able "to maintain up-to-the-minute premium, loan
and insurance records of 29 million policyholders. It also [would] handle inquiries from and answers to the Field."[56] This customized system probably did
not involve true time-sharing, but it may have gone beyond simple data transmission. In any case, it would handle premium bill payments for both ordinary insurance policies and "account policies," previously called industrial insurance policies, collected weekly or monthly at homes.[57] It was scheduled to
be up and running in 1969.

From 1963 through 1969 articles about it ran in company publications, fa-
miliarizing employees with the concept. At the 1965 IASA meeting, Herman
Seltzer, assistant vice president, described the system and showed samples of
the "bar-coded data cards."[58] He ended with a rhetorical flourish emphasizing
the new options that the system created for the firm: "Yesterday's challenges
have become today's opportunities. We are confident that today's opportunities will, in turn, become tomorrow's accomplishments." In 1969, when the
equipment was already installed in most of the offices, the targeted premium
billing service was finally being converted for use on it.[59] Metropolitan Life
had long since moved on from its initial, single-function (actuarial) computer
application to an integrated premium billing and accounting function, but
now it was also incorporating—and perhaps shaping, given the joint press
release—innovative telecommunications technology and procedures to integrate field office and headquarters, extensively transforming existing processes. By the early 1970s, connections to one of four different computer centers around the country supplemented those to the home office (fig. 7.3).[60]

Installing this system with its bar codes and telecommunications network had taken between six and eight years to complete. The company's cost ratios did not show any clear improvement on completion (see fig. 6.5), though the system might have improved service rather than cut costs.[61] In fact, sometime in the mid-1960s, Prudential overtook Metropolitan Life as the largest insurance firm.[62] Nevertheless, the system may have been essential to maintaining the growth that kept Metropolitan Life well ahead of all insurance firms except Prudential.

Over time, new computer capabilities were emerging. By the mid-1970s, the largest computer firms were putting pressure on vendor firms to increase hardware capacity to accommodate their huge numbers of policies and the greater level of integration among processes they were now achieving.[63] The hardware enabled and constrained different insurance processes, but realizing those possibilities awaited firms willing and determined to implement them. Most insurance companies still adopted new hardware slowly, and the ultimate economic impact was still in question. Moreover, software was just as important as hardware to successful computer use.

## The Insurance Industry Faces the Challenges of Software

As Prudential's case showed, acquiring a computer was only the first step in computerization; the subsequent programming of applications could stretch on for years. In the early days, programming costs, consistently underestimated in advance, ran anywhere from 33% to 100% of hardware rental.[64] According to the rough tally that Franklin Life provided in 1962, for example, its conversion costs—which included data entry, programming, and operational costs, but no overhead—came to just under two-thirds of the purchase and installation costs.[65] Insurance firms adopted computers to cut clerical costs in routine data-processing tasks, but during the early 1960s they were realizing, according to Bruce McBeath of Country Life Insurance Company, "the tremendous costs being incurred by companies in the area of systems design and programming required to install computers to perform these various functions." Indeed, he saw these costs as high enough to make firms reconsider the value of computers: "In far too many cases we began hearing that companies were becoming disheartened and dissatisfied with computers. They were pointing out that programming costs had far exceeded predictions, and the anticipated cost savings were not forthcoming."[66] A common pattern of eliminating low-level clerical jobs and creating programming, systems development, and managerial jobs did not necessarily improve the overall cost picture.[67] Programming was becoming a critical bottleneck impeding further advances in insurance computing. From the mid-1950s well into the 1970s, insurance would influence (as well as be influenced by) computer software much more actively than hardware.

## Programming Languages and Operating Systems

During the first decade of commercial computing, vendors and various users worked together to develop higher-level symbolic programming languages— farther from machine language and closer to English—to speed up and simplify programming. Grace Hopper of Remington Rand devised the first language intended for business programming, FLOWMATIC, for the UNIVAC.[68] Metropolitan Life helped shape that language by providing its initial testing ground, one of its new computers, in 1956. FLOWMATIC would, in turn, influence the most important subsequent development.

In 1959 the U.S. Department of Defense, which wanted to be able to port its business programs from machine to machine rather than reprogram them from scratch for every new computer, established the Committee on Data Systems and Languages (CODASYL), representing computer manufacturers, users, and government agencies, to design a new standard language for business data processing. This committee was further divided into a short-range and an intermediate-range committee.[69] By 1960 the short-range committee, made up of programming experts from vendors and government agencies, had created the first version of COBOL (Common Business Oriented Language). Initially conceiving this effort as an interim solution until the intermediate-range committee created the real product, committee members leaned heavily on existing vendor-specific languages, especially FLOWMATIC. No entirely new product was forthcoming, however; instead, COBOL would evolve from this original version, dominating business computing for the next several decades. Users, including several insurance firms, were members of the intermediate-range committee, shaping the language's continued development.[70] Under pressure from the Department of Defense, all hardware manufacturers soon provided COBOL compilers, or programs translating COBOL into machine language, thus decreasing insurance programming costs.

Operating systems, a machine-specific software layer that would mediate between the compiler and the application software, were also problematic. Early computers came without operating systems, though the various computer vendors provided their customers access to libraries of preprogrammed routines that would eventually be consolidated into operating systems. Users sometimes collaborated to develop operating systems. The SHARE user group of IBM 704 users shared operating systems as well as other software, and GUIDE, established in 1956, did the same for business users of IBM 650, 702, and 705 computers, presumably including some of the many insurance firms that adopted those models.[71] When IBM announced the System/360 in 1964, it promised to deliver an operating system with it. That promise proved difficult to live up to, however, and in 1965 IBM provided the initial machines with 1401 emulators.[72] John R. Redfern, then an IBM salesman, later asserted that emulator use masked the potentially revolutionary change offered by System/360: "I don't think anybody, even within the industry, realized the quantum leap when . . . we went from 1401 to 360, no one really realized how powerful that machine was. One of the reasons they didn't is the 360 was announced with OS [operating system], was never delivered with OS. . . . We got to the point with slippages and deliveries, that what we did is we delivered it with a 1401 emulator. So people could use their 360 to run [1401 software] just like it ran [on] the 1401 [but] ten times faster."[73] The 360 was so much more powerful than the 1401 (and the 7070) that even with software emulation it achieved significant speed gains. Using emulators, rather than the operating system designed to take advantage of the 360's power, allowed life insurance firms to continue their incremental migration of processes without fundamental transformation, easing the transition to the System/360 line.

Higher-level programming languages, libraries of routines, operating systems, and emulators all helped decrease programming time, especially for large firms that needed to program their own customized systems. But these improvements still did not eliminate the thorny problems insurance firms encountered in programming applications. Off-the-shelf application software for insurance, emerging from the interaction of major equipment vendors with the insurance industry, addressed this dilemma for many medium-sized or small insurance firms. The computer equipment manufacturers had initially offered hardware customers access to their libraries of programmed routines for general functions like report generation.[74] As programming difficulties and costs became more salient, such libraries were not sufficient, and vendors began to develop application programs for several large user industries, including insurance. Before IBM unbundled its software from its hardware in 1969, hardware vendors were the primary external sources of insurance application programs. After the unbundling, an application software industry grew up to serve the insurance industry, reconfiguring insurance companies' options.[75] During the 1960s, insurance actively shaped software, more than hardware, resulting in a continuation of the integrated operation first suggested in the Society of Actuaries committee report and its consolidated functions approach.

## Application Software before Unbundling

Apparently the first and certainly the best known of the vendor-produced insurance software packages was IBM's '62 CFO, designed for its popular 1401 tape computer.[76] This set of programs was not intended for (or used by) the largest firms, both because those firms needed larger computers to handle all their insurance policies and because they preferred to develop their own systems around what they perceived as unique needs. According to Prudential's Malcolm MacKinnon, for example, "We liked to do things the Prudential way."[77] But for small and medium-sized firms that were considering acquiring a 1401, '62 CFO could reduce programming time and costs enormously. Based on the consolidated functions approach that the Society of Actuaries committee had designed a decade earlier, this set of programs handled premium billing, accounting, and related functions for ordinary insurance. Country Life's McBeath explained the program's origins:

> IBM, one of the computer manufacturers, being close to the problem [of high application programming costs] and aware of its impact on their market set out to do something about it. In addition to engineering changes in computers to simplify programming, they assembled a systems and programming team to develop a Consolidated Functions System for Ordinary Life Insurance with three primary objectives:
>
> 1. To develop a systems approach for computers that will allow automatic processing of all scheduled transactions and requested processing for all nonscheduled transactions involving Ordinary Life contracts.
> 2. To write a series of computer programs for the 1401 which will perform all record-keeping functions on a daily, monthly, or annual cycle for Ordinary Life Insurance contracts and miscellaneous accounting applications that are directly related to Ordinary Life Insurance contracts.
> 3. To test and document these computer programs to such an extent that they

can be used broadly throughout the Life Insurance Industry as operational computer programs or as a guide in the development of personalized total systems on an individual company basis.[78]

The Society of Actuaries report shaped this software product from the beginning. Moreover, according to Aetna's O'Neil, present at the spring 1962 workshop where IBM unveiled the still-unfinished software, IBM had worked with an actuarial consultant and several life insurance firms during '62 CFO's development.[79]

This software's progress in the insurance industry may be traced in IASA presentations. At the 1963 meeting, the application software package was only on the horizon, with no presenting firms yet using it. In discussing how to implement the consolidated functions plans on small-scale computers, two representatives of small insurance firms referred to '62 CFO as something to consider, though they were not yet ready to endorse it.[80] By the following year, however, it had caught on among medium-sized firms represented at the IASA conference, with three presenters discussing how their firms were using it. As McBeath described, Country Life adopted the package with only minor modifications: "The programs are flexible enough to be modified to conform to the desires of almost any company. Any program can be modified as long as the basic philosophy of it is not violated. If you begin to change the philosophy, your program modifications will conflict with all programs, since all programs are tied together for the ultimate result."[81] Although enthusiastic, he added that the package did not eliminate all the work involved in conversion: "In closing I would like to illustrate my appraisal of '62 CFO in this manner. . . . We now have an objective we wish to reach—automatic processing of ordinary life insurance—'62 CFO is the Santa Fe Trail for this objective. It is clearly marked and documented. There will be some hardships along the way. However, if you follow the trail, I'm sure you will reach the objective." Speaking for Republic National Life, Robert Baines discussed using '62 CFO in a modified form on his firm's new 1410 computer.[82] He even described having "collaborated with the '62 CFO programmers" to develop one particular variation. Finally, Provident Mutual's W. K. Headly explained that although his firm's particular 1400 series hardware configuration did not work with '62 CFO, his company found the package very useful as a guide for activities ranging from broad problem definition to training.[83]

The insurance industry apparently widely shared these favorable impressions. In that same year, a western regional '62 CFO user group was established, the first of three such user groups to be formed.[84] By 1972, seventy-five life insurance companies attended meetings of this regional '62 CFO user group. IASA papers over the next few years demonstrate that the package was widely accepted and that both insurance users and IBM benefited from it. In 1965 Douglas Smith quantified the savings '62 CFO offered, based on Guarantee Mutual Life's experiences: "If a company were to adopt CFO in its entirety, about 35 man-years of research, planning, and programming would be saved. We realized a savings of approximately 22 man-years in our [significantly modified] installation."[85] As IBM hoped, the software attracted customers to the hardware. For example, George Tindall of the North American Company claimed that his firm "decided to order an IBM 1401, specifically to utilize the IBM 'package' of programs for Life Insurance known as '62 CFO."[86] Indeed, insurance industry sources then and now consider '62 CFO, used by 250–300 insurance companies, to be the most successful insurance software package ever.[87] The reciprocal influences of the insurance industry on IBM's software and of that software on the industry were strong.

Further, the 1401 computer and the '62 CFO software reinforced each other's popularity in the insurance industry. IBM's decision to create such a life insurance package made sense, since insurance was, according to contemporary sources, the second most intense computer user industry during the 1960s.[88] By reducing the programming time and cost each firm had to invest, IBM made it easier for the many small and medium-sized firms to adopt a 1401 computer. The North American Company, for example, converted the firm's life and health policies onto '62 CFO using only one and one half months' work from a team of three.[89] This increased ease of adoption both broadened the 1401's market and helped prevent these small insurance firms from going to other vendors with less expensive equipment. Moreover, IBM's choice of the consolidated functions ordinary application illustrates the ongoing influence of the Society of Actuaries committee. Still, some firms implemented only a few of the package's subroutines, suggesting that they were not yet ready to take full advantage of the 1401's capabilities. In general, however, the '62 CFO package encouraged further convergence of ordinary insurance methods and organization among small firms, helping them to begin consolidating related functions in a single application.

IBM had established its reputation, in both the tabulator and computer eras, as providing full customer service, not just equipment—an example of what

Alfred D. Chandler Jr. has called "long-term functional learning" in the marketing and customer services areas.[90] According to one history of computing, "only IBM guaranteed a complete solution to business problems," rather than equipment and a new set of problems.[91] Thus IBM's leadership in offering such an application package was not surprising. Although bundling software with hardware was common practice among the era's computer vendors, IBM did so most aggressively.[92] UNIVAC offered only general-purpose routines for functions such as report generation, contributing to its competitive disadvantage vis-à-vis IBM. But Honeywell, another firm that marketed heavily to the insurance industry, attempted to compete in providing targeted software applications, as well as its H-200 computer, designed to be plug-compatible with the IBM 1401. This head-on competition had already led it to offer the Liberator program for translating 1401 software to the H-200, encouraging what it positioned as an upgrade to a faster machine. But by the late 1960s Honeywell also developed its own competitive package, called the TIP (Total Information Processing) system.[93] D. W. Stinson, a former IBM software developer, later characterized TIP as "the CFO system . . . put into Honeywell language with front and rear extensions" and an example of "IBM competition recognizing the importance of industry-oriented software."[94] Still, IBM's '62 CFO dominated sessions at IASA and LOMA conferences, reflecting IBM's lead in this market.

Although IBM's external competition in life insurance application software was not strong, when it launched the 360 range of computers, it put itself in competition with its own product. IBM provided support for emulating the 1401 on the 360 and continuing to use '62 CFO, an approach adopted by many firms; however, that approach did not take full advantage of the speed and other new capabilities the 360 architecture offered, including direct-access storage and inquiry and telecommunications capabilities.[95] Thus in 1964, only two years after the introduction of '62 CFO, IBM insurance marketers met a group of insurance industry representatives to discuss IBM's development of a consolidated functions insurance package for the System/360.[96] During the next year, when the first IBM 360 machines were shipped, IBM began work on the new software system, this time with the ongoing participation of insurance representatives. The package suffered multiple delays, making its belated official appearance only in 1969. Writing from the vantage point of the early 1990s, Gregory Jordahl noted, "While the 360 quickly became overwhelmingly successful, the insurance software systems written for it by IBM in 1965—

ALIS (Advanced Life Insurance System) and PALIS (Property and Liability Insurance System)—did not."[97]

ALIS was intended to extend, not just replicate, '62 CFO. It processed a single daily run to accomplish all routine policy functions and special periodic runs for reporting purposes.[98] Moreover, as Allen Johnson, IBM insurance industry specialist, explained to IASA members, it would use the 360's direct-access storage and telecommunications capabilities "to provide status and several types of quotations via a teleprocessing terminal" that allowed individuals within the home office (and potentially at regional offices) to make direct online inquiries—a limited form of time-sharing—rather than waiting for the next batch processing.[99] Dale Pearson, of Equitable Life of Iowa, pointed out that "the availability of mass storage facilities with immediate access capabilities" was particularly attractive to potential users.[100] Based on these projected capabilities, industry representatives initially discussed future conversion to ALIS quite enthusiastically.[101]

As the package reached beta test stage, however, representatives from at least two of the five insurance companies testing it were less pleased.[102] In explaining that the ALIS rate file would be on tape rather than disk, Pearson noted that "the monitor companies did not agree with this philosophy, but IBM felt the disk approach would raise the minimum machine configuration needed to install and operate ALIS."[103] Then he elaborated what he saw as the basic problem with the ALIS development effort: "Herein lies one of the basic problems that must have contributed substantially to the unexpected delays in the completion of the ALIS project. The company was committed to provide software for a minimum configuration and this restriction worked hardships on the project team." The wide range of machines in the 360 line, from smallish machines to quite large ones, were all, in theory, compatible, but ALIS's program design depended on the configuration chosen. IBM designed ALIS for the 360/30, close to the minimum configuration, so as to target the same segment that had used '62 CFO.[104] This approach fit IBM's marketing strategy, but it disappointed big insurance firms that had looked forward to using this package when they adopted the larger 360 models.

The long delay in releasing ALIS also created problems for insurance firms that received their 360 machines well before the software, partially accounting for the many companies that either adapted '62 CFO to the 360 system or developed their own systems, sometimes in the same time or less.[105] Prudential, for example, conceived its AOS (Advanced Ordinary System) for integrating multiple processes before the System/360 was announced and implemented it in the year IBM released ALIS.[106] The delayed 1969 release posed another problem: only months later, in the face of government antitrust activity, IBM would fundamentally change the market by unbundling its hardware and its software, thus changing ALIS from a "free" product to a costly one. In light of all these negative factors, ALIS, unsurprisingly, enjoyed much less success than '62 CFO. For example, in 1972, when seventy-five user firms attended one of four regional '62 CFO user groups, only twenty-nine attended the single ALIS user group.

A company's alternative to using vendor-provided software or developing its own was hiring a third-party service provider either to develop the software or to provide data-processing services that included software. Although this approach was unusual before unbundling, it was possible.[107] Software companies that created customized application software for their clients appeared early, though sparsely. Prudential was a prominent early insurance client for such customized applications. As early as 1956 it funded Computer Usage Corporation's (CUC) development of an actuarial program that ran on the IBM 650 computer; CUC, which has claimed to be "the world's first computer software company," considered this its "first nontechnical application."[108] The packaged software industry getting started in the mid- to late 1960s was even less significant before unbundling.[109] Nevertheless, in 1969 Prudential purchased Mark IV, a proprietary file management system, from the Advanced Information Systems Division of Informatics to allow a nonprogrammer to generate pension reports.[110] Some firms thus addressed the programming problems and expenses by hiring firms to do custom development or by purchasing the rare general-purpose packaged software.

The computer service companies offered more than the application software itself—they offered services, as well. Electronic Data Systems Corporation (EDS), which Ross Perot, a dissatisfied former IBM salesman, founded in 1962, was one such company.[111] It offered what came to be known as facilities management services—a contract to run a firm's entire data-processing operation. Perot targeted the life insurance industry early on, acquiring Dallas-based Mercantile Securities Life as the first of many insurance company clients. By the mid-1960s, EDS hired two people from the life insurance industry who had installed '62 CFO in their former life insurance firms to develop software for and sell services to other life insurance firms.[112] The EDS facilities management approach offered fairly comprehensive packages of application software and computer services but required that the clients relinquish control of their own facilities, and many companies were not willing to do so. Other service companies also attempted to gain life insurance customers, though typically offering a less comprehensive bundle of services.[113]

The SPAN Data Processing Center represented a final service arrangement. This service organization was created in 1955, when Aetna Insurance Company (a fire and casualty firm) persuaded three other small fire and casualty insurance companies, each too small to support a large computer independently, to combine forces and jointly buy a computer.[114] SPAN—named for the four companies: Springfield, Phoenix, Aetna, and National—first acquired an IBM 705 and later progressed to the IBM 7070 and 7074, in each case developing software to serve all four companies. These programs were not widely available packages such as '62 CFO, but all four member firms used them, gaining some software development economies by enforcing some standardization across the four. In 1963, after two of the four had withdrawn from the arrangement because they had been acquired, Aetna Life Insurance Affiliated Companies ultimately bought SPAN, though it continued to serve its former owners as well as Aetna Life.

In the face of rising programming costs that threatened the gains promised by computers, insurance firms turned to several sources of relief, from vendor-provided software to computer services firms, with the most popular solution being IBM's '62 CFO software shaped by the 1952 report of the Society of Actuaries committee. It promised to transform insurance processes by integrating the insurance functions kept separate through most of the tabulator period, but in practice it reinforced the incremental approach to this change already comfortable to many companies. Because the package had many separate programs, it allowed firms to integrate at their own pace—probably a factor in its popularity. While IBM's '62 CFO was the most important package for life insurance, software applications for less core functions, such as pension management, also emerged during this period.[115] The software landscape as it existed in the late 1960s was about to undergo a profound change, however, that permanently altered insurance firms' options, encouraging a greater variety of approaches.

## Unbundling and the Emergence of Packaged Application Software for Insurance

A general market for packaged programs was just beginning to develop in the late 1960s. The IBM System/360 provided the "first stable industry-standard platform," allowing a very few products such as the Mark IV file management system to appear on the market.[116] According to one computer history, "the market for software packages was still in its infancy, however, with fewer than fifty products on open sale." This market development was "dramatically accelerated" in December 1968, when IBM announced that it would unbundle its software from its hardware over the next year, pricing the two separately.[117] In that same month, Control Data Corporation filed a private antitrust suit against IBM, citing violations of IBM's 1956 consent decree, starting what has been called "A Generation of Litigation."[118] Although IBM claimed publicly that it decided to unbundle primarily in response to the rising software development costs, the move probably responded primarily to the antitrust threat.[119]

Whatever the impetus for IBM's decision, its effect was to spur the development of software firms and software products, including those aimed at insurance.[120] According to a founder of Cybertek Computer Products, who was previously on the IBM programming team that developed '62 CFO, "nearly all the software companies that were founded right after IBM unbundled started out by providing the peripheral functions a company needed to make '62 CFO more versatile."[121] Cybertek's main products included systems designed to augment that package and ALIS.[122] Taking another approach to the new opportunities, Tracor Computing Corporation (TCC), started in 1969, developed its own consolidated functions system, called Life 70, to compete with '62 CFO.[123] By 1971, EDS had also developed a standard insurance software package to offer as part of its facilities management contract.[124] Reflecting the active role insurance firms had frequently taken in shaping many information technology developments for their use, fifteen relatively large life insurance firms combined forces in 1969 to found Insurance Systems of America (ISA), with a stated mission "to develop applications systems and related installation services for the life insurance industry." ISA offered "applications packages, consulting services, and custom contract services."[125] Similarly, Equitable collaborated with Informatics, a general software vendor, in creating Equimatics, a joint venture to design life insurance software application packages. Whether founded by users or by software and service providers, these and many other start-ups contributed to an expanding market for insurance application software.

Insurance firms and existing service companies initially struggled to understand unbundling's impact on their own operations.[126] Clearly, prices associated with software per se would rise, since vendor software had previously been "free" to those who used it. Beyond that, the speakers at the 1970 IASA program knew only that the repricing of hardware and software would make all of them "think quite differently in the future."[127] One speaker attempted to map the new territory, identifying four types of software firms an insurance company could turn to in computerizing the pension business: service bureaus; system development firms, which built customized programs for the firm; proprietary package firms, which sold off-the-shelf packages; and firms marketing packages created from proprietary systems developed by insurance companies.[128] Thus the emerging software industry was beginning to take form.

By 1971, the IASA conference program reflected a better understanding of and a more proactive approach to the new opportunities appearing in the wake of unbundling. In one panel, representatives of three different life insurance firms evaluated insurance software systems and services for IASA members.[129] The Berkshire Life Insurance Company's Robert Plageman, for example, attempted to give a balanced assessment of packaged software: "Let me assure you that it is not the pot of gold at the end of the rainbow. It is usually, but not always, quicker to achieve results, but for this you must pay more dollars. It may be more error free, but for this you have to fit your operation into their package; it may save you some analysis and programming time to implement, but you may pay for this by more time to adapt and maintain through its life-time. These and many other items are to be weighed in the evaluation of a proposal."[130] Despite this cautious introductory note, he ended his talk by affirming the role of packaged software in the insurance industry: "There is no doubt in my mind that package software is in its infancy. We should see it grow and mature and play a bigger part in our processing lives over the next five years. . . . The concept is sound and we'd better learn how to live with [software packages] and maximize profits from them if we hope to continue to grow in this computer age."[131] This comment proved to be prophetic.

Indeed, by 1972 insurance firms were taking advantage of the proliferating software firms, products, and services. In that year, LOMA issued its first software catalog in response to "the vast number of software packages being developed" for insurance, the "increasing utilization of these packages by the life insurance industry," and the many software-related inquiries made to its offices.[132] The catalog was based on a membership survey to find out what vendors were being used, followed by a survey of the vendors named. It contained data on eighty-one vendors and more than 275 software packages broken down into twenty-five categories, of which the most numerous were individual insurance—life, actuarial, CFO support systems, and ALIS support systems.

Some firms built products around IBM's '62 CFO or created CFO-related applications for IBM 360 or 370 computers.[133] Some developed alternatives to ALIS to help '62 CFO users move to IBM 360 hardware, and others developed similar application packages for non-IBM hardware, such as Network Data Processing Corporation's LILA (Life Insurance Logistics Automated) and related programs for the Burroughs, Honeywell, UNIVAC, and NCR hardware.[134] Many had multiple packages, adding new application areas from file management systems to real estate and mutual funds applications.

Subsequent LOMA publications also attempted to evaluate software.[135] Similarly, the 1972 IASA conference program included several papers evaluating software packages. Rayford Freemon of Beneficial Computer Services claimed that his firm had evaluated twenty software packages or services in the preceding four years, of which it had purchased fourteen.[136] Some new software companies presented their own software packages at these conferences, including, for example, one intended to assist in underwriting.[137] These many publications and presentations helped LOMA and IASA member firms choose from the expanding options in custom and packaged software as well as computer services.

As the programming task had grown more enormous, an insurance software and services industry had begun to emerge. By separating the software and hardware decisions and by making the cost of software visible, IBM's unbundling decision spurred this emergence. Even though smaller insurance firms, especially, were giving up the notion that they could do all their own development work, the insurance industry continued its tradition of influencing the information-processing industry by engaging with the new software vendors, both individually and through industry associations. The expansion of the software and services industry around insurance supported the continued incremental migration of processes. Initially the majority of packages centered around the consolidated functions plan. As more firms achieved this core application, however, the industry offered new packages to handle unrelated functions, allowing movement into new arenas and continued change of insurance processes to take advantage of new hardware capabilities.

## Insurance Use of Computers into the 1970s

Insurance adoption of hardware and application software reveals a central trend of gradual migration toward (and ultimately beyond) a consolidated functions application to manage ordinary insurance operations as an integrated whole. That trend, however, does not reflect the full range of insurance computer use into the 1970s. Insurers also computerized other processes and focused individually and collectively on other related issues, as period studies and LOMA and IASA proceedings demonstrate.

The 1964 LOMA survey discussed earlier presented a snapshot of computer applications achieved by the mid-1960s, reflecting the ongoing influence of the consolidated functions plan as a goal that was yet to be attained.[138] All responding firms had some computer applications in the ordinary life insurance line, with premium billing and accounting the most common, closely followed by commission calculation and accounting and policy loans and accounting. These applications were all part of a consolidated functions plan, but companies were not asked whether they used prepackaged software such as '62 CFO but rather what insurance functions they had computerized and whether these functions were consolidated with others. Still, their responses suggest that even those with '62 CFO often were not using all the program modules. Those companies with IBM 1400 series computers, for which it was developed, consolidated from none to thirty-eight different life insurance applications into a subsystem, suggesting wide disparities in how it was used.[139] Among all firms with medium-scale computers, those using even the two most popular applications dropped rapidly from 88% (premium billing) to 51% (dividend calculation). The proportion that used each of these two applications integrated with any others was even lower (75% and 32%). Several firms claimed to be studying additional functions for consolidation, suggesting that they were still progressing toward but had not yet achieved the consolidated functions approach originally envisioned by the Society of Actuaries committee.[140]

Meanwhile, several applications unrelated to a consolidated functions plan had appeared in a few companies. The survey revealed, for example, policy-writing applications in 20% of firms with medium-scale computers and 46% of those with large-scale computers, actuarial research and analysis in 24% and 59%, and underwriting in 4% and 5%.[141] The survey also revealed that many insurance firms had diversified their business, and computer applications, into additional insurance areas, including individual health insurance, group life and health insurance, and debit weekly and monthly insurance (industrial insurance).[142] Finally, many firms had general computer applications, including most commonly payroll, income tax withholding statements, general ledger accounting, and mortgage accounting and servicing, uses that were roughly half as common as those included in the consolidated functions approach to ordinary life insurance but still more common than underwriting or actuarial analysis.[143] A very few firms were using computers for forecasting, "one of the newer fields of computer usage," focusing on managers' earnings, available cash, and income tax. In the mid-1960s, then, insurance computer users focused most heavily on the operational processes pertaining to ordinary life insurance and on firmwide functions such as payroll and mortgage accounting. Other applications were less common, and more advanced uses such as forecasting were quite rare.

The shifting concerns of LOMA and IASA members from the late 1950s to the late 1970s demonstrated what they considered most important. The triennial Loma Systems Forums focused on the following topics, as summarized by Charles Cissley:

1959—Programming and debugging; converting from punched cards; organizing the DP effort

1962—Revising first-generation systems; data validation and control

1965—Integrating systems; total systems concepts; data security and control

1969—Consolidation of functions; direct-access processing; teleprocessing

1971—Role of the user in systems development and operation; management science applications

1974—Management of the systems function; data base management and data communications

1977—Physical and data security; privacy; image processing; satellite communications[144]

The issues that dominated the first two forums were practical implementation issues. In the mid- to late 1960s, integrated and consolidated systems for ordinary life insurance took center stage, and only in the 1970s did they finally become less central to these meetings, allowing issues such as teleprocessing, management science, and database applications to emerge more prominently.

Annual IASA proceedings give a finer-grained view of such concerns. Although the 1960s started with a big question, when Continental Casualty Company's Carl Orkild asked whether computers could be justified—a question he ultimately answered positively—interests quickly focused on the practical details of programming methods and costs, maintaining data controls, and implementing particular applications.[145] By 1962 premium billing and accounting applications, as well as consolidated functions applications on various hardware bases, dominated.[146] For the first time, conference speakers discussed problems in converting from one computer to another, indicating that firms were migrating from first-generation to second-generation machines.[147] Paul McAnarney of Franklin Life assessed successes and failures of that firm's data-processing efforts—predictably emphasizing the successes more than any failings.[148] Discussions of the '62 CFO program and other consolidated functions methods dominated the 1963–65 conferences.[149] By 1965, IASA members increasingly introduced new approaches and applications such as the integration of health policies into the CFO system, an electronic policy index allowing random access, and data transmission both within and between sites.[150] The 1966 and 1967 conferences focused on both implementations of consolidated functions plans and new and innovative technologies and applications.

By 1968 and 1969, IBM's ALIS package, still being developed, was the most popular topic, with many papers exploring what it would offer and complaining about its shortcomings and delayed release.[151] Perhaps the most interesting new applications allowed employees dispersed within the main office or at a district office to make real-time queries. George Lukens described Travelers' fairly advanced "on-line real-time system" using UNIVAC computers, IBM teleprocessing equipment, and Western Union leased lines to allow inquiries and policy record changes, more or less in real time.[152] These new applications, though still the minority, embraced new models of working enabled by the new technologies. In the 1968 through 1970 IASA conferences, sessions focused on training and retaining EDP personnel, suggesting that firms were now turning to longer-range issues of building EDP departments.[153]

IBM's software unbundling and its implications for the emerging software industry dominated the early 1970s conferences. At the same time, some presenters discussed new applications such as pension programs and annual statement preparation, whether as packages offered by the new software vendors or as systems developed within insurance firms.[154] Using computers to improve service to insurance policyholders was also an important topic.[155] Based on papers presented, many companies were interested in online inquiry systems, innovative data entry methods such as those involving optical character recognition, and database systems, among other topics.[156] Franklin Life's Cranwill, for example, considered his firm's direct input on a cathode-ray tube (CRT) console an "unusual" EDP application, indicating that it was still pioneering new uses of technology.[157] The 1973–75 conferences focused on EDP management issues, including training and retaining personnel, but also EDP project management and "non-in-house" or externally contracted EDP.[158] These topics reflect industry concerns about computerization costs that continued to rise.

The early 1970s IASA conferences also considered the notion of management information systems (MIS).[159] Recent research has explored the emergence in the 1950s and ultimate decline in the late 1960s of the "'totally integrated management information system' (MIS)—a comprehensive computerized system designed to span all administrative and managerial activities."[160] Coming from the broad systems and procedures movement, the "systems men" who championed MIS attempted to establish their authority over computers and management. In 1968, a backlash against the original MIS concept gained momentum in the broad U.S. information systems community, especially among corporate management and accountants, resulting in its replacement by a watered-down version.[161] During the 1960s, presenters at LOMA and IASA meetings did not show much interest in MIS, focusing more on the insurance industry's consolidated functions approach than on broader trends in computing.[162] Only in the early 1970s did the MIS concept attract life insurance attention, as the industry opened to external influences. By this time, however, insurance had missed the height of the MIS fad and was considering the watered-down version. As the mid-1970s approached, online systems and telecommunications, along with databases, record keeping, and EDP management, seemed to dominate the literature.

Cissley's 1977 LOMA-sponsored book surveyed insurance computing in the late 1970s, closing out the period studied. From this vantage point Cissley reported that the industry had started with "the major home office housekeeping functions: billing, accounting, policyowners' dividends, and agents' commissions."[163] Insurers developed computer applications for these functions first because they were easy to define, offered clear cost benefits, provided relatively simple applications with which firms could learn about computers and programming, and had typically already been automated by punched-card processing, allowing easier conversion. Despite these advantages, however, companies computerized these initial processes unevenly and did not realize the benefits unequivocally.[164] According to Cissley, system design on the first-generation, vacuum tube–based computers such as the UNIVAC or the IBM 650 drew on the unit-record concept from punched-card tabulators, while system design on second-generation, transistor-based computers such as the IBM 1401 focused on consolidating previously separate files into one, as in '62 CFO.[165] Only after they adopted third-generation hardware with "miniaturized" or integrated circuits, such as the IBM 360 and 370 systems, did firms move on to more complex tasks such as actuarial analysis, statistical forecasting, reserve valuation, and teleprocessing.

Cissley's general trajectory from single applications based on unit records, to consolidated file applications, to more complex tasks fits the pattern traced above. It was not, however, driven by hardware alone, as Cissley implies, but also by insurance firms' use of new technologies to migrate very gradually from old to fundamentally new processes, rather than to transform themselves all at once. Even on first-generation computers, firms such as Franklin Life and Pacific Mutual, which embraced rapid transformation, implemented consolidated applications, while by 1964, even though the third-generation IBM 360 had just been announced, most firms were still focused on consolidating files and applications. By the late 1960s and early 1970s, many—though not all—firms had achieved an initial integrated application and were seeking more innovative ways of using computing technologies, as well as better ways of organizing the EDP operation.

By the mid-1970s, then, insurance computerization had finally and gradually progressed to and even beyond the consolidated functions approach proposed by the Society of Actuaries committee and based on the integrated premium billing and accounting applications of the late tabulator era. Results of this activity are difficult to judge. Expense ratios for ordinary insurance gradually *increased* rather than *decreased* from the 1950s to the mid-1970s (fig. 7.4), perhaps reflecting the enormous resources poured into computerization. Yet by the later 1970s the expense ratio began to drop again.[166] Was this reduction a delayed payoff for computerization, an indication that firms had not, until the 1970s, made the organizational changes necessary to gain full benefit from their hardware and software investments? In the mid-1960s George Delehanty suggested this organizational explanation for weak results to date.[167] More recently, economists of information technology have made similar arguments in accounting for the productivity paradox.[168] Clearly the card-based vision of data-processing hardware and the consolidated functions vision of insurance applications, both originating in the tabulator era, shaped

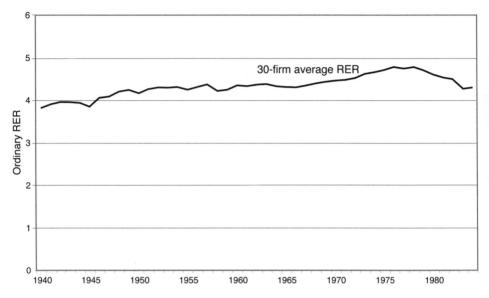

*Fig. 7.4.* Average ordinary renewal expense ratio for the largest thirty firms rose from 1940 to 1974 and then fell from 1975 into the 1980s. *Best's,* 1940–85.

insurance computing until the mid- to late 1960s, when other types of hardware and applications rose in importance. Most firms achieved fundamentally different, integrated operating processes not by rapid transformation but by incremental migration. This gradual process began in the 1950s and dominated the industry's computerization until the 1970s.

# CHAPTER 8

# Case Studies in Insurance Computing

New England Mutual Life and Aetna Life

The previous two chapters have demonstrated how insurance firms typically moved from tabulators to computers. This chapter shows how the influence of the tabulating past and the tension between the desire for overnight transformation and the preference for incremental migration played out in two moderately large insurance firms—New England Mutual Life Insurance Company and Aetna Life Insurance Company.[1] These firms were larger than Pacific Mutual, Franklin Life, and most other firms but significantly smaller than Metropolitan Life, Prudential, and Equitable. Like Pacific Mutual and Franklin Life, they lacked the volume that allowed Metropolitan Life to acquire its initial computer for only one function. Like the giants, however, they had too many policies for a consolidated functions application on a UNIVAC or an IBM 1401 to handle. These cases highlight, among other things, how both individual actors and institutionalized structures shape evolving computer use.

## New England Mutual Life

New England Mutual Life, "the first mutual life insurance company chartered in America," ranked eleventh in assets in 1952.[2] It was more than three times larger than Pacific Mutual or Franklin Life but still less than half the size of John Hancock and one-seventh that of Metropolitan Life.[3] In its earliest days, New England Mutual Life, having acquired several Arithmeters, led insurance firms in the use of computational technology; it did not, however, play a comparable leadership role in the tabulator and early computer eras.[4] Only in the 1970s and 1980s did one executive, supported by others above and below him in the company hierarchy, propel it again to the forefront.

In the 1940s and early 1950s, the firm lagged behind many insurance companies in technology use, depending on miscellaneous, unrelated office equipment to accomplish various tasks. For example, it used Addressographs to issue premium bills, Burroughs' Moon-Hopkins accounting machines to handle policy loans, and IBM punched-card tabulators to perform actuarial (but not operational) work.[5] In 1951, when many insurance firms were acquiring IBM 604 electronic calculators and studying how they might use computers when they became available, New England Mutual Life's in-house monthly publication described its newest office machines, "Convé files," which were large desk-type file cabinets with an electrical foot pedal for advancing the contents to a designated place.[6] Remington Rand had specially designed these relatively low technology units for the company. As late as 1955, the Actuarial Department added an IBM 407, not even the newer 604 electronic tabulator, to its installation.[7] In office machines, New England Mutual Life was a frequent, though not exclusive, customer of Remington Rand.[8]

In early 1955, as the first firms adopted UNIVAC or IBM 650 computers, New England Mutual Life established its Electronic Data Processing (EDP) Committee, as well as a task force to consult with manufacturers and peer organizations and to receive computer training.[9] In announcing this move internally, it demonstrated its sensitivity to employment concerns, announcing that, should the company "go electronic," two rules would apply: "No employee will lose a job because of the machine," and "An intensive training program will be set up to train present employees for the new methods and machines."[10] This announcement began a series of related articles appearing in the in-house magazine over subsequent months.[11] They attempted to debunk fear of "automation," which had reemerged since the war, extending from the factory floor into the office.[12] Arguing that automation would by itself neither "create a glorious new world" nor "destroy our society altogether," one article laid out the committee's view of computers: "Computers cannot think and they are not brains, electronic or otherwise. Nor is automation a force beyond the control of man. It is simply an industrial technique, whose results will depend upon the human beings who control it."[13] The same article pictured the new IBM 407 accounting machine that the Actuarial Department had just acquired, with a caption beginning, "The right machines in the right places are essential to the efficient operations of a prosperous company." This juxtaposition clearly signaled continuity between pre-computer and computer technology.

The series continued these themes, attempting to inform employees about future EDP at New England Mutual Life, thus reducing their anxieties. The articles frequently reiterated that computers were nothing without human intelligence to run them ("The so-called electronic brain is in effect a moron with a filing system"; "The hard-working obedient moron which is an electronic computer is helpless without the direction of a human mind"). In addition, they emphasized that jobs were not in danger ("No one will lose his job, job status, or salary level") and that, in fact, automation was necessary to achieve the efficiency needed to keep the company competitive and growing ("Everyone's job security will be increased as [New England Mutual Life] strengthens its sales position in a highly competitive industry").[14] One article described computer applications at some other insurance firms, including both Metropolitan Life's initial actuarial application and "the so-called combined operations approach" ("by far the most popular approach" to EDP) that Franklin Life and many other relatively small firms were adopting.[15] In describing the latter, it explained that centralizing all data on in-force insurance policies and manipulating it at lightning speed made such "mass routine operations" more efficient than possible in a nonautomated system. New England Mutual Life's EDP Committee was clearly following developments in insurance adoption and use of computers and learning much about where computers were expected to be most useful. The May 1956 editorial that ended the series made two points forcefully.[16] First, it noted that "automation, of which EDP is a part, is a new chapter in an old book," and it stressed continuity, not discontinuity, between pre-computer and computer technologies. Second, the editorial argued, "Far from threatening mass unemployment, automation gives new hope that—by working hard—industry can produce sufficient goods and services to meet the growing demands." Like other firms, New England Mutual Life emphasized that growth, not layoffs, would result from adopting computers.

One month after the final editorial, four members of New England Mutual Life's EDP Committee met with UNIVAC sales representatives "to commence work on a proposal for a UNIVAC II System as applied to Ordinary Life Insurance Operations."[17] Now that the committee had completed its preliminary study, it was turning not to IBM but to another familiar vendor to develop detailed plans. The Remington Rand customer contact report on this meeting listed the primary applications the two parties discussed: "File Maintenance," "Premium Billing and Accounting," "Commission Accounting," "Reserve and Dividend Calculation and Accounting," "Agency and Home Office Statistics," and "Premium and Policy Loan Accounting."[18] Probably the EDP Committee members planned eventually to integrate these applications into a consolidated functions application. Although surviving records do not indicate whether this group pursued proposals from IBM or other potential vendors, as well, its talks concerning the UNIVAC must have continued successfully. In April 1957, New England Mutual Life's president signed a lease-to-buy contract for a UNIVAC II, to be installed two years later.[19] This new model, which had been announced but would not be available until 1958, was a magnetic-tape computer with vacuum tubes, like the original UNIVAC but with twice the memory and speed.[20] According to the in-house magazine, the $1.6 million computer "will bring the miracle of electronic data processing to New England Life."[21] Although this dramatic announcement suggested a greater technological discontinuity than the committee had claimed in the article series, an incremental approach maintaining continuity with the past was clear on the applications side.

Work on programming began in March 1959.[22] A progress report that appeared in the in-house magazine four months later stated that premium billing, previously done by Addressograph, was the first major application mounted on the UNIVAC II. Using the computer, the home office would prepare the bills in advance so it could send them to the agencies for mailing, as in the past. Eventually, the home office would also mail them. New England Mutual Life had also used the computer to perform small jobs such as printing new rate and dividend books and would soon use it to value policy reserves for the Actuarial Department. At the 1960 IASA conference, Donald Ryan spoke about the firm's computerized commission accounting system, the first computer-related talk anyone from New England Mutual Life had given at these conferences.[23] With the commission accounting system and the premium billing application, the company was gradually assembling elements of a consolidated functions application.

The next stages of New England Mutual Life's progress are less well documented in available records. In the early 1960s, the firm acquired a transistor-based UNIVAC III in addition to its UNIVAC II. In 1964, the president and executive vice president announced a reorganization from eight divisions to eleven, listing computer use as one of several factors making it necessary.[24] The new Policyholders and Data Processing Services division absorbed data-processing equipment from throughout the firm, as well as functional insurance units dealing directly with policyholders, such as Premium and Renewal Service and Policy Loan. By creating this division, the top executives centralized data processing. How much progress the company had made in integrating various life insurance functions into a consolidated application, however, is not clear.

In 1967 New England Mutual Life began its next advance in computer use when, after evaluating proposals from IBM as well as Sperry Rand's UNIVAC Division, the company ordered the new UNIVAC 1108 computer, the first of this model ordered by an insurance company.[25] It would replace the UNIVAC II and supplement the UNIVAC III, calculating ten times faster than the latter computer. The 1108, like the IBM System/360, was a third-generation computer that used integrated circuits as well as transistors and that, in later models, could support multiprocessing.[26] As the in-house magazine proclaimed, "The 1108's greatest asset is that it is capable of bringing the 'real time' concept to the Company." The company established an ambitious project, called "Milepost," to translate its old batch-processed computer systems to an integrated online system, the new holy grail of the late 1960s and early 1970s. Robert Shafto, hired from Electronic Data Systems (EDS) in 1972 to help run the effort, described it retrospectively: "Milepost was the fundamental translation of punch cards to on-line. The best way to describe it is, punch cards bring the work to the computer; on-line brings the computer to the work. So, we went from a punch card overnight batch-based system, which was the predecessor where you bring the work to the computer, to an on-line interactive system where you put the terminals in the user department at an on-line interactive data base."[27] Milepost Phase I would make the home office systems interactive, while Phase II would connect agencies to the home office system, using telecommunications to provide online access from afar. New England Mutual Life would ultimately achieve both objectives, but only after problems became so severe that the project became known internally as Millstone, rather than Milepost.[28]

The project's problems, which centered around the UNIVAC 1108, emerged

*Fig. 8.1.* Robert Shafto with the UNIVAC 1108 at New England Mutual Life.
New England Financial Archives.

gradually. In early 1968, New England Mutual Life headquarters received the
new computer with great fanfare, but Phase I soon became completely bogged
down.[29] Thus when Robert Shafto, a former insurance man who now designed
and installed insurance computer systems for EDS, approached New England
Mutual Life in 1971, executives welcomed him to study their needs, thinking
that perhaps EDS could help them.[30] Ultimately, New England Mutual Life rejected Shafto's EDS proposal because it required the firm to give full control of
data processing to EDS as facilities manager; nevertheless, the company managed to hire Shafto away from EDS to become its second vice president for data
processing and to work with the company from the inside (fig. 8.1).[31]

Hiring Shafto in 1972 was a key inflection point in New England Mutual

Life's computer use. Shafto had led EDS's insurance business, working with many different insurance firms and applications, including successfully piloting an insurance client's online application for Policy Owner Services administration in 1968.[32] Since then, he had worked with three companies to develop a "comprehensive data processing system designed to serve the needs of the life insurance industry."[33] Shafto thus had wide-ranging knowledge about life insurance applications in general and online systems in particular. With the knowledge and confidence developed during his EDS years, he took charge of New England Mutual Life's computing and would ultimately turn a troubled laggard in computer use into a leader.[34]

Looking back twenty years later, Shafto identified two primary problems the company faced when he arrived: "one a Univac problem and secondarily, the fact that [company executives] didn't understand how big the [programming] problem was they were facing."[35] On the latter issue, he quickly convinced the top executives that ten programmers could not make adequate progress on what was essentially a "400 man-year project." By moving some programmers from the old system to the new, and by staffing up further, he finally began to make progress on the Milepost project.

This new approach, however, only highlighted the first problem faced by New England Mutual Life: "During this process, we found that Univac did not have the mix and memory and essentially the compute power necessary to support an insurance company at a reasonable price."[36] Contrary to Shafto's initial hopes, his staff determined that the 1108, even with fully expanded memory, would fail to meet the firm's demands by the mid-1970s, even before Milepost Phase I was fully installed. By late 1974 Shafto's staff, which now included Fred Knier, who had been hired away from the UNIVAC sales force, recommended moving to the UNIVAC 1110 the following year, rather than waiting until 1977, when it would become absolutely necessary.[37] During this period New England Mutual Life, like other large insurance firms, was pushing current hardware capacity and pressuring vendors to provide more.[38] Indeed, within a year Shafto's data-processing staff feared that the 1110, too, was inadequate: "The current 1110 operating system [used with the 1108 and 1106 hardware at this time] is clearly not tuned toward a business environment in which there are large Cobol programs, a compute bound interpretive data management system, and compute bound business Cobol logic doing minimal input/output due to their use of direct access files. This environment describes not only New England Mutual Life but most large business data processing environments in the United States."[39] Input/output had become less important in such integrated online applications and rapid direct access more important. Based on excessive downtime and slow online speeds, the data-processing group concluded that making this configuration work for New England Mutual Life required major hardware changes.

This realization initiated a prolonged struggle between New England Mutual Life and Sperry Rand's UNIVAC division, in which the former expressed escalating displeasure over the problems and demanded support and responsiveness, while the latter promised but never delivered studies and solutions.[40] As the largest East Coast UNIVAC contract, New England Mutual Life was an important customer, and it could conceivably have helped UNIVAC innovate for the large insurance market.[41] But instead of serving both parties, the relationship deteriorated into recriminations and defensiveness.

Meanwhile, in 1976 New England Mutual Life began talking to IBM, since the IBM 370/168 was a possible alternative to the UNIVAC 1110.[42] Since its initial computer adoption, the insurance company had centered its primary applications around UNIVAC equipment, though it had also used an IBM 1401 (replaced in 1969 by the smallest IBM 360) in a less central application.[43] Still, New England Mutual Life was not yet seriously considering changing over its central Milepost system to IBM hardware.[44] The firm's executives had always assumed that IBM was more expensive than UNIVAC, and they knew that a complete switch-over would be a huge undertaking. Still, Shafto and his staff were exploring IBM possibilities to give New England Mutual Life an alternative bid, thus ratcheting up pressure on Sperry Rand/UNIVAC. As Shafto later said, "So we brought IBM in to compete against UNIVAC—you know this game. Come to find out, IBM did have the equipment . . . It had in one machine the MIPS and megabytes we needed, and it was competitively priced."[45] Persuading first himself, then his staff and other New England Mutual Life executives, that they should make the switch would, however, take time. In March 1976, Shafto and Knier met with Sperry Rand/UNIVAC's vice president of Eastern Operations Marketing and, according to their contemporaneous documentation, emphasized UNIVAC's competitive shortcomings:

- We have done extensive comparison of IBM vs. Univac in the last month. The Univac 1110 is not priced competitively with the IBM 370/168 and offers less performance in the areas of the central processor and peripherals. We emphasized to Univac that they must propose the 1100/80 "future system" if they are to compete with IBM.

- In general, Univac products do not match up well to the profile of our large scale business data processing.[46]

Although they were still primarily attempting to push UNIVAC into developing some aspects of the technology, these comparisons gave Shafto and Knier something to think about.

As New England Mutual Life's conflict with Sperry Rand/UNIVAC escalated, Shafto became more interested in the IBM option. In documenting another face-to-face meeting, Knier described where the disagreement stood: "Mr. Shafto and I emphasized that the key issue is whether Univac's products will meet our data processing needs over the next 8–10 years. The issue is no longer simply the short range costs and performance of the 1110."[47] Shafto and Knier had given the UNIVAC executives attachments including a table comparing the IBM 370/168 and the UNIVAC 1110 on cost and performance (fig. 8.2). The comparison clearly favored IBM—for example, the first three rows of the table revealed that while the IBM 370 had 4 megs of memory and the 1110 configuration had only 2.75 megs, the UNIVAC's purchase price exceeded IBM's by 2% and its maintenance price by 84%. Shafto and his staff, meanwhile, were becoming increasingly serious about the IBM option.[48] When James Zilinski, an IBM marketing manager, was initially invited to talk to the firm with the largest UNIVAC contract on the East Coast, he assembled a team hoping to secure at least some of this business.[49] He presented two options to New England Mutual Life: a gradual migration from UNIVAC to IBM equipment, which would not begin with the core Milepost application, and an immediate and total conversion.[50] His letter documenting this first detailed discussion suggested that the gradual migration was much more likely; given New England Mutual Life's commitment to UNIVAC technology, he recognized that total conversion would involve enormous disruption. He reckoned without Shafto.

In October 1976, after considerable, and often unpleasant, negotiation with the Sperry Rand/UNIVAC sales executives, New England Mutual Life agreed to rent a UNIVAC 1110 until the UNIVAC 1100/80 was available for testing.[51] Even before signing this one-year contract, however, Shafto (now executive vice president) had convinced other New England Mutual Life executives to consider converting completely to IBM, with the decision to be made "as soon as possible, but no later than June 1, 1977, the last day on which NEL [New England Mutual Life] can cancel the Univac contract by paying a retroactive penalty."[52] By now, Shafto had established an in-house committee chaired by

| | IBM 370/168 | UNIVAC 1110 (1108 COSTS NOT INC.) | COMMENTS |
|---|---|---|---|
| Configuration | 370/168-1 ( 4 meg) | Full System 3X2 1110 (2.75 meg) | Equivalent number peripherals |
| Purchase | $7,099,011 | $7,195,338 | Univac + 2% Purchase $ |
| Maint/Mo | $14,069 | $25,200 | Univac + 84% Maint $ |
| CPU Portion | $4,930,000 | CPU Section $4,300,074 | 3X2 196/524 vs. 168-4 Univac CPU is less powerful |
| Larger Univac CPU Equal Univac CPUs | | $4,492,000 $4,492,000 | − 12% on price 3X2 262/524 Cost 3X2 262/786K (4.0 meg, Avg) |
| Megabytes Speed | 4 meg 400ns + 16K cache | .75   + 2.00(No Cache) @500 @900ns, i.e., Avg Speed = 790 ns | Univac = 30% memory size |
| MIPS | 3.10 (3 meg) MIPS | 2.56 MIPS | Univac − 20% MIP Performance |
| Larger IBM CPU | $5,618,000 | | 5 meg, 2 Blk, 2 Byte, 2 Selector |
| Disc Capacity | 8.4 billion | Disc Section 3.6 billion | IBM is 2 1/2 times storage at − 43% price |
| Disc Technology | 2 Controls "3350" Disc | 5 Controls "8433" Disc | |
| Tape Capacity | Tape Section 2 Controls − 16 tapes 11 6250 bpi 4 62050/1600 bpi 1 800 bpi | 3 Controls 20−U−20 1600 bpi | IBM is 6250 bpi capability at − 26% price |
| Tape Technology | 6250 bpi | 1600 bpi | |
| Paper Peripherals | Printers/Readers 4 Prt @2000 LPM 2 Rdr 1 Pch | 6 Prt @1100 LPM 2 Rdr 1 Pch | IBM is − 18% price |
| Terminals | Communications $18,577 (R&M) $560,211 (Purchase) | $22,080 $716,479 | Univac (CMS/CTMC), IBM 68 CRT, 38 PRT (In−house) |
| Multiprocessor Memory Mgt Software TP Capability Software Cost | Other No Virtual−paged MVS/IMS/SNA SNA $2,000/mo | Yes Real−banked 1100 OS/DMS/TIP Unknown Unbundled | |

*Fig. 8.2.* New England Mutual Life's table comparing UNIVAC 1110 with IBM 370/168 clearly favored IBM. Attachment to memo, Knier to file, Subject: April 2, 1976, UNIVAC Visit, April 5, 1976, Fibiger Files, New England Financial Archives.

former UNIVAC salesman Knier (now second vice president of New England Mutual Life) to study whether to convert to IBM. Within a month of the short-term agreement, Knier's committee recommended to President Edward E. Phillips and Executive Vice President John A. Fibiger that the company convert to IBM immediately, without waiting to test the UNIVAC 1100/80.[53] The committee urged immediate commitment to this plan because Milepost Phase I was now complete, under Shafto's leadership, and staff should not begin working on Phase II (to connect agents and field offices to the home office system) on the costly and unstable UNIVAC 1110. Further, Knier pointed out that two other large life insurance firms, Travelers and Connecticut General, were converting from UNIVAC computers, suggesting that these computers might not be viable for large insurance firms much longer.[54] Phillips and Fibiger accepted the committee's recommendation.

Later that month, Shafto briefed Fibiger on what exactly to tell Sperry Rand's UNIVAC Division.[55] New England Mutual Life and Sperry Rand/UNIVAC would continue legal wrangling over the contract termination for several more years, but New England Mutual Life had now committed irreversibly to its decision.[56] It converted rapidly and efficiently, turning off the last UNIVAC machine in early 1980 and running a now completed Milepost system entirely on IBM equipment.[57]

Several IBM employees involved at the time later attributed New England Mutual Life's willingness to undertake the bold hardware switch-over to Shafto's capability and background in insurance computing, as well as his personal confidence.[58] As Edward Kelley commented, "You must not underestimate the change brought about when Bob Shafto arrived at The New England. He has transformed that company." Shafto became well known both internally—he ultimately became chief executive officer (CEO)—and externally. He actively shared his knowledge about computer use within the industry and beyond. For example, he started the regional "Life Insurance Systems" group for systems executives in medium-sized firms.[59] He also shared the company's experiences at IASA and other industry meetings.[60] Under his leadership, New England Mutual Life moved from lagging to leading in insurance computerization and established a strong ongoing relationship with IBM.[61] He could not, as structuration theory implies, have transformed existing company structures single-handedly.[62] Key subordinates such as Knier made the case for the necessary hardware change, and Phillips and Fibiger in top management accepted his recommendation. Without their support and the active cooperation of lower-level employees he could not have achieved this change so successfully.

Tracking business results of New England Mutual Life's computer use is, as usual, difficult. As figure 8.3 shows, New England Mutual Life's cost ratio remained below that of the thirty-firm average throughout the period, suggesting that it used both UNIVAC and IBM computers reasonably successfully. The firm's costs remained relatively even until the mid-1950s and then rose very gradually until 1978, when costs finally began to fall. Its costs turned down slightly later than those of the thirty-firm average but caught up quickly and dropped well below the line. The long, gentle rise occurred during the UNIVAC and Milepost years, perhaps reflecting the problems the firm was facing, while

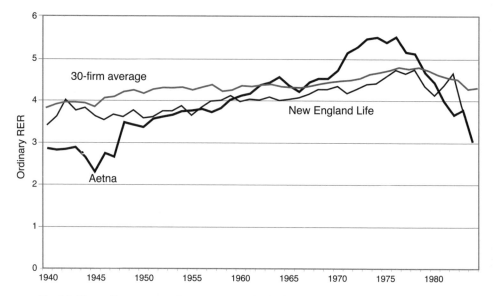

*Fig. 8.3.* The ordinary renewal expense ratio for both Aetna Life and New England Mutual Life started below the thirty-firm average, but Aetna's rose throughout the 1950s, 1960s, and up to the mid-1970s, exceeding the trend line significantly until 1980. Still, Aetna's turned downward in 1976, two years earlier than New England Mutual Life's, and dropped more rapidly. *Best's,* 1940–85.

the reduction coincided with the conversion to IBM equipment. Still, any causal relationship must be speculative.

This case study highlights several themes established earlier. Like many other firms, New England Mutual Life initially followed an incremental path in its hardware adoption, remaining with a familiar vendor from the pre-computer era. Perhaps both because its tabulator use was minimal and because it had worked with Remington Rand to develop customized equipment such as the Convé files, it chose that vendor, rather than IBM. Thus the firm's first computer, acquired relatively late, was a UNIVAC rather than an IBM machine. It followed the already established pattern of moving very gradually toward a consolidated functions–type application. Like other firms, by the late 1960s it also became interested in time-sharing and online applications, stretching its original goals first to include an integrated policy-handling application accessible via time-sharing throughout the home office and then to extend the online system to district offices.

Finally, however, following the incremental path failed as Milepost bogged down and UNIVAC computers seemingly could not fulfill New England Mutual Life's gradually evolving needs. Had the firm not hired EDS's Robert Shafto in 1972, it might have remained mired for years in a failed attempt to implement its online Milepost system. Shafto, with his broader knowledge of computer capabilities and insurance applications, became increasingly impatient with Sperry Rand/UNIVAC's unresponsiveness and ultimately convinced top management to incur the cost of converting to IBM hardware, a rapid and disruptive transformation of vendor and equipment, though not of application, which was already being developed. New England Mutual Life finally joined many other insurance firms in using IBM computers, a latecomer that quickly excelled. Shafto propelled New England Mutual Life from the lagging to the leading edge of computerized insurance applications. By using his own knowledge and by assembling and leading a team of others who were knowledgeable in insurance computing, Shafto transformed New England Mutual Life's approach to computing and completed the ambitious Milepost project successfully. As a historian of the firm noted, "Perhaps the best evidence of the high quality of Shafto's work was the formation of InterNEL in 1983, a subsidiary which was set up to market EDP services from NEL to other companies."[63] By the early 1990s, Shafto had risen from data-processing management to CEO, a career path that was quite unusual then, both in insurance firms, which were typically run by actuaries, and in other businesses.[64] He attributed his rise to his focus not on the technology itself but on the insurance business.

## Aetna Life Insurance Company

In 1952 Aetna Life Insurance Company, part of a Hartford-based insurance cluster, ranked ninth, with 40% greater assets than New England Mutual Life but only roughly one-fifth those of Metropolitan Life.[65] A century earlier Aetna Life had broken off from Aetna Insurance Company, the fire insurance firm that became one of SPAN's co-founders in the 1950s.[66] Unlike most very large firms, Aetna Life was a stock rather than a mutual life insurance company.[67] Based on its permissive Connecticut charter, it also became a multiline insurance provider quite early, adding accident, health, and liability insurance to life insurance by 1900 and automobile insurance shortly thereafter.[68] To deal with state regulatory differences in how different insurance lines could be combined, Aetna created several subsidiary companies—including Aetna Casualty and Surety and the Aetna Automobile Insurance Company—under Aetna Life Affiliated Companies.[69] Aetna's early and extensive multiline strategy, atypical among life insurance companies until the 1950s, when relevant regulations eased up, had implications for its computer use. Life insurance firms typically led other insurance firms in using early computers, but within Aetna this was not initially the case. Indeed, because individuals whose roles were unrelated to the core ordinary life insurance operations became key players in Aetna's computerization, the noncore business lines and functions led Aetna's data-processing development.

Aetna had demonstrated interest in information-processing technology long before the computer. During the nineteenth century, the firm employed a mechanical calculating device similar to the one New England Mutual Life used.[70] In 1910, Aetna first rented Hollerith tabulating equipment, on a one-time basis, to tabulate its mortality experience.[71] By the mid-1920s, it had a Hollerith Department that handled several distinct business lines and functions, beginning with premium accounting in its casualty insurance area.[72] It had at least three Hollerith Departments—the Life Hollerith Department, the Casualty Hollerith Department, and the Fire and Marine Hollerith Department—by 1931. The company continued to upgrade its Hollerith equipment and techniques through the 1930s and 1940s, and by the early 1950s it had acquired an IBM 604 electronic calculator.[73] Nevertheless, in 1955 Robert G. Espie, the chief accounting officer of Aetna Life Affiliated Companies, saw the firm as not being very highly mechanized: "There are large areas of our operations where we have not yet converted to punched cards."[74] So the firm entered the computer era with a mixed record in information technology use.

In the early 1950s, Aetna's executives began considering computers. They determined that the UNIVAC was too expensive for their uses and the IBM Card-Programmed Calculator too limited.[75] Thus in early 1954, Espie ordered an IBM 650.[76] Given the firm's long-term commitment to "Hollerith" equipment, IBM was the obvious vendor choice, and without any pressing need for abrupt transformation, Aetna decided to start with the small, card-based 650. Ten Aetna representatives, including Espie himself and Nathan D. O'Neil, from the casualty insurance area, attended an IBM 650 programming class, alongside eight from Connecticut General, two from Travelers, one each from Connecticut Mutual and Phoenix group, and one each from two noninsurance companies.[77] Soon O'Neil, who would help shape Aetna's computerization efforts, had written his first program, for auto liability insurance.[78] In 1955 two

650 computers arrived, one for group insurance and one for casualty.[79] The first 650, which Aetna claimed was the "first of its kind to be used by a Connecticut insurance company, and third among all insurance companies," was "put immediately to work determining the distribution of premiums on group insurance policies."[80] The second went to the Casualty Department, which used it to analyze automobile premiums.

At the 1955 IASA conference Espie described the philosophy behind this application: "We felt that the best way to introduce this new equipment to our organization was to try to take some procedures which were already on punched cards and convert them, so that we would not mingle with the introduction of our electronic equipment any of the animosity that tends to arise when you take jobs away from clerical people and put them on punched cards. We didn't want the two concepts to get mixed up. Once we have established the 650 and/or its successors as acceptable operations and have built up an area of confidence for them, then we will continue to mechanize further areas."[81] Thus Espie began with an explicitly incremental plan for computerizing, converting processes directly from tabulators to computers. Interestingly, he argued that computerizing a tabulator application was less likely to trigger employee fears than mechanizing (whether on tabulators or computers) an application previously handled clerically, underlining how incremental the move from tabulators to the IBM 650 appeared to the firm.

Espie's background and role initially shaped Aetna's incremental migration path, which turned in an atypical direction. In 1956, he created the Central Data Processing Development Department (CDPDD), separate from the tabulating departments.[82] Because Espie, the firm's chief accountant, oversaw the department, it became very accounting-oriented, focusing its data-gathering and -processing efforts on accounting needs, rather than on the needs of business unit managers.[83] Espie's influence aligned the company more with early noninsurance computer users than with other insurance users, directing efforts away from the consolidated functions application central to most early life insurance computer use.[84] Moreover, Espie's work as actuary for group insurance before becoming chief accountant, along with O'Neil's previous and ongoing association with casualty insurance, encouraged an initial focus on those two areas rather than ordinary life insurance operations.

Aetna's incremental approach included combining 650s with existing IBM tabulating equipment where appropriate. Moreover, the in-house publication stressed this continuity, as in this 1958 description of IBM equipment in the

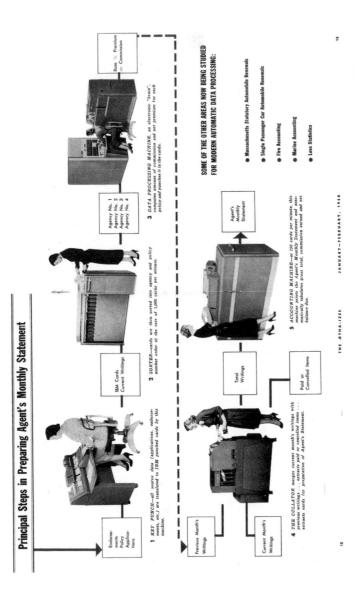

*Fig. 8.4.* Aetna's "Principal Steps in Preparing Agent's Monthly Statement" showed the 650 (in step 3) being used with tabulating equipment on either side. "Automation at the Aetna," *Aetna-izer,* Casualty, Bonding, Fire, and Marine Edition, January/February 1958, 12–13. Reprinted with the permission of Aetna Inc.

casualty area: "The Aetna Life Affiliated Companies have kept careful watch on the development of modern office machinery, and adopted new machines whenever studies showed they would make desirable improvements in economy or speed of operations. The result is that today certain sections of the home office contain row on row of great grey machines, whirring and clicking industriously, as they produce, compute, sort and stack millions of punched cards, providing an endless stream of records and statistics."[85] The "great grey machines" included IBM tabulating devices as well as the IBM 650 computer.[86] Preparing monthly statements for casualty insurance agents, for example, integrated both types of IBM information-processing equipment (fig. 8.4). The seamless combination of older and newer technology to perform insurance functions provided clear advantages.

Nevertheless, Espie, O'Neill, and others saw that the 650s would not fulfill the firm's long-term needs. Consequently, in 1956 Aetna began exploring further options. The firm tentatively ordered the tape-based IBM 705 and in early 1957 sent several employees to the small IBM-organized "Life Insurance Data Processing Seminar" discussed earlier.[87] In O'Neil's summary of it, he noted that representatives of the twelve insurance firms present (four of which already had 700 series machines installed) distributed and explained each firm's current or intended master records for its life insurance files.[88] They also discussed personnel issues and the rent-versus-buy decision. The Aetna attendees took this forum, like LOMA and IASA meetings, as an opportunity to learn from other insurance firms. Ultimately, however, Aetna did not acquire a 705, instead purchasing time on SPAN's 705 to serve its group insurance computing needs.[89]

Shortly after the IBM seminar, Espie also decided to order a Burroughs (ElectroData) Datatron 205, "a medium size computer, midway between the IBM 650, of which we now have one in the Group Division and one in Central Tabulating, and the IBM 705 now on order for the Group Division."[90] He based his decision on size, price, and a desire not to be "inescapably wedded to IBM." After placing a tentative order, he scheduled a pilot test of the programs and equipment at a small New York City insurance firm.[91] O'Neil and the two subordinate programmers who conducted the test found that their programs were quite successful, thus validating the CDPDD's growing programming proficiency, but that the Burroughs hardware was plagued by machine problems.[92] Moreover, the Datatron 205 did not perform much better than the IBM 650s Aetna already had. When Espie and O'Neil determined that the Datatron 205 lacked adequate capacity and performance, Burroughs tried to convince Aetna that it needed a Datatron 220, a larger-capacity, tape-based machine, instead.[93] The test had, however, cooled Espie's interest in this vendor; after he canceled the original order, he did not place another.

Throughout this period, IBM demonstrated its famed marketing capabilities, acting in ways that would ultimately help it keep Aetna's business. Although not as large as Metropolitan Life or Prudential, Aetna was certainly large enough to warrant considerable efforts from IBM's marketing and sales and was part of an industry IBM certainly saw as worth wooing. IBM's life insurance data-processing seminars offered Aetna information about IBM products and training and an opportunity to exchange information with other life insurance firms. In addition, IBM sales representatives sent letters and other documents designed to encourage Aetna to work with IBM. For example, early in 1957 Don Mastriforte sent Nathan O'Neil Prudential's press release about how it used the IBM 702 and 705 to prepare life insurance premium notices.[94] A few months later, he wrote to Espie, describing various software resources IBM's Applied Science Department could make available (including, for example, the SOAP I and II assembler programs for the 650 and Autocoder for the 705) and noting that such software offerings "every day prove IBM's awareness of its responsibility to its customers, above and beyond that of hardware alone."[95] The following month O'Neil received a list of other insurance firms' computers, in place or ordered, including ninety-five card-based IBM 650s, fifteen tape-based 650s, twenty-one tape-based IBM 700 series computers, and eleven IBM RAMACs, all in contrast to ten UNIVACs in place or ordered and one each Bizmac and Datatron.[96]

In addition to these marketing efforts, IBM provided excellent support for Aetna's 650s, responding to O'Neil's requests from the IBM 650 Program Library and stationing a 650 customer engineer on site every day throughout the main shift to assure adequate 650 performance.[97] Ultimately, Espie was probably influenced by all these factors. Moreover, remaining with a single, familiar vendor while following the incremental migration path provided by the 650 and the 1401 was an easier choice than changing vendors and starting over on programming applications. In September 1961, Aetna installed two card-based IBM 1401s and a year later four additional tape-based 1401s, releasing the 650s and one card-based 1401 back to IBM.[98]

Soon after, however, Aetna began considering large-scale computers, not limited to IBM's. After visiting Honeywell in 1962, O'Neil reported that the vendor was "aware that we are as yet uncommitted to medium or large scale equipment," and he claimed to be "impressed by the Honeywell hardware, software, and personnel."[99] Around the same time, however, he attended an IBM course on '62 CFO, noting that the system manual he brought back "should serve as an excellent guide and check list for our own studies" and that "my own knowledge has been greatly enhanced by attendance at the course."[100] Later that year Aetna settled the issue, at least for the immediate future, when it bought the SPAN Data Processing Center. SPAN, which already handled Aetna's group insurance on a service contract, had exclusively IBM computer equipment, including 1401s, 705s, a 7070, and multiple tape drives.[101] As Aetna's wholly owned subsidiary, SPAN subsequently bought one IBM 7074 and rented another and acquired dozens of tape drives. Aetna solidified its commitment to IBM technology in 1965 when Espie ordered the newly announced IBM System/360 equipment, "which should obsolete most of the equipment" already owned or rented from IBM.[102] Its first 360/65 was installed in 1966, and the annual report that year lauded Aetna's leadership in this area: "Aetna continued to seek out the most modern methods of handling its expanding volume of business. One of the largest IBM computers was installed, the first of its kind to be put into commercial use."[103] In the late 1960s, Aetna used two General Electric computers when it first established a time-sharing network, but by the early 1970s it used IBM machines for this function, as well.[104] Through the mid-1970s, IBM 360s and 370s dominated the firm's ever growing hardware capacity.

In its allegiance to IBM as its primary vendor, Aetna followed a steady incremental hardware migration path; nevertheless, by the mid-1960s Aetna was encountering significant software problems, especially in its life insurance operation.[105] Life insurance, which included group life insurance, was by far the biggest of the affiliated companies. In Aetna's centennial year (1953), statistics broken down by affiliated company showed that Aetna Life Insurance Company had assets over $2 billion, Aetna Casualty and Surety Company had just over $250 million, and the automobile and fire companies were much smaller still.[106] Within the Aetna Life Insurance Company, group insurance accounted for $10 million insurance in force, compared with ordinary life's $3 million, but the firm had more than fifty-five times as many ordinary life policies as group policies to manage. Still, Aetna's ordinary life business lagged behind both group insurance and casualty insurance in data-processing capability. This gap reflected both Espie's and O'Neil's current and former associations with the group and casualty insurance businesses, on the one hand, and Espie's preference for accounting rather than operational applications, on the other.[107]

Aetna reinforced these preferences by centralizing the data-processing function during the late 1950s and 1960s. Although group insurance operated as a relatively autonomous profit center with its own computer group and SPAN contract, all other computer operations became increasingly centralized.[108] Formed in the late 1950s, the CDPDD absorbed several tabulating units by the early 1960s.[109] Centralizing data-processing operations was relatively common, in insurance and elsewhere, at this time.[110] Because the CDPDD did not focus very much on life insurance operations, however, centralization retarded that area's development. During this period the CDPDD had grown faster than the firm's general administration in staff, budget, and specialties, a fact that concerned Aetna's upper management.[111]

In April 1959, upper management finally established the Life Integrated Data Processing (LIDP) Committee, with its most experienced data-processing expert, O'Neil, as member and full time consultant to committee chair Espie.[112] In Espie's words, this committee's mandate was to explore

> the establishment of a central source file from which, by use of an electronic computer and its peripheral equipment, we could develop data for
>
> 1. Preparation of the policy and of the various forms for disseminating policy-issue data
> 2. Policy issue and in-force statistics for Agency Department purposes
> 3. Premium billing and accounting
> 4. Policy Loan, Cash Value, and Dividend calculation and accounting
> 5. Policy Reserves for valuation
> 6. Premiums due and unpaid, deferred, and paid in advance for annual statements
> 7. Policy exhibit data for annual statements[113]

This mandate indicates that Espie was at last considering a consolidated functions–type application for life insurance. IBM would not develop its '62 CFO software for three more years, and even then the 1401 on which that program ran lacked adequate capacity to handle Aetna's large operations. Thus Aetna began work on its own application.

The CDPDD initially allowed three to five years for the LIDP project, recognizing that the department would face significant implementation problems.[114] Still, Aetna expected to have the "advantage of profiting from [the] experience of others" because the firm was following, rather than leading, in this area. It does not appear to have benefited fully from this position, however. The LIDP Committee started out *very* slowly, first tackling not actual applications but the data that the computer systems would use—and produce: "The LIDP Method of Data Analysis provides a systematic means for the defining, recording, and maintaining of pertinent information regarding a complete data processing system. It is expressly effective in that it requires a complete explanation of the characteristics and utilization of each piece of data, each document, and each file in the system. What probably represents the newest concept in a method of this type is the fact that all data, document, and file information is recorded and maintained on punched cards, making an unlimited variety of analyses possible."[115] The committee saw this approach's advantages as including "a definite and orderly method of documenting systems requirements, independent of the processing media"; detection of "omissions, inconsistencies, and duplication," prompting report consolidation; decrease in "the possibility of misunderstandings between management and operating departments"; flexibility to add, delete, or correct on punched cards; and creation of a "valuable reference tool."[116] Three years later, the committee had still not completed this data analysis.[117]

Meanwhile, the committee was also converting the old, Addressograph-based system for premium billing to a punched-card-based 650 application, an incremental step that would ready it for later conversion to a consolidated application on an IBM 7070 or similar machine.[118] By late 1960, only two of the firm's seventy-two working 650 programs belonged to the life insurance line; in contrast, seventy programs were associated with auto, casualty, or marine insurance or with general accounting, personnel, or payroll applications.[119] In late 1962, Aetna was just testing one piece of the proposed life insurance application—accounting for life insurance premiums and agents' commissions— using both an IBM 1401 and the larger IBM 7074.[120] Creating an integrated life insurance application was proving more difficult than anticipated.

By May 1963, a fundamental disagreement about how to proceed had emerged within management. After an LIDP Committee meeting Frank Havens wrote to Espie (now vice president and assistant comptroller and Havens' boss) about the "rather staggering costs [for an ordinary life data-processing system] quoted at the meeting."[121] He attributed these costs to two factors, the daily cycle model, and data transmission allowing agencies to report bill collections and request status on loans. He proposed instead to do away with the daily cycle and to eliminate need for data transmission by centralizing collections. Espie forwarded this memo to O'Neil, adding his support: "I am far from satisfied that the daily cycle, daily print-out, or daily status answer is the ideal approach."[122] O'Neil unequivocally disagreed with this position. In notes prepared for a meeting with Irwin Sitkin, assistant secretary of the Accounts Department and member of the LIDP Committee, he explained why daily cycling was advantageous and why a large computer configuration was needed even without daily cycling. He concluded:

> Until Aetna needs are known in detail and until a proposal based on these needs has been prepared, I feel strongly that any conclusions such as Frank's (and Mr. Espie's) are ill-timed. I also feel, and I hope that Aetna's proposal to integrate when it comes will conclusively demonstrate, that a cycle less frequently than daily will be an inefficient use of the equipment since the system will of necessity be built around manual processing instead of computer processing. It is not out of the realm of possibility that Aetna will achieve such growth in this decade that in order [to] serve other than the needs of HQ accounting (and shouldn't the needs of agents and policyholders be served first?) twice daily cycle will be required.[123]

O'Neil perceived Havens and Espie as placing accounting needs above operational needs; in contrast, he felt that operational needs should be paramount.

The records do not reveal exactly how this disagreement was resolved. On the same date Sitkin sent out the agenda for a future meeting, with the following stated purpose: "To reinforce the successful meeting held with IBM representatives May 14, 1963 at which we discussed data processing developments in the ordinary life business, I have arranged for a review of what the Aetna is doing in this area to be presented to members of the Comptrollers Department."[124] Sitkin's draft of his introduction to that meeting, dated the same day, discussed "what has been accomplished by the LIDP Committee and by the 3,000 man hours of effort invested by the clerical and technical personnel assigned to it."[125] The progress he reported, however, was only in research and, as a by-product, education; no completed design or coding for an integrated life application yet existed. The committee members had documented Aetna's own files, requirements, and goals; studied other companies' integrated systems; and created a "representative" plan and "a rough description of the steps for the development of an integrated system and for the conversion to it." As a by-product, they had educated themselves and, to a lesser extent, the life departments about converting to an integrated system. Sitkin enumerated the benefits both of creating a central file and of processing it by computer. He concluded with the limited claim that "the LIDP Committee has prepared the Company for the changes to come. It has provided documentation of Company procedures that will facilitate development of detailed integration plans." O'Neil's files show no further decisions or progress for the next two years.

In 1964, while the LIPD committee was dormant, an important organizational change set the stage for ending the stalemate in ordinary life data processing. In April, the board of directors decentralized responsibility for application development to the operating divisions, such as Casualty Insurance and Life Insurance, and replaced the Central Data Processing Development Department with the centralized Computer Services Department (CSD).[126] The new CSD, in charge of the firm's computer operations and equipment, reported to a newly created vice president for data processing rather than to the comptroller. This organizational change was intended to decrease the growth rate of computer expenses, which had exploded during the late 1950s and early 1960s, and to deal with the extended development times, "a host of problems and some failures," computer personnel growth, and "proliferating" titles and specialties.[127] In addition, it broke up a log jam that had impeded progress toward a life insurance application; as long as data-processing development reported to the comptroller, it seemed to focus on accounting needs more than on the needs of the operating divisions and their customers.

Sitkin, who became secretary of the decentralized Data Processing Development Department within the Casualty Division, resurrected his proposal, which Espie had earlier turned down, for a "total information system" for Casualty. This idea resulted in a cutting-edge networked system for automobile and home owners insurance called SAFARI (System by Aetna for Fast Access and Rate Information), which linked field offices to the home office to administer these casualty policies.[128] Sitkin emphasized to his subordinates that the department "serve[d] an insurance business," not data processing per se.[129] In this role, they contributed "better information" on the dimensions of accuracy, timeliness, economy, and scope.[130]

By decentralizing application development to insurance divisions, the organizational change reinvigorated computerization efforts within the ordinary life insurance business, as well. Abandoning its attempts to build a system from scratch, Aetna became a beta test site for IBM's proposed ALIS life insurance package for the IBM System/360 line, even though Aetna had never implemented its predecessor and model, '62 CFO. At LOMA's 1968 Automation Forum Robert McComb related that the company "first became involved with IBM's Advanced Life Information System (ALIS) shortly after it was announced, in November 1964, that IBM was in the process of developing a new, comprehensive systems approach to maintaining, processing and servicing individual life insurance contracts."[131] This commitment to ALIS probably reflected the new structure, with the life insurance operating unit supporting an integrated life application package.

Challenges remained, however. First, Aetna itself was ill prepared for the conversion, with many life operations still handled through manual and mechanical processes.[132] Thus it planned to adjust the application to its current system and needs. In addition, IBM was slow in completing ALIS and disappointed beta test sites like Aetna that acquired the larger machines in the System/360 range, since it was designed for the minimum 360/30 configuration and did not take advantage of Aetna's 360/65 system. In 1967 O'Neil hosted visitors from Prudential who wanted to compare their nearly completed Advanced Ordinary System (AOS) with Aetna's planned implementation of the proposed ALIS system. That meeting produced "an interesting exchange of ideas" but also made visible Aetna's lag in this application area. In a five-year plan written later that spring, ALIS was hardly mentioned.[133]

Finally, in 1972, Aetna launched an integrated life insurance application that networked between field offices and home office, known as LIAS (Life Insurance Administration System). LIAS went beyond an integrated home office system to add networking and online field office access, reflecting the industry's current interest in time-sharing and online applications with remote access. An internal history of Aetna's data processing states that the firm "modified a commercial product to meet its own specification and requirements," suggesting that the initial core of LIAS was either ALIS or another system purchased from a software vendor but that it was altered enough to make LIAS distinct—and more effective.[134] According to this account, LIAS was "one of the most sophisticated on-line conversational systems in the industry." Aetna had finally completed its transformation of ordinary insurance processes.

Although available records do not reveal how most Aetna employees felt about computerization, the firm's—and industry's—rapid growth meant that computerization did not require layoffs. Indeed, Aetna's home office staff grew 61% in the decade from 1953 and 1963, when the firm acquired its early computers; 32% during the next decade; and a whopping 75% between 1973 and

1983, after it put LIAS into operation.[135] Moreover, although some concerns about technological displacement emerged early in the computerization process, Aetna "always had a full employment practice, and so people didn't really fear for their jobs. They wondered whether they could cope with the new technology or whether they could learn it or learn how to get it to help them do what they wanted to do better."[136] Thus training and trainability, not employment, were the central issues. Sitkin described some individuals who still, twenty-five years later, worked with the older, punched-card technology and others who had shifted to computers.

During the 1950s and 1960s, managers and technical personnel taking part in Aetna's computerization efforts learned from and interacted extensively with peers in other firms, through bilateral exchanges, organizations, courses, and government-sponsored standards efforts. O'Neil, for example, corresponded with individuals from other insurance companies, including direct competitors such as Connecticut General, about their computer adoption and use.[137] Aetna also belonged to or participated in national insurance organizations such as IASA and LOMA and computer interest groups unrestricted to insurance, such as the National Machine Accountants Association, later renamed the Data Processing Management Association, and the Spring Joint Computer Conference.[138] In addition, Aetna shared information about hardware and applications through vendor- or firm-sponsored educational or training events, including those IBM organized in 1957 and 1962. Moreover, when Aetna bought SPAN, it inherited membership in GUIDE, a group of IBM business users, and a center through which to run training courses.[139] In Sitkin's words, "In effect, we created the class and sold some seats to some of our contemporaries around Hartford . . . to help us to lower our unit cost."[140] Finally, in 1967 Aetna became involved in the government-organized Committee on Data Systems and Languages (CODASYL) effort, sending O'Neil to join a task force extending COBOL to handle database mass storage.[141] In his recommendation that Aetna participate, R. G. Goodwin, assistant secretary of computer services, explained his reasoning: "When we participate in an industry project, we incur some expense and I know we must weigh the potential returns carefully against our investment. We gain by having opportunity to influence the pattern of development. We also become among the best informed of all corporations using large scale equipment and we gain the first benefits of a new language, such as GIS [an IBM development]."[142] Contacts with the twenty task force participants—including those from insurance firms such as Allstate and

Travelers; vendors such as General Electric, RCA, Burroughs, and UNIVAC; and other large commercial firms such as General Motors and American Telephone and Telegraph (AT&T)—also benefited the firm.[143] Thus Aetna's data-processing managers and top technical personnel learned from peers within and outside the insurance industry.

This case study, like that of New England Mutual Life, reflects several themes from previous chapters while also raising some new ones. Aetna, with its varied business lines and its heavy dependence on IBM punched-card tabulating equipment, briefly considered other vendors but, with good service and encouragement from IBM, ultimately followed a fairly typical incremental hardware path, moving from the 650 to the 1401 to the 7070 to the 360 and 370, using IBM hardware almost exclusively through the mid-1970s. Unlike New England Mutual Life, it did not ultimately run into a vendor capability constraint that drove it to a massive switch. In the software arena, however, it followed a less traveled and more bumpy path. The two individuals most active in Aetna's early computerization, Espie and O'Neil, shaped initial development toward the casualty and group insurance business areas and toward accounting and reporting, rather than operational, applications. Although this put Aetna ahead in those areas, in ordinary life insurance, most applications simply translated individual, tabulator-based accounting and reporting systems to small IBM 650 and 1401 computers. When the board of directors decentralized application development from the comptroller's office to the operating divisions, it reinvigorated the stalled work on an ordinary life integrated application. Even then, however, Aetna's large size, which required a large computer to run such a program, and IBM's problems with ALIS, designed for the System/360, further delayed the project. Only in the late 1960s and early 1970s was a more advanced, integrated system, LIAS, introduced to handle routine processing of ordinary insurance. Its late appearance, however, allowed LIAS to benefit from Aetna's applications in other business areas, such as the advanced SAFARI system. Aetna's computer managers and personnel also benefited from various contacts with peers elsewhere working on similar problems. Thus its incremental migration path, though unusual, eventually led it to transformed processes that resembled New England Mutual Life's.

Like New England Mutual Life, Aetna struggled with both personnel and budget growth in its computer operations. Within the ordinary life insurance area, as figure 8.3 shows, Aetna's ordinary renewal expense ratio started climbing in the mid-1940s and, except for a brief downturn in the mid-1960s, kept growing until the mid-1970s, when it greatly exceeded the thirty-firm average ratio. At that point the cost ratio finally began to drop, perhaps responding to the 1972 LIAS installation—although it is, of course, impossible to link them definitively. Nevertheless, throughout this period Aetna Life was rising in asset-based rank. Between 1952 and 1962 it moved from ninth largest to sixth largest, and by 1982 it was fourth largest.[144] Asset growth reflects many factors other than computerization, but Aetna's progress up the ranks indicates that it was not losing ground vis-à-vis other large firms. Whereas much smaller firms such as Franklin Life and many adopters of '62 CFO could get an entire integrated package for their firms' life insurance business onto the UNIVAC or the IBM 1401, larger firms needed much larger equipment, such as that provided by the IBM 360 and 370 series. Significantly, Aetna initially innovated more in its other, smaller businesses than in ordinary life. The oldest and largest of Aetna's businesses, ordinary life, followed rather than led the other business areas in computerization.

## Common Themes

Although these two cases are not representative, they illustrate in more detail some dynamics that unfolded in the first decades of insurance computerization. First, they show that the incremental hardware path, when readily available, attracted insurance firms. Both New England Mutual Life and Aetna adopted early computers from their primary office equipment vendors. For Aetna this incremental hardware decision led to a relatively smooth hardware migration up IBM's developing line. New England Mutual Life started later and had a much less satisfactory hardware experience with Sperry Rand's UNIVAC computers. Although it initially liked the UNIVACs, eventually it reached a crisis point when Shafto and his staff determined that the UNIVAC 1108 and 1110 would soon not meet its capacity needs. Although Sperry Rand was unable or unwilling to improve the situation, IBM was ready to fill the void. Still, New England Mutual Life might not have made its decisive transition from UNI-VAC to IBM equipment (indeed, IBM's marketing staff did not expect it) except for Robert Shafto's attitudes and actions. He had extensive knowledge of insurance data processing, the self-confidence to make a difficult call, and the ability to convince others around him to support it.

Software, in particular application development in the ordinary life insurance area, posed an even tougher challenge than hardware for these firms, both too large for '62 CFO. New England Mutual Life followed the more typical software path, constructing a consolidated functions application piece by piece. Although the firm had not completely integrated these pieces on its UNIVAC II and III computers, in the late 1960s it devised the more ambitious Milepost system for the UNIVAC 1108, supplementing integrated operations with on-line connections. In this case, both inadequate hardware and a misjudgment of how much software development was needed blocked progress until Shafto arrived in the early 1970s. Under his guidance, the firm finally switched from UNIVAC to IBM computers and got Milepost functioning by the late 1970s. Aetna, on the other hand, followed an atypical application development path from the beginning. Its ordinary life insurance applications lagged considerably behind operational applications in the casualty and group insurance areas and behind accounting applications. Size probably played a role here, too, since the smaller businesses such as casualty insurance were easier to computerize, especially before the 360 became available. But only after top management decentralized control of computer development efforts to the operating divisions in 1964 did Aetna finally devote resources to an integrated system for managing ordinary life operations. Initially, it turned to IBM's ALIS development, in which Aetna's beta-testing role exemplified insurance industry engagement with the computing industry, which was focused more on software than hardware by the 1960s. When ALIS turned out to be inadequate, it built its own LIAS system based on, but going beyond, existing products. Despite the false starts, LIAS was operational by 1972, several years before Milepost.

The two case studies also highlight how difficult large insurance firms found it to reduce ordinary life expenses during this period.[145] Expense ratios for these firms, like those for the thirty-firm average, begin to fall only in the mid- to late 1970s. Until that point, computerization may have contributed to rising, not falling, costs, more examples of the productivity paradox. By the late 1970s, these firms had finally succeeded in migrating to large-scale computers and using them in ways that transformed the old tabulator-based processes and that were likely to lower costs. Of course, even before the late 1970s, computer use might have reduced the growth rate for expenses, but these case studies suggest good reasons that computerization's full benefit might not be felt until the 1970s. As figure 8.3 shows, New England Mutual Life's expense ratios never rose as steeply or to as high a level as Aetna's, but after Aetna finally achieved the critical ordinary life integrated application, it turned the expense ratio growth around earlier than New England Mutual Life did and brought it down more steeply.[146] If the ordinary renewal expense ratio in fact reveals the influence of ordinary insurance computer applications, then Aetna's strategy of ignoring integrated ordinary life applications led to higher-than-expected costs in the 1960s and early 1970s. However, Aetna began to lower its costs earlier than New England Mutual Life, possibly reflecting its earlier completion of its integrated online application for ordinary life operations, LIAS. Learning from systems developed in Aetna's other insurance businesses may also have helped make LIAS a success. New England Mutual Life's incremental software strategy prevented its costs from climbing as high as Aetna's, but its hardware switch before full implementation of the Milepost system delayed the largest benefits from computerization.

Finally, both cases highlight how individual managers and technical experts can shape a firm's adoption and use of computers. As Giddens notes, structures exist only by virtue of individual actions.[147] At New England Mutual Life, Shafto's knowledge and confidence helped that firm move from UNIVAC to IBM hardware abruptly, rather than gradually. He could not have made the change alone, however. The actions of knowledgeable top executives such as Phillips and Fibiger and of subordinates such as Knier supported Shafto's willingness to walk away from UNIVAC hardware.[148] At Aetna, individual influence both constrained and enabled development. Espie's accounting responsibilities and interest in group insurance, along with O'Neil's work for casualty insurance, both shaped the order in which Aetna computerized various business lines and functions and the effort put into each. Firm structures such as the initial placement of computer operations within the comptroller's domain apparently encouraged accounting applications and discouraged the ordinary life insurance operating application.[149] Only when application development became the operating divisions' responsibility did Aetna finally achieve an integrated life insurance application. At that stage, Sitkin, with his belief that data processing should serve the business divisions, helped reinforce the new development direction.

Less prominent employees also figured in computerization. The New England Mutual Life case illustrates how important assuaging the workers' fears of technological displacement was to insurance firms. New England Mutual Life, like many other firms, initiated an information campaign in its in-house magazine before bringing any machines into the firm. Available records reveal less about how Aetna handled this area, but in both cases, rapid growth of life insurance and of computer personnel within insurance firms (generally insurance employees trained to work with computers) obviated the need to displace clerical workers. In both firms, educating middle-level insurance managers and technical employees through exchanges with peers in the industry also helped develop staffs capable of carrying out the strategies key management figures designed.

# Conclusion

Life insurance has been a major user of information technology from the tabulator era through the early computer era. As such, it provides a useful focus for examining technology adoption, use, and transitions. Its story is, of course, unique to the industry. Nevertheless, some broader patterns and influences emerge that seem likely to characterize other commercial users of information technology during the same period and that provide insight into the adoption and application of new information technologies yesterday and today.

## Patterns of Continuity and Change

Two primary themes underlie this story: the reciprocal influence of information technology and its use by firms, and the influence of past technology and technology-in-practice on firms' adoption and application of new technologies.

### Reciprocal Influence of Technology and Use

During the tabulator era, the technology and its use in life insurance clearly exerted reciprocal influences. Initially, Hollerith tabulating technology enabled life insurance user firms to sort, count, and add more rapidly. Thus the equipment allowed them to continue the current trend of subdividing their tasks into ever smaller pieces, rather than to do things in fundamentally new ways. In the second decade of the twentieth century, however, insurance companies felt constrained in their applications of tabulating technology because it lacked the printing capability available on adding and calculating machines. Some life insurance firms, such as Metropolitan Life and Prudential Assurance Company, worked directly with inventors such as Pierce or with producers such as Powers' British subsidiary to develop tabulating equipment with printing capabilities, first numerical and then alphabetical. Other, smaller firms influenced the technology through market forces, by switching to the vendor that provided this capability soonest and best. These reciprocal influences resulted in what I have elsewhere termed a co-evolution of tabulating technology and its use.[1] When insurance associations such as the Life Office Management Association (LOMA) and later the Insurance Accounting and Statistical Association (IASA) added equipment exhibits to their annual meetings, they opened another avenue of influence between vendors and users. At these exhibits, vendors often demonstrated particular applications in the insurance context. IBM's exhibit at the 1935 LOMA conference, for example, demonstrated how insurance firms could use its tabulating equipment for "Premium Accounting and Premium Notice and Receipt Writing," an early version of the integrated premium billing and accounting application that insurance companies designated as a goal during both the late tabulator era and, in a more developed form, the early computer era.[2]

This reciprocal influence between technology artifacts and their use also appeared in the early computer era. The characteristics of new information technology clearly influenced its use in insurance. Given the size and price of the UNIVAC, for example, medium-sized firms such as Pacific Mutual and Franklin Life had an incentive to adopt a consolidated functions application to justify the cost, whereas very large firms such as Metropolitan Life and John Hancock could apply the computer to a single task, testing its capabilities in less risky applications. The IBM 650, with its small capacity and card input/output, made translating tabulating applications directly onto it, with no change in the underlying business process, very attractive for most firms. Moreover, its tabulator-like design made it fit right into existing tabulator installations, not requiring the massive space renovations needed to install a UNIVAC. Later, third-generation computers such as the IBM 360/370 lines brought new capabilities such as time-sharing that allowed online insurance applications. Computer software, as well as hardware, influenced and was influenced by insurance use. While most insurance users initially struggled to develop their own software, in 1962 IBM developed and bundled a software application package for life insurance with its Type 1401 computer. Its '62 CFO, itself based on the consolidated functions approach devised by the Society of Actuaries committee, further encouraged incremental progress toward the integrated application, one function at a time. Other vendors offered similar packages, but with less widespread influence.

The reciprocal influence of insurance users and applications on the technology artifacts during the early computer era has typically been overshadowed by the military and government influence.[3] As I have shown, however, the insurance industry played a significant role in adapting computers and software to commercial uses. Berkeley's negotiations on Prudential's behalf, reinforced by interactions with the Society of Actuaries, LOMA, and IASA committees, prompted Eckert and Mauchly to develop card input and output as well as high-speed printers for the UNIVAC, thus shaping a characteristic that was much more important in commercial applications than military ones. Life insurance firms also exerted a market-based influence when they (along with many other commercial firms) rushed to rent or buy the IBM 650 computer with its familiar look, card input/output, and compatibility with tabulator peripherals. Internal IBM projections for the 650 undershot actual demand by a factor of ten, and insurance contributed to overturning this low expectation.[4] By March 1957, according to the final report of the Society of Actuaries committee, 640 IBM 650s had been installed, of which 40 were in life insurance firms and another 45 in all other types of insurance, so that insurance as a whole accounted for 13% of the market to that point.[5] The surprise success of the 650 both helped IBM navigate the transition from tabulators to computers and showed it clearly how attractive the incremental migration path was to many commercial users. The IBM 1401 was similarly successful among insurance and other commercial firms. The case studies in Chapter 8 highlight the extent to which large insurance firms pushed the capacity limits of computers, with the inadequate capacity of the UNIVAC 1108 and 1110 triggering Aetna's switch to IBM computers.

In the 1960s and 1970s, the influence insurance users exerted on the technology increasingly shaped software even more than hardware. For example, insurance firms played a role in developing general business software by participating in efforts such as the Committee on Data Systems and Languages' development of the COBOL language. Most obvious, IBM's incredibly popular '62 CFO package for the 1401 was based on the consolidated functions approach that the Society of Actuaries committee had proposed a decade earlier for computerizing ordinary insurance operations. This software in turn shaped insurance hardware adoption and use, making the 1401 even more attractive and allowing incremental, module-by-module implementation, thereby assuring that the committee's vision would be the goal of most life insurance applications into the 1970s. Several life insurance firms were also very involved in IBM's ALIS development effort, which brought the consolidated functions application onto its 360 computers and expanded it. IBM was more responsive to the many smaller firms that would adopt models such as the 360/30 than to the large firms that planned to adopt 360/65s and other powerful models, however, thus probably contributing to ALIS's failure to take off. Still, companies such as Aetna and Prudential created their own consolidated applications with online access by adding their own software development resources. Even after an independent software industry emerged, most vendors that produced packaged software worked with members of targeted industries such as life insurance to develop desirable packages. Thus the insurance industry's shaping of technology during the computer era increasingly shifted into the software realm.

In general, according to Giddens, "technological change is not something that occurs independently of the uses to which agents put technology, the characteristic modes of innovation, etc."[6] During this period firms shaped what has been called *technology-in-practice,* or the ways in which the technology is actually used.[7] In Whisler and Meyer's 1967 study of insurance computer use, they described what they saw as a rather surprising outcome: "Throughout our study, one fact stood out clearly: Information technology has been shaped and applied in a variety of ways, with a variety of organizational effects. It is harder to find a pattern or trend than it is to see the variations. Although it is difficult to prove, we strongly suspect that not only does information technology affect the shape of the organization, but the character of the organization affects the shape of the technology."[8] Beyond shaping the hardware and software as it was *developed,* an influence that most social construction literature emphasizes, insurance firms also influenced *technology-in-practice.* Particular organizational structures and managerial actions shaped what technology companies acquired and how they used it, a complex and interrelated series of choices about hardware, software, and use, each of which reflected the organization's "character." For example, Franklin Life's space crisis encouraged it to adopt a UNIVAC, and its small size shaped the firm's choice of a consolidated functions application; Metropolitan Life's unwillingness to risk disrupting policyholder relations along with its extremely large size led executives to choose an actuarial application for its first UNIVAC; Shafto's leadership was crucial in converting New England Mutual Life rapidly and completely from UNIVAC to IBM when he and his staff determined that the UNIVAC line was inadequate; and Aetna's Espie and O'Neill favored accounting and group insurance applications based on their backgrounds and organizational roles, neglecting ordinary insurance applications for many years.

Life insurance firms and the people making them up influenced information technology configuration and use, just as information technology influenced how its users conducted their business. The user shaping of technology-in-practice presented in this book, however, differs from that increasingly visible in the social shaping of technology literature, which focuses on the individual level of analysis, primarily on the "social appropriation of technologies" by individual consumers.[9] Instead, I have focused on a technology too large and expensive to be a consumer technology. Tabulating installations and early computers were large-scale technologies that only firms and organizations needed and could afford to acquire. Although individual agents clearly played critical roles, they could not act alone but had to mobilize those above and below them in the company hierarchy, as well as their peers, to acquire and apply such technology. Moreover, industry structures were also important. Insurance firms cooperated through professional and trade associations such as the Society of Actuaries, LOMA, and IASA to study new technologies, interact with their producers, and explore how the technologies might best be used. This firm and industry focus illuminates a level thus far studied on the producer side but rarely on the user side.[10]

## Influence of Past Practices on Technology Adoption and Use

The ongoing reciprocal influences of technology and its use also operate over long periods and across technology changes. Thus organizational practices related to earlier technologies significantly influenced how life insurance firms adopted and used new technology when they made the transition from tabulating installations to computers starting in the 1950s.[11] On the equipment side, life insurance firms were accustomed to working with IBM (or occasionally Remington Rand) tabulators, sales representatives, and technical support people; moreover, they possessed millions of eighty-column punched cards full of data. Although tempted by the notion of immediate and radical transformation via the UNIVAC, initially most firms preferred to maintain continuity as they changed by retaining a familiar vendor and using their existing punched cards on a small IBM 650 computer. Even firms adopting the magnetic-tape UNIVAC wanted the security of card, as well as tape, data storage. Moreover, the 650's close visual resemblance to the top end of the tabulator range emphasized its continuity with tabulating technology. A few firms—motivated by strong and immediate needs (e.g., Franklin Life's space crisis), felt a need to take a leadership role (e.g., Metropolitan Life), or other factors strong enough to overcome a preference for gradual change—adopted the large and unfamiliar UNIVAC. The vast majority chose the incremental hardware migration path, using the 650 as a stepping-stone to the 1401 and maybe to a 7070. A few compromised, starting with the larger, tape-based 702 or 705 but still maintaining vendor continuity. Only in the mid- to late 1960s did most companies take the larger step to the IBM 360 series, the UNIVAC 1108, or another third-generation computer. The 360s were radically different from tabulators, but most firms had taken an incremental hardware path to reach them, never losing the continuity between past and present.

On the application side, past processes also structured present ones. Managers used initial tabulating applications just to automate discrete manual tasks, continuing the functional subdivision of processes they had already begun. By the late tabulator era, however, an integrated premium billing and accounting application was beginning to gain popularity. The consolidated functions approach that emerged from the Society of Actuaries committee and dominated early insurance computing extended that integration further. IBM's bundling of its '62 CFO software, based on the committee's plan, with its 1401 computer increased that model's popularity. The '62 CFO software package became enormously successful, in part because its modular structure allowed firms to follow an incremental strategy of first computerizing all the discrete functions, then gradually integrating them. Thus tabulator applications shaped application development in computers for the first two decades of computer use.[12]

The electronic stored-program computer was, in many ways, radically different from what preceded it; as the Society of Actuaries committee members had indicated, insurance firms needed to reengineer or transform their existing processes to take full advantage of the technology. Nevertheless, most insurance firms favored an adoption and use pattern of incremental migration, starting with current tabulator applications on the smallest computers and moving gradually to larger computers and more elaborate integrated applications. Without a strong impetus, such as Franklin Life's space crisis, most insurance firms clearly preferred to adopt and use new technology in the least disruptive way possible, creating as much continuity with past practices as possible. Ultimately, this incremental migration also transformed existing processes, but it did so gradually, not overnight. The New England Mutual Life and Aetna case studies demonstrated the twists and turns possible even when firms desired continuity. New England Mutual Life chose a familiar vendor, if not machine, in Remington Rand's UNIVAC. After following an incremental path for a decade, it encountered a dead end—its hardware could not support its chosen software path. Eventually it accepted sudden and complete hardware and vendor change so as to continue developing the Milepost application it wanted. Aetna, in contrast, successfully maintained hardware continuity but did not initially pursue the standard consolidated functions application for ordinary life insurance, developing it only much later, after false starts and alternative paths in other insurance functions and businesses. Still, both attempted to follow the incremental path throughout. Communication historian Carolyn Marvyn has explained this conservative tendency as follows: "Early uses of technological innovations are essentially conservative because their capacity to create social disequilibrium is intuitively recognized amidst declarations of progress and enthusiasm for the new. . . . Inevitably, both change and the contemplation of change are reciprocal events that expose old ideas to revision from contact with new ones. This is also how historical actors secure in the perception of continuity are eternally persuaded to embrace the most radical of transformations. The past really does survive in the future."[13] This explanation refers to individual users of technological innovations, but it clearly applies to firm users, as well. By transferring old applications onto the most familiar-looking new equipment, the firms began their slow progress into the computer age.

The preferred incremental migration path followed by most insurance firms may shed light on the so-called productivity paradox, as well. In the late 1980s and 1990s, many economists and managers lamented what they saw as information technology's failure to boost the productivity rate of firms investing in it.[14] They suggested various explanations, from mismeasurement and time lags for learning and adjustment to redistribution of profits and mismanagement.[15] Social theorist Manuel Castells, turning to economic history accounts of earlier productivity lags related to broadly significant technological innovations, suggested that organizational and cultural changes were necessary precursors of productivity gains: "For new technological discoveries to be able to diffuse throughout the whole economy, thus enhancing productivity growth at an observable rate, the culture and institutions of society, business firms, and the factors intervening in the production process need to undergo substantial change. This general statement is particularly appropriate in the case of a technological revolution centered around knowledge and information."[16] Although more recently the paradox seems to have lessened or disappeared as

U.S. productivity has grown, this study of one user industry supports the theory that productivity growth lagged significantly behind the initial computer investment because organizational changes were needed to realize the gain. The average ordinary renewal expense ratio (ordinary RER) suggests that the lag was as long as two decades. Most insurance firms acquired their initial computers in the mid-1950s, but the expense ratio rose despite these investments until the mid-1970s, when it finally turned around. This lag far exceeds the two to five years assumed by managers and scholars discussing the productivity paradox in the 1990s, though it accords with historical accounts of the productivity impact of prior technologies.[17] Of course, there are several caveats to this explanation. First, the ordinary RER is admittedly an imperfect measure that does not, for example, correct for inflation.[18] Moreover, factors discussed below, such as regulation and ideology, may have slowed learning and change in the insurance industry more than in other industries, resulting in a longer lag. In addition, evidence from early insurance computerization does not rule out contributions from other possible explanations, such as mismeasurement or mismanagement. Finally, computer use could have been preventing the ordinary RER from rising even higher for other reasons. Nevertheless, a lag brought about by incremental migration rather than sudden transformation seems plausible in this context, and the insurance industry clearly exemplifies the conservative tendency Marvin considers widespread in early technology use.

Users' preference for continuity may also help explain why IBM survived the technology transition to dominate the early computer industry just as it had the tabulator market. The common wisdom in studies of technological innovation is that market incumbents are unlikely to survive a radical discontinuity in core technology.[19] Nevertheless, there have always been some glaring exceptions to this pattern, of which IBM is one.[20] The insurance and computing story sheds light on how it bridged that technological discontinuity successfully. The tiny 650 computer, a stopgap measure to keep customers on board as IBM played catch-up on larger commercial and scientific computers, succeeded in the insurance market partly because it looked like an electronic tabulator and used the same cards. IBM learned from the 650's unexpected success that insurance companies and other commercial users preferred an incremental migration path over a sudden and radical transformation in hardware and in applications. It built on this desire for incremental migration by developing its card-based 1401, buying itself more time as it developed its more advanced 360 range of computers.

Both the reciprocal influence of technology and its use and the influence of past practices on the adoption and application of new technology reflect the dynamic structuring process. "The structural properties of social systems exist only in so far as forms of social conduct are reproduced chronically across time and space," according to Giddens.[21] It is this reproduction of structures across time and space that characterized insurance acquisition and application of information technology. The structurational lens, which suggests that individuals typically reproduce existing structures but can always choose to do otherwise, has led me to examine more closely under what conditions the incremental migration pattern was likely to dominate and under what conditions individuals and firms decided on another path. Franklin Life's incredibly rapid growth, its focus on sales more than on home office matters, and its space crisis all combined to make it receptive to A. C. Vanselow's championing of the new technology. Structuration's focus on the ongoing interplay of individual actions with institutionalized structures also helps us understand New England Mutual Life's rapid and wholesale shift from UNIVAC to IBM equipment. Shafto's previous experience and consequent recognition of the firm's problems made him willing to abandon the incremental hardware path and leap rapidly from UNIVAC to IBM; by that time he had also assembled a team that could successfully enact this transition. This lens highlights both continuity and change in life insurance use of information technology.

## Other Important Structuring Factors

Along with these overarching patterns of continuity and change, other institutionalized structures also shaped the life insurance industry's interaction with tabulating and computing technology. Focusing on firms, rather than individuals, as users broadens the scope of potential structuring factors, since both individuals within them and structures within, across, and around them may play a role. I will discuss these factors in two general categories: *industry context,* and *ideology and culture.*

### Industry Context

The life insurance industry context played a particularly important role in influencing firms' adoption and use of information technology. Perhaps most salient is the insurance business's sheer information intensity. The increasingly large volume of data that firms needed to store safely and process repeatedly meant that firms and associations could not afford to ignore the improvements promised first by tabulating and then by computer technology. They hoped that computers might reverse the steady rise of cost ratios since the mid-1930s. Thus insurance companies were among the first commercial firms to study computers and among the first to adopt them in the 1950s. By the mid-1970s, Booz, Allen and Hamilton reported that data-processing costs accounted for 20% of total expenses in the insurance industry, putting it second only to the securities industry, at 30%.[22] Around this time cost ratios in the thirty largest firms in the industry finally turned downward, though computers may have flattened the rise earlier.

The labor shortages and rapid life insurance growth in the postwar era, just as computers were being developed for commercial use, also significantly influenced how insurance companies viewed computers. The labor shortages that developed during World War II did not vanish after the war, as firms had expected, increasing their incentives to adopt technologies that would reduce clerical labor. At the same time, the insurance market's rapid growth shielded firms from the need to lay off workers as they automated more clerical processes. In the mid-1960s, the Bureau of Labor Statistics revealed that total office employment in insurance firms had continued to rise (though the growth rate declined from 4.2 to 2.4% per year) and that retraining and attrition had generally precluded any layoffs.[23] The absence of technological displacement in this industry undoubtedly reduced employee resistance to computerization, as did many insurance firms' attempts to anticipate and defuse fears and hostile reactions through educational and publicity campaigns.[24]

Regulation was another key facet of the industry context. Because the states, rather than the federal government, regulated life insurance, life insurance firms had to report to up to fifty different regulatory bodies. Although states coordinated many requirements, differences remained. These frequent and varied reporting requirements and the consequent repetition and reuse of insurance policy information reinforced insurance firms' attraction to both tabulating and computing technology from the start. Moreover, in a few cases specific regulatory changes encouraged firms to adopt technologies at particular times. For example, the Guertin laws of the late 1940s, which mandated that insurance firms base their rates on a new experience table, encouraged them to acquire additional, often updated, tabulating equipment to make the change. In addition, expectations about whether regulators would accept new technologies had a prospective influence on their adoption. When the Society of Actuaries committee debated whether insurance companies should eliminate cards in favor of magnetic tape when they adopted computers, it decided that firms must retain "a visual record . . . which would be generally accepted by the courts and regulatory bodies—at least until wide use of tape has become commonplace."[25] As with other industries and earlier technologies such as carbon copying, regulatory acceptance was important in adoption decisions.[26]

Regulation also shaped the competitive landscape within the insurance industry, which in turn structured its technology acquisition and application. In the mid-1960s, an economist analyzing insurance computer use noted that the industry lacked strong competitive incentives to use the technology in the most innovative and efficient ways: "In general, these structural variables indicate strong competition for new business and to achieve high growth rates. This competition takes the form, though, of selling effort, including product variation. Price competition, given the regulated character of the industry and the wide availability of mortality data, does not appear to be widespread. . . . Thus it would appear that desires for reduced administrative costs through innovation may not be as strong as if the industry structure generated vigorous price competition."[27] This economist attributed the lack of strong price competition to regulation, which allowed life insurance firms to compete primarily on sales and growth, rather than on prices and thus costs, during this period. Because competition to cut costs was not high, firms had decreased incentives to take a more risky (but potentially higher-return) approach to adopting and using computers. Consequently, the competitive environment of the 1950s to 1970s reinforced firms' preferences for an incremental migration, rather than a sudden transformation, of processes.

The competitive landscape for vendors, as seen from the life insurance industry's perspective, also structured evolving information technology use in life insurance. During both eras the primary vendor rivalry for the insurance business was between Hollerith/IBM, on the one hand, and Powers/Remington Rand/UNIVAC, on the other. In the tabulator era, competition between Hollerith and Powers generated considerable technological innovation. Moreover, insurance firms encouraged developments they valued, such as printing capability, by shifting from one rival firm's products to the other's. Accounts of the early computing era typically describe IBM's competitors as the Seven Dwarfs, of which Remington Rand/UNIVAC (later Sperry Rand) was just one.[28] For the life insurance industry, however, the rivalry between IBM and Remington Rand/UNIVAC was still central, and all other vendors were peripheral. Because insurance firms typically had large tabulating installations and thus had established sales and service relationships with one of the two tabulator vendors, IBM and Remington Rand had an edge with users who desired vendor continuity. Initially, the UNIVAC computer was seen as very new and distinct; when Remington Rand acquired the struggling Eckert-Mauchly Computer Corporation in 1950, however, UNIVAC became associated with a known vendor. This association of UNIVAC with Remington Rand did not seem very important to the first UNIVAC adopters, but once the shock of the new passed, later-adopting insurance firms such as New England Mutual Life may have found purchasing computer equipment from a familiar vendor easier than establishing new vendor service and support relationships. Some insurance firms turned to computer vendors outside the office machines industry, such as RCA and Honeywell, but most insurance industry accounts from this period saw these vendors as a distant third, behind IBM and UNIVAC. During the first two decades of life insurance computer use, the old two-sided rivalry, with IBM holding a lopsided advantage, reproduced itself.

Insurance associations also played an important role in structuring insurance adoption and use of information technology. Associations flourished in the insurance industry, encouraged by ideological and cultural factors discussed below. In the early tabulator era the Actuarial Society of America (precursor of the Society of Actuaries) organized multifirm experience studies that spread knowledge of and experience with punched-card tabulating. Later, trade associations such as LOMA and IASA played a critical role. Special committees established within such associations created an opportunity for firms to collaborate even more closely on this subject. In the early computer era, first the Society of Actuaries and then both LOMA and IASA provided forums for sharing information about the new technology and its application. Reciprocally, the associations provided a mechanism through which insurance companies could communicate with vendors. The special committees, for example, regularly interacted with vendors, thus potentially influencing the evolving technology in desirable directions. The associations spread knowledge about the new technologies and their uses; in addition, they shaped applications for information technology, as in the Society of Actuaries committee's highly influential consolidated functions approach.

Changes in the insurance business itself influenced technology use by affecting the identity of technology "lead users."[29] These motivated users, in this case firms rather than individuals, adopted technology early and were most likely to influence it directly. During the tabulator era, the lead users typically specialized in industrial insurance, since these firms had to process many more policies much more frequently than did firms with ordinary insurance only. Thus Metropolitan Life and Prudential both took more aggressive actions to shape tabulating technology—including building the Gore sorter and hiring Pierce to make custom equipment—than did Equitable, New York Life, or Mutual Life of New York. Similarly, Prudential Assurance, the huge British industrial insurance firm, collaborated with the British Powers agency to develop tabulator printing capabilities. By the 1950s, however, the industrial insurance market was stagnating, and ordinary insurance was growing rapidly. In interacting with Eckert and Mauchly, for example, Prudential's Berkeley focused on that firm's premium billing for ordinary insurance rather than on its industrial insurance processes, and the early test applications that several firms developed in conjunction with various vendors also focused on ordinary insurance. Many of the early adopters of computers (e.g., Franklin Life and Pacific Mutual) offered ordinary but not industrial insurance. Thus changes in the insurance business affected which users took the lead in adopting the technology, and for which uses.

Clearly, various factors in the industry context—and this list is certainly not comprehensive—shaped technology adoption and use by insurance firms. Yet when scholars of technology focus primarily on individual consumers and societal effects, they ignore this industry-level influence.

## Ideology and Culture

A second set of structuring factors, ideology and culture, also shaped insurance adoption of tabulator and computer technology. After the 1905 Armstrong Hearings, which had exposed a late nineteenth-century insurance culture of corruption and managerial abuses, most insurance firms cleaned house and adopted the view, already characteristic of fraternal life insurance companies and some mutuals, that the business of life insurance was special—a quasi-public service to be made as widely available as possible. Lower costs became desirable not to increase profits but to achieve growth goals held by firms and the industry. Life insurance firms somewhat belatedly turned to the systematic management ideology. This managerial philosophy had initially emerged in manufacturing, but by the early twentieth century it had entered the office. In insurance, unlike in manufacturing, office work did not just manage production—it *was* production. Thus efficient office management was doubly important. The public service and systematic office management ideologies worked together to support adopting information-handling technologies such as Hollerith's tabulating equipment to reduce costs and promote growth.

These ideologies manifested themselves on the industry level, as well as in firms, particularly in the many insurance associations. Although a few associations such as the Actuarial Society of America were founded before the Armstrong Hearings, many more were founded after that watershed event, as the public service ideology took root and encouraged cooperation to serve the public interest. In supporting collaboration across firms, associations such as LOMA regularly invoked the notion of public service. Such associations were part of a larger national movement toward associational activities, but in insurance they had an added attraction.[30] Moreover, LOMA's stated intention to share existing knowledge and to create new knowledge about efficient home office management of insurance processes was also grounded in the systematic management ideology. LOMA (and later IASA) helped spread office management techniques and technologies, educating members about tabulating equipment and its uses in insurance companies through papers, workshops, and exhibits at association meetings. The public service ideology may also help explain why firms' representatives typically shared their experiences with such technologies quite openly, rather than hoarding their knowledge as a potential source of competitive advantage. Firms may have received some economic benefits from such sharing, through increased leverage with vendors and mutually beneficial information exchanges with other firms, but it seems likely that they also incurred costs. Thus one factor determining the extent to which firms engaged in these joint activities may have been an ideologically motivated sense that cooperating was the right thing to do. Whatever the motives, insurance firms certainly embraced many and varied industry associations.

Another broadly cultural factor that shaped insurance adoption and use of information technologies was the attitude toward employees that they shared. Although firms varied in specific culture, most tended to be fairly paternalistic, extending their public service ideology to employees as well as customers. Many took great care in educating their employees about the nature of and need for computers, often promising that no one would lose his or her job because of computerization. Although insurance firms were not alone in making such pledges, they did so fairly consistently and seemed to have stood by them, perhaps even beyond what greater price competition would have allowed. Most firms trained their own programmers and operators from within rather than hiring from outside, both because they had committed not to lay off employees and because they believed that insurance was a special business not easily understood by outsiders. The mid-1960s Bureau of Labor Statistics study of insurance computer use reported that 72% of electronic data-processing employees were recruited from within firms. Thus cultural and ideological factors, as well as or in conjunction with other industry factors, shaped insurance acquisition and application of computers.

## Implications for Other Users and Technologies

This book has focused on life insurance firms, individually and as an industry, as information technology users during two different technology eras. Although this story's details are specific to the insurance context, the overarching pattern of reciprocal influence between technology and its use by firms and industries should shed valuable light on how other firm-level users adopt and apply technologies. Organizational technology use may influence the technology artifact to a greater or lesser extent depending on how important a particular user firm or industry is to the vendor's market and whether the technology is important enough to the user firm to encourage its engagement with the vendor. Even in cases in which the organizational user has no perceptible effect on the vendors' offerings, it will shape the technology-in-practice, that is, the way the company or organization applies the technology. The technology's reciprocal influence on the organization also depends on how central it is to that organization's work, but it will almost always have some effect, however small. Similarly, the influence of past technologies and processes on adoption and use of new technologies seems to be a general pattern. How great an influence past practices wield on future use is likely to vary, depending on the cultural and ideological context and on industry pressures.

This study also suggests that transitions from one dominant technology to another are unlikely to look as sharp and as clean from the user organization's perspective as they do externally and retrospectively. Both continuity and change are likely to appear in varying proportions. Moreover, change is better understood as an ongoing process rather than simply as a one-time event or even a process limited to a predefined implementation period. The life insurance industry followed a predominantly incremental migration path toward transformed processes for almost twenty years before it achieved and surpassed its initial vision—itself shaped by past practices—and before it began to reduce costs. This analysis from the user industry's point of view also suggests that

IBM successfully made the transition from tabulators to computers in part because it recognized that many commercial users wanted such an incremental path and that IBM could help them follow that path.

Finally, these observations suggest that historians and scholars of contemporary technological change may gain new perspective by recognizing and exploring the corporate user's point of view on transitions in large-scale, non-consumer technologies. Recent scholars have increasingly looked at individual consumers and even societies as consumers, but very few have focused on user organizations other than the military and government.[31] Ultimately, the reciprocal influences suggest that the experience of large user organizations, taken in aggregate, if not individually, shape technology, just as technology shapes the user organizations.

# Notes

## Introduction

1. Of course, information and communication played important roles elsewhere in the world, but this book focuses on the United States, generally acknowledged to be a leader in information use and technology. Chandler and Cortada, *Nation Transformed by Information*, makes the argument that information has been central throughout the life of the United States, and some of the scholars represented in it have elsewhere more fully traced the U.S. preoccupation with information to earlier eras (e.g., Brown, *Knowledge Is Power*, and John, *Spreading the News*). Meanwhile, a small but growing body of scholarly literature has demonstrated the important role of information use, as well as the techniques and technologies that facilitate it, during the past century (e.g., Beniger, *Control Revolution*; Yates, *Control Through Communication*; and Cortada, *Before the Computer*).

2. See, in particular, Bijker, Hughes, and Pinch, *Social Construction of Technological Systems*, and Bijker, *Of Bicycles, Bakelites, and Bulbs*. For other works focusing on how users shape technology, see, for example, Douglas, *Inventing American Broadcasting*, and Fischer, *America Calling*.

3. See, for example, Mackay and Gillespie, "Extending the Social Shaping of Technology Approach"; Oudshoorn and Pinch, *How Users Matter*; and Mackay et al., "Reconfiguring the User." "Technology-in-practice" comes from Orlikowski, "Using Technology and Constituting Structures."

4. Mackay and Gillespie, "Extending the Social Shaping of Technology Approach," 698–699. See also Oudshoorn and Pinch, *How Users Matter*.

5. Haigh, "Chromium-Plated Tabulator," begins to address this question for the broader arena of administrative data processing.

6. The claims and counterclaims for technological priority can be gained by scanning several volumes of *Annals of the History of Computing*, for example. Campbell-Kelly and Aspray provide a guide to some of this partisan literature in their bibliographic essay for chapter 4 of *Computer*, 307–308.

7. Cortada, *Before the Computer*, looks at pre-computer vendors of information technology. In *Inventing the Electronic Century*, Chandler looks at the vendors of early computers, classifying them in part according to whether they had started out as vendors of other business machines. Several writers of varying historical credentials and with varying amounts of focus on the technology itself have looked at the history of IBM as it made the transition from the tabulator into the computer era, including Sobel (*IBM*); Pugh, (*Building IBM*); and Bashe et al. (*IBM's Early Computers*).

8. For example, Flamm, *Creating the Computer*, and Stern, *From ENIAC to UNIVAC*.

9. Treatments of commercial information technology users in general include, for example, Norberg, "High Technology Calculation"; Cortada, "Commercial Applications of the Digital Computer in American Corporations"; Haigh, "Chromium-Plated Tabulator"; and Usselman, "Fostering a Capacity for Compromise."

10. James L. McKenney and his colleagues looked at banking industry use: Fisher and McKenney, "Development of the ERMA Banking System"; Fisher and McKenney, "Manufacturing the ERMA Banking System"; and McKenney, *Waves of Change.* Caminer et al., *World's First Business Computer,* focus on a user that became a vendor. Most recent and most specifically focused on computer use is Cortada's *Digital Hand,* which gives an overview of computer use in the manufacturing, transportation, and retail industries. Information systems scholars are more likely to consider users' roles, though they rarely take a long-term view and typically aim more at managing systems development than at understanding technology use. For a discussion of various user classifications, including his own, see Friedman, *Computer Systems Development.*

11. I refer to life insurance as an industry throughout this book. Although it is also part of the larger insurance industry, it functioned quite separately from other insurance types during this period for regulatory and other reasons; even its trade associations were usually solely for life insurance (with the Insurance Accounting and Statistical Association [IASA] as an important exception). Other types of insurance adopted and used tabulating technology, as well, but typically at a somewhat slower rate and somewhat less extensively because they lacked the immense numbers of policies common in life insurance and had more variation in the policies themselves (see Charles H. Cissley, *Systems and Data Processing in Insurance Companies* [New York: Life Office Management Association, 1977], 13–16). Moreover, though other types of insurance grew over the twentieth century, a 1965 Bureau of Labor Statistics study noted that at that time more than half of all insurance employees were employed in life insurance (U.S. Department of Labor, Bureau of Labor Statistics [hereafter cited as BLS], "Impact of Office Automation in the Insurance Industry" [Washington, D.C.: U.S. Government Printing Office, 1965], p. 1). Thus I have chosen to limit my user industry analysis to life insurance, and unless otherwise stated, references to insurance should be taken to mean life insurance.

12. The best extended historical treatments of this industry are still Zelizer, *Morals and Markets;* Keller, *The Life Insurance Enterprise;* and Stalson, *Marketing Life Insurance.*

13. Yates, "Co-evolution of Information Processing Technology and Use" and "Early Interactions between the Life Insurance and Computer Industries"; Orlikowski, "Using Technology and Constituting Structures."

14. For a review of literature on this subject as of the early 1990s, see Brynjolfsson, "Productivity Paradox of Information Technology"; for the disparity's disappearance from more recent statistics, see Brynjolfsson and Hitt, "Beyond the Productivity Paradox."

15. See, for example, Norberg, "High Technology Calculation"; Campbell-Kelly, "Punched-Card Machinery"; Cortada, *Before the Computer;* Yates, "Co-evolution of Information Processing Technology and Use"; and Haigh, "Chromium-Plated Tabulator."

16. For example, Campbell-Kelly and Aspray, *Computer,* and Ceruzzi, *History of Modern Computing.* Somewhat older histories occasionally mention tabulating technology as used by government but not by business (e.g., Goldstine, *Computer from Pascal to von Neumann*).

17. On the level of technology architecture, see Ceruzzi, "Crossing the Divide." An exception to this neglect is Haigh, "Chromium-Plated Tabulator."

18. Giddens, *Constitution of Society*.

19. Yates, "Using Giddens' Structuration Theory to Inform Business History." See also Scranton, "Giddens' Structuration Theory and Research on Technical Change," and Borg, "'Chauffeur Problem' in the Early Auto Era."

20. Giddens, *Constitution of Society*, 25.

21. Orlikowski, "Duality of Technology."

22. Giddens, *Constitution of Society*, 15.

23. This theme may, of course, be approached without the structurational lens, as in Marvin, *When Old Technologies Were New*.

ONE: Insurance at the Turn of the Twentieth Century

1. In *Morals and Markets*, Zelizer traces the early history of the life insurance industry in the United States. For a brief history of voluntary mutual aid organizations, see Beito, *From Mutual Aid to the Welfare State*, 5–16.

2. Zelizer, *Morals and Markets*, 1–7.

3. Ibid., 91.

4. Stalson (*Marketing Life Insurance*) argues that growth in the 1840s derived from the agency system, in which agents personally solicited business. Zelizer (*Morals and Markets*, esp. 41–117), however, more persuasively argues that the emergence and success of the agency system responded to changes in attitudes.

5. Zelizer, *Morals and Markets*, 18–19; Collier, *Capital Ship*, 1.

6. Keller, *Life Insurance Enterprise*, 42.

7. Zelizer, *Morals and Markets*, 101–105.

8. Ibid., 117.

9. Insurance in force is a common metric for measuring firm size. Total assets is another metric for judging this.

10. Stalson, *Marketing Life Insurance*, 798–799, table B.

11. Keller, *Life Insurance Enterprise*, 42.

12. Ibid., 62.

13. U.S. Bureau of the Census, *Historical Statistics of the United States: Colonial Times to 1957* (Washington, D.C.: U.S. Department of Commerce, Bureau of the Census, 1960), ser. X 458, p. 674.

14. Keller, *Life Insurance Enterprise*, 16.

15. Litterer has explored this phenomenon in "Systematic Management: The Search for Order and Integration"; "Alexander Hamilton Church and the Development of Modern Management"; and "Systematic Management: Design for Organizational Recoupling in American Manufacturing Firms." See also Yates, *Control Through Communication*, 1–20, and Shenhav, "From Chaos to Systems." This movement fits with the broader societal ideology of this era, as traced by Wiebe in *Search for Order, 1877–1920*.

16. Systematizers had two common themes: (1) the need to transcend individuals by standardizing and documenting processes and procedures, and (2) a systematic approach to gathering and analyzing data. See Litterer, "Systematic Management: Design for Organizational Recoupling," p. 389; Yates, *Control Through Communication*, 10–15. For

some of the differences in how the ideology played out in different types of manufacturing, see Scranton, *Endless Novelty*, 18–19.

17. Zunz has called this trend "the cult of efficiency" in *Making America Corporate*, 116.

18. Yates, *Control Through Communication*, 1–20. For the application of systematic management to the office, the best example is William Henry Leffingwell, *Office Management: Principles and Practice* (New York: A. W. Shaw Co., 1927).

19. In discussing life insurance sales agents, Kwolek-Folland talks about "two streams of managerial theory, the rational and the impressionistic" (*Engendering Business*, 77). The former, which is based on systematic management, is more relevant to my story of insurance use of information processing than the latter, based on interpersonal skills.

20. See Campbell-Kelly, "Large-Scale Data Processing in the Prudential," for an account of how large-scale but entirely manual insurance work was systematized in a British life insurance firm.

21. Keller describes a "disturbing phenomenon"—"the stubborn association of growth with high, and rising, costs" (*Life Insurance Enterprise*, 52).

22. Ibid. Some of that rise was attributable to the growth in industrial insurance, which had an inherently higher cost structure.

23. See, for example, Stalson, *Marketing Life Insurance*. Frederick L. Hoffman, a Prudential officer, later characterized the two types as *class* and *mass* insurance (Carr, *From Three Cents a Week*, 13).

24. Keller, *Life Insurance Enterprise*, 56–57; North, "Entrepreneurial Policy and Internal Organization in the Large Life Insurance Companies," 142–143. A tontine is essentially a gambling pact in which all the proceeds go to the last surviving member.

25. Keller, *Life Insurance Enterprise*, 10. See also Carr, *From Three Cents a Week*; Davis, *Industrial Life Insurance in the United States*, and Dublin, *Family of Thirty Million*.

26. Although the vast majority (95% and higher) of insurance agents from1890 to 1930 were men (Kwolek-Folland, *Engendering Business*, 77–78), almost from the beginning a few women made their way into this primarily masculine profession (Carr, *From Three Cents a Week*, 23–24).

27. Beito, *From Mutual Aid to the Welfare State*, 24.

28. Carr, *From Three Cents a Week*, 10–22.

29. A ratio of 119% for Metropolitan Life, compared with 49% for the Big Three, according to Keller, *Life Insurance Enterprise*, 53. Keller also notes greater awareness of costs in industrial insurance (58).

30. Buley, *American Life Convention*, 1:61–63. Elizur Wright, Massachusetts insurance commissioner beginning in 1858, is widely credited with being the first important regulator of life insurance (see also, e.g., Collier, *Capital Ship*, 3–4, 43–46, and Hooker, *Aetna Life Insurance Company*, 41). By 1890, seventeen states had regulatory commissions (Keller, *Life Insurance Enterprise*, 194).

31. Keller, *Life Insurance Enterprise*, 8; Zelizer, *Morals and Markets*, 105.

32. Keller, *Life Insurance Enterprise*, 32.

33. Buley, *American Life Convention*, 1:84–85; Keller, *Life Insurance Enterprise*, 194.

34. Superintendent George W. Miller of New York, as quoted in Buley, *American Life Convention*, 1:84.

35. As historian Morton Keller has noted, "In general, company management was

not a concern of the regulatory system; substantial action in this field came after 1905" (*Life Insurance Enterprise*, 199).

36. Moorhead, *Our Yesterdays*, 18–19; Buley, *American Life Convention*, 1:55; Keller, *Life Insurance Enterprise*, 8–9.

37. Buley, *American Life Convention*, 1:55–56.

38. Moorhead, *Our Yesterdays*, 29–31, 45–46, 50; Kwolek-Folland, *Engendering Business*, 81.

39. Buley, *American Life Convention*, 1:xiii.

40. Abbott, *System of Professions*. Actuaries are not typically included in studies of the professions, but they seem to fit the criteria set out by Abbott and others. The educational requirements and certification restrict entry to a profession. See Moorhead, *Our Yesterdays*, for a history of actuarial professionalization.

41. These two criteria come from Goode, "Theoretical Limits of Professionalization." The actuaries, like others in insurance firms, embraced the public service ideology of insurance, at least in rhetoric. For a discussion of the attitudes of early British actuaries toward quantification, on the one hand, and the need for professional judgment, on the other, see Porter, *Trust in Numbers*, 101–113.

42. Moorhead, *Our Yesterdays*, 12, 17–42.

43. Ibid., 17–42. Shenhav, "From Chaos to Systems," sees professionalization, broadly construed, as related to systematization.

44. Clayton C. Hall, speaking in 1909, from *Transactions of the Actuarial Society of America* (hereafter cited as *TASA*) 11 (1909–10): 28, as quoted in Moorhead, *Our Yesterdays*, 43.

45. See Porter, *Trust in Numbers*, 101–113, for this argument in relation to actuaries in England.

46. Keller, *Life Insurance Enterprise*, 60–63, quotation at p. 60.

47. D. P. Fackler, from *TASA* 3 (1893–94): 165, as quoted in Moorhead, *Our Yesterdays*, 67.

48. Buley, *American Life Convention*, 1:315, 440.

49. A typical definition of a trade association is as follows: "A trade association is a group of businesses within an industry that work together to build industry awareness, advocate certain political goals and provide services to members" (www .socialstudieshelp.com/EcoNon_Profits.htm, accessed August 14, 2003). A critical element of this definition is business membership. Another element commonly associated with trade associations is lobbying for political goals, though this element is not an essential aspect of a trade association.

50. Gerri Lynn Flanzraich, "The Role of the Library Bureau and Gaylord Brothers in the Development of Library Technology, 1876–1930" (Ph.D. diss., Columbia University, 1990); Yates, *Control Through Communication*, 56–57.

51. Herbert E. Davidson of the Library Bureau to Frank Wells, secretary, ALIMD, May 5, 1890, as quoted in Flanzraich, "Role of the Library Bureau," 296. Such a list lowered risk for all the subscribing firms, but it was, of course, a form of blacklist.

52. Buley, *American Life Convention*, 1:440, 450–453, 465–467, 579–585, 591, passim. The MIB ultimately merged with a similar service founded by the American Life Convention's Medical Section.

53. Kwolek-Folland suggests that "the combination of messianic message and cut-

throat methods was in some ways unique to the [life insurance] industry" and one reason for the negative image of insurance sales (*Engendering Business*, 90).

54. For discussion of occupations, see Van Maanen and Barley, "Occupational Communities." For the fraternal aspects of insurance sales, see Kwolek-Folland, *Engendering Business*, 90–91. By virtue of its firm (rather than individual) membership, NALU was also, of course, a trade association.

55. Kwolek-Folland, *Engendering Business*, 91.

56. In addition to the home office, firms generally also had district or regional offices and sales offices. This section focuses exclusively on the home office.

57. This level of information use exceeded that in British insurance firms, in which a single annual valuation of policies in force was the major actuarial task; most British firms continued to use nineteenth-century mortality tables well into the twentieth century and did not typically maintain internal cost accounting systems to monitor costs and to aid in pricing products. While the difference in actuarial reporting reflected more extensive state regulation of the U.S. insurance industry, the presence of cost systems in the U.S. industry but not in the British reflected the turn-of-the-century preoccupation with systematization and statistical analysis prevalent in the American business community as a whole. Campbell-Kelly, pers. comm., January 1993; Yates, *Control Through Communication*, 1–20.

58. Before 1905, however, firms offering such insurance were criticized, often accurately, for structuring policies so that lapses benefited the firm, thus creating an incentive for allowing policy lapses (Keller, *Life Insurance Enterprise*, 58).

59. B. F. Dvorak, "Application of Office Machinery," *Proceedings of the Life Office Management Association* (1924): 20. Manuscript version in Home Office Study Committee, cabinet 13, MetLife Archives, New York.

60. Dublin, *Family of Thirty Million*, 230–231. Although Metropolitan Life focused primarily on industrial insurance, it also offered ordinary insurance.

61. James, *Metropolitan Life*, 129.

62. Dublin, *Family of Thirty Million*, 288. By 1915, Metropolitan Life had 1,170 typewriters in its home office (Zunz, *Making America Corporate*, 114).

63. Quoted from a contemporary report of the insurance superintendent of the state of New York in Dublin, *Family of Thirty Million*, 235.

64. James, *Metropolitan Life*, 130, cited from Metropolitan Life's *Souvenir Number of the Weekly Bulletin* (1897): 55.

65. Buley, *Equitable Life Assurance Society of the United States*, 1:355 and, more generally, 349–381.

66. Moorhead, *Our Yesterdays*, 333–334.

67. Ibid; also Phyllis E. Steele to John Huss, memo, November 10, 1992, The New England Financial Archive (part of MetLife Archives), Chronological File, 1992, box 1 (hereafter cited as NEF/file, folder and/or box number).

68. Stalson, *Marketing Life Insurance*, 798–799; Nunis, *Past Is Prologue*, 19–20. Pacific Mutual had been the beneficiary of Elizur Wright's consulting.

69. The Armstrong Hearings have received considerable attention from a few scholars. For the period around the turn of the century, including the lead-up to the hearings and the fallout from them, the most thorough source is Keller, *Life Insurance Enterprise*. A more detailed look at certain aspects of the hearings appears in North, "Life Insurance

and Investment Banking" and "Entrepreneurial Policy and Internal Organization in the Large Life Insurance Companies."

70. North, "Life Insurance and Investment Banking," 210; increase in total assets computed from figures in n. 6.

71. Computed from figures in Stalson, *Marketing Life Insurance,* 798–799.

72. Keller, *Life Insurance Enterprise,* 16–17, 21–22.

73. Ibid., 16.

74. Buley, *American Life Convention,* 1:209–224; Keller, *Life Insurance Enterprise,* 157–184 and elsewhere.

75. North, "Life Insurance and Investment Banking." The parallels to the business scandals of 2001/2002 are striking.

76. Keller, *Life Insurance Enterprise,* 235–240, 288.

77. Quoted in Buley, *American Life Convention,* 1:199.

78. Keller, *Life Insurance Enterprise,* 22.

79. Ibid., 247–248.

80. Paul Morton, who had previously held executive positions at both the Chicago, Burlington and Quincy Railroad and the Atchison, Topeka and Santa Fe Railroad.

81. Buley, *American Life Convention,* 1:193–199.

82. Ibid., 209–210.

83. See North, "Entrepreneurial Policy and Internal Organization in the Large Life Insurance Companies."

84. Keller, *Life Insurance Enterprise,* 243–253.

85. Buley, *American Life Convention,* 1:220–223; Keller, *Life Insurance Enterprise,* 42–47, 52–53; May and Oursler, *The Prudential,* 132–141; Dublin, *Family of Thirty Million,* 64–68.

86. Keller, *Life Insurance Enterprise,* 57–58, 170–172; Buley, *American Life Convention,* 1:222–223.

87. Keller, *Life Insurance Enterprise,* 270–271.

88. McCurdy and Armstrong both as quoted in Buley, *American Life Convention,* 1:216.

89. Keller, *Life Insurance Enterprise,* 43.

90. Buley, *American Life Convention,* 1:269–275.

91. Ibid., 279–281.

92. Stalson, *Marketing Life Insurance,* 799–800; size in terms of insurance in force.

93. Keller, *Life Insurance Enterprise,* 287.

94. Paul Morton, "The Executive as an Expert," *System* 6 (July 1904): 4, as quoted in Zunz, *Making America Corporate,* 90; see also pp. 47 and 91 for Morton's previous career.

95. George E. Delehanty, "Computers and the Organization Structure in Life-Insurance Firms: The External and Internal Economic Environment," in Charles A. Myers, ed., *The Impact of Computers on Management* (Cambridge: MIT Press, 1967), 61–98.

TWO: First Impressions of Tabulating, 1890–1910

1. *New York Tribune,* April 25, 1890, as quoted by Austrian, *Herman Hollerith,* 83.

2. The pre-computer information-processing industry could be defined even more broadly to include office supplies and office furniture as well as office appliances or busi-

ness machines themselves. For discussion of the definitional problems, see Cortada, *Before the Computer*, 3–4 and elsewhere. For treatment of other information-handling devices, see Yates, *Control Through Communication* and "Business Use of Information and Technology from 1880–1950."

3. Austrian, *Herman Hollerith*, 238; Norberg, "High Technology Calculation," 764.

4. In 1911, Hollerith's Tabulating Machine Company (TMC) merged with three other business machine manufacturers, and Hollerith became a technical adviser (Austrian, *Herman Hollerith*, 306–314).

5. Campbell-Kelly, *ICL*, 8–9; Campbell-Kelly and Aspray, *Computer*, 22–23.

6. Austrian, *Herman Hollerith*, 1–6; Campbell-Kelly, "Punched-Card Machinery," 124.

7. I use "system" here to refer just to the technical artifacts, though this book as a whole, of course, deals with a sociotechnical system that shapes and is shaped by human actors, organizations, and interests (see, e.g., Bijker, Hughes, and Pinch, *Social Construction of Technological Systems*, and Bijker, *Of Bicycles, Bakelites, and Bulbs*).

8. Unless otherwise indicated, the description of early tabulating equipment in the next several paragraphs is based on Truesdell, *Development of Punch Card Tabulation*, 43–56; Austrian, *Herman Hollerith*, 10–83 and passim; and Bashe et al., *IBM's Early Computers*, 2–6.

9. Campbell-Kelly, *ICL*, 14, 21, 35.

10. In Martin Campbell-Kelly's study of the manual information-processing methods in the British census, he notes that these methods did not result in substantially longer processing time than those used in the U.S. census but rather in more limited analysis attempted by the British ("Information Technology and Organizational Change in the British Census").

11. Campbell-Kelly, *ICL*, 13; John H. Blodgett, "Herman Hollerith: Data Processing Pioneer" (thesis, Drexel Institute of Technology, 1968), 89. Blodgett attributes the rental practice entirely to Hollerith's displeasure with the few early customers who bought the equipment, whose improper maintenance, in Hollerith's view, led to a need to replace the equipment. Both factors seem likely to have influenced Hollerith.

12. Campbell-Kelly, "Punched-Card Machinery," 133–134.

13. Yates, *Control Through Communication*, 1–20, and "Business Use of Information and Technology from 1880–1950."

14. Cortada, *Before the Computer*.

15. *New York Tribune*, April 25, 1890, as quoted in Austrian, *Herman Hollerith*, 82–83. Further details of this installation are from the same source.

16. Number of policies from May and Oursler, *The Prudential*, 109; ranking in dollars of insurance in force from Stalson, *Marketing Life Insurance*, 799. In 1890 Prudential ranked eighth by that metric.

17. Moorhead, *Our Yesterdays*, 338; David Parks Fackler, "Regarding the Mortality Investigation, Instituted by the Actuarial Society of America and Now in Progress," *Journal of the Institute of Actuaries* 37 (1903): 1–15. Prudential used the Gore sorters in statistical work and in sorting weekly issue cards.

18. Moorhead (*Our Yesterdays*, 338), May and Oursler (*The Prudential*, 308), and Blair Olmstead ("Prudential's Early Experience with Computers," Prudential internal typescript, February 1, 1978, p. 1) all report 15,000 cards/hour, equivalent to 250 cards/minute (Olmstead also notes that while that is the average rate, "in a single run one machine actually sorted 200,000 cards in 8 hours," for a rate of more than 400 cards/

minute). Fackler ("Regarding the Mortality Investigation") claims that for the ASA mortality study, it sorted 25,000 cards/day, a much slower rate.

19. Charles and Ray Eames (by the office of), *A Computer Perspective: Background to the Computer Age,* new ed. (Cambridge: Harvard University Press, 1990), 31.

20. John K. Gore to Herman Hollerith, May 23, 1901, container 10, Herman Hollerith Collection, Library of Congress, Washington, D.C.

21. By the time of Gore's letter, Hollerith's new sorter was only a few months from introduction, and thus its development was assuredly at or near completion. The considerable adjustment required to make the two systems compatible would probably have taken longer than the introduction of Hollerith's new and equally fast sorter.

22. Campbell-Kelly, "Punched-Card Machinery," 140.

23. May and Oursler, *The Prudential,* 351.

24. This reluctance is similar to much more recent cases of unwillingness to abandon sunk investments in information technology (Philip Scranton, pers. comm., ca. September 25, 2003).

25. Moorhead, *Our Yesterdays,* 338; May and Oursler, *The Prudential,* 308.

26. Computed from Stalson, *Marketing Life Insurance,* 799.

27. May and Oursler, *The Prudential,* 112.

28. Arthur, "Competing Technologies, Increasing Returns, and Lock-in by Historical Events"; David, "Understanding the Economics of QWERTY." Pinch ("Why You Go to a Piano Store to Buy a Synthesizer") has argued the importance, from a social construction perspective, of examining *path creation* as well as *path dependence.*

29. David, "Understanding the Economics of QWERTY."

30. Thomas P. Hughes, *Networks of Power: Electrification in Western Society, 1880–1930* (Baltimore: Johns Hopkins University Press, 1983), 14.

31. Donald MacKenzie, "Missile Accuracy: A Case Study in the Social Processes of Technological Change," in Bijker, Hughes, and Pinch, *Social Construction of Technological Systems,* 197.

32. Campbell-Kelly, *ICL,* 14–16.

33. Ibid., 15.

34. Ibid., 14.

35. Austrian, *Herman Hollerith,* 199–206.

36. Campbell-Kelly, *ICL,* 15.

37. Flanzraich, "Role of the Library Bureau," 332–334; Austrian, *Herman Hollerith,* 133–134, 166. Flanzraich says that the contract was terminated in 1899, but in 1901 Hollerith was still corresponding with H. E. Davidson of the Library Bureau about possible insurance customers that might be handled by Library Bureau (Hollerith to Davidson, March 5, 1901, and May 8, 1901, and Davidson to Hollerith, March 8, 1901, and April 30, 1901, container 10, Hollerith Collection), so they seem to have continued at least an ad hoc relationship.

38. According to a 1924 pamphlet advertising the Library Bureau's services in various areas, its Statistical Service Bureau offered services to insurance firms then, though for reasons of confidentiality it mentioned no specific clients (Library Bureau, *Recorded Experience* [Boston: Library Bureau, 1924]).

39. Louis F. Butler to Hollerith, March 13, 1901, container 10, Hollerith Collection. The second quotation in this paragraph is also from this letter.

40. In 1895, Travelers was ranked fifteenth in insurance in force, but the companies

ranked first and second at that point handled more than ten times as much insurance (Stalson, *Marketing Life Insurance,* 799). Prudential had roughly 3.5 times as much insurance in force, but as an industrial insurance company, it had a proportionately greater number of policies.

41. For example, an April 3, 1900, letter from John B. Lunger, managing actuary of New York Life, to Hollerith (container 10, Hollerith Collection) asked about getting special punches made for New York Life, like those Hollerith had made for the Prudential. In Hollerith's reply (April 20, 1900), he mentioned that he was selling the same small punches to some Hartford insurance companies.

42. JoAnne Yates, "Information Systems for Handling Manufacturing and Marketing Data in American Firms, 1880–1920," *Business and Economic History,* 2d ser., 18 (1989): 207–217.

43. Hollerith to Davidson, May 8, 1901, container 10, Hollerith Collection.

44. Campbell-Kelly, *ICL,* 15.

45. Hollerith to Davidson, 8 May 1901, container 10, Hollerith Collection.

46. Truesdell, *Development of Punch Card Tabulation,* 84, 86.

47. This account is based on Fackler's "Regarding the Mortality Investigation," presented in 1902 to the British professional association for actuaries, the Institute of Actuaries. The passages from McClintock's paper, entitled "The Objects to Be Attained in Future Investigations of Mortality and Death Loss," are as quoted on p. 1 of Fackler's paper.

48. This committee included actuaries from the companies then ranked first, second, third, seventh, and eleventh in insurance in force. Names of the committee members come from Fackler, "Regarding the Mortality Investigations"; affiliations from Moorhead, *Our Yesterdays,* 51; and ranks of the companies in 1900 from Stalson, *Marketing Life Insurance,* 799, table B.

49. Moorhead (*Our Yesterdays,* 66–67) quotes statements revealing this unease from presidential and other addresses to the ASA by B. J. Miller, D. P. Fackler, and R. W. Weeks, all members of the ASA committee organizing the study.

50. Hollerith corresponded with Louis F. Butler and H. J. Messenger of Travelers Insurance; Emory McClintock of Mutual Life; John Tatlock of the Actuarial Society of America; John B. Lunger, Rufus Weeks, and A. R. Grow of New York Life; and D. H. Wells of Connecticut Mutual Life in the period from December 1900 through May 1901 (container 10, Hollerith Collection).

51. For example, Lunger to Hollerith, November 27, 1900; D. H. Wells (Connecticut Mutual Life Insurance Company) to Hollerith, December 12, 1900; Hollerith to Wells, December 31, 1900; Wells to Hollerith, January 5, 1901, all in container 10, Hollerith Collection.

52. Hollerith to Lunger, May 8, 1901; A. R. Grow (New York Life) to Hollerith, May 15, 1901; Hollerith to Emory McClintock (Mutual Life), May 16, 1901; John Tatlock Jr., secretary of the ASA, to Hollerith, May 20, 1901; Hollerith to Tatlock, May 21, 1901; Hollerith to Gore, May 21, 1901; Hollerith to Tatlock, May 23, 1901; Gore to Hollerith, May 23, 1901, all in container 10, Hollerith Collection. Gore responded with his statement (quoted earlier) about the potential complementarity of the Gore and Hollerith systems.

53. Austrian, *Herman Hollerith,* 177. Leon Truesdell, historian of use at the U.S. Census Bureau, suggests that Hollerith introduced the sorting machine as a direct response to problems faced by the agricultural census (Campbell-Kelly, "Punched-Card Machin-

ery," 140). Hollerith's correspondence from 1900 and 1901 indicates, however, that life insurance was also exerting pressure to improve his system's sorting capabilities.

54. Truesdell, *Development of Punch Card Tabulation,* 86–87.

55. Hollerith to Henry C. Adams, April 6, 1905, and May 24, 1906, container 10, Hollerith Collection.

56. Campbell-Kelly, "Punched-Card Machinery," 140.

57. Arthur Hunter, "Method of Making Mortality Investigations by Means of Perforated Cards, Sorting and Tabulating Machines with Special Reference to the Medico-Actuarial Mortality Investigation," *TASA* 11 (1909–10): 252–275.

58. Austrian, *Herman Hollerith,* 306–314.

59. Arthur Hunter, "Note on an Approximate Method of Making Mortality Investigations," *TASA* 10 (1907–8): 361; Hunter, "Method of Making Mortality Investigations," 268–269. See also New York Life Insurance Company, *A Temple of Humanity* (New York: New York Life Insurance Co., 1909). New York Life's rank (by insurance in force) is from Stalson, *Marketing Life Insurance,* 800.

60. Hunter, "Method of Making Mortality Investigations," 268–269.

61. Davidson to Hollerith, April 30, 1901, container 10, Hollerith Collection.

62. Hunter, "Method of Making Mortality Investigations," 256, 265, quotations at 265. Forty-five-column cards were the largest of three standard configurations available at this time.

63. Henry N. Kaufman, "Some Uses for the Hollerith Machines," *TASA* 11 (1909–10): 276–295, quotations at pp. 282, 291. Kaufman's company is not identified, but a November 9, 1911, letter from Kaufman to Hollerith on the latter's retirement (container 10, Hollerith Collection) reveals his title and affiliation. Phoenix was ranked 19th out of 214 firms in 1910 (Stalson, *Marketing Life Insurance,* 800, 821).

64. Kaufman, "Some Uses for the Hollerith Machines," 290.

65. Ibid., 295.

66. Giddens (*Constitution of Society*) suggests that all structures constrain as well as enable human action.

67. Stalson, *Marketing Life Insurance,* 800. Since both firms deal predominantly with ordinary, not industrial, insurance, the amount of insurance in force is a very rough proxy for number of policies and thus amount of data to be processed.

68. Kaufman to Hollerith, November 9, 1911, container 10, Hollerith Collection. It is not clear whether the number referred to all individual devices (card punches, sorters, or tabulators) or just to the tabulators.

69. Brochure draft, 1983, Record Group 50, Data Processing Records, Exhibit Files, Aetna Inc. Archives, Hartford, Connecticut (hereafter cited as Aetna Archives). Interestingly, the brochure draft notes that the thirty-five women temporarily hired to help the actuary compile and tabulate this experience were segregated and permitted access only through a rear entrance, since then president Morgan G. Bulkeley objected to having women in the office.

70. [Signature unclear] to Hollerith, November 8, 1911, container 10, Hollerith Collection.

71. 1911 Annual Report of the Tabulating Machine Company, March 31, 1912, Hollerith Collection.

72. Hunter, "Method of Making Mortality Investigations," and Moorhead, *Our Yesterdays,* 64.

73. Hunter, "Method of Making Mortality Investigations," 253.

74. Ibid., 252–253.

75. Metropolitan Life Insurance Company, *The Metropolitan Life Insurance Company: Its History, Its Present Position in the Insurance World, Its Home Office Building and Its Work Carried on Therein* (New York: Metropolitan Life Insurance Co., 1914), 70.

76. Income calculated from a table entitled "The Tabulating Machine Company Rental and Card Sales," container 10, Hollerith Collection.

77. Chandler, *Scale and Scope*, 8, 35.

78. Austrian, *Herman Hollerith*, 238–256.

79. Metropolitan Life Insurance Company, *Metropolitan Life Insurance Company*, 70.

80. Kaufman, "Some Uses for the Hollerith Machines," 278.

81. C. L. Hayes to Mr. Braitmayer, November 25, 1912; Braitmayer to Hayes, December 3, 1912, container 10, Hollerith Collection.

82. Kaufman, "Some Uses for the Hollerith Machines," 279. Kaufman's sample cards expressed years in two, rather than four, digits, illustrating that the shortcut that would eventually lead to the widely anticipated Y2K computer problem was already in use. See sample cards on pp. 280, 283, 284, 287, and 289.

83. "Tabulating Machine Co. Operating Revenue and Operating and Selling Expense, 1909 to 1913," container 10, Hollerith Collection.

THREE: The Push toward Printing, 1910–1924

Much of the material in this chapter first appeared in Yates, "Co-evolution of Information Processing Technology and Use."

1. TMC was a unit within CTR until 1924, when the entire organization took the name International Business Machines (IBM).

2. Ward, *Down the Years*, 93–95, 102–113; Buley, *American Life Convention*, 1:495.

3. Buley, *American Life Convention*, 1:523–525, 486–561, passim.

4. Stalson, *Marketing Life Insurance*, app. 26, provides data for insurance in force. Data for national income and population come from U.S. Bureau of the Census, *Historical Statistics of the United States: Colonial Times to 1957*, ser. F-7, p. 139, and ser. A-2, p. 7.

5. Stalson, *Marketing Life Insurance*, 800–801.

6. In a quantitative study based on ten selected firms studied from 1906 to 1933, Harry A. Hopf, former life insurance manager turned management consultant, showed that, with the exception of some fluctuations, the trend in costs generally went down as the size of insurance firms grew, until at some very large point it stabilized, then drifted up slightly. Hopf, "Measuring Management in Life Insurance," *Proceedings of the Life Office Management Association* (hereafter cited as *Proceedings of LOMA*) (1934): 35–68.

7. In 1926, a representative of Connecticut Mutual Life Insurance Company stated that competition for office clerks (even "girl clerks") was stiff in Hartford, both among the various life insurance companies and between insurance firms and other businesses, increasing firm interest in any type of office machinery that reduced demand or turnover. W. B. Barber Jr., "The Application of Office Machinery to Home Office Clerical Operations," *Proceedings of LOMA* (1926): 38–40.

8. Yates, *Control Through Communication*; Yates, "Business Use of Information and Technology from 1880–1950," 107–135.

9. Melvil Dewey, "Office Efficiency," and Samuel F. Crowell, "Office Equipment,"

both in Howard P. Dunham, comp. and ed., *The Business of Insurance: A Text Book and Reference Work Covering All Lines of Insurance,* 3 vols. (New York: Ronald Press Co., 1912). 3:272–316 and 3:317–328, respectively.

10. Dewey, "Office Efficiency," 3:272. Dewey even advocated a simplified spelling system for the office.

11. Crowell, "Office Equipment," 3:322.

12. An overview of Hopf's career at Germania and, to a lesser extent, after he left there appears in Rapone, *Guardian Life Insurance Company,* 130–142. In 1910, Germania ranked twenty-first in insurance in force, with $126 million (Stalson, *Marketing Life Insurance,* 800).

13. Rapone, *Guardian Life Insurance Company,* 136–138.

14. He apparently achieved this reputation in part through a speech at the 1912 meeting of the Medical Section of the American Life Convention and a consequent mention of him in a book entitled *The American Office* (published in 1913) as an "insurance office specialist connected with the Germania Life Insurance Company" (Rapone, *Guardian Life Insurance Company,* 139).

15. Harry A. Hopf, "Home Office Organization," *Proceedings of the American Life Convention* (1917): 26–41, with discussion transcribed on pp. 41–46. The section "Methods, Equipment and Standardization" is on pp. 38–40.

16. Discussion, ibid., p. 43.

17. More than a decade later an insurance executive and chair of an industry committee on home office organization cited that 1917 paper as the only major treatment of home office organization by a national life insurance association before 1928. F. L. Rowland, "Committee Report: Home Office Organization," *Proceedings of LOMA* (1928): 182.

18. June 1914 letter quoted in Austrian, *Herman Hollerith,* 332–333.

19. "Tabulating Machine Co. Operating Revenue and Operating and Selling Expense, 1909 to 1913," container 10, Hollerith Collection.

20. [Unreadable signature] to Hollerith, March 26, 1916, container 3, Personal Correspondence, 1916–18, Hollerith Collection.

21. For his work with electric utilities, see W. E. Freeman, "Automatic Mechanical Punching, Counting, Sorting, Tabulating and Printing Machines Adaptable to Various Lines of Accounting and Statistical Work Essential for Public Service Corporations with Particular Reference to Improvements in the Art of Mechanical Accounting," paper presented at the annual convention of the National Electric Light Association, San Francisco, June 7–11, 1915.

22. Based on 1915 insurance in force from Stalson, *Marketing Life Insurance,* 800.

23. Austrian, *Herman Hollerith,* 134.

24. Percy C. H. Papps, "The Installation of a Perforated Card System with a Description of the Peirce Machines," *TASA* 15 (1914): 49–61.

25. "Report on the Royden System of Perforated Cards," March 9, 1912, addressed to the President's Commission on Economy and Efficiency, signed by M. O. Chance, F. H. Tonsmeire, and E. H. Maling, container 3, Hollerith Collection. The PCEE was also known as the Taft Commission on Economy and Efficiency.

26. Prospectus for a new company, the Royden Company, with cover letter from Arthur C. Sherwood to James R. Morse, September 24, 1912, stamped "Personal/HH," container 10, Hollerith Collection. The Royden Company intended to take over these

patents but probably failed, since I've seen no further references to that name while Peirce Patent Company continued to exist and to manufacture machines. Since Metropolitan Life was not listed among the backers for Peirce's company prospectus, Peirce was probably not yet working for that firm.

27. F. S. Cleveland, chairman, PCEE, to the secretary of the Treasury, April 17, 1912, attached to PCEE report in container 10, Hollerith Collection.

28. The prospectus (container 10, Hollerith Collection) lists a "Mr. Stevenson, Comptroller of the Mutual Life Insurance Company," though the company was probably the Mutual *Benefit* Life Insurance Company, given the involvement between Peirce and Mutual Benefit revealed in Papps, "Installation of a Perforated Card System."

29. Papps, "Installation of a Perforated Card System."

30. Ibid., p. 51.

31. Ibid., p. 61.

32. Discussion on Papps, "Installation of a Perforated Card System," *TASA* 15 (1914): 414.

33. Percy C. H. Papps, "Essential Policy Records," *Proceedings of LOMA* (1924): 28–32, quotation at p. 29. See Bashe et al., *IBM's Early Computers,* 9–10, for the buyout of Peirce. In a brief aside, Papps lamented the loss of Peirce's printing punch. TMC and IBM had not adopted the card punch feature that allowed it to type numbers at the top of the cards at the same time it punched them. The printing punch may have been one of the many features that, according to one TMC/IBM employee, would never have been practical for IBM to copy for mass production (Bashe et al., *IBM's Early Computers,* 10). By 1929, however, a LOMA report on home office appliances (R. A. Taylor, "Accounting and Calculating Machines," *Proceedings of LOMA* [1929]: 21) noted IBM's recent introduction of "The Interpreter," a device that took already punched cards and printed the corresponding information on the top of the card, in any specified configuration. The key punch plus the interpreter, then, could achieve the same result as Peirce's printing punch, but with two machines and two processes, rather than one. Powers lagged in this development, producing an interpreter only several years later (Campbell-Kelly, *ICL,* 96).

34. J. D. Craig, discussion on Papps, "Installation of a Perforated Card System," *TASA* 15 (1914): 414. Metropolitan Life's public accounts of when Peirce was retained were contradictory (Dublin, *Family of Thirty Million,* 253, 397), suggesting as early as 1907 and as late as 1913, but other evidence (series of contractual letters between J. Royden Peirce and J. M. Craig, actuary for Metropolitan Life, dated May 29 through June 23, 1913, Peirce Machine Matter, cabinet 2, MetLife Archives) suggests that the latter date is most likely. J. D. Craig is the son of J. M. Craig (Dublin, *Family of Thirty Million,* 379, 387).

35. James, *Metropolitan Life,* 186. This quotation comes from the notice announcing Metropolitan Life's hiring of Dr. Frankel to get the organization involved in welfare work. Zunz argues that "with Metropolitan, promoting social welfare became a business" and indeed that "Metropolitan is a particularly good example of the way in which big business could coopt the reformers' program" (*Making America Corporate,* 92).

36. Metropolitan Life Insurance Company, *Metropolitan Life Insurance Company,* 55–56.

37. Ibid., 128.

38. Series of contractual letters between Peirce and J. M. Craig, May 29 through June 23, 1913, Peirce Machine Matter, cabinet 2, MetLife Archives.

39. Hollerith's biographer has noted that in 1914 Hollerith was spurred on to file a

patent for automatic control (which had the same effect of eliminating the need for stop cards), in great part because "one competitor, urged on by a customer, was now working on a means of getting around the use of stop cards entirely"—an apparent reference to Peirce. Austrian, *Herman Hollerith,* 334.

40. Metropolitan Life Insurance Company, *Metropolitan Life Insurance Company,* 71–72.

41. Ibid.

42. Commentary by J. D. Craig on Papps, "Installation of a Perforated Card System," *TASA* 15 (1914): 409–413.

43. Undated internal report from Lawrence Washington to Henry Bruere, third vice president, Peirce Machine Matters, cabinet 2, MetLife Archives. Context and other references to it make 1916 the likely date. In it, he notes that "Mr. Pierce [*sic*] is now nearly finished with the work he is doing for the Actuarial Division." Elsewhere, however, a handwritten note identified some Peirce cards as being "used on the Peirce sorters and tabulators in Actuarial Division from 1918–1925," suggesting that it would be another two years before Peirce had the machines in working order (Peirce Machine Cards, cabinet 4, MetLife Archives). Washington's report also notes the doubled final cost of the key machine. One internal pre-contract memo to J. M. Craig questioned whether Peirce's original price was *too* high: "Shall we continue to negotiate with them and after the plans are complete have them submit a definite bid or is the price prohibitive?" (unidentified to Craig, May 7, 1913, Peirce Machine Matters, cabinet 2, MetLife Archives). Craig initialed an affirmative reply (that is, to continue to negotiate), and the negotiations resulted in a contract at a figure within the range initially quoted.

44. Drawings marked "Confidential" and "Peirce Patents Company," May 20, 1913, Peirce Machines Matters, cabinet 2, MetLife Archives.

45. Peirce to J. M. Craig, Metropolitan Life, December 18, 1916, Peirce Machine Matters, cabinet 2, MetLife Archives.

46. Ibid., italics added.

47. Memorandum of agreement between Metropolitan Life, Peirce himself, and Peirce Patents Company, April 23, 1918, Peirce Machine Matters, cabinet 2, MetLife Archives. The list of devices had been lengthened and specialized since the 1916 proposal, but related surviving materials do not reveal whether that process was driven primarily by Peirce, by Metropolitan Life, or by the interaction of both.

48. Unsigned to Mr. Fiske, vice president, March 23, 1918, Peirce Machine Matters, cabinet 2, MetLife Archives.

49. The history of Peirce's other contracts is traced in an internal Metropolitan Life report, "A Study of the Peirce Machines," March 1, 1926, Peirce Machine Study, cabinet 2, MetLife Archives. See also Peirce to Metropolitan Life, January 21, 1919, and February 5, 1919, with attached notes from Metropolitan executives, Peirce Machine Matters, cabinet 2, MetLife Archives.

50. Unsigned memorandum addressed to Home Office Study Committee, November 7, 1924, Home Office Organization Study, cabinet 13, MetLife Archives. This committee was initiated to address a space crisis in the home office but dealt with a broad range of operating processes. Mechanization of clerical processes was seen as one way to save space.

51. J. D. Craig to Bruere, third vice president and chairman of the Home Office Study Committee, December 22,1924, Home Office Organization Study, cabinet 13, MetLife Archives.

52. Ibid.

53. Austrian, *Herman Hollerith,* 272–274, 291.

54. A certain amount of patent litigation took place between the Hollerith and Powers organizations in the United States and in Europe, but ultimately, a cross-licensing arrangement was reached for use of the basic tabulating patents, removing them from the competitive arena. Some later patents that were relevant to the competition will be noted as necessary. James Connolly, *A History of Computing in Europe* (New York: IBM World Trade Corporation, 1967), 13; Campbell-Kelly, *ICL,* 35, 64, 88–90.

55. Cortada, *Before the Computer,* 152.

56. Ibid., 156–157. By 1926, both firms sold the cards, which provided considerable cash flow, and Hollerith sold mechanical key punches (William Henry Leffingwell, ed., *Office Appliance Manual* [n.p.: National Association of Office Appliance Manufacturers, 1926], 168). By 1933, however, all Powers machines could be purchased as well as rented (with rental fees, including maintenance, set at 2% of the purchase price and maintenance charges for purchased equipment set at 2.5% per year), indicating that Powers changed its policy sometime in between (L. J. Comrie, *The Hollerith and Powers Tabulating Machines* [London: Printed for private circulation, 1933]). This policy shift may reflect Remington Rand's acquisition of Powers in 1927 (Campbell-Kelly, *ICL,* 69), the loss of compatibility between the two firms' equipment after IBM's 1928 introduction of the eighty-column card, and Remington Rand's reaction to the 1932 antitrust suit filed against IBM and Remington Rand (on the antitrust suit, see Cortada, *Before the Computer,* 116–118).

57. "Powers Machinery: I. Origin and Development" (first of a six-part series), *Prudential Bulletin* (December 1934): 2664–2665.

58. Norberg, "High Technology Calculation," 765.

59. For instance, see samples in Home Office Study Committee, cabinet 13, MetLife Archives.

60. Campbell-Kelly, *ICL,* 35.

61. Bruere to Craig, November 20, 1924; Craig to Bruere, November 22, 1924; Bruere to Craig, November 25, 1924, Home Office Study Committee, cabinet 13, MetLife Archives.

62. Although Hollerith ceased to be head of TMC in 1911, when it was merged into CTR, insurance users continued to refer to the equipment as Hollerith machines for decades.

63. This paragraph draws on Campbell-Kelly, "Large-Scale Data Processing in the Prudential," 128–130.

64. J. Burn, actuary of Prudential Assurance Company, Ltd., to Mr. Hegeman, vice president, Metropolitan Life, November 7, 1917, Peirce Machine Matters, cabinet 2, MetLife Archives.

65. Hegeman to Burn, February 12, 1918, Peirce Machine Matters, cabinet 2, MetLife Archives.

66. Campbell-Kelly, *ICL,* 44–45.

67. Technically, it was TMC's British affiliate, British Tabulating Machine Company, that lost the Prudential Assurance business, but TMC was certain to know and feel the loss.

68. Campbell-Kelly, *ICL,* 35–6.

69. Austrian (*Herman Hollerith,* 334–335) and Bashe et al. (*IBM's Early Computers,* 9) date the introduction to 1921, while Campbell-Kelly ("Punched-Card Machinery," 141)

says it was announced to the sales force in 1919 and introduced in 1920. For simplicity in the ensuing discussion, I will use 1921 as the date of introduction.

70. Campbell-Kelly (*ICL,* 63–64) offers the standard view, while George Jordan ("A Survey of Punched Card Development" [master's thesis, Massachusetts Institute of Technology, 1956]) argues that TMC developed its printing tabulator in response to a postwar crisis of surplus machinery and a need to expand demand. The gap between the development of the first TMC printing tabulator in 1917 and the commercial marketing of the first such tabulator in 1921, however, undercuts this theory.

71. Bashe et al., *IBM's Early Computers,* 7–8. An internal comparison of Powers, Hollerith, and Peirce equipment at the Metropolitan in the mid-twenties revealed a clear preference for the verifier over other methods of verifying accuracy, but other issues, including printing and alphabetical printing capability, were more important. Report to Mr. Dobbins, file copy unsigned, February 2, 1926, Home Office Study Committee, cabinet 13, MetLife Archives.

72. Quoted in Craig to Bruere, memo, November 22, 1924, Home Office Study Committee, cabinet 13, MetLife Archives.

73. Undated document from A. C. Carpenter in 1923–26, Home Office Study Committee, cabinet 13, MetLife Archives. Metropolitan Life continued to work with Peirce to develop machinery for its ordinary insurance business.

74. Campbell-Kelly, *ICL,* 43–45.

75. "Powers Machinery: I. Origin and Development," 2665.

76. Campbell-Kelly, *ICL,* 48.

77. Ibid., 45.

78. "Report on Perforated Card Systems of English Companies, January 1924" (dated December 13, 1923, at the end of the report itself), item 63.33.3, cabinet 2, MetLife Archives; Campbell-Kelly, "Large-Scale Data Processing in the Prudential," 131–132. Presumably it was written in December (possibly in England) but typed and delivered only on the contingent's return.

79. B. F. Dvorak, "Application of Office Machinery, with Particular Reference to the Hollerith and Powers Tabulating Equipment, to the Actuarial, Statistical and Accounting Work in Life Insurance Offices," *Proceedings of LOMA* (1924): 22.

80. Campbell-Kelly, "Large-Scale Data Processing in the Prudential," 131.

81. Ibid., 132. Of course, as Dvorak remarked in 1924, the technology by itself "cannot replace careful planning by which alone a sound foundation for efficient office organization can be laid" ("Application of Office Machinery," 22), and Burn must have understood this.

82. As Campbell-Kelly (*ICL,* 73) explains, Powers-Samas was founded in 1929 to be the dedicated sales company for the machines being manufactured for the Acc and Tab, and the British Powers agency soon became known solely as Powers-Samas, even though the Acc and Tab still manufactured the machines.

83. "Report on Perforated Card Systems of English Companies, January 1924." It is unclear whether Powers ever marketed this thirteen-character version in England.

84. Ibid. These "full" alphabetic tabulators printed twenty-four letters, using the same character for U and V and the same character for S and 5.

85. Home Office Organization Study, 1924, cabinet 13, MetLife Archives. See esp. entries for June 13–July 12, pp. 52–56. This notebook, assembled by the office of Henry Bruere, third vice president and chairman of the committee, includes logs of meetings and phone calls as well as copies of memos and reports exchanged.

86. April 2, 1925, MetLife Archives. The date probably indicates when the sample sheet was created, not necessarily when this machine was first successfully run. Standard treatments of the history of tabulating equipment date introduction of alphabetical tabulating by Powers to 1924 (Campbell-Kelly, "Punched-Card Machinery," 142; Norberg, "High Technology Calculation," 768), and the log of the Home Office Study Committee places the first successful demonstration of the alphabetical attachment on November 19, 1924 (see pp. 66–71).

87. In working with Powers to develop this alphabetical tabulator, according to the committee's logs, one Metropolitan Life employee devised several mechanical changes to the equipment that the insurance firm wanted to patent, to "furnish us protection against undue charges for the Powers machines, should we come to a final arrangement" (June 16–July 12, 1924, pp. 55–56, Home Office Organization Study, January 1924, cabinet 13, MetLife Archives). Other entries indicate that patent issues became more problematic later, as IBM informed Metropolitan Life that its Peirce patents invalidated Powers' patents (July 9, p. 56; September 1–8, p. 61; December 1–31, p. 72).

88. Jordan, "Survey of Punched Card Equipment," 20; Campbell-Kelly, "Punched-Card Machinery," 142.

89. Bashe et al, *IBM's Early Computers*, 9–10. Until 1926 Peirce continued to work independently for Metropolitan Life in the shop built for him within that firm's home office, as well as for IBM (contract between Metropolitan Life and IBM, August 12, 1926, Peirce Machine Matters, cabinet 2, MetLife Archives). In that year, IBM took over Peirce's contracts with Metropolitan Life, Prudential, and the Veterans Bureau. Interestingly, although Metropolitan Life continued its independent work with Peirce, the committee also conducted experiments with other punched-card equipment, including one involving industrial actuarial work using Hollerith equipment (A. C. Carpenter, unaddressed and undated memo, ca. 1923, in 1923–26, Home Office Study Committee, cabinet 13, MetLife Archives). This experiment began using solely Hollerith equipment but over time replaced the sorters with Powers sorters and replaced a few other pieces of equipment with Powers equipment, illustrating again the ease with which such firms could use their market power by picking and choosing among compatible systems.

90. Bashe et al., *IBM's Early Computers*, 10.

91. At this time, the largest industrial insurance firms fit both characteristics of lead users defined in von Hippel, *Sources of Innovation*, 107: (1) they faced information-handling needs that would be experienced by all life insurance firms (and many other types of firms, as well), but they faced them significantly earlier than other firms; and (2) they would benefit significantly by obtaining solutions to those needs. The large number of transactions required by industrial insurance brought on problems of data management much sooner than in ordinary insurance.

92. MacLeod, "Strategies for Innovation," 301.

93. Dvorak, "Application of Office Machinery." Dvorak is listed as unaffiliated with any insurance company, though he may have earlier served as a Powers representative.

FOUR: Insurance Associations and the Flowering of the Tabulator Era

1. LOMA is considered a trade association, since membership is by firms rather than by individuals. Today, as in 1924, however, LOMA describes itself as an association in

which member firms cooperate on research and educational activities (www.loma.org/IndexPage-AboutLOMA.htm, accessed April 16, 2003), rather than on lobbying activities.

2. Franklin B. Mead, "Opening Remarks of Temporary Chairman," *Proceedings of LOMA* (1924): 5, presented at first annual meeting of LOMA, Fort Wayne, Indiana, September 1924. Buley (*American Life Convention,* 1:622–623) tells us that the chair of the American Life Convention, a general life insurance association, registered objection to the formation of yet another insurance association as unnecessary, but Mead and others at the meeting were clearly not deterred by this objection.

3. After 1931 there was some reduction in membership numbers—both because economic conditions forced a few member firms to merge or have their business reinsured by others and because the organization raised dues significantly in 1934 to create a permanent headquarters and salaried staff—but the low membership in 1935 still amounted to 136 firms, well above its starting point of 87, and it would soon start growing again. F. L. Rowland, "Report of Executive Secretary," *Proceedings of LOMA* (1935): 300–303.

4. Top twenty-five firms by assets, according to Stalson, *Marketing Life Insurance,* 801. Attendance at meetings listed in *Proceedings of LOMA* (1930) and *Proceedings of LOMA* (1950).

5. In some cases an attendee was identified as having two titles (e.g., vice president and secretary), in which case both were counted. In a few cases no title was listed for an attendee. For secretary's responsibilities, John B. Lunger, "Office Organization in Life Insurance," 1905 Yale Insurance Lectures, extracted and reproduced in *Proceedings of LOMA* (1928): 195.

6. Arthur F. Hall, "Address of Welcome," *Proceedings of LOMA* (1924): 8.

7. Ibid., 9.

8. A handful of life insurance firms maintained memberships in the broader American Management Association of the Office Managers' Association, but this activity was outside the life insurance industry itself (Dr. Henry Wireman Cook, "Influence of the Administration of the Office Organization upon the Home Office Activities of Life Insurance Companies," *Proceedings of LOMA* [1924]: 11).

9. E. E. Reid, "Presidential Address," *Proceedings of LOMA* (1927): 8. Reid, acting president in 1927, replaced an elected president who had moved to a bank.

10. E. E. Reid, "Presidential Address," *Proceedings of LOMA* (1928): 6.

11. Henry Holt, "Mechanical Appliances in Home Office Operations," *Proceedings of LOMA* (1927): 204–208, quotation at p. 204.

12. George A. Drieu, "Report of Committee: Office Machinery and Equipment," *Proceedings of LOMA* (1938): 229; see also George A. Drieu, "Survey of New Office Machines and Equipment Applicable to Life Office Operations," *Proceedings of LOMA* (1939): 161. The timing probably in part reflects greater emphasis on costs during the depression.

13. James Scott, "Round Table Conference: Classification of Home Office Accounts to Permit Operating Control," *Proceedings of LOMA* (1925): 35.

14. See Yates, *Control Through Communication,* 9–20.

15. Adolph A. Rydgren, chairman, Round Table Conference No. 6, "Procedure for Establishing Standard Practice Written Routines," *Proceedings of LOMA* (1924): 105–109, quotations by Rydgren at pp. 105–106.

16. B. J. Perry, O. G. Sherman, and G. A Drieu, "Committee Report: Equipment Stan-

dardization," *Proceedings of LOMA* (1928): 202. Perry's title comes from the attendance list in *Proceedings of LOMA* (1924): 135.

17. William Henry Leffingwell, "The Present State of the Art of Office Management," *Proceedings of LOMA* (1926): 21–37; see also, for example, a paper by Dr. Harlow S. Person, identified as a managing director of the Taylor Society, entitled "Principles of Scientific Management as Applied to Office Institutions" (*Proceedings of LOMA* [1932]: 11–19).

18. For discussions of the welfare movement, see, for example, Brandes, *American Welfare Capitalism;* Eilbirt, "Development of Personnel Management in the United States"; Jacoby, *Employing Bureaucracy,* 49–67; and Wren, *Evolution of Management Thought,* 202–203.

19. Gillespie, *Manufacturing Knowledge,* 29–30; Jacoby, *Employing Bureaucracy,* 126–129.

20. Henry Wireman Cook, "Presidentiaal Address," *Proceedings of LOMA* (1926): 11.

21. Dvorak, "Application of Office Machinery," 20–27, quotation at p. 20. In the *Proceedings,* Dvorak is identified only as living in Chicago and not affiliated with any life insurance company. An internal Metropolitan Life document from this same year describes him as "an expert accountant and systematizer frequently employed by the Powers Machine Company" (Home Office Organization Study, 1924, cabinet 13, MetLife Archives, log entries by Bruere, third vice president and chairman of the committee, for May 26–June 14, 1924, p. 47).

22. Reid, "Presidential Address," *Proceedings of LOMA* (1928), 6.

23. Buley, *American Life Convention,* 2:877.

24. Ibid., 2:707, 732. The Dow Jones Industrial Average lost almost half its value between June 30 and the end of 1931.

25. Dublin, *Family of Thirty Million,* 101; Buley, *American Life Convention,* 2:744–752, 876.

26. Moorhead, *Our Yesterdays,* 136–137.

27. Buley, *American Life Convention,* 2:838–862, 876; Dublin, *Family of Thirty Million,* 22.

28. Buley, *American Life Convention,* 2:681–877; Moorhead, *Our Yesterdays,* 131–138.

29. See, for example, Adolph A. Rydgren, "Influence of Present Economic Conditions on Life Company Management," presidential address, *Proceedings of LOMA* (1931): 7–12; H. S. Arnold, "Home Office Activities Aiming to Promote Conservation of Business," *Proceedings of LOMA* (1931): 124–140; F. L. Rowland, "Application of the N. R. A. Code to Home Office and Branch Personnel," *Proceedings of LOMA* (1933): 187–222.

30. G. W. Skilton, "Co-operative Management Research in the Life Office," presidential address, *Proceedings of LOMA* (1934): 8–9.

31. L. R. Menagh Jr., chairman, "Committee Report: Home Office Departmental and Functional Costs," *Proceedings of LOMA* (1937): 117–148; L. R. Menagh Jr., chairman, "Report of Committee: Departmental and Functional Costs." *Proceedings of LOMA* (1938): 131–219.

32. As described by Lloyd K. Crippen, "The Life Office Management Association Institute," presidential address, *Proceedings of LOMA* (1945): 2.

33. Crippen's 1945 presidential address quotes this passage from a 1942 report, on p. 3. This public relations function for the industry is another aspect of trade associations as defined in Chapter 1.

34. Thomas F. Meagher, "Report of Office Planning and Equipment Committee," *Proceedings of LOMA* (1941): 104.

35. Ralph W. Beeson, "Opening Remarks by Association President," *Proceedings of LOMA* (1942): 1.

36. Captain Daniel J. Reidy, "Premium Allotments among Members of the Armed Forces," *Proceedings of LOMA* (1942): 7–22. See, for example, coverage of the other topics in James B. Slimmon, "Adjusting Life Office Operations to War Conditions," presidential address, *Proceedings of LOMA* (1943): 1–6.

37. Moorhead, *Our Yesterdays*, 146–151. Alfred N. Guertin, actuary of the New Jersey Insurance Department, chaired the National Association of Insurance Commissioners' committee to modernize insurance valuation, first formed in 1937.

38. Slimmon, "Adjusting Life Office Operations to War Conditions," 2.

39. Edmund Fitzgerald, "Looking Ahead to 1944," presidential address, *Proceedings of LOMA* (1945): 4.

40. Helen L. Washburn, "Recruiting Office Workers," *Proceedings of LOMA* (1946): 337.

41. Ibid., 337–338. Washburn suggests putting returning young veterans into some positions formerly staffed by women.

42. E. L. Baldwin, on panel entitled "Recruiting and Retaining Clerical Employees," LOMA Special Conference, "Making Management Policies Effective on the Employee Level," *Proceedings of LOMA* (1947): 283. See also Edward J. Thomas Jr., on panel entitled "Recruiting and Retaining Clerical Employees," LOMA Special Conference, "Making Management Policies Effective on the Employee Level," *Proceedings of LOMA* (1947): 285–294. Baldwin provides supporting figures (282–283).

43. *The First Three Decades of I.A.S.A., 1928–1958: Historical Development of the Insurance Accounting and Statistical Association* [n.p.: IASA, ca. 1959], 5.

44. Ibid. The story is framed as part of a telephone call to George Westermann of the Peoria Life Insurance Company, who is also acknowledged in the preface by IASA's History Committee as the source "for much of the material covering the first few years" (n.p.).

45. Ibid., 92.

46. Ibid., 16–17.

47. Ibid., 13.

48. Ibid., 22. The abbreviation IASA remains, but today it stands for the Insurance Accounting and Systems Association (www.iasa.org/about2.asp, accessed April 28, 2003).

49. *First Three Decades of I.A.S.A.*, 33–35.

50. Ibid., 49–53, 90–91; *Proceedings of LOMA* (1948): 306. Of the five largest firms, Metropolitan Life, Prudential, and John Hancock (all younger industrial insurance firms) joined, but not traditional insurance giants Equitable and New York Life. Attendance Roster, *Proceedings of the Insurance Accounting and Statistical Association* (hereafter cited as *Proceedings of IASA*) (1947): 364–369. Ranking based on *Best's Insurance Reports—Life/Health* (hereafter cited as *Best's*), 1947.

51. *First Three Decades of I.A.S.A.*, 90–91. In 1936 IASA met in Philadelphia, at the home office of its first non-midwestern member firm.

52. Ibid., 36–37.

53. Ibid., 41–45. Because IASA had corporate membership, it was still a trade association by the most common definition.

54. There were other firms competing for European business, including British Tabulating Machine Company (BTM), which had an agreement with IBM and its predecessors, and the Accounting and Tabulating Corporation of Great Britain Limited (the Acc and Tab), later renamed Powers-Samas. Campbell-Kelly *(ICL)* provides a thorough account of the evolution of these firms. By the mid-1930s, there were also firms such as Powers GMBH marketing Remington Rand products designated Powers-Siemens and Halske in Germany (Cortada, *Before the Computer,* 155). But in the American market, IBM and Remington Rand were the sole competitors by this time.

55. Henry Holt, "The Application of Office Machinery to Home Office Operations," *Proceedings of LOMA* (1925): 129, 136. The addressing machines were almost all Addressograph equipment.

56. Ibid., 134.

57. Barber, "Application of Office Machinery to Home Office Clerical Operations," M. D. Johnson, Lincoln National Life, 45–53; George A. Drieu, Connecticut General Life, 53–57; and D. N. Warters, Bankers Life Company, 57–60.

58. Fewer references to Powers equipment may have reflected in part the lesser attention paid to industrial than ordinary insurance in LOMA. Otis Grant, chair of a 1929 discussional conference titled "Home Office Problems Having to Do with Industrial Insurance," noted the previous omission of anything about industrial insurance methods from LOMA and other international insurance conventions, even though industrial insurance accounted for more than three-quarters of existing policies, though certainly not of insurance in force (Otis P. Grant, "Home Office Problems Having to Do with Industrial Insurance," discussional conference, *Proceedings of LOMA* [1929]: 156).

59. Otis P. Grant, "The Application of Machine Methods to Industrial Insurance," *Proceedings of LOMA* (1929): 157–160. Life and Casualty Insurance Company had assets roughly 1/300th the size of Metropolitan Life's (calculated based on figures from *Best's,* 1927).

60. Log book entry for December 1–21, 1924, p. 72, Home Office Study Committee, January 24, 1924, cabinet 13, MetLife Archives.

61. Cortada, *Before the Computer,* 155; Campbell-Kelly, *ICL,* 69.

62. Attendance Roster, *Proceedings of LOMA* (1927): 256–257. IBM was still listed as the Tabulating Machine Company in 1927 and 1928, though its name had changed to IBM in 1924.

63. Attendance Roster, *Proceedings of LOMA* (1928): 236–237.

64. Attendance Roster, *Proceedings of LOMA* (1929): 211–212.

65. Campbell-Kelly, *ICL,* 65–66.

66. Campbell-Kelly, "Punched-Card Machinery," 142. Cortada (*Before the Computer,* 102) speculates that the expanded card was a product of accountants' influence, but insurance users had at least as strong a reason to desire a larger card, especially once alphabetical fields were added for names.

67. Norman O. Mick, "Some Recent Developments in the Field of Office Appliances," *Proceedings of LOMA* (1928): 55–64. He also mentioned IBM's new subtracting machine (useful in accounting applications, including those used by insurance), its improved verifier (important for obtaining the accuracy insurance firms felt necessary), and its automatic gang punch (for simultaneously punching identical information into batches of cards, useful in many insurance applications).

68. Bashe et al., *IBM's Early Computers,* 10.

69. Connolly, *History of Computing in Europe,* 25.
70. Campbell-Kelly, *ICL,* 82.
71. Bashe et al., *IBM's Early Computers,* 11, text and photo.
72. Campbell-Kelly, *ICL,* 82. This method of compression was similar to that used by Peirce.
73. Memo, May 13, 1925, Peirce Machine Matters, cabinet 2, MetLife Archives. The memorandum asserted that Hollerith cards were going to expand from forty-five to eighty-six fields, rather than to eighty, but focused on the future incompatibility. The hoped-for competitive advantage could have come simply from the larger card capacity. Alternatively, a salesperson could have leaked the information to encourage Metropolitan Life not to continue working with Remington Rand as well as IBM, since doing so would eventually cause compatibility problems.
74. R. Wells Leib, chairman, "The Use of Punched Cards in Home Offices," discussional conference, *Proceedings of LOMA* (1931): 225.
75. Ibid.
76. Logan J. Massee, "New Machines and Machine Improvements, during the Past Three Years, in the Adding, Accounting and Calculating Machine Field," *Proceedings of LOMA* (1932): 84, 80–89, in R. A. Taylor, chairman, "Recent Developments in Office Machinery and Equipment," *Proceedings of LOMA* (1932): 79–97. This episode prefigures insurance demand for card-to-tape conversion equipment to facilitate the move to computers.
77. R. W. Leib, "Committee Report: Punched Cards in the Life Insurance Office," *Proceedings of LOMA* (1930): 257–311.
78. Ibid., 257. He noted that the committee sent the questionnaire to 122 companies. The indented quotation is also from 257.
79. Ibid., 260–261.
80. Ibid., 258 (two subsequent quotations are also from this page).
81. G. W. Skilton, chairman, "Committee Report: Premium Accounting and Related Activities," *Proceedings of LOMA* (1930): 22–204. (Eight reports from individual firms, along with the chairman's introduction, constituted the committee report).
82. Frank E. Fricke, "Report of Premium Accounting and Related Activities," the Phoenix Mutual Life Insurance Company, in Skilton, "Committee Report," 148–169. According to Stalson (*Marketing Life Insurance,* 800–801), Phoenix Mutual was in twenty-fourth place by size in both 1925 and 1935 but did not make it into the top twenty-five in 1930, suggesting that it was just below that level in 1930.
83. Phoenix first installed punched-card equipment in 1908 (D. N. Clark, "Premium Accounting by Punched Cards in the Phoenix Mutual," *Proceedings of LOMA* [1936]: 79).
84. Fricke, "Report of Premium Accounting and Related Activities," 150.
85. This and the next quotation are from ibid.
86. Skilton, discussion following "Committee Report," 198–202.
87. Clark, "Premium Accounting by Punched Cards," 87–89.
88. Leib, "Use of Punched Cards in Home Offices," 216–226.
89. Campbell-Kelly, *ICL,* 91–92.
90. See 1932 *Fortune* magazine article about IBM, as quoted in Campbell-Kelly, *ICL,* 77–78.
91. Cortada, *Before the Computer,* 152.
92. Sobel, *IBM,* 71.

93. Cortada, *Before the Computer,* 156.
94. Calculated from ibid., 153.
95. Norberg, "High Technology Calculation," 771.
96. See the sections entitled "Exhibit of Office Equipment" in *Proceedings of LOMA* for 1933–35; internal evidence suggests they were submitted by the vendors and printed with few, if any, changes.
97. "Exhibit of Office Equipment," Remington Rand section, *Proceedings of LOMA* (1935): 323–325.
98. See, for example, "Exhibit of Office Equipment," Remington Rand section, *Proceedings of LOMA* (1933): 247–248, and "Exhibit of Office Equipment," Remington Rand section, *Proceedings of LOMA* (1935): 323–325.
99. "Exhibit of Office Equipment," IBM section, *Proceedings of LOMA* (1935): 318–319.
100. "Parade of the Business Machines," *Business Week,* October 19, 1935, 10–11. According to Cortada (*Before the Computer,* 107), the Type 601 was developed in conjunction with utility companies that needed to multiply rates in order to compute bills, but the *Business Week* article suggests that IBM also had insurance uses in mind.
101. Clark, "Premium Accounting by Punched Cards," 78–80.
102. G. E. Cannon, "Alphabetical Tabulator for Premium Notice Production," *Proceedings of LOMA* (1936): 90–100, quoted phrase at p. 90.
103. Ibid., 90, 99.
104. Jordan, "Survey of Punched Card Development," 52; Herman Knauss, "Recent Developments in Office Machinery, Equipment and Methods Applicable to Life Office Operations," Report of the Office Planning and Equipment Committee, *Proceedings of LOMA* (1946): 76.
105. "Renewal Premium Notices and Receipts and Premium Billing Routines," prepared by LOMA Staff Office, Report No. 2 of the Office Machinery and Equipment Committee of the Life Office Management Association, September 1, 1938, in MetLife Archives.
106. Lester H. Van Ness, "Application of Tabulating Equipment to Rate Book Making," *Proceedings of LOMA* (1937): 69–76.
107. Menagh, "Committee Report: Home Office Departmental and Functional Costs," 117–148.
108. LeVita, "Prepared Discussion," in ibid., 139–140.
109. Ralph W. Beeson, chair, Industrial Insurance Seminar, "Home Office Routines and Procedures for Handling Industrial Insurance," *Proceedings of LOMA* (1937): 162–217. See, for example, Hill Montague, "Use of Punched Card Equipment and the Actuarial Card for the Purpose of Issuing New Policies and Writing and Re-running Registers," *Proceedings of LOMA* (1937): 177.
110. H. J. Volk, in response to question by Chairman Beeson, within Montague, "Use of Punched Card Equipment," 181–184.
111. Frank J. Beebe, "Application of Punched Card Accounting Machines," *Proceedings of LOMA* (1947): 190–202.
112. Ralph W. Beeson, "Organization and Routine Changes in the Development of a Life Insurance Company," *Proceedings of LOMA* (1939): 80, 84–86.
113. William P. Barber Jr., "Indicated Trends in Life Office Management," presidential address, *Proceedings of LOMA* (1940): 6–7.

114. Milton Effros, "New Developments in Punched Card Equipment Applicable to Life Office Operations," *Proceedings of LOMA* (1944): 137.

115. Jordan, "Survey of Punched Card Development," 52.

116. "Exhibit of Office Equipment," *Proceedings of LOMA* (1941): 259.

117. Effros, "New Developments in Punched Card Equipment," 137–138.

118. Knauss, "Recent Developments in Office Machinery, Equipment and Methods," 76.

119. "Exhibit of Office Equipment," *Proceedings of LOMA* (1946): 433.

120. Logan J. Massee, "Mailing of Premium Notices from the Home Office versus Mailing from Field Offices," *Proceedings of LOMA* (1946): 99.

121. For example, *L.O.M.A. Bulletin* 17 (1951) includes three items about conversions of billing operations to punched cards: May 15, p. 25; July 15, p. 40; November 15, pp. 63–64; see also H. G. Fogg, "Premium Billing with Punched Cards," *Proceedings of IASA* (1948): 59–64.

122. W. V. Cassara, "Survey of Premium Billing and Accounting," *Proceedings of IASA* (1952): 66–76.

123. Roland A. Mangini, "Developments in Office Methods and Machinery during the Past Year," *Proceedings of LOMA* (1947): 104–105. See also Bashe et al., *IBM's Early Computers,* 44–46, 59–68.

124. Mangini, "Developments in Office Methods and Machinery," 105.

125. Ibid. This development was evident in the 519 end printing summary punch and reproducer, as well as in the 602 multiplier and the 055 verifier.

126. Yates, "Structuring of Early Computer Use in Life Insurance."

127. Mangini, "Developments in Office Methods and Machinery," 105.

128. Edmund C. Berkeley, "Electronic Sequence Controlled Calculating Machinery, and Applications in Insurance," *Proceedings of LOMA* (1947): 116–129.

129. Bashe et al., *IBM's Early Computers,* 176–177.

130. Cortada (*Before the Computer,* 102) attributes the key role in shaping the technology to accountants, and they undoubtedly played a large role, as evidenced by IBM's substitution of the term *electronic accounting machine* (EAM) for the name *tabulator* in its 400 series announced in 1931 (Campbell-Kelly, *ICL,* 91). But the evidence amassed here shows that life insurance firms, too, were key and active customers.

131. Ralph J. Hasbrouck, "Comparative Analysis of Forms Included in Portfolio No. 1 of Industrial Insurance Forms," Industrial Seminar, *Proceedings of LOMA* (1941): 175–185.

132. This result is in line with what Giddens' structuration theory (*Constitution of Society*) would lead us to expect most of the time, though he would also allow for individual actors to do otherwise.

FIVE: Early Engagement between Insurance and Computing

1. Cortada has identified the period from 1945 to 1952 in computer history as one in which "commercial uses were nonexistent" and "businesses . . . did not see an economic advantage in commercial applications of digital computers" ("Commercial Applications of the Digital Computer in American Corporations," 19). The life insurance industry, however, was clearly an exception to this timetable.

2. See, for example, Goldstine, *Computer from Pascal to Von Neumann;* Flamm, *Creat-*

*ing the Computer;* Stern, *From ENIAC to UNIVAC;* Campbell-Kelly and Aspray, *Computer;* and many articles in the *Annals of the History of Computing.*

3. Goldstine, *Computer from Pascal to von Neumann,* 86–86.

4. Campbell-Kelly and Aspray, *Computer,* 62–63.

5. Moreau, *Computer Comes of Age,* 27–29; Goldstine, *Computer from Pascal to von Neumann,* 115–118.

6. For example, remote data entry and floating point arithmetic.

7. Ceruzzi, *History of Modern Computing,* 18.

8. Ceruzzi, "Crossing the Divide," 10.

9. Ceruzzi, *History of Modern Computing,* 19. See also Bashe et al., *IBM's Early Computers,* 68–71.

10. Ceruzzi, "Crossing the Divide," 10.

11. The role of lead users in technological innovation is explored in von Hippel, *Sources of Innovation.*

12. The story presented in these two paragraphs is summarized primarily from Campbell-Kelly and Aspray, *Computer,* 69–76, with additional details from Goldstine, *Computer from Pascal to Von Neumann,* 111–114, 117–119, illustrations, and Bashe et al., *IBM's Early Computers,* 25–33.

13. Campbell-Kelly and Aspray (*Computer,* 74) cite the account in Thomas and Marva Belden, *The Lengthening Shadow* (Boston: Little, Brown, 1962), 260–261.

14. This account is based primarily on Ceruzzi, *History of Modern Computing,* 15–24, and Campbell-Kelly and Aspray, *Computer,* 85–104.

15. Ironically, it would not be completed until shortly after the war was over (Campbell-Kelly and Aspray, *Computer,* 95). J. Presper Eckert Jr. was unrelated to IBM's Wallace Eckert.

16. Ibid., 94–95.

17. Ibid., 109.

18. See, for example, Moorhead, *Our Yesterdays,* chap. 9, "How Actuaries Calculated," 331–348.

19. "Office Robots," *Fortune* 45 (January 1952): 82.

20. Life insurance in force calculated from U.S. Bureau of the Census, *Historical Statistics of the United States, Colonial Times to 1957,* ser. X 435–440, p. 672; life insurance policies, as well as subsequent employment statistics, from BLS, "The Introduction of an Electronic Computer in a Large Insurance Company," *Studies of Automatic Technology,* no. 2 (Washington, D.C.: U.S. Government Printing Office, 1955).

21. E. William Phillips, "Binary Calculation," *Journal of the Institute of Actuaries* 67 (1936): 187–203.

22. E. William Phillips, "Finelli and Electronic Procedures," *Review* (London), March 4, 1960, as quoted in Moorhead, *Our Yesterdays,* 345.

23. Berkeley is better known to computer historians as the author of the first popular book on computers, the 1949 *Giant Brains; or, Machines That Think* (New York: John Wiley and Sons, 1949), as well as a founder of the Association for Computing Machinery after he left the insurance industry. Berkeley's background and activities are described and documented in detail in Yates, "Early Interactions between the Insurance and Computer Industries." Much of the material in this section and the next section was originally reported in that article.

24. E. C. Berkeley to H. J. Volk, November 10, 1941, Berkeley Collection, box 3, folder

34, Charles Babbage Institute, University of Minnesota, Minneapolis (hereafter cited as Berkeley/CBI, followed by box and folder numbers).

25. Berkeley to Volk, February 9, 1942, Berkeley/CBI 3:35.

26. There may also have been other such interactions of which no record exists or has yet surfaced. Phillips' ("Finelli and Electronic Procedures") assertion that John J. Finelli had been a follower of binary electronic computers since 1936, for example, along with a passing reference to his handling of a large-scale computational job shortly thereafter, suggests that he may have had similar interests and perhaps contacts.

27. Moorhead, *Our Yesterdays*, 354–359.

28. Ibid.; see also Philip M. Morse, *In at the Beginnings: A Physicist's Life* (Cambridge: MIT Press, 1977), 184.

29. Moorhead, *Our Yesterdays*, 354–355.

30. Carr, *From Three Cents a Week*, 106–107.

31. Yates, "Early Interactions between the Life Insurance and Computer Industries," 65.

32. Moorhead, *Our Yesterdays*, 359.

33. Similar to the role of technology brokering described by Hargadon and Sutton in "Technology Brokering and Innovation in a Product Development Firm."

34. Berkeley to Volk, C. B. Laing, and E. F. Cooley, September 17, 1946, Berkeley/CBI 8:52.

35. Ibid.

36. Bashe et al., *IBM's Early Computers*, 47–49; Campbell-Kelly and Aspray, *Computer*, 74, 115.

37. Berkeley to Volk, Laing, and Cooley, September 30, 1946, in accession 1825, Unisys Records, box 83, in Hagley Museum and Library, Wilmington, Delaware (hereafter cited as Unisys/Hagley, followed by the box number).

38. E. C. Berkeley, "List of Some Questions for Discussion at Meeting Called for May 14, 1947 . . . in Mr. F. B. Gerhard's Office," May 13, 1947, Berkeley/CBI 8:55. The fact that Berkeley made detailed notes in preparation for a meeting about this subject suggests that he recognized that his argument against IBM as a potential vendor might be unpopular among executives of Prudential.

39. Berkeley to Cooley, January 6, 1947, Berkeley/CBI 3:51.

40. Berkeley to Volk, Laing, and Cooley, September 30, 1946, Unisys/Hagley 83.

41. He claimed that this problem, which involved a complex set of table look-ups and computations to figure the costs for a change of policy, was the first insurance problem ever run on a sequence controlled calculator.

42. Berkeley to Volk, November 5, 1946, Unisys/Hagley 78.

43. As this and other Berkeley documents in the CBI's Berkeley Collection show, he was thinking in terms of a general purpose, relatively high-speed central processor, not, as Stern (*From ENIAC to UNIVAC*) has argued, only of high-speed input and output equipment.

44. Berkeley listed what he must have known to be an unrealistically low price of $10,000 to $20,000 per machine, on a mass production basis (Berkeley to Volk, November 5, 1946, Unisys/Hagley 78).

45. Berkeley to Volk, Laing, and Cooley, "New Machinery to Handle Information-Path of Development. Report No. 2: Finding and Studying Applications," February 17, 1947, Berkeley/CBI 8:53.

46. Berkeley's reports from this period did not even mention the recomputation of life experience tables due to changes in the Guertin laws, the application that, according to Stern (*From ENIAC to UNIVAC*), drove Prudential's investigation into computers.

47. H. T. Engstrom to Prudential Insurance Company of America (attn., Berkeley), January 21, 1947, Berkeley/CBI 8:53; Berkeley to Volk, Laing, and Cooley, February 7, 1947, Berkeley/CBI 8:53; Raytheon Manufacturing Company, "Proposal for an Automatic Digital Calculator for the Prudential Insurance Company," March 31, 1947, Berkeley/CBI 8:54.

48. Berkeley to Volk, Laing, and Cooley, "Symposium on Large Scale Digital Calculating Machinery at the Harvard Computation Laboratory, Cambridge, Massachusetts, January 7 to 10, 1947—Report," January 13, 1947, Berkeley/CBI 8:52.

49. In a March 13, 1947, letter, J. W. Mauchly to Berkeley (in Unisys/Hagley 48), Mauchly refers to Berkeley's "three memoranda dated January 13, January 28 and February 27." The two men may have met even before this point, but the correspondence makes clear that they certainly interacted at this symposium.

50. Yates, "Early Interactions between Life Insurance and Computing," 68.

51. Electronic Control Company, "Proposal for the Construction of a Group of Electronic Sequence Controlled Calculators," February 18, 1947, Berkeley/CBI 8:53.

52. On one item, floating point capabilities, Mauchly pointed out that "a so-called floating decimal point is actually undesirable for accounting work," at the same time stating that if Berkeley needed this capability for a particular problem, "instructions in the form of a subroutine can provide its equivalent" (ibid.).

53. Subsequent informal correspondence between the two men (see, e.g., Mauchly to Berkeley, February 26, 1947, Berkeley/CBI 8:53) and the second, more detailed proposal (Electronic Control Company, "Application of High Speed Computing Machines to Certain Problems of the Prudential Life Insurance Company," May 16, 1947, Unisys/Hagley 48) both reveal that Berkeley insisted on conversion equipment that would provide humanly readable cards that could be verified.

54. In one letter to Eckert and Mauchly, Berkeley even commented that although Harvard's Howard Aiken had suggested to him that a special-purpose machine developed especially for insurance might be even more useful to Prudential than the more general machine it was contracting with ECC about, "we are convinced that we should have general purpose machinery" (Berkeley to Mauchly and J. P. Eckert, July 8, 1947, Unisys/Hagley 79). This choice may have reflected a wariness about following the path that had led to a technological dead-end with the Gore and then Peirce machines in the earlier period.

55. Arthur L. Norberg, "New Engineering Companies and the Evolution of the United States Computer Industry," *Business and Economic History* 22 (1993): 186.

56. Electronic Control Company, "Application of High Speed Computing Machines to Certain Problems of the Prudential Life Insurance Company," May 16, 1947, Berkeley/CBI 8:55.

57. Berkeley to Gerhard, Laing, Cobb, and Cooley, May 24, 1947, Berkeley/CBI 8:55. Ironically, Berkeley had already eliminated IBM, which understood a great deal about insurance applications based on its tabulator business.

58. Mauchly and J. Presper Eckart Jr. to the Prudential Insurance Company, August 4, 1947, Unisys/Hagley 80, and Berkeley/CBI 3:56.

59. An undated draft of this purchase agreement may be found in Unisys/Hagley 78.

An internal Prudential report by B. E. Olmstead ("Prudential's Early Experience with Computers," 8) says Prudential's executive committee approved the contract on November 23, 1948, and Stern (*From ENIAC to UNIVAC,* 286) states that it was signed on December 8, 1948.

60. Berkeley had been working on a Prudential "hazards project" that identified nuclear war as one of the greatest threats to humanity. When Prudential abandoned the project and told Berkeley he could no longer work on it, even on his own time, Berkeley felt it was his moral imperative to oppose nuclear war, so he left the firm to do so. Pat Hennessy, "Edmund C. Berkeley Papers" (archival finding aid), CBI, 1990.

61. The undated draft of the contract (Unisys/Hagley 78) and Olmstead's internal report, "Prudential's Early Experience with Computers" (p. 12), both state the contract purchase price as $297,976. In contrast, Stern (*From ENIAC to UNIVAC,* 286), drawing on EMCC records, says the contract was for $150,000. In either case, it was significantly lower than the $1,250,000 price Remington Rand would ask for the UNIVAC.

62. Olmstead ("Prudential's Early Experience with Computers," 12) and Stern (*From ENIAC to UNIVAC,* 297–299) give somewhat different but not inconsistent accounts of how Remington Rand succeeded in canceling the contract, including its use of threats (to set up EMCC as a separate company and allow it to go bankrupt, or to initiate an expensive lawsuit) as well as inducements (its offer to return the development money Prudential had already supplied).

63. George Boyd, in a session entitled "Remington Rand Univac," in *Proceedings of IASA* (1954): 445. Boyd was general manager for insurance markets at Remington Rand ("Remington Rand Forum on the Use of Electronics in the Insurance Industry," as reproduced in Kenneth M. Hills, *Insurance Data Processing: Property—Liability—Life* [Philadelphia: Chilton Co.–Spectator, 1967], 138).

64. Dr. Herbert F. Mitchell, "Practical Adaptations to Insurance," in *Proceedings of IASA's First Electronics Conference,* "Electronics and Its Future in the Insurance Industry," held April 20–21, 1953, in New York (hereafter cited as *IASA's First Electronics Conference*), 26.

65. Berkeley to Volk, Laing, and Cooley, September 17, 1946, Berkeley/CBI 8:52. In a later internal document, Berkeley recorded the high points of a policy discussion on sequence controlled machines (E. B. Berkeley, "Electronic Machinery for Handling Information—Policy Discussion," May 13, 1947, Berkeley/CBI 8:55). In it, he summarized Prudential's policy on sharing with other interested parties "any general nonconfidential knowledge or expectations we have about facts, experimental results, and possibilities," while "keep[ing] confidential particular proposals made to us" by vendors.

66. Moorhead, *Our Yesterdays,* 165, 344. To avoid confusion, I refer to the organization as the Society of Actuaries throughout this discussion, whether before or after the name change.

67. Knauss, "Recent Developments in Office Machinery, Equipment and Methods," 71–86.

68. Mangini, "Developments in Office Methods and Machinery," 99–115.

69. Berkeley, "Electronic Sequence Controlled Calculating Machinery, and Applications in Insurance," 116–129.

70. Ibid., 117; Olmstead, "Prudential's Early Experience with Computers," 10. During 1947 Berkeley also talked at a May meeting of the Society of Actuaries (manuscript labeled "Electronic Machinery for Handling Information, and Its Uses in Insurance: Pre-

sented to the Actuarial Society of America at Its Meeting May 8, 1947," Berkeley/CBI 3:53, published in *TASA* 48 [1947]: 36–52) and at a meeting of IASA (see Moorhead, *Our Yesterdays*, 345–346).

71. George C. Boddiger, "Recent Developments in Office Machinery and Equipment," *Proceedings of LOMA* (1948): 169–183; "Exhibit of Office Equipment," *Proceedings of LOMA* (1949): 440–455.

72. Hess T. Sears, "Recent Developments in the Equipment Field," *Proceedings of LOMA* (1950): 354.

73. Olmstead, "Prudential's Early Experience with Computers," 10.

74. Edmund C. Berkeley, "Sequence Controlled Calculators," *Proceedings of IASA* (1947): 39–44.

75. Ibid., 43.

76. Ibid., 44.

77. H. T Engstrom, "Computation—A Look into the Future," *Proceedings of IASA* (1950): 114–119.

78. Hills, *Insurance Data Processing*, 137–139. The other two insurance associations were the Insurance Accountants Association and the Association of Casualty and Surety Accountants and Statisticians.

79. Ibid., 139.

80. Ibid.

81. Berkeley, "Electronic Machinery for Handling Information, and Its Uses in Insurance."

82. William P. Barber, Edward H. Wells, and Edward A. Rieder, *TASA* 48 (1947): 278 ff.; quotations are from unpaginated manuscript form of comments, found in Berkeley/CBI 3:54.

83. M. E. Davis, W. P. Barber Jr., J. J. Finelli, and W. Klem, "Report of Committee on New Recording Means and Computing Devices," Society of Actuaries, September 1952. See also Moorhead, *Our Yesterdays*, 344.

84. Moorhead, *Our Yesterdays*, 344; M. Paul Chinitz, in "The Univac Conference," CBI Oral History #200, session 3, pp. 10, 102 (conference organized by CBI, the Smithsonian Institution, and Unisys Corporation, May 17–18, 1990, Smithsonian Institution, Washington, D.C.); William D. Bell, *A Management Guide to Electronic Computers* (New York: McGraw-Hill, 1957), 4, 280.

85. Moorhead, *Our Yesterdays*, 344. For timing of the change in chairmen, see designations of chair on the three reports: Davis (chairman) et al., "Report of Committee," September 1952; M. E. Davis (chairman), W. P. Barber Jr., H. F. Rood, J. W. Ritchie, R. E. Slater, and J. J. Finelli, "Current Status of Magnetic Tape as a Recording and Data Processing Medium," Report of Committee on New Recording Means and Computing Devices, Society of Actuaries, June 1955; and J. J. Finelli (chairman), W. P. Barber Jr., J. W. Ritchie, M. R. Cueto, H. F. Rood, A. D. Murch, R. E. Slater, and D. H. Harris, "Application of Electronic Data Processing Equipment to Office Operations," Report of Committee on New Recording Means and Computing Devices, Society of Actuaries, October 1957.

86. Ranked by assets, *Best's*, 1947. In Part II, I depend primarily on assets to rank the size of firms, as that information is more readily available than insurance in force for recent years.

87. Council minutes, Actuarial Society, May 12, 1948, as quoted in Moorhead, *Our Yesterdays*, 344. Ellipses are in the passage as quoted.

88. Davis et al., "Report of Committee," 1952, v and 3.

89. The report does not name vendor firms, but internal as well as external evidence clearly reveals their identities.

90. Davis et al., "Report of Committee," 1952, both quotations at p. 4.

91. Ibid., 10.

92. Ibid., 14.

93. Ibid., 16.

94. Ibid.

95. Ibid., 22–23.

96. Ibid., 26.

97. Ibid. Whether this company was Metropolitan Life or some other firm represented on the committee is not clear, but the card-based computer initially used in developing the application was the IBM SSEC. The committee later learned that the smaller and less complex CPC could do the application nearly as well (ibid., 23, 27).

98. Ibid., 46.

99. Ibid., 37.

100. To enable the committee to limit the number of permanent cards, alphabetical name and address information was not in punched form but instead typed onto the punched notice-writing card. A photoelectric scanning machine, of "the same kind which has been used for magazine addressing in recent years" (ibid., 35), was used to print name and address on the bill. Photoelectric technologies had been gaining insurance attention since the war. Metropolitan Life was examining mark-sensing technology by at least 1945, when a War Accounting Service report entitled "Electronics and Pencil Marks," produced by IBM's Department of Logistics, was circulated within the company as an attachment to *Ways and Means: A Review of Management Thinking and Practice* of June 15, 1945. Interestingly, in 1952 when the consolidated functions approach was unveiled, Metropolitan Life was installing its own punched-card system for preparing premium notices and receipts for ordinary insurance policies ("Preparation of Ordinary Premium Receipts and Notices Being Mechanized," in "What's Going on at Metropolitan," *Ways and Means,* October 1952, 1–2). Its new system, using 400 series IBM tabulating equipment, encoded alphabetical as well as numerical information on punched cards and printed the receipts, notices, and accounting stubs on continuous fan-fold forms. The process nevertheless included the use of a "mark-sensing" reproducing punch (a photoelectric device that read pencil marks and converted them into punched holes) for handling certain numerical information. Moreover, "while punch card equipment will be used initially, the procedure has been developed with a view to possible conversion to a more advanced mechanical or electronic system as may be perfected in the future" (p. 2). Thus the committee's sample plan, as reported by Metropolitan Life's Finelli, did not fully mirror what Metropolitan Life was doing internally.

101. Davis et al., "Report of Committee," 1952, 33.

102. Ibid.

103. Ibid., 35.

104. Ibid., 48.

105. Ibid. In this respect, insurance differed, for example, from railroads, which typically hired computer experts from outside the railroad business to run computing installations.

106. Ibid., 49.

107. Moorhead, *Our Yesterdays,* 344. In many respects this rhetoric is echoed several decades later in the rhetoric around the Internet. See, for example, Iacono and Kling, "Computerization Movements," or Turner, "From Counterculture to Cyberculture."

108. Metropolitan Life, for example, had formed its own internal committee by 1948 (Finelli, "Installing Electronic Procedures—A Progress Report," pamphlet [Cambridge University Press] reprinted from *Journal of the Institute of Actuaries* 86 [1960]: 162); Franklin Life had initiated its explorations in 1951 (John Diebold and Associates, Inc., *Univac Applications in Two Insurance Companies: Franklin Life Insurance Company; Metropolitan Life Insurance Company,* an Automatic Data Processing Methods Report [Chicago: Cudahy Publishing Co., 1956], 4).

109. M. E. Davis, "The Use of Electronic Data Processing Systems in the Life Insurance Business," *Proceedings of the Eastern Joint Computer Conference* (New York: Institute of Radio Engineers, 1953), 17.

110. *IASA's First Electronics Conference;* "First Three Decades of I.A.S.A.," 62.

111. *IASA's First Electronics Conference,* 91.

112. Ibid., 5. The schedule for the two days is on pp. 7–8.

113. Mitchell, "Practical Adaptations to Insurance," 26.

114. Ibid.

115. Ibid., 26–27.

116. This and the following quotation come from ibid., 27.

117. George Runyan, in "Report on Electronics Conference, Panel Discussion," George Hamilton, chairman, *Proceedings of IASA* (1953): 27.

118. Ibid.

119. For a brief account of IBM's shock at the first sales of the UNIVAC and its attempts to catch up in the business market, see Campbell-Kelly and Aspray, *Computer,* 123–128; for a more detailed, technical account, see Bashe et al., *IBM's Early Computers,* 73–186.

120. General Session (James B. Clancy, of the IASA Electronics Committee, chairman), *IASA's First Electronics Conference,* 73.

121. Bashe et al., *IBM's Early Computers,* 162.

122. See ibid., 158–164; see also Ceruzzi, *History of Computing,* 34–36, for a brief discussion of this machine and the 702.

123. Bashe et al., *IBM's Early Computers,* 176.

124. General Session, *IASA's First Electronics Conference,* 73.

125. E. C. Carlson, in "Report on Electronics Conference Panel Discussion," George Hamilton, chairman, 28–29.

126. Ibid., 28.

127. Ibid, 29.

128. Kermit Lang, in "Report on Electronics Conference Panel Discussion," George Hamilton, chairman, 29–30.

129. Ibid., 29.

130. Ibid., 30. The remaining quotations in this paragraph are also from this page.

131. E. F. Cooley, in "Report on Electronics Conference Panel Discussion," George Hamilton, chairman, 30–31. At this time, Prudential had tested the UNIVAC and decided not to purchase it at the higher price asked by Remington Rand.

SIX: Insurance Adoption and Use of Early Computers

1. Much of the material in this chapter appeared in Yates, "Structuring of Early Computer Use in Life Insurance," 5–24.

2. The view of the computer as a radical innovation was reflected, for example, in Berkeley's book title, *Giant Brains; or, Machines That Think.*

3. Ceruzzi, "Electronics Technology and Computer Science," 262.

4. The 700 series computers outsold UNIVACs as early as 1956; still, "it was not the large-scale 700 series that secured IBM's leadership of the industry, but the low-cost Magnetic Drum Computer [the 650]" (Campbell-Kelly and Aspray, *Computer*, 127).

5. Olmstead, "Prudential's Early Experience with Computers," 12–13. For a description of this application, see *Premium Billing and Dividend and Commission Calculation,* a pamphlet published in 1951 by the Eckert-Mauchly Computer Corporation, a division of Remington Rand (NBS #5109825, box 21, folder 5, U.S. National Bureau of Standards Computer Literature Collection, CBI).

6. *Premium Billing and Dividend and Commission Calculation,* 3.

7. Olmstead, "Prudential's Early Experience with Computers," 14.

8. Ibid.

9. "Univacs Completed to Date," February 8, 1956, unsigned typed list, 1956 chronological file, Unisys/Hagley. In 1954 Remington Rand shipped eight UNIVACs, two to government agencies, two to U.S. Steel, one to DuPont, one to General Electric (the first one shipped), and two to life insurance companies, Metropolitan Life and Franklin Life.

10. Davis, "Use of Electronic Data Processing Systems in the Life Insurance Business," 11–17; BLS, "Introduction of an Electronic Computer in a Large Insurance Company"; Finelli, "Installing Electronic Procedures," 161–214; typescript "Introduction and Growth of EDP in Metropolitan," March 23, 1962, MetLife Archives, box 19 03 01, folder: Electronics Installations 1952–59 #1; John Diebold and Associates, Inc., *Univac Applications in Two Insurance Companies,* 16–24.

11. BLS, "Introduction of an Electronic Computer in a Large Insurance Company."

12. Assets based on *Best's,* 1952; number of policies and size ranking from John Diebold and Associates, Inc., *Univac Applications in Two Insurance Companies,* 16.

13. Davis, "Use of Electronic Data Processing in Life Insurance," 15.

14. Ibid.

15. Ibid.

16. Finelli, "Installing Electronic Procedures," 163.

17. Davis, "Use of Electronic Data Processing in Life Insurance," 15. The four-year payback estimate is from p. 16.

18. Ibid., 15–16. The following quotation is from p. 15.

19. Ibid., 16.

20. Subgroups of the first two organizations, similar to the committees established in the Society of Actuaries, the IASA, and LOMA, were the relevant organizing parties: the Professional Group on Electronic Computers of the Institute of Radio Engineers and the Committee on Computing Devices of the American Institute of Electrical Engineers (*Proceedings of the Eastern Joint Computer Conference*).

21. Ibid., 17. The Blackett quotation was referenced as follows: "'Operational Research,' paper published by British Association for the Advancement of Science, vol. V, no. 17; April, 1948."

22. *Proceedings of the Eastern Joint Computer Conference*, 17.

23. "Univac I Schedule," February 8, 1956 (unsigned typed list, 1956 chronological file, Unisys/Hagley), lists machines #28 and #29 as allocated to Metropolitan Life and tentatively scheduled for installation in April of that year; the information about the 1958 applications comes from Peggy Courtney, ed., *Business Electronics Reference Guide*, vol. 4 (New York: Controllership Foundation, 1958), 119. Volume 3 of the same series, published in 1956, lists Metropolitan Life as possessing three UNIVACs (installation completed in August 1956) but having only actuarial applications (Herbert F. Klingman, ed., *Business Electronics Reference Guide*, vol. 3 [New York: Controllership Foundation, 1956], 33).

24. Figured from *Best's*, 1952. Its assets had increased from under $1 billion in the late 1930s to $3.5 billion in the early 1950s (*Best's*, 1937, 1952). According to another source, John Hancock was also the eleventh largest U.S. business in the mid-1950s (R. Hunt Brown, *Office Automation: Insurance*, first revision 1960, loose-leaf handbook [New York: Automation Consultants, 1959], pt. 3, sec. D 13–1, in CBI). For John Hancock's labor shortages, see Brown, *Office Automation*, pt. 3, sec. D 13–1.

25. H. F. Hatch, "Installing and Preparing for Premium Billing on Univac," *Proceedings of IASA* (1956): 93.

26. Ibid.

27. In 1950 Raytheon Manufacturing Company, an electronics and control firm, studied John Hancock's operations and how these could be computerized ("The Application of Automatic Electronic Digital Techniques to the Operations of the John Hancock Mutual Life Insurance Company," Raytheon Manufacturing Company, Waltham, Massachusetts, August 1950, in CBI, box 1: John Hancock: Raytheon). It concluded that "a fairly detailed appraisal of the requirements of an insurance company has revealed no insurmountable obstacles to large-scale computer operation" (p. 63). While the study was as much for the benefit of Raytheon as for John Hancock, the latter's cooperation with the study shows that pockets of interest remained in it throughout this period. See Campbell-Kelly and Aspray, *Computer*, 128, on Raytheon's brief role in this market.

28. Hatch, "Installing and Preparing for Premium Billing on Univac," 93. The 1950 Raytheon study and the contacts made through it undoubtedly put the Datamatic into this set, though Raytheon would not remain in this market much longer. In looking at IBM's offerings, the committee ignored the card-based 650, which it adopted for smaller jobs, apparently without considering it a real computer (E. F. Shepherd, "Using the 650 for Weekly Premium Insurance Operations in the Actuarial Department," *Proceedings of IASA* [1956]: 146–148; Bashe et al., *IBM's Early Computers*, 171). The choice of application may be found in Brown, *Office Automation*, pt. 3, sec. D 13–1; "Premium Billing by Univac: John Hancock Mutual Life Insurance Company, Boston, Massachusetts," undated, ca. 1956, accession 1825, box 347, Hagley Museum and Library.

29. Hatch, "Installing and Preparing for Premium Billing on Univac," 93–94.

30. Ibid., 94.

31. Ibid., 93; Brown, *Office Automation*, pt. 3, sec. D 13–1; "Univac Performs at John Hancock," *Journal of Machine Accounting* 7:5 (1956): 22.

32. "Premium Billing by Univac."

33. Ibid.

34. It is perhaps a measure of the difference in size between the two companies that even with the premium billing application installed, the computer was used for only one

shift, enabling the second shift to be used by the Chesapeake and Ohio Railroad and the Bureau of Ships until John Hancock had coded more applications (Hatch, "Installing and Preparing for Premium Billing on Univac," 95).

35. *IASA's First Electronics Conference,* 46. In 1952, Pacific Mutual was twenty-fifth in size by assets, and Franklin Life was thirty-first (*Best's,* 1952). In the late 1950s Pacific Mutual had more than $2 billion of life insurance in force (some ordinary insurance and some group insurance), while in 1952, when it ordered its UNIVAC, Franklin Life had roughly $1 billion (to exceed $2 billion by the end of 1955) (Nunis, *Past Is Prologue,* 48, 56). Pacific Mutual had just over $600 million of life insurance in force in 1938, after losing 5% in 1937; by 1959, it had increased its life insurance in force by more than $2 billion (Paul McAnarney, "The Successes and Failures of EDP to Date," *Proceedings of IASA* [1962]: 552; O'Brien, *Fabulous Franklin Story,* 142, 148). Pacific Mutual had $440 million in assets in 1952, rising to $566 million in 1957, while Franklin Life had $223 million in 1952, rising to $420 million in 1957 (*Best's,* 1952, 1957).

36. D. K. Swinnerton, "Installing a Daily Cycle Data Processing System," *Proceedings of IASA* (1956): 97. Note the similarity to early adoption of tabulator equipment by the large New York Life and the moderate-sized Phoenix Mutual (see Chapter 2).

37. O'Brien, *Fabulous Franklin Story,* 143; Brown, *Office Automation,* pt. 3, sec. D 8–1, "First revision" (internal evidence suggests the case study was revised in 1959). Although Franklin Life placed its order for a UNIVAC before any firm except Prudential (whose order had by then been canceled and not renewed), it received its computer later than Metropolitan Life did, either because Metropolitan Life had finished necessary preparations for housing the large system earlier or because it had taken over Prudential's earlier order.

38. Peter B. Laubach, *Company Investigations of Automatic Data Processing* (Boston: Division of Research, Graduate School of Business Administration, Harvard University, 1957).

39. Charles E. Becker, "Life Insurance Gets the Univac," unpaginated two-page reprint from *Systems Magazine* 18:3 (March 1954). Vanselow put the increase since 1939 at more than 900% (A. C. Vanselow, "Electronics in a Life Company," *Proceedings of IASA* [1954]: 489).

40. O'Brien, *Fabulous Franklin Story,* 134, 142. In assets, Franklin had risen to thirty-first by 1952 (*Best's,* 1952).

41. Becker, "Life Insurance Gets the UNIVAC"; A. C. Vanselow, "Programming the Electronic Computer for Clerical Production," paper presented to the Office Management Conference, American Management Association, New York, October 20–22, 1954, in the Holburton Collection, box 23, Franklin Life Insurance Company, CBI), 4; Brown, *Office Automation,* pt. 3, sec. D 8-1-14.

42. Vanselow, "Programming the Electronic Computer for Clerical Production," 5. The figure of $1 billion in ordinary insurance, considerably lower than the $1.75 cited elsewhere as insurance in force in 1954, probably reflects 1951 levels. Indeed, Franklin Life attained its second billion dollars of insurance in force in less than five years, between 1950 and 1955 (O'Brien, *Fabulous Franklin Story,* 148).

43. John Diebold and Associates, Inc., *Univac Applications in Two Insurance Companies,* 8. Franklin Life was thus one of the few companies to avoid being trapped into eighty-column files, based on eighty-column cards.

44. A. C. Vanselow, "Electronics at Work in Life Insurance Accounting," *Proceedings*

*of the High Speed Computer Conference,* Louisiana State University, March 5–8, 1957, 161–163. According to Brown, *Office Automation,* pt. 3, sec. D 8–11, first revision, the conversion was completed in December 1957.

45. Vanselow, "Insurance Accounting: Two Computer-Operation," *Data Processing Annual* 3 (1961): 151–153.

46. Ibid., 152.

47. McAnarney, "Successes and Failures of EDP to Date," 552–556.

48. Ibid., 552.

49. Ibid., 556.

50. Nunis, *Past Is Prologue,* 45–57.

51. Despite its name, Pacific Mutual was a stock company before it went bankrupt in 1935; the decision to mutualize was made during the reorganization, approved by sufficient policyholders in 1946, and completed in 1959. See Moorhead, *Our Yesterdays,* 326.

52. R. D. Dotts, "An Approach to Electronics by a Medium Sized Company," *Journal of Machine Accounting* 5:11 (1954): 5, 7–9; Wesley S. Bagby, "Deciding upon an Electronic Data Processing System," *Journal of Machine Accounting* 7:11 (1956): 19–20, 22.

53. Dotts, "Approach to Electronics by a Medium Sized Company," 5.

54. Ibid.

55. Ibid., 6; subsequent quotation from same page.

56. Ibid., 9.

57. Bagby, "Deciding upon an Electronic Data Processing System," 19.

58. This aspect of the system is explained in detail in Swinnerton, "Installing a Daily Cycle Data Processing System," 97–99.

59. Ibid., 97.

60. R. D. Dotts, "Univac System: A Case Study," *Journal of Machine Accounting* 7:10 (1956): 23.

61. Ibid.

62. Dotts, "Approach to Electronics by a Medium Sized Company," 9.

63. Electrodata Company would be taken over by Burroughs in 1956. For information on Electrodata and Computer Research Corporation, see Campbell-Kelly and Aspray, *Computer,* 128–129.

64. Dotts, "Approach to Electronics by a Medium Sized Company," 9.

65. Dotts, "Univac System," 23

66. Giddens, *Constitution of Society.* See also Orlikowski, "Duality of Technology."

67. Berkeley, *Giant Brains,* 201–202.

68. "Office Robots," 118.

69. Bix, *Inventing Ourselves out of Jobs?*

70. J. A. Dollard, "Evolution of the Application of Office Machinery to Industry," *Proceedings of LOMA* (1955): 74–75.

71. For Hatch's attitude, see, for example, his statements about taking away cards before employees were ready, during his informal presentation transcribed within Quentin Lane, "Policyholder Billing and Accounting by Univac 1," *Proceedings of IASA* (1957): 635–638.

72. Hatch, "Installing and Preparing for Premium Billing on Univac," 94.

73. BLS, "Introduction of an Electronic Computer in a Large Insurance Company," 1–2.

74. Ibid., 1. The study does not name Metropolitan Life, but internal evidence (dates, size, application, and so on) as well as many references elsewhere make the identity obvious.

75. "A Genius of Sorts," *Home Office* (Metropolitan Life internal publication), June 1954, MetLife Archives.

76. BLS, "Introduction of an Electronic Computer in a Large Insurance Company," 1.

77. "Two More Univacs, but There's Still a Need for Additional Clerks," *Home Office,* June 1956, 6–9, MetLife Archives.

78. No author or recipient, "Re: Re-Assignment of Employees due to Electronic Installation," August 20, 1956, MetLife Archives, box 19 03 01, Electronics Installations 1952–59, #1.

79. Personal letter from R. M. Hutches, Franklin Life Insurance Company, March 26, 1998.

80. Frances Elizabeth Holberton, in "The Univac Conference," CBI Oral History #200, session 2, quotations at p. 49.

81. Vanselow, "Programming the Electronic Computer for Clerical Production," 5. He used almost identical words in Vanselow, "Electronics in a Life Company," 490.

82. Vanselow, "Programming the Electronic Computer for Clerical Production," 5–6.

83. The acquisition of the UNIVAC received relatively little attention in O'Brien's *Fabulous Franklin Story,* 143, 145, while the growth story dominates this section of the book.

84. McAnarney, "Successes and Failures of EDP to Date," 552. He does not, unfortunately, tell us who these key personnel were and what their jobs and levels were.

85. Ibid., 556. Next quotation is from the same page.

86. Upper management of Franklin Life used the technology to "informate" (Zuboff, *In the Age of the Smart Machine*) rather than just to automate aspects of sales, thereby getting better reactions from them.

87. Morgan W. Huff, in "The Univac Conference," CBI Oral History #200, session 1, p. 49.

88. Dotts, "Approach to Electronics by a Medium Sized Company," 7.

89. Bagby, "Deciding upon an Electronic Data Processing System," 22. Subsequent quotation is from the same page.

90. Dotts, "Univac System," 44.

91. Nunis, *Past Is Prologue,* 61–62.

92. Finelli, "Installing Electronic Procedures," 208.

93. The problem with judging performance, given the mix of mutuals and stock companies, is discussed in more detail by Delehanty, "Computers and the Organization Structure in Life-Insurance Firms," 70–72. He also speculated that the industry had had some slack in costs, based on favorable trends in investments and mortality as well as on growth.

94. Three expense ratios were reported to regulatory agencies and published by the industry periodical, *Best's.* One of these, the ordinary renewal expense ratio (ordinary RER), is the most relevant measure for which consistent and complete data for all the companies were publicly reported over a long period. The differences in ordinary RER ratios between stock and mutual firms between 1940 and 1980 were slight, with the average stock firm having expense ratios that went slightly higher and peaked slightly later

than the average mutual. North ("Entrepreneurial Policy and Internal Organization in the Large Life Insurance Companies") also found little difference between stock and mutual life insurance firms in the period before the Armstrong Hearings.

95. Inflation was significant during parts of the period studied, but the ratio has not been indexed for inflation, since doing so poses insurmountable problems of information and computation. The numerator, costs, is generally in current dollars and thus could be indexed. However, the denominator, ordinary insurance in force, is the sum of values of policies bought in (and thus valued in dollars from) a wide array of years. This distribution varies from firm to firm. Fast-growing firms such as Franklin Life, for example, would have a younger policy distribution than an old, large firm such as Metropolitan Life. Thus all graphs use the ratios as reported in *Best's* each year.

96. A regression line for the thirty-firm average slopes upward for 1940–74 and downward for 1975–90. The break point was initially determined by eye, and then was tested using a Chow test, which gave a value of 11.63, considerably larger than the $f$ distribution value of 0.523, suggesting that 1975 is the appropriate break point for stability. This pattern may reflect what has been called the "productivity paradox"—the issue of why the expected gains in productivity from information technology did not originally show up. Some recent scholarship has suggested both that information technology does lead to productivity gains (based on studies of more recent information technology investment) and that there is a lag before its effects are realized, in part because these gains are heavily dependent on complementary changes in organizational structure, work practices, and so on (see, e.g., Brynjolfsson and Hitt, "Beyond the Productivity Paradox").

97. "Two More Univacs, but There's Still a Need for Additional Clerks," 6–9; "Metropolitan Life's Electronic Computer Center," *Eastern Underwriter,* March 1, 1957, 3, 6.

98. Bob Volante, retired from John Hancock Insurance Company, interview by author and Bob Hancke, Boston, July 22, 1993.

99. J. Howard Ditman, chairman, "Present Status of Electronics Applicable to Life Office Operations," Panel Discussion, *Proceedings of LOMA* (1955): 98.

100. Lane, "Policyholder Billing and Accounting by Univac 1," 632–635.

101. BLS, "Impact of Office Automation in the Insurance Industry," 10.

102. This was the only one of the fourteen IBM 702s built to go to an insurance firm. Hurd, "Computer Development at IBM," 410; Ceruzzi, "Electronic Technology and Computer Science," 262.

103. Flamm, *Creating the Computer,* 83.

104. For example, Sun Life's L. M. Clark and J. F. Emms talked about life insurance applications of the IBM 604 electronic calculator, the most advanced electronic addition to the tabulating line, and Pacific Mutual's Dotts described how his firm had decided to buy its UNIVAC (L. M. Clark and J. F. Emms, "Some Life Office Applications of the Electronic Calculating Punch Machine," *Proceedings of LOMA* [1954]: 46–69; R. D. Dotts, "An Approach to Electronics by a Medium Sized Company," *Proceedings of LOMA* [1954]: 309–316). The Dotts paper on Pacific Mutual appeared in the *Journal of Machine Accounting* that same year. Similarly, the IASA conference, in addition to sessions on tabulating technology, featured several "electronics sessions," including one on the UNIVAC and one on the IBM 702 (George Boyd and James B. Clancy, "Remington Rand Univac," *Proceedings of IASA* [1954]: 445–452; James B. Clancy, "IBM Type 702—Description of Machine and Its Application by Manufacturer's Representative," *Proceedings of IASA* [1954]: 439–445).

105. Paul Knaplund, "Description of the IBM Type 650 Magnetic Drum Processing Machine," *Proceedings of IASA* (1954): 437; George Hamilton, chairman, "Panel Discussion of Life Insurance Applications of the IBM Magnetic Drum Calculator Type 650," *Proceedings of IASA* (1954): 462–470, quotation at p. 462.

106. Hamilton, "Panel Discussion of Life Insurance Applications," 462.

107. Knaplund, "Description of the IBM Type 650 Magnetic Drum Processing Machine," 437.

108. The separate electronics sessions appeared alongside sessions on life insurance, debit insurance (industrial insurance), group insurance, fire and casualty insurance, and so on through 1963, though by the early 1960s many papers on computer applications were listed within sessions on the specific types of insurance, and the separate electronics session dwindled in size until it was entirely subsumed within the other sessions.

109. UNIVAC: J. R. Slights, "Life—Univac File Computer," *Proceedings of IASA* (1956): 53–59; Hatch, "Installing and Preparing for Premium Billing on Univac," 93–96; Swinnerton, "Installing a Daily Cycle Data Processing System," 97–99. IBM 702: Emerson F. Cooley, "Prudential Experience with 702," *Proceedings of IASA* (1956): 104–105. IBM 650: for example, Walter L. DeVries, "Equitable's Experience in Programming for the Type 650 Machine," *Proceedings of IASA* (1956): 124–131; A. S. Kuenkler, Waid J. Davidson Jr., and Theodore C. Morrill, "650 Magnetic Tape System," *Proceedings of IASA* (1956): 106–109.

110. Kermit Lang, chair, "Panel Discussion of Life Applications on the 650," *Proceedings of IASA* (1956): 123.

111. Harold B. Doyle, "Expense Accounting (Including Payroll) on the 650," *Proceedings of IASA* (1956): 60; Ian Morrison, "Loss Accounting Using IBM Type 650 for Loss Reserve File Updating and Multiple Loss Distributions," *Proceedings of IASA* (1956): 160–166.

112. Finelli et al., "Application of Electronic Data Processing Equipment to Office Operations," 14. J. Stanley Hill, "Programming the Burroughs Datatron for Life Insurance Applications," *Proceedings of IASA* (1957): 639–642. The twelve large-scale computers included UNIVACs, IBM 702s and 705s, and perhaps one or two others such as the Burroughs Datatron. According to Hill, a Datatron "cost us about $355,000 FOB, Pasadena and about $400,000 installed including spare parts, magnetic tape and 25 tons of auxiliary air conditioning" ("Programming the Burroughs Datatron for Life Insurance Applications," 630). He describes the Datatron as "the poor man's Univac, or 705," significantly larger than the 650 and magnetic-tape-based, but not as large as the other two machines.

113. Bashe et al., *IBM's Early Computers,* 171; Lang, "Panel Discussion of Life Applications on the 650," 148.

114. J. A. Daley, "Conversion to and Installation of IBM 705 Systems at the Prudential," *Proceedings of IASA* (1958): 365–366.

115. Olmstead, "Prudential's Early Experience with Computers," 17.

116. Davis et al., "Current Status of Magnetic Tape as a Recording and Data Processing Medium."

117. Berkeley to Gerhard, Laing, Cobb, and Cooley, July 25, 1947, Berkeley/CBI 3:56.

118. The 1956 consent decree that required IBM to offer its tabulators and computers for sale as well as rent clearly precluded such a situation after that time.

119. Bashe et al., *IBM's Early Computers,* 175–178.

120. As early as 1949, a two-day meeting including Thomas J. Watson Jr. and various

department heads considered "the competitive threat to IBM punched-card installations, specifically in the insurance accounting field, posed by the increasingly active computer-development groups. Chief of these was the Eckert-Mauchly Computer Corporation" (ibid., 193–194). There was further reaction within IBM to the competitive threat posed by the UNIVAC when the Census Bureau took delivery of its machine in 1951.

121. Ibid., 171.

122. Panel discussion segment of Ditman, "Present Status of Electronics Applicable to Life Office Operations," 96.

123. In general, insurance firms were considered more interested in buying than other types of customers. As John K. Swearingen, who worked for GE when it purchased a UNIVAC, commented at the 1990 UNIVAC Conference, "Except for life insurance companies for which purchase had a financial advantage and the government agencies where it generally didn't make any difference, I think most commercial operations there were concerned about spending several million dollars outright because that was then a capital investment" ("The Univac Conference," CBI Oral History #200, session 1, p. 11). Moreover, according to Fisher, McKie, and Mancke, (*IBM and the U.S. Data Processing Industry*, 21), IBM and some other computer vendors offered short-term leases on early computer systems, reducing the risk even further.

124. Bashe et al., *IBM's Early Computers*, 574–576.

125. Glenn O. Head, "650 Planning at United States Life," *Proceedings of IASA* (1955): 465–466.

126. Brown, *Office Automation*, pt. 3, sec. D 4–1.

127. Carl O. Orkild, "Approaching Automation in a Casualty Insurance Company," *Computers and Automation* 4:2 (1955): 19. He did not consider the UNIVAC, which had to be purchased.

128. Blackburn H. Hazlehurst, "Using the 650 as a Proving Ground for Electronics," *Proceedings of IASA* (1956): 70–72, quotation at p. 72.

129. Mackay and Gillespie, "Extending the Social Shaping of Technology Approach," 692–694.

130. Hazlehurst, "Using the 650 as a Proving Ground for Electronics," 70.

131. Chinitz, in "The Univac Conference," CBI Oral History #200, session 3, p. 58.

132. G. J. Williams, "Premium Billing and Related Functions on the IBM Type 650 Machine," *Proceedings of IASA* (1957): 689–692.

133. Hazlehurst, "Using the 650 as a Proving Ground for Electronics," 70.

134. Nathan D. O'Neil, "Procedures on IBM 650—Maintenance of Mortgage Loan Due File," *Proceedings of IASA* (1957): 677–681.

135. DeVries, "Equitable's Experience in Programming for the Type 650 Machine," quotation at p. 124.

136. A. L. Wright, "Setting up Punch Card Records with the 650," *Proceedings of IASA* (1956): 76–78, quotations at p. 76.

137. Lang,"Panel Discussion of Life Applications on the 650," 131.

138. Glenn O. Head, co-chairman (with Dudley M. Pruitt and Robert Espie), "Advanced Seminar on IBM 650," part of the electronics sessions, *Proceedings of IASA* (1955): 437.

139. Glenn O. Head, "Changeover Procedures at United States Life," *Proceedings of IASA* (1956): 72–76.

140. Waid J. Davidson Jr., "650 Planning and Application at the Pan-American Life Insurance Co.," *Proceedings of IASA* (1956): 133.

141. Life Office Management Association [hereafter cited as LOMA], "EDP Applications in Life Insurance Companies," LOMA Automation Report No. 10, February 1965, 4, 8.

142. Kermit Lang, chairman, "Procedures on IBM 650," *Proceedings of IASA* (1957): 677.

143. ElectroData was one of the small start-ups of the early phase of computing, bought up by Burroughs in 1956. Its computer was also drum-based but was a more sophisticated scientific computer than the 650. Ceruzzi, *History of Modern Computing,* 66. Aetna ultimately did not purchase it.

144. R. Walden, "Life Applications on the 650," *Proceedings of IASA* (1956): 86, 87.

145. Lloyd E. Gross, "An Approach to Automation," *Journal of Machine Accounting* 7:9 (1956): 11–12, 21; quotation at p. 12. At this stage Gross himself may have been one of the department heads.

146. He did not indicate whether there were any salary differences based on gender.

147. Gross, "Approach to Automation," 12.

148. T. L. Whisler and H. Meyer, *The Impact of EDP on Life Company Organization,* Personnel Administration Report No. 34 (New York: Life Office Management Association, 1967).

149. Ibid., 15.

150. Campbell-Kelly and Aspray, *Computer,* 127.

151. Bashe et al., *IBM's Early Computers,* 178.

152. *IASA's First Electronics Conference,* 75, 76–77; on the IBM 702, see Bashe et al., *IBM's Early Computers,* 176.

153. Campbell-Kelly and Aspray, *Computer,* 126.

154. Fisher, McKie, and Mancke, *IBM and the U.S. Data Processing Industry,* 30.

155. "Life Insurance Data Processing Seminar, January 24–25, 1957," list of attendees, in Nathan D. O'Neil, Data Processing Records, Record Group 50, Chronological File 1954–59, Aetna Archives (hereafter cited as O'Neil DP/Aetna/chronological file designation).

156. O'Neil, supervisor, Electronic Data-Processing Development Department, to S. W. Palmer, assistant secretary, memo, January 30, 1957, Subject: Life Insurance Data-Processing Seminar—January 24, 25, 1957, O'Neil DP/Aetna/Chronological File 1954–59.

157. *Best's,* 1952. Size based on assets.

158. Brown, *Office Automation,* pt. 3, sec. D 7–1. Except as otherwise indicated, this section is summarized from the case study of Equitable, pt. 3, sec. D 7–1 to sec. D 7–10.

159. Ibid., D 7–1.

160. Ibid.

161. Details of Equitable's premium billing and accounting application are provided in C. E. Thompson, "Ordinary Premium Billing and Accounting on IBM No. 705," *Proceedings of IASA* (1962): 86–91.

162. Brown, *Office Automation: Insurance,* pt. 3, sec. D 7–4.

163. Ibid., D 7–10.

164. Ibid., D 7–7. Training supervisors and clerks to handle both old and new systems during the conversion period was particularly difficult.

165. Ibid.

166. Rousmaniere, *Life and Times of the Equitable,* 230. Later, CAPS came to stand for Computerized (rather than Cashiers') Automatic Processing System.

167. Ibid., 231.

168. Daley, "Conversion to and Installation of IBM 705 Systems at the Prudential," 366. Prudential was second in assets only to Metropolitan Life in the early 1950s, and by 1967 it would exceed Metropolitan Life on this measure (*Best's,* 1967).

169. Daley, "Conversion to and Installation of IBM 705 Systems at the Prudential," 365. Daley's title is from Olmstead, "Prudential's Early Experience with Computers," 19.

170. Olmstead, "Prudential's Early Experience with Computers," 21.

171. Ibid., 22–24.

172. Daley, "Conversion to and Installation of IBM 705 Systems at the Prudential," 366.

173. Ibid.

174. Ibid; Olmstead, "Prudential's Early Experience with Computers," 22–24.

175. Prudential had a South Central Home Office in Jacksonville, a North East Home Office in Boston, and a Western Home Office in Los Angeles.

176. Daley, "Conversion to and Installation of IBM 705 Systems at the Prudential," 369; the following quotation is from same page.

177. Olmstead, "Prudential's Early Experience with Computers," 29.

178. Ibid., 24–30.

179. Ibid., 26; the next quotation is from p. 27.

180. Ibid., 27.

181. Ibid., 27–28.

182. Francis S. Quillan, second vice president, to the Vice Presidents' Council, April 1958, as quoted in ibid., 28.

183. According to Campbell-Kelly and Aspray (*Computer,* 196), the term *software* came into use around 1959–60.

184. BLS, "Impact of Office Automation in the Insurance Industry," iii, 1. Life insurance employed more than half of all insurance employees.

185. They could, of course, wait for a time, and some firms chose that path.

186. A. E. DuPlessis, "Conversion to and Installation of a Large Scale Electronic Data Processing System," *Proceedings of IASA* (1958): 358–360.

187. J. Howard Ditman, "The Application of Data Processing Equipment to Life Office Operations," *Proceedings of LOMA* (1955): 83–84.

188. Campbell-Kelly and Aspray, *Computer,* 127.

189. As quoted in ibid.

SEVEN: Incremental Migration during the 1960s and 1970s

1. Delehanty, "Computers and the Organization Structure in Life-Insurance Firms," 67–68.

2. American Council of Life Insurance, *1992 Life Insurance Fact Book,* 14, 16. The following statistics are from the same pages.

3. BLS, "Impact of Office Automation in the Insurance Industry," 2. These figures cover 1954–64.

4. Ibid.

5. Charles H. Cissley and Jean Barnes, *EDP Systems and Applications in Life Insurance* (New York: Life Office Management Association, 1972), 9.

6. BLS, "Impact of Office Automation in the Insurance Industry," 4. The study surveyed more than 400 firms accounting for about 89% of all insurance employees. Based on first-round responses, they surveyed more than 300 firms responding that they already had computers or had them on order (p. 3).

7. Cited in Cissley, *Systems and Data Processing in Insurance Companies*, 17. In 1970, one expert put banking first and insurance second, so the order was shifting during the 1970s (Walt Bohne, "Software Traveling Specialization Road," *Electronic News*, May 4, 1970, sec. 2, p. 55).

8. Although in practice hardware and software were closely intertwined over the next decade or two, I have discussed them separately in this chapter.

9. Bashe et al., *IBM's Early Computers*, 473.

10. Campbell-Kelly and Aspray, *Computer*, 131–132. The 1403 chain printer that was packaged as part of the system turned out to be a customer hit in its own right, since it printed 600 lines per minute, four times as rapidly as a popular printing tabulator, and the entire system rented for only twice as much. Campbell-Kelly and Aspray speculate that "it was an unanticipated motive for IBM's customers to enter the computer age, but no less real for that" (134).

11. Ibid., 134.

12. Of the ninety-one companies with medium-scale computers, eighty-two reported a specific computer. Of these, sixty-two had 1400 series computers (mostly 1401s, but a smattering of the 1410 or 1440 models). LOMA, "EDP Applications in Life Insurance Companies," table 10. Unfortunately, the report does not include the computer types of the companies with large-scale computers, in part because these firms typically had multiple computers.

13. Chandler, *Inventing the Electronic Century*, 86.

14. LOMA, "EDP Applications in Life Insurance Companies," table 10. Campbell-Kelly and Aspray, *Computer*, 142, 135, for descriptions of some of the machines listed.

15. Gray, "UNIVAC Solid State Computer," 1–4, quotation at p. 4.

16. Campbell-Kelly and Aspray, *Computer*, 142.

17. Ibid., 142–144.

18. Pugh, Johnson, and Palmer, *IBM's 360 and Early 370 Systems*, 35–37; Bashe et al., *IBM's Early Computers*, 465. The 7090 and 7080 were aimed more at the scientific market, the 7070 at the commercial data-processing market.

19. Whisler and Meyer, "Impact of EDP on Life Company Organization." Whisler was professor of industrial relations at the Graduate School of Business, University of Chicago. According to Haigh ("Inventing Information Systems," 34–35), a 1958 *Harvard Business Review* article by Harold J. Leavitt and Whisler ("Management in the 1980s," vol. 36, pp. 41–48) is cited by most (but not all) writers on this subject as being the first to use the term *information technology*.

20. Ceruzzi, *History of Modern Computing*, 162.

21. Cissley, *Systems and Data Processing in Insurance Companies*, 11–12.

22. Hills, *Insurance Data Processing*, 155.

23. Robert C. Goshay, *Information Technology in the Insurance Industry: The Impact of Electronic Data Processing on Managerial Processes and Insurance Functions* (Homewood, Ill.:

Richard D. Irwin, 1964), 28. Goshay is identified as assistant professor of business administration, University of California, Berkeley.

24. For example, Lawrence F. Haug, "Premium Billing and Accounting on an IBM 1401 Card System," *Proceedings of IASA* (1962): 76–81.

25. For example, the system adopted by Canadian Crown Life Insurance Company, described by Lloyd G. Rollerson, "Living with Consolidated Functions at the Crown Life," *Proceedings of IASA* (1962): 156–160.

26. Bashe et al., *IBM's Early Computers*, 574–576.

27. Martin J. Amlung, "Analysis of Lease-Buy Decisions," *Proceedings of IASA* (1969): 286.

28. O'Neil to Palmer, memo, January 30, 1957, Subject: Life Insurance Data-Processing Seminar.

29. Goshay, *Information Technology in the Insurance Industry*, 28.

30. Ibid., 29.

31. James N. Cranwill, "Computer Acquisition," *Proceedings of IASA* (1969): 286.

32. Amlung, "Analysis of Lease-Buy Decisions," 289.

33. He included third-party leasing, along with purchase and monthly rental from the manufacturer, as a third alternative.

34. Cranwill, "Computer Acquisition," 286.

35. Goshay, *Information Technology in the Insurance Industry*, 30.

36. Cranwill, "Computer Acquisition," 286.

37. Goshay, *Information Technology in the Insurance Industry*, 30.

38. Ibid.

39. Campbell-Kelly and Aspray, *Computer*, 143. The information in this paragraph is from pp. 143–148. The authors note that the 360 was really more generation 2.5 than generation 3, since it lacked true time-sharing capabilities and used something halfway between transistors and integrated chips. They argue that it was marketing, not technology, that made this line seem so revolutionary. Still, on technical dimensions its capabilities were clearly well beyond those of the 1401 or 7070.

40. George Gray, "The UNIVAC 1108," *Unisys History Newsletter* 3:2 (1999, rev. 2000): 1.

41. Ibid., 2, and Fisher, McKie, and Mancke, *IBM and the U.S. Data Processing Industry*, 140.

42. Pugh, Johnson, and Palmer, *IBM's 360 and Early 370 Systems*, 291–345. The next section provides detail on operating system and application software issues with regard to the System/360.

43. Cissley, *Systems and Data Processing in Insurance Companies*, 10. The snapshots of computing resources at the three companies are on pp. 11–12.

44. Campbell-Kelly and Aspray, *Computer*, 148.

45. For this complicated story, see Pugh, Johnson, and Palmer, *IBM's 360 and Early 370 Systems*, 355–367.

46. Cissley, *Systems and Data Processing in Insurance Companies*, 20–22.

47. Fisher, McKie, and Mancke, *IBM and the U.S. Data Processing Industry*, 387.

48. "New Method of Renewal Premium Billing at Nationwide Insurance," "The Editor Selects" column, *Journal of Machine Accounting* 6:11 (1955): 20.

49. Robert K. Kissinger, "Recent Advances in Data Transmission," *Proceedings of IASA* (1960): 231–232.

50. Ibid.

51. BLS, *Impact of Office Automation in the Insurance Industry,* 4.

52. Ibid., 20–23.

53. Cissley and Barnes, *EDP Systems and Applications in Life Insurance,* 140. For more on minicomputers, see Ceruzzi, *History of Modern Computing,* 124–141.

54. "Operation Univac Away," *Home Office,* December 1966, 16–17, MetLife Archives.

55. Gilbert W. Fitzhugh, president, "Message from the President: Company to Install New Computer Communication System," final approved copy to be used in the Metropolitan Life *Home Office* bulletin, initialed September 24, 1963, MetLife Archives, box 19 03 01, folder: Electronics Installations, 1960–69, box 1: 1963A. Language is almost identical to that in press release from Honeywell, dated for release September 30, 1963, MetLife Archives, box 19 03 01, folder: Electronics Installations, 1960–69, box 1: 1963B.

56. Fitzhugh, "Message from the President: Company to Install New Computer Communication System."

57. "New Metropolitan EDP Hook-Up," *Insurance,* October 24, 1964, MetLife Archives, box 19 03 01, folder: Electronics Installations, 1960–69, box 1: 1964C. For description of account policies, see "The Case of the Computer That Telephones at Night," *Home Office,* November 1964, 7–11, MetLife Archives, box 19 03 01, folder: Electronics Installations, 1960–69, box 1: 1964E.

58. Herman Seltzer, "Data Communications at Metropolitan," *Proceedings of IASA* (1965): 89–94.

59. "It's in the Cards: Wire Communications in Quincy, Mass.," *Metropolitan,* February–March 1969, 21–23, MetLife Archives, box 19 03 01, folder: Electronics Installations, 1960–69, box 1: 1969E.

60. Photocopied segment of pamphlet, in MetLife Archives, box 19 03 02, folder: Electronics Installations 1970–86, box 1: 1970+.

61. Metropolitan Life's ordinary RER fell beginning in 1961, before the new system was even announced, and continued to fall until 1967, well before the system was completed (see fig. 6.5). It rose again beginning in 1967 and did not decline again until 1975, well after the system was in place.

62. *Best's,* 1927–92. Size is ranked by assets.

63. Edward W. Kelley, IBM Marketing, interview by author and Robert Hancke, Boston, August 6, 1993.

64. H. Gordon Goodwin, "Technical Developments in EDP—Programming Methods," *Proceedings of IASA* (1960): 234. Goodwin estimated this figure at 33% for the SPAN Data Processing Center but said that the Defense Department estimated it at 67–100%.

65. McAnarney, "Successes and Failures of EDP to Date," 552. This section draws heavily on Yates, "Application Software for Insurance in the 1960s and Early 1970s."

66. Bruce K. McBeath, "Up-to-Date-Appraisal of '62 CFO Package," *Proceedings of IASA* (1964): 16–18.

67. See, for example, employment statistics from two firms in Delehanty, "Computers and Organization Structure in Life-Insurance Firms," 94–95.

68. Bashe et al., *IBM's Early Computers,* 364.

69. For an account of these events, see Sammet, "Brief Summary of the Early History of COBOL." Briefer accounts appear in Campbell-Kelly and Aspray, *Computer,* 191–192, and Bashe et al., *IBM's Early Computers,* 364–366. A long-range committee was also an-

ticipated but never formed, according to Sammet ("Brief Summary of the Early History of COBOL," 290).

70. In 1967, for example, Aetna was invited to send a representative to the medium-range committee. According to Nathan O'Neil, other members then were from Travelers and Allstate, as well as General Motors, ATT, and several vendors. H. G. Goodwin, assistant secretary, to Ragnar E. Anderson, assistant vice president, memo, February 28, 1967, and O'Neil to Goodwin, memo, June 13, 1967, O'Neil DP/Aetna/Chronological File 1964–70.

71. Fisher, McKie, and Mancke, *IBM and the U.S. Data Processing Industry,* 31–32. Campbell-Kelly, *From Airline Reservations to Sonic the Hedgehog,* 31–34.

72. The IBM historians of the 360 and 370 ranges have described the traumas of developing operating systems (they tried four different systems) for the 360 (Pugh, Johnson, and Palmer, *IBM's 360 and Early 370 Systems,* 291–345).

73. John R. Redfern, formerly of IBM, interview by author and Robert Hancke, Boston, August 16, 1993.

74. Norbert W. Schultz, "Conversion Problems during the Initial Conversion to Electronic Data Processing," *Proceedings of IASA* (1962): 593–599.

75. For the story of software development before and after unbundling, see Campbell-Kelly, *From Airline Reservations to Sonic the Hedgehog,* esp. chap. 4.

76. In some places this software is referred to as '62 CFO and in others as CFO '62. I use the former except in quotations as appropriate.

77. Malcolm MacKinnon, interview by Robert Hancke, Sunapee, New Hampshire, July 21, 1994.

78. McBeath, "Up-to-Date Appraisal of the '62 CFO Package," 16–17.

79. O'Neil, systems supervisor, to Irwin J. Sitkin, assistant secretary, Accounts Department, memo, May 9, 1962, O'Neil DP/Aetna/Chronological File 1959–63.

80. George R. Van Wyck, "Consolidated Functions—Small Scale Computers," *Proceedings of IASA* (1963): 80–82; Gilbert M. Whitfill, "Consolidated Functions—Small Scale Computers," *Proceedings of IASA* (1963): 82–83.

81. McBeath, "Up-to-Date Appraisal of the '62 CFO Package," 16–18, both quotations at p. 18.

82. Robert E. Baines, "1410 Computer Applications at Republic National Life Insurance Company," *Proceedings of IASA* (1964): 35–40, quotation at p. 37.

83. W. K. Headley, "The CFO Package as a Guide," *Proceedings of IASA* (1964): 13–16, quotation at p. 13.

84. D. W. Stinson, "Long-Range Computer Systems Planning—Software," *Proceedings of IASA* (1972): 140–141.

85. Douglas L. Smith, "Experiences of a Functioning CFO '62 Operation," *Proceedings of IASA* (1965): 13–17.

86. George R. Tindall Jr., " '62 CFO for Health Policies, a History and Evaluation of One Installation," *Proceedings of IASA* (1966): 225.

87. Stinson, "Long-Range Computer Systems Planning—Software," 140; Jordahl, "Software Explosion."

88. Bohne, "Software Traveling Specialization Road," sec. 2, p. 55. Bohne lists banking as the most intense user, with insurance second. As noted earlier, according to a study by consulting firm Booz, Allen and Hamilton, insurance was second in 1975, as well, but

in that year it was second to the securities business, with banking after that (cited in Cissley, *Systems and Data Processing in Insurance Companies*, 17).

89. Tindall, " '62 CFO for Health Policies," 225.

90. Chandler, *Inventing the Electronic Century*, 3–4, 87.

91. Campbell-Kelly and Aspray, *Computer*, 153.

92. Bundling as a competitive tool is discussed by Fisher, McKie, and Mancke, *IBM and the U.S. Data Processing Industry*, 23–25.

93. Hills, *Insurance Data Processing*, 161.

94. Stinson, "Long-Range Computer Systems Planning—Software," 141.

95. Richard W. Longing, "A Look at C.O.S. for C.F.O. on 360," *Proceedings of IASA* (1967): 327–329.

96. Stinson, "Long-Range Computer Systems Planning—Software," 140.

97. Jordahl, "Software Explosion," 28.

98. Longing, "Look at C.O.S. for C.F.O. on 360"; Allen M. Johnson, "ALIS and PALIS for Health Processing," *Proceedings of IASA* (1967): 123–126.

99. Johnson, "ALIS and PALIS for Health Processing," 123; see also Thomas P. Maher, "The IBM Advanced Life Information System," *Proceedings of IASA* (1968): 118–122.

100. Dale H. Pearson, "An Evaluation of IBM's ALIS," *Proceedings of IASA* (1967): 319.

101. See, for example, James R. Robinson, "A & S ALIS at Occidental," *Proceedings of IASA* (1967): 126–133; Ralph Roseman, "ALIS Implementation—One Company's Experience," *Proceedings of the LOMA Automation Forum* (1968): 192–196.

102. Robert W. McComb Jr., "The IBM ALIS Package—Modification, Conversion, and Implementation Problems," *Proceedings of the LOMA Automation Forum* (1968): 189–191; O'Neil, administrator, Computer Services, to Goodwin, assistant secretary, Computer Services, memo, "Progress Report January 13 to January 26, 1967," January 27, 1967, O'Neil DP/Aetna/Chronological File 1967–68; Pearson, "Evaluation of IBM's ALIS," 319–321.

103. Pearson, "Evaluation of IBM's ALIS," 320.

104. In the System/360 line, only the 360/20 was smaller (Cerruzzi, *History of Modern Computing*, 158).

105. See, for example, Pearson, "Evaluation of IBM's ALIS."

106. O'Neil, to Goodwin, "Progress Report January 13 to January 26, 1967"; Malcolm MacKinnon, "A Brief History of the Development and Installation of Prudential's Advanced Ordinary System (1963–73)," stenciled internal Prudential document with hand notation of date and author, "presented at lunch to commemorate completion of AOS on Dec. 11, 1973." Document obtained from Malcolm MacKinnon and confirmed as correct by him in 1994 interview.

107. Campbell-Kelly, *From Airline Reservations to Sonic the Hedgehog*, chap. 3.

108. Kubie, "Reflections of the First Software Company," 65, 67.

109. Fisher, McKie, and Mancke, *IBM and the U.S. Data Processing Industry*, 322–325; Haigh, "Software in the 1960s as Concept, Service, and Product," 7–8.

110. J. H. Talbot Jr., "The Mark IV Programming System Used by the Prudential Insurance Company of America," *Proceedings of IASA* (1969): 7–9.

111. Levin, *Irreconcilable Differences*, 27–30.

112. Robert Shafto, CEO, New England Mutual Life, formerly of EDS, interview by author and Hans Godfrey, Boston, September 1, 1993; Raymond A. Duncan, "Facilities

Management: Why Would an Established Life Insurance Company Contract for Computer Services with a Facilities Management Company?" *Proceedings of the LOMA Systems Forum* (1971): D4–1.

113. Stinson, "Long-Range Computer Systems Planning—Software," 141.

114. SPAN Data Processing Center, Inc., "Developments—June 1960 to Date," report, November 16, 1964, in box 1/SPAN: 1960–64, Aetna Archives.

115. For example, William Waugh of Babb Computer Systems, Inc., stated that "the insurance industry began to use software firms to computerize pension functions around 1966" (William W. Waugh Jr., "Computerization of Pension Programs: Who, What, How and Why," *Proceedings of IASA* [1970]: 339).

116. Campbell-Kelly and Aspray, *Computer,* 203, quotation in the next sentence also from this page; Campbell-Kelly, *From Airline Reservations to Sonic the Hedgehog,* 99–104. See also Haigh, "Software in the 1960s as Concept, Service, and Product," 7–9. While he points to the use of software application packages in the 1960s, most of them are fairly general ones (e.g., inventory management), and he says that they are not an important part of the data-processing manager's concern.

117. Campbell-Kelly and Aspray, *Computer,* 203. Haigh ("Software in the 1960s as Concept, Service, and Product," 11) argues that the development of this market was "reinforced." For others who emphasize the importance of the unbundling, see Jordahl, "Software Explosion," 32, and Fisher, McKie, and Manke, *IBM and the U.S. Data Processing Industry,* 323.

118. Sobel, *IBM,* 254–276.

119. Campbell-Kelly and Aspray, *Computer,* 203–204; Fisher, McKie, and Manke, *IBM and the U.S. Data Processing Industry,* 323; and Sobel, *IBM,* 250–252.

120. Campbell-Kelly (*From Airline Reservations to Sonic the Hedgehog,* 99) distinguishes legally and economically between software *packages* and *products,* but I have used them synonymously here.

121. Quoted in Jordahl, "Software Explosion," 28.

122. Cissley and Barnes, *EDP Systems and Applications in Life Insurance,* 73.

123. Ibid.; LOMA, "EDP Software Catalog," Operations and Systems Report No. 38, 1977.

124. Jerry Grisham, "EDS Will Offer Life Insurance Mgmt. Package," *Electronic News,* April 19, 1971, 58.

125. Cissley and Barnes, *EDP Systems and Applications in Life Insurance,* 73.

126. For example, Jack K. Jones, "Unbundle?!" *Proceedings of IASA* (1970): 92–94; Donovan L. Wilson, "Computer Related Services: Unbundling," *Proceedings of IASA* (1970): 92–93.

127. Jones, "Unbundle?!" 92.

128. Waugh, "Computerization of Pension Programs: Who," 340–341.

129. For example, H. Gordon Goodwin, "Evaluation of Computer Software Systems," *Proceedings of IASA* (1971): 49–55; Robert L Plageman, "Experience with and Evaluation of Computer Software Packages," *Proceedings of IASA* (1971): 46–49; Earle A. McKever, "Experience with and Evaluation of Computer Software Services," *Proceedings of IASA* (1971): 53–55.

130. Plageman, "Experience with and Evaluation of Computer Software Packages," 47.

131. Ibid., 49.

132. James F. Foley Jr., "LOMA Develops EDP Software Services Catalog," *Proceedings of IASA* (1972): 23–26. This first software catalog was actually split into two LOMA Systems and Procedures Reports: LOMA, "EDP Software and Service Companies" and "EDP Software Catalog," Systems and Procedures Reports #14, 1972, and #15, 1972, respectively.

133. For example, Cybertek, as revealed in LOMA, "EDP Software Catalog," Operations and Systems Report No. 38.

134. Jordahl, "Software Explosion," 32; LOMA, "EDP Software Catalog," Operations and Systems Report No. 38, 35–44; Cissley and Barnes, *EDP Systems and Applications in Life Insurance,* 73–74.

135. Cissley and Barnes, *EDP Systems and Applications in Life Insurance;* LOMA, "Evaluation of Software Packages," Systems and Procedures Report #16, 1972, 197.

136. Rayford A. Freemon, "Fourteen Software Packages in Four Years," *Proceedings of IASA* (1972): 27–28.

137. Vaughn W. Morgan, "Computer Assisted Underwriting," *Proceedings of IASA* (1972): 48–56.

138. LOMA, "EDP Applications in Life Insurance Companies," figures from table 1, pp. 8–9.

139. Ibid., table 10, n.p.

140. Ibid., table 1, pp. 8–9.

141. Ibid. Of these, policy writing and underwriting were generally consolidated with some other set of programs, while the actuarial programs were generally freestanding.

142. Ibid., tables 1–8, summarized pp. 4–7.

143. Ibid., table 9, p. 24; also summary, pp. 6–7. Although 91% of all responding firms had computerized premium billing, only 50% had computerized mortgage accounting.

144. Cissley, *Systems and Data Processing in Insurance Companies,* 13.

145. Carl O. Orkild, "Can Computers Be Justified?" *Proceedings of IASA* (1960): 236–243. See, for example, Lloyd E. Gross, "Getting Started in Electronics," *Proceedings of IASA* (1960): 456–459, and R. P. Bennett, "Getting Started in Electronics," *Proceedings of IASA* (1960): 459–465.

146. For example, Haug, "Premium Billing and Accounting on an IBM 1401 Card System"; Rollerson, "Living with Consolidated Functions at the Crown Life."

147. B. P. Richardson, "Conversion Problems from the 305 to the 1401 Tape System," *Proceedings of IASA* (1962): 591–593; Louis W. Kaltschmidt, "Conversion Problems of Going from One Large Computer to Another," *Proceedings of IASA* (1962): 606–608.

148. McAnarney, "Successes and Failures of EDP to Date."

149. For example, Van Wyck, "Consolidated Functions—Small Scale Computers"; McBeath, "Up-to-Date Appraisal of '62 CFO Package"; Smith, "Experiences of a Functioning CFO '62 Operation."

150. G. R. Ferdinandtsen, "Integration of Health Policies in the CFO System," *Proceedings of IASA* (1965): 203–209; Louis W. Kaltschmidt, "MONY's Electronic Policy Index," *Proceedings of IASA* (1965): 34–36; Rayford A. Freemon, "The Future Is Here in Data Transmission," *Proceedings of IASA* (1965): 88–89; Seltzer, "Data Communications at Metropolitan," *Proceedings of IASA* (1965): 89–94.

151. For example, David M. Horman, "The Latest on IBM's ALIS Package," *Proceed-*

*ings of IASA* (1968): 113–118; Perry B. Lewis, "The Experiences of an ALIS User," *Proceedings of IASA* (1969): 161–164.

152. George P. Lukens, "Travelers On-Line Real-Time System Cross+Country [*sic*] Link with the Data Center," *Proceedings of IASA* (1968): 141–142. The system required the query to be written down as a policy number and a two-digit action code. This was in turn entered by a "flexowriter operator" onto a paper tape. The paper tape was then sent to the headquarters computer, which found the information and transmitted the reply back to the field office, where it was printed out. Thus it took a little time, but not much in comparison with overnight batch processing.

153. For example, Paul A. Bennett, "Training and Retaining EDP Personnel," *Proceedings of IASA* (1968): 77–79; Donald R. Williams, "Training and Retention of Accounting and EDP Personnel," *Proceedings of IASA* (1969): 379–381; Robert R. Van Brocklyn, "Replacement, Training and Evaluation of Programmers," *Proceedings of IASA* (1970): 285–289.

154. Waugh (representing Babb Computer Systems, Inc.), "Computerization of Pension Programs"; Warren C. Cleven, "Annual Statement Preparation Including EDP Applications," *Proceedings of IASA* (1972): 117–118.

155. Charles W. Anglin, "Application of a Terminal Oriented New Issue System to Policy Holder Service," *Proceedings of IASA* (1970): 22–28; Leonard Guberman, "The Equitable's Computer Assisted Policyowner Service System," *Proceedings of IASA* (1972): 92–95.

156. For example, Harold Shew, "Online Insurance Systems," *Proceedings of IASA* (1973): 22–23; Harold N. Innell, "Data Capture Via Key-Disk and O.C.R.," *Proceedings of IASA* (1973): 311–313; Robert A. Shafto, "Building the Data Base," *Proceedings of IASA* (1973): 250–253.

157. J. N. Cranwill, "Unusual EDP Applications—Input Via CRT," *Proceedings of IASA* (1972): 86–89.

158. Larry Battani, "Project Management in a Sophisticated Data Processing Environment," *Proceedings of IASA* (1975): 180–188; Elmer Joseph, "A Better Way, Non-in-House EDP," *Proceedings of IASA* (1973): 60–63. Today this increasingly popular strategy would be called "information technology out-sourcing."

159. For example, Ralph G. Bull, "MIS Revisited," *Proceedings of IASA* (1970): 39–41; Howard F. Arner, "What Is MIS?" *Proceedings of IASA* (1972): 15–17.

160. Haigh, "Inventing Information Systems," 15.

161. Ibid., 52–55. Indeed, the talks sometimes questioned the notion of MIS, for example, "MIS—EDP—Why?" (L. Guy Dillahunty, *Proceedings of IASA* [1971]: 29–31) and "What Is MIS?" (F. R. Kimball, *Proceedings of IASA* [1972]: 14–15). They also sometimes conflated it with other popular topics such as user-based systems development, for example, "User Development of Management Information Systems" (Roland C. Baker, *Proceedings of IASA* [1971]: 17–20), and databases, for example, a panel entitled "MIS—Let's Get Specific," of which the first paper is entitled "Building the Data Base" (Shafto, 250–253). Databases, in particular, Haigh ("Inventing Information Systems," 55) has noted, were central to one of the most important 1970s watered-down notions of MIS.

162. The closest reference to this trend visible in most of the LOMA and IASA (life insurance section) proceedings of the 1960s is the occasional use of the term *total system,* which Haigh ("Inventing Information Systems," 38–40) notes as a code word for

this MIS approach, in reference to the systems that insurance firms might build based on the '62 CFO system. (e.g., McBeath, "A Total System Design," *Proceedings of IASA* [1966], 271–273). It is clear, however, that *total system* was used in a more limited sense here, since '62 CFO did not at all attempt to achieve the total system originally conceived as MIS.

163. Cissley, *Systems and Data Processing in Insurance Companies*, 6.

164. One academic study of insurance computing conducted in 1966 found that "the impact of computers on the firms studied and probably on the industry as well has not been great," a fact the author of the study attributed primarily to lack of economic incentives for insurance companies to reduce costs, more than just to weak management (Delehanty, "Computers and the Organization Structure in Life-Insurance Firms," 95).

165. Ibid., 7.

166. As noted earlier, the regression line for 1940 to 1974 has an upward slope, while that for 1975 to 1990 slopes slightly downward. The 1970s suffered high inflation, and indexing this ordinary insurance renewal expense ratio for inflation is desirable. Unfortunately, it could not be indexed for reasons explained earlier (see Chapter 6, note 95). Nevertheless, because inflation was high both before and after the expense ratio finally began to drop again, it does not seem likely to be the cause of the delayed decline.

167. Delehanty, "Computers and the Organization Structure in Life-Insurance Firms."

168. Brynjolfsson and other contemporary economists of information technology made such an argument to explain the absence of any productivity growth that could be linked to information technology investment in the 1980s (see, e.g., Brynjolfsson, "Productivity Paradox of Information Technology," 67–77. and Brynjolfsson and Hitt, "Beyond the Productivity Paradox."

EIGHT: Case Studies in Insurance Computing

1. New England Mutual Life Insurance Company was the legal name of that firm until it became a wholly owned stock subsidiary of MetLife at the end of August 1996, when its legal name changed to New England Life Insurance Company. It has also had a series of short marketing names or service marks, as follows: New England Mutual (1835–1956), New England Life (1956–86), The New England (1986–98), and New England Financial (1998–present). (Pers. comm. from Phyllis Steele, last New England Financial archivist before the archives were folded into the MetLife Archives, October 7, 2004.) Because the legal name remained the same throughout the period I studied, I use the (shortened) legal name New England Mutual Life throughout the text to avoid going through the name changes in the service mark names. I refer to the archives as the New England Financial Archives, as they are called today, even though they have now been combined with the MetLife Archives.

2. The claim is quoted from the title page of *New England Mutual Life Insurance Company: The New Home Office Building* (Boston: New England Mutual Life Insurance Company, 1942), a pamphlet found in NEF/Building Files, 1875–1988, box 1. Although New England Mutual Life was chartered in 1835, it began operating in 1843.

3. Asset rank and figures from *Best's*, 1952.

4. Phyllis E. Steele to John Huss, "Changing Technology at the New England: Highlights from the Period 1844 to 1967," October 11, 1992, NEF/Archives Research and Reference Files, Technology Folder, 1992; Moorhead, *Our Yesterdays*, 9–11, 333–334.

5. *New England Mutual Life Insurance Company: The New Home Office Building*, photo and text (n.p.), NEF/Photograph Files, Photo No. 880, 1942; *Machine Accounting Methods for Life Insurance Company as Used by the New England Mutual Life Insurance Company, Boston, Massachusetts*, pamphlet (Detroit: Burroughs, 1937), NEF/Archives Vertical Files, A31VF; "Burroughs Machine and Multilith Now Being Used for Consolidated Premium Bills in Pension Cases," *Spinning Wheel* (New England Mutual Life's internal monthly newsletter), August 1953, in NEF (all *Wheel* newsletters cited in notes are in NEF); Steele to Huss, "Changing Technology at the New England." Steele noted that the Addressograph-Multigraph Corporation saw New England Mutual Life as a pioneering user of its equipment for premium billing, as the corporation highlighted in a 1936 booklet entitled "Modern Business Office Methods Used by New England Mutual Life Insurance Company" (a copy of this booklet is in NEF), but this path of innovation did not lead forward into the computer era as did use of tabulating equipment for this purpose.

6. "Addressograph and Premium Collection Departments Receive New Equipment," *Spinning Wheel*, December 1951.

7. Steele to Huss, "Changing Technology at the New England"; "Automation—What It Is and Is Not," *Spinning Wheel*, April 1955, 4–5.

8. In addition to its design and production of the Convé files, Remington Rand was also the source of the microfilm photographic unit described in "Special Machine Used to Microfilm Records, 700,000 Essential Documents Already Done," *Spinning Wheel*, December 1950.

9. Article in January 1955 *Spinning Wheel*, as summarized and quoted in Steele to Huss, "Changing Technology at the New England."

10. Ibid., n.p.

11. At the end of the final article a note indicates that the series has been prepared by the chairman of the committee and three committee staff members and checked with an independent automation consultant ("The Alternatives," editorial, *Spinning Wheel*, May 1956, 2).

12. Bix, *Inventing Ourselves out of Jobs?*, 242–243.

13. "Automation—What It Is and Is Not," 4.

14. "EDP—the Moron with a System," *Spinning Wheel*, October 1955, 5; "EDP: Thinking for a Computer," *Spinning Wheel*, November 1955, 6; "Automation—EDP at an HO," *Spinning Wheel*, July 1955, 3.

15. "Automation—EDP at an HO," 3.

16. "The Alternatives," (*Spinning Wheel* editorial), 2.

17. Customer Contact Report, Remington Rand Division of Sperry Rand Corporation, of contact June 19–29, 1956, with New England Mutual Life Insurance Company, July 5, 1956, accession 2015, ERA Collection, Hagley Museum and Library.

18. Ibid.

19. "Univac Contract Signed by Pres. Anderson; 'Giant Brain' Ordered," *New England Life's Wheel*, April 1957, 1. *New England Life's Wheel* is a continuation of the *Spinning Wheel*. On September 25, 1956, a year after the firm began to refer to itself as New England Life, the old company emblem of Priscilla Alden at her spinning wheel was replaced by a picture of the Constitution (Old Ironsides), and the in-house publication

changed from the *Spinning Wheel* to *New England Life's Wheel,* with the image of the ship and a ship's wheel on the masthead (Collier, *Capital Ship,* 122).

20. Gray, "UNIVAC III Computer" 1–2. The delays in the UNIVAC II's release, according to Gray, allowed the IBM 705 to capture the large business market in the meantime.

21. "Univac Contract Signed by Pres. Anderson," 1.

22. "A Progress Report on Univac II," *New England Life's Wheel,* August 1959, 2.

23. Donald F. Ryan, "New England Life's Commission Accounting System under Univac," *Proceedings of IASA* (1960): 419–425. For cases of non-computer-related talks, see, for example, William M. Finn, "Budgeting," *Proceedings of IASA* (1958): 127–129.

24. "Major Changes in Company Organization Are Announced," *New England Life's Wheel,* Special Edition, Annual Meeting, March 18, 1964.

25. "$2½ Million Computer Contract Is Signed; 1108 Arrives in 68," *New England Life's Wheel,* July 13, 1967, 1–2. According to an IBM salesman working with insurance firms at the time, New England Mutual Life had asked IBM as well as UNIVAC for a proposal at this point, as had John Hancock at about the same time. John Hancock had gone with IBM and New England Mutual Life with UNIVAC. (Kelley, interview.) Another IBM salesman of that period confirmed this story and attributed IBM's (and his) failure to win the initial bid to the fact that New England Mutual Life's former senior vice president of data processing had previously worked for and was very committed to UNIVAC. (Redfern, interview.)

26. Gray, "UNIVAC 1108," 1–3.

27. Shafto, interview.

28. Collier, *Capital Ship,* 146–147.

29. "The 1108 Computer Arrives—Saturday, March 2," *New England Life's Wheel,* March 7, 1968; "1108 Arrives, " *New England Life's Wheel,* March 21, 1968.

30. Shafto, interview.

31. Collier, *Capital Ship,* 146–147.

32. Shafto, "On-Line Applications," *Proceedings of IASA* (1971): 100–104.

33. Ibid., 100.

34. Both Ed Kelley, of the IBM sales force, and Jim Zilinski, initially of IBM and later of New England Mutual Life, attributed the bold move that ultimately followed, with its dramatic positive effects, to Shafto's decisive leadership. (Kelley, interview; James W. Zilinski, New England Mutual Life, interview by author, Boston, August 27, 1993.)

35. Shafto, interview.

36. Ibid.

37. F. Knier and R. Montalto to R. A. Shafto, memo, Subject: Computer Equipment, 1975–80, December 11, 1974, in Administrative Files of John A. Fibiger, president, accession #90–1, ser. 2, The New England Archives (hereafter cited as NEF/Fibiger Files). See also undated (but ca. November 1974) document "1110 Hardware Acquisition Considerations," NEF/Fibiger Files. Edward Kelley, salesman for IBM, identified Fred Knier as "the salesman that sold New England Life the UNIVACs," and he stated that Shafto had hired him at New England Mutual Life to make the conversion from UNIVAC to IBM (Kelley, interview). Knier had moved to New England Mutual Life well before the decision was made to convert, however, as this memo from him to Shafto indicates.

38. Kelley, interview; Zilinski, interview. Zilinski had been with IBM before being hired by Shafto to work at New England Mutual Life. Both men stated, based on their

IBM experience, that the insurance industry was IBM's largest commercial computer customer at this time.

39. Knier to File, memo, Subject: 1110 Configuration Problems, December 4, 1975, NEF/Fibiger Files.

40. For example, Shafto, New England Mutual Life, to William Murphy, Sperry Rand/ UNIVAC, May 19, 1975, and Murphy to Shafto, June 11, 1975, both in NEF/Fibiger Files.

41. Zilinski, interview.

42. Knier to File, memo, Subject: March 19, 1976, Visit to UNIVAC, March 23, 1976, NEF/Fibiger Files.

43. "Sunbright IBM 360 debuts at NEL," *New England Life's Wheel,* July 24, 1969, 1, 8.

44. Shafto, interview.

45. Ibid.

46. Knier to File, memo, March 23, 1976.

47. Knier to File, memo, Subject: April 2, 1976, UNIVAC Visit, April 5, 1976, NEF/ Fibiger Files.

48. For example, see Shafto, "Univac vs. IBM Report," August 26, 1976, attached to memo from Shafto to E. E. Phillips and J. A. Fibiger, Subject: UNIVAC vs. IBM Report, August 26, 1976, NEF/Fibiger Files.

49. Zilinski, interview. He noted that the 1975 recession enabled him to get greater resources to use in what was viewed by IBM as a high-risk sales effort at New England Mutual Life.

50. J. W. Zilinski, IBM marketing manager, to Fibiger, executive vice president, New England Mutual Life, May 25, 1976, NEF/Fibiger Files. Zilinski also stated in his 1993 interview that his strategy at this time had been to mount a "two-pronged attack," initially using a new application to get a foot in the door, then convincing New England Mutual Life to migrate its entire business to IBM.

51. Harry A. Steinberg, Sperry Rand/UNIVAC, to Fibiger, New England Mutual Life, October 14, 1976, NEF/Fibiger Files.

52. Stephanie Cole to distribution (including Shafto, Knier, and other executives), memo, Subject: UNIVAC vs. IBM Strategy Discussion, September 10, 1976, NEF/Fibiger Files.

53. F. W. Knier, "IBM Conversion Study," November 12, 1976, NEF/Fibiger Files. For titles of Phillips and Fibiger at this time, see Collier, *Capital Ship,* 164–167.

54. Knier, "IBM Conversion Study," 4. Connecticut General had decided to shift from RCA Spectra computers, at this point owned by UNIVAC (RCA's computer operations had been bought up by Sperry Rand's UNIVAC division in 1971), to IBM computers. "New Computer Equipment to be Added for CG and Aetna Use," *Life in General* (Home Office Weekly, Connecticut General Life Insurance Company), no. 589, January 27, 1969, 1; "New IBM Computer Put in for CG, Aetna," *Life in General,* no. 914, April 30, 1975, both in box 1, CIGNA Archives, Hartford, Connecticut. Travelers had also been an RCA user, so it was probably also shifting away from Sperry Rand–owned RCA computers.

55. Shafto to Fibiger, memo, Subject: Key Points to Communicate to UNIVAC Executive Vice President Relative to IBM Conversion Decision, November 23, 1976, NEF/ Fibiger Files.

56. A detailed chronological summary of the troubled relationship through May 1977 was prepared by the law firm Bingham, Dana and Gould, "Overview of New En-

gland Life—Sperry Univac Relationship," May 16, 1977, NEF/Fibiger Files. The final release agreed to between the two companies is documented in a memo from Donald J. Sullivan and Jeremiah A. Shafir to Fibiger, March 31, 1980, and a letter acknowledging that the UNIVAC computer had been removed (after installation of the IBM equipment was complete) was sent from Joseph J. Kroger, Sperry Rand/UNIVAC, to Fibiger, May 22, 1980, both in NEF/Fibiger Files.

57. Michael Brown to Fibiger, memo, January 10, 1980, NEF/Fibiger Files.

58. Zilinski, interview, and Kelley, interview; quotation is from Kelley interview.

59. Shafto, interview.

60. For example, Shafto, "Building the Data Base," 250–253.

61. Zilinski, interview.

62. Giddens, *Constitution of Society.*

63. Collier, *Capital Ship,* 147.

64. Haigh ("Chromium-Plated Tabulator," 96) discusses the fundamental divide in administrative computing between data processing and general management.

65. *Best's,* 1952.

66. The original Aetna Insurance Company (from which Aetna Life Insurance Company broke off in 1853) was ultimately acquired by Connecticut General, which then merged to form part of CIGNA ("Cigna: Historical Background Report: 200 Years of Results," March 1992, 8 and unpaginated time line, CIGNA Archives).

67. Only two of the top ten firms in asset size in that year were stock companies—Travelers and Aetna, ranked eighth and ninth. A total of eight of the top thirty firms in asset size that year were stock companies, with one more ranked fourteenth (Connecticut General) and the rest ranked between twentieth and thirtieth. (Asset rank and figures from *Best's,* 1952.) Mutual life insurance companies dominated the industry at this time.

68. Hooker, *Aetna Life Insurance Company,* 103–105. Travelers and Aetna both had Connecticut charters that allowed such diversification as long as it did not take them into fire insurance; combining fire and life insurance was strictly forbidden, given the dangers of large urban fires that wiped out fire insurance firms (Hal Keiner, former archivist, CIGNA, pers. comm. August 16, 2002).

69. Between the 1964 and 1965 company annual reports, it changed its name from Aetna Life Affiliated Companies to Aetna Life and Casualty.

70. Annual Statement, 1895, in Data Processing Topical File, Aetna Archives. In this case, it was an arithmometer.

71. Brochure draft, 1983, Aetna Archives. To run the tabulating equipment, women were hired on a temporary basis and segregated from men.

72. Thomas F. Tarbell, "Accounting Methods for Casualty Companies by Use of the Hollerith System," *Casualty Actuarial Society* 12 (1925): 215–237.

73. Irwin J. Sitkin, "From Punched Holes to ASCII Bits—A Personal History," May 21, 1979, 2, Aetna Biographies, box 1, Sitkin 5, Aetna Archives (hereafter cited as Aetna Biographies/file name and number). Internal evidence makes clear that this document was originally presented as a speech.

74. Robert G. Espie, "Using the IBM Magnetic Drum Data-Processing Machine Type 650: Automobile B.I. and P.D. Written Premium Analysis," *Proceedings of IASA* (1955): 438.

75. Nathan D. O'Neil, "Speech for Orientation Seminar," Spring 1965, manuscript in O'Neil DP/Aetna/Chronological File 1964–70. My primary source documents for this

case study come from two boxes of O'Neil's rich (but limited in point of view) Data Processing Files, preserved in the Aetna Archives. Unfortunately, this archive is now closed to the public.

76. Brochure draft, 1983, Aetna Archives, 2. Irwin Sitkin identifies Bob Espie as the person who ordered Aetna's first IBM 650 in Sitkin's address "DPMA [Data Processing Managers' Association] Computer Sciences Man of the Year," November 1, 1978, New Orleans, in Aetna Biographies/Sitkin 3.

77. Class list, Programming Class, IBM 650 Magnetic Drum Data Processing Machine, February 16, 1954, O'Neil DP/Aetna/Chronological File 1954–59.

78. O'Neil to Al Brown, IBM, August 13, 1954, O'Neil DP/Aetna/Chronological File 1954–59; see also O'Neil, "Speech for Orientation Seminar," Spring 1965. The program was an Auto Liability and Property Damage insurance premium application.

79. O'Neil, "Speech for Orientation Seminar," Spring 1965. The Group Insurance Department operated independently of the Life Department even though Group Insurance included group life insurance.

80. Hooker, *Aetna Life Insurance Company,* 181.

81. Espie, "Using the IBM Magnetic Drum Data-Processing Machine Type 650," 438.

82. O'Neil, "Speech for Orientation Seminar," Spring 1965.

83. Irwin Sitkin, Aetna, interview by Leith Johnson, May 4, 1989, typescript in Aetna Biographies/Sitkin 6.

84. Haigh ("Chromium-Plated Tabulator") describes the typical uses of what he terms "administrative data processing."

85. "Automation at the Aetna," *Aetna-izer,* Casualty, Bonding, Fire, and Marine Edition, January/February 1958, 11, Aetna Archives.

86. The IBM 650, like the tabulators of this era, was gray and had round corners. The square corners and blue color that became recognized as the IBM look and were reflected in the firm's nickname, "Big Blue," came in subsequent computers (e.g., the IBM 1401). Martin Campbell-Kelly, pers. comm., July 17, 2003.

87. Brochure draft, 1983, Aetna Archives, 3; "Company Ordering IBM 705," item in [IBM] *Good Word,* May 21, 1956, found in O'Neil DP/Aetna/Chronological File 1954–59; "Life Insurance Data Processing Seminar, January 24–25, 1957," list of attendees, in O'Neil DP/Aetna/Chronological File 1954–59.

88. O'Neil to Palmer, memo, January 30, 1957, Subject: Life Insurance Data-Processing Seminar—January 24, 25, 1957, O'Neil DP/Aetna/Chronological File 1954–59.

89. Brochure draft, 1983, Aetna Archives, 3; O'Neil to T. Fujita, Mitsui Mutual Life Insurance Company, December 27, 1960, O'Neil DP/Aetna/Chronological File 1954–59. By 1961, Aetna was experimenting with IBM's successor to the 705, the 7070, and SPAN purchased the 7070 and started converting applications from the 705 to the 7070 in 1962 (O'Neil, "Speech for Orientation Seminar," Spring 1965; SPAN Data Processing Center, Inc., "Developments—June 1960 to Date"). Aetna bought up and absorbed SPAN in 1963, making the ownership of these computers moot (O'Neil, "Speech for Orientation Seminar," Spring 1965).

90. R. G. Espie to M. B. Brainard, R. W. Conly, G. E. Mann, F. P. Perkins, J. B. Slimmon, and C. A. Spoerl, memo, April 10, 1957, Subject: Electronic Equipment, O'Neil DP/Aetna/Chronological File 1954–59.

91. Espie to W. F. Bardo, memo, July 12, 1957, Subject: Datatron Equipment, O'Neil DP/Aetna/Chronological File 1954–59.

92. O'Neil to Espie, memo, January 28, 1958, Subject: Datatron Testing Success, O'Neil DP/Aetna/Chronological File 1954–59. It is interesting to note that one of the two programmers was a woman. The presence of female programmers here and at Pan-American Life, as noted earlier, may indicate that insurance firms such as Aetna were less hardened than other types of firms in the gender roles they imposed on this new occupation, perhaps in part because insurance firms had brought women into the clerical ranks earlier than many other types of firms had. See Haigh, "Chromium-Plated Tabulator," 96, for a discussion of gender roles in administrative (as opposed to scientific/technical) computing.

93. John J. Connell to Espie, August 7, 1958, O'Neil DP/Aetna/Chronological File 1954–59.

94. Don Mastriforte, IBM, to O'Neil, January 28, 1957, O'Neil DP/Aetna/Chronological File 1954–59.

95. Mastriforte, IBM, to Espie, Aetna, April 11, 1957, O'Neil DP/Aetna/Chronological File 1954–59.

96. List dated May 29, 1957, in O'Neil Data Processing Records, RG 50, IBM Correspondence, Aetna Archives.

97. O'Neil, Aetna, to F. E. Ross, IBM, December 6, 1957, IBM Correspondence, and O'Neil, Aetna, to H. T. Moore Jr., Glens Falls Insurance Company, February 2, 1959, Chronological File 1954–59, both in O'Neil Data Processing Records, RG 50, Aetna Archives.

98. O'Neil, "Speech for Orientation Seminar," Spring 1965.

99. O'Neil to Sitkin, assistant secretary, Accounts Department, memo, May 8, 1962, O'Neil DP/Aetna/Chronological File 1959–63.

100. O'Neil to Sitkin, memo, May 9, 1962, O'Neil DP/Aetna/Chronological File 1959–63.

101. O'Neil, "Speech for Orientation Seminar," Spring 1965; SPAN Data Processing Center, Inc., "Developments—June 1960 to Date." Two of the four original partners in SPAN had withdrawn by then, and SPAN started out by soliciting Aetna to join the remaining two, but ultimately Aetna decided it was better simply to buy the entire operation.

102. O'Neil, "Speech for Orientation Seminar," Spring 1965. O'Neil says the order was placed in 1965, but Robert W. McComb, in his paper at the 1968 LOMA Automation Forum ("IBM ALIS Package"), claims that Aetna joined the ALIS development effort in November 1964, when it was first announced. Thus Aetna must have been committed to the 360 line by late 1964.

103. Aetna Life and Casualty, 1966 Annual Report, 7, Aetna Archives.

104. Brochure draft, 1983, Aetna Archives.

105. Sitkin, interview, 14. In this 1989 interview, Sitkin said, "Unquestionably we were a leader then as I think we still are in implementing technology in our business." In his 1979 autobiographical sketch "From Punched Holes to ASCII Bits," however, he was more candid about the difficulties Aetna faced on the applications side.

106. Hooker, *Aetna Life Insurance Company,* 224–228.

107. Sitkin, interview, 11.

108. Ibid.; this "partially centralized" structure is described in O'Neil to Fujita, December 27, 1960, O'Neil DP/Aetna/Chronological File 1959–63. Here, O'Neil refers to the "Group Division," but elsewhere it is called the Group Insurance Department.

109. O'Neil, "Speech for Orientation Seminar," Spring 1965.

110. See, for example, the conclusions about centralization in Whisler and Meyer, "Impact of EDP on Life Company Organization," 4–8; but also see Delehanty, "Computers and the Organization Structure in Life-Insurance Firms," 89–91, on why it is difficult to see any centralization in decision making in insurance firms at this time.

111. Sitkin, "From Punched Holes to ASCII Bits," 5.

112. Espie to officers and department heads, memo, April 7, 1959, Subject: Life Integrated Data Processing Committee, O'Neil DP/Aetna/Chronological File 1954–59.

113. Ibid.

114. Handwritten notes attached to a memo from Espie to Palmer, secretary, November 12, 1959, O'Neil DP/Aetna/Chronological File 1959–63. It is not clear whether notes are by Palmer or, as suggested by their location in the archives, by O'Neil.

115. William D. Slysz, CDPDD, to Sitkin, assistant secretary, Accounts Department, memo, February 28, 1961, Subject: LIDP Data Analysis, O'Neil DP/Aetna/Chronological File 1959–63.

116. Ibid.

117. W. D. Slysz to I. E. Doxsee, senior systems analyst, March 14, 1962, Subject: LIDP Status (Current Activities), O'Neil DP/Aetna/Chronological File 1959–63.

118. O'Neil to Fujita, January 27, 1960, O'Neil DP/Aetna/Chronological File 1959–63; O'Neil to K. F. McCreery, assistant secretary, memo, December 12, 1962, O'Neil DP/Aetna/Chronological File 1959–63.

119. O'Neil to Fujita, January 27, 1960, O'Neil DP/Aetna/Chronological File 1959–63; "650 Programs as of November 10, 1960," O'Neil DP/Aetna/Chronological File 1959–63. The two programs were life renewal billing and life renewal deferred premium, both part of premium billing.

120. O'Neil to McCreery, assistant secretary, memo, December 12, 1962, Subject: Paid Premium Accounting and the Preparation of Agents' Earned Commission Reports, O'Neil DP/Aetna/Chronological File 1959–63.

121. Frank E. Havens, Administrative Assistant, Planning Department, to Espie, vice president and assistant comptroller, Subject: Life Data Processing, May 20, 1963, O'Neil DP/Aetna/Chronological File 1959–63.

122. Espie to O'Neil, system supervisor, Planning Department, May 24, 1963, O'Neil DP/Aetna/Chronological File 1959–63.

123. [O'Neil], notes dated May 31, 1963, O'Neil DP/Aetna/Chronological File 1959–63. The notes have Sitkin's initials written on top, apparently in O'Neil's handwriting. The last few words of the quotation are not completely legible.

124. Sitkin to Espie, May 31, 1963, O'Neil DP/Aetna/Chronological File 1959–63.

125. [Sitkin], typed notes, May 31, 1963, with handwritten emendations, "Introduction" to meeting called for June 13, in O'Neil DP/Aetna/Chronological File 1959–63.

126. O'Neil, "Speech for Orientation Seminar," Spring 1965; Sitkin, "From Punched Holes to ASCII Bits," 6.

127. Sitkin, "From Punched Holes to ASCII Bits," 5.

128. Sitkin, interview, 23; Leith G. Johnson, comp. and ed., "From Punched Cards to Satellites, and Beyond: A History of Data Processing at Aetna Life and Casualty Prepared for an Exhibit Held in the Aetna Institute Gallery," April 5, 1984, typescript from Data Processing, RG 50, Aetna Archives.

129. Sitkin to Data Processing Development Department, October 29, 1965, O'Neil DP/Aetna/Chronological File 1964–70.

130. When Sitkin became head of the Corporate Data Processing Services (CDPS) Department in 1969, he further articulated the structure and duties of this centralized department, as opposed to the decentralized data-processing development departments (John H. Filer, executive vice president, Administration and Planning, to all officers, memo, April 1, 1969, O'Neil DP/Aetna/Chronological File 1964–70; Aetna Life and Casualty Divisions, "Chronology," O'Neil DP/Aetna/Chronological File 1964–70).

131. McComb, "IBM ALIS Package," 189. As noted in note 102 above, at around the same time Aetna probably ordered the 360/60 or 360/62 machine, both of which were announced in April 1964 but replaced in April 1965 by the 360/65 (not released until the end of that year—see Pugh, Johnson, and Palmer, *IBM's 360 and Early 370 Systems*, table 3.1, p. 171). This sequence would be consistent with evidence elsewhere that Aetna ordered its 360/65 in 1965.

132. McComb, "IBM ALIS Package," 189.

133. Aetna Life and Casualty, "Five Year Data Processing Projection, 1967–1971," March 31, 1967, in O'Neil DP/Aetna/Chronological File 1964–70.

134. Johnson,"From Punched Cards to Satellites, and Beyond," 6.

135. Collier, *Capital Ship*, 202.

136. Sitkin, interview, 16.

137. Firm managers communicated with both noncompetitive firms, such as Glens Falls Insurance Company (O'Neil to Moore, February 2, 1959, O'Neil DP/Aetna/Chronological File 1954–59) and Mitsui Life Insurance Company (O'Neil to Fujita, January 27, 1960, O'Neil DP/Aetna/Chronological File 1959–63), and competitive firms, such as Connecticut General Life Insurance Company of Hartford (John A. Bevan, actuary, Connecticut General, to Robert G. Perry, associate actuary, Aetna, October 7, 1964, O'Neil DP/Aetna/Chronological File 1964–70). The letter from Bevan offered information about Connecticut General's current services, as well as asking for Aetna's. A handwritten note indicated that Perry passed it on to O'Neil to respond. Such exchanges, even among direct but friendly competitors such as Aetna and Connecticut General, appear to have been common.

138. See, for example, the following LOMA and IASA publications by Aetna representatives: Nathan D. O'Neil, "Controlling Data Processing Procedures," typescript, IASA, 1964, O'Neil DP/Aetna/Chronological File 1964–70, also listed in *Proceedings of IASA* (1964) under "Conference Papers Appearing in the Interpreter"; McComb, "IBM ALIS Package," 189–191; Otmar A. Klee, "Evaluation of Commercial Packages at Aetna Life and Casualty," in LOMA, "Evaluation of Software Packages," 14–17. Sitkin's speech "DPMA Computer Sciences Man of the Year" describes his involvement with that organization. According to Haigh, this organization's name change "ultimately expressed the evolutionary progression through which the new institutions of data processing formed around the older ones of tabulating" ("Chromium-Plated Tabulator," 94). Aetna was quite involved in this organization, and in 1978 Irwin Sitkin, then Aetna's vice president of Corporate Data Processing and Administrative Services, was selected the DPMA Computer Sciences Man of the Year (news release, Data Processing Management Association, "Irwin Sitkin Selected as DPMA's 1978 Computer Sciences Man-of-the-Year," in Aetna Biographies/Sitkin 4). For participation in the Spring Joint Computer Conference, see

O'Neil, administrator, CDP Support, to Sitkin, assistant vice president, Corporate Data Processing, memo, June 24, 1969, O'Neil DP/Aetna/Chronological File 1964–70.

139. O'Neil to Goodwin, memo, June 13, 1967, O'Neil DP/Aetna/Chronological File 1964–70.

140. Sitkin, interview, 24.

141. Goodwin, assistant secretary, to Anderson, assistant vice president, memo, February 28, 1967, O'Neil DP/Aetna/Chronological File 1964–70; O'Neil to Goodwin, memo, June 13, 1967, O'Neil DP/Aetna/Chronological File 1964–70.

142. Goodwin to Anderson, February 28, 1967.

143. O'Neil to Goodwin, memo, June 13, 1967, O'Neil DP/Aetna/Chronological File 1964–70. Only thirteen of the twenty members were represented at the first meeting O'Neil attended.

144. Based on figures in *Best's,* 1952–82.

145. Haigh ("Chromium-Plated Tabulator") argues that administrative data processing didn't reduce costs for most firms adopting it.

146. The average stock firm's expense ratios went slightly higher and peaked slightly later than the average mutual's. Aetna, a stock firm, performed worse than the average stock firm until the late 1970s, when its cost ratio moved below the average cost ratio for stock firms. New England Mutual Life's cost ratio rose to the level of the average mutual firm by the mid-1970s and stayed closer to that average until 1979, when it began to go below that line.

147. Giddens, *Constitution of Society.*

148. These key players are similar to the three key roles that, James L. McKenney suggests, need to be represented in a pioneering and innovative information technology user firm: a CEO who guides change, here presumably Phillips, though Fibiger seems to have been equally involved; a technology maestro, a strategist and change agent role that Shafto fits well; and a technical team, here represented by Knier and others working with Shafto (McKenney, *Waves of Change,* 143–147).

149. Such positioning of computing within the organization was more typical in noninsurance firms adopting computers for administrative data processing (Haigh, "Chromium-Plated Tabulator," 81–82) than in insurance firms, which typically applied computers to life insurance operations.

## Conclusion

1. Yates, "Co-evolution of Information Processing Technology and Use."

2. "Exhibit of Office Equipment," IBM section, *Proceedings of LOMA* (1935): 318.

3. See, for example, Flamm, *Creating the Computer,* and Ceruzzi, *History of Modern Computing.*

4. Fisher, McKie, and Mancke, *IBM and the U.S. Data Processing Industry,* 16–18.

5. Finelli et al, "Application of Electronic Data Processing Equipment to Office Operations," 14. Thus insurance sales alone equaled almost half of the initial demand projections of 200–250.

6. Giddens, *Constitution of Society,* 178.

7. Orlikowski, "Using Technology and Constituting Structures."

8. Whisler and Meyer, "Impact of EDP on Life Company Organization," 102.

9. See, for example, Mackay and Gillespie, "Extending the Social Shaping of Tech-

nology Approach"; Oudshoorn and Pinch, *How Users Matter;* Mackay et al., "Reconfiguring the User."

10. McKenney's *Waves of Change* is an exception, though he approaches the subject from a managerial perspective. A very recent exception, also not part of the social shaping of technology literature, is Cortada's *Digital Hand,* which takes a business and economic approach to understanding how several industries have adopted and used computers.

11. This influence operated in the tabulator era, as well, with tabulating equipment being used to continue the subdivision of tasks begun before the technology was available. But the structure of my study makes this influence of past on present clearest for the transition from tabulators to computers in insurance.

12. This influence of past technology use on the present has been noted by cultural and interpretive scholars of technology and its use such as Marvin, *When Old Technologies Were New,* and Boczkowski, *Digitizing the News.*

13. Marvin, *When Old Technologies Were New,* 235.

14. For literature review, see Brynjolfsson, "Productivity Paradox of Information Technology"; see also Paul David's historical treatment of this paradox with regard to a different technology by identifying the extended lag between the emergence of the electrical dynamo and its impact on productivity and economic growth (Paul David, "Computer and Dynamo: The Modern Productivity Paradox in Historical Perspective," Working Paper #172, Stanford University Center for Economic Policy Research, 1989).

15. Brynjolfsson, "Productivity Paradox of Information Technology."

16. Manuel Castells, *The Rise of the Network Society,* 74.

17. Ibid., 75; David, "Computer and Dynamo."

18. As noted earlier, correcting it for inflation would be extremely difficult. Although the numerator of the ratio, expenses, reflects the current inflation rate, the denominator, insurance in force, is the sum of insurance bought at many preceding times. Thus each company would have a different portfolio of insurance bought at various times, and that portfolio would change each year, depending on the previous year's sales.

19. See, for example, Michael L. Tushman and Philip Anderson, "Technological Discontinuities and Organizational Environments," *Administrative Science Quarterly* 31 (1986): 439–465, and Rebecca M. Henderson and Kim B. Clark, "Architectural Innovation: The Reconfiguration of Existing Product Technologies and the Failure of Established Firms," *Administrative Science Quarterly* 35 (1990): 9–30.

20. Similarly, both Rolls Royce and Pratt and Whitney made the transition from piston to jet engines in aircraft propulsion. Philip Scranton, pers. comm., ca. September 25, 2003.

21. Giddens, *Constitution of Society,* xxi.

22. Quoted by Cissley, *Systems and Data Processing in Insurance Companies,* 17, from a Booz, Allen and Hamilton 1975 unpublished report entitled "Information Resource Management (IRM)—A New Concept."

23. BLS, "Impact of Office Automation in the Insurance Industry," 5.

24. Bix (*Inventing Ourselves out of Jobs?*) discusses these fears and employee resistance, though more in the 1930s than in the later period. Educational campaigns such as Metropolitan Life's were not limited to insurance firms.

25. Davis et al., "Report of Committee," 1952, 16.

26. For the carbon paper case, see Yates, *Control Through Communication,* 48–49.

27. Delehanty, "Computers and the Organization Structure in Life-Insurance Firms," 69.

28. This standard description has appeared in any number of accounts; a recent version appears in Chandler, *Inventing the Electronic Century*, 94–117.

29. Von Hippel, *Sources of Innovation*.

30. Hawley, *Great War and the Search for a Modern Order*, 76–77.

31. Cortada's *Digital Hand* is an exception to this statement, providing general surveys of how selected industries used computers and other digital technologies. He does not, however, examine the reciprocal interactions between technology and its use.

# Selected Bibliography

This section contains a descriptive note on the primary sources used in this study and an alphabetical listing of most secondary sources cited. Many secondary sources receive critical discussion in the notes, especially those to the introduction and conclusion.

Because I have taken the perspective of insurance users, I sought insurance archives rather than vendor archives. Some of the insurance firms, including Metropolitan Life Insurance Company, Aetna Life Affiliated Companies, and New England Mutual Life Insurance Company, have—or had when I did my research—archives available to researchers; Aetna's archive is no longer open to the public, and New England Mutual Life's (now known as New England Financial) archive can be accessed only through the MetLife Archives. The MetLife Archives are still open to the public. These firm records were invaluable for getting a sense of how technology acquisition and application decisions were made, in some cases illuminating internal conflicts. I also used three other general archives. The Herman Hollerith Collection at the Library of Congress in Washington, D.C., contains much of Hollerith's correspondence with insurance firms and other customers during the decades surrounding 1900. Although Prudential Insurance Company does not, unfortunately, have an archive, I found a very extensive and rich set of materials from Edmund Berkeley's own files at the Charles Babbage Institute (CBI) at the University of Minnesota in Minneapolis. These records included the many internal memorandums he wrote to document virtually everything he did and thought about during his years at Prudential. In addition, the Unisys archives at Hagley Museum and Library in Wilmington, Delaware, provided an array of useful materials on Eckert Mauchly Computer Company and its successors regarding the development and marketing of Univac computers, including draft versions of the contract with Prudential.

For the computer era, though not for the tabulating era, interviews and oral histories supplemented these archival sources. I interviewed several individuals involved in insurance computing during those years—primarily people working for insurance firms but also one person who had been an IBM salesman for the insurance market. In addition, I used the transcript of the Univac Conference sponsored by the CBI, the Smithsonian Institution, and Unisys Corporation in 1990 to provide a similar perspective on Univac. As with all retrospective reconstructions, these memories are no doubt partial and distorted by time, but they add details and perspectives otherwise unavailable to the researcher, serving to fill in the picture emerging from other sources.

Trade publications and published proceedings and reports of various life insurance associations also provided rich contemporary treatments of technology adoption and

use. *Best's Insurance Reports—Life/Health* (New York: Alfred M. Best Co.), an annual publication, provided all the data for the charts of Ordinary Renewal Expense Ratios for various firms. Although this ratio is far from a perfect measure, *Best's* reported it every year
for all firms during the period of my study (as well as before and after that period). The
proceedings of the Life Office Management Association (LOMA) and the Insurance Accounting and Statistical Association (IASA), along with the *Transactions of the Actuarial
Society of America* (*TASA*) in the tabulator era and publications of the Society of Actuaries, were rich with the details of individual firm decisions about and experience with various technologies and applications. The LOMA and IASA proceedings for the relevant
period even include transcriptions of the discussions following presentations. Although
*TASA* and publications of the Society of Actuaries are available through many libraries,
the LOMA and IASA proceedings and reports were more difficult to locate. I found some
of them in the insurance company archives I was using and many more at the Insurance
Association Library of Boston. LOMA, IASA, and the Society of Actuaries, all three of
which survive, have back copies of their proceedings, as well.

## Secondary Sources

Abbott, Andrew. *The System of Professions: An Essay on the Division of Expert Labor.* Chi-
cago: University of Chicago Press, 1988.
American Council of Life Insurance. *1992 Life Insurance Fact Book.* Washington, D.C.:
American Council of Life Insurance, 1992.
Arthur, W. Brian. "Competing Technologies, Increasing Returns, and Lock-in by Histor-
ical Events." *Economic Journal* 99 (1989): 116–131.
Austrian, Geoffrey D. *Herman Hollerith: Forgotten Giant of Information Processing.* New
York: Columbia University Press, 1982.
Bashe, Charles J., Lyle R. Johnson, John H. Palmer, and Emerson W. Pugh. *IBM's Early
Computers.* Cambridge: MIT Press, 1986.
Beito, David T. *From Mutual Aid to the Welfare State: Fraternal Societies and Social Services,
1890–1967.* Chapel Hill: University of North Carolina Press, 2000.
Beniger, James R. *The Control Revolution: Technological and Economic Origins of the Infor-
mation Society.* Cambridge: Harvard University Press, 1986.
Bijker, Wiebe E. *Of Bicycles, Bakelites, and Bulbs: Toward a Theory of Sociotechnical Change.*
Cambridge: MIT Press, 1995.
Bijker, Wiebe E., Thomas P. Hughes, and Trevor Pinch, eds. *The Social Construction of Tech-
nological Systems: New Directions in the Sociology and History of Technology.* Cambridge:
MIT Press, 1987.
Bix, Amy Sue. *Inventing Ourselves out of Jobs? America's Debate over Technological Unem-
ployment, 1929–1981.* Baltimore: Johns Hopkins University Press, 2000.
Boczkowski, Pablo J. *Digitizing the News: Innovation in Online Newspapers.* Cambridge: MIT
Press, 2004.
Borg, Kevin. "The 'Chauffeur Problem' in the Early Auto Era: Structuration Theory and
the Users of Technology." *Technology and Culture* 40:4 (1999): 797–832.
Brandes, Stuart D. *American Welfare Capitalism, 1880–1940.* Chicago: University of Chi-
cago Press, 1976.

Brown, Richard D. *Knowledge Is Power: The Diffusion of Information in Early America, 1700–1865*. New York: Oxford University Press, 1989.

Brynjolfsson, Erik "The Productivity Paradox of Information Technology." *Communications of the ACM* 36 (December 1993): 67–77.

Brynjolfsson, Erik, and Loren Hitt. "Beyond the Productivity Paradox." *Communications of the ACM* 41 (August 1998): 49–55.

Buley, R. Carlyle. *The American Life Convention, 1906–1952: A Study in the History of Life Insurance*. 2 vols. New York: Appleton-Century-Crofts, 1953.

———. *The Equitable Life Assurance Society of the United States*. New York: Appleton-Century-Crofts, 1959.

Caminer, David, John Aris, Peter Hermon, and Frank Land. *The World's First Business Computer: User-Driven Innovation*. London: McGraw-Hill, 1996.

Campbell-Kelly, Martin. *From Airline Reservations to Sonic the Hedgehog: A History of the Software Industry*. Cambridge: MIT Press, 2003.

———. *ICL: A Business and Technical History*. Oxford: Oxford University Press, 1989.

———. "Information Technology and Organizational Change in the British Census, 1801–1911." *Information Systems Research* 7:1 (Spring 1996): 22–36.

———. "Large-Scale Data Processing in the Prudential, 1850–1930." *Accounting, Business and Financial History* 2:2 (1992): 117–139.

———. "Punched-Card Machinery." In William Aspray, ed., *Computing before Computers*, 122–155. Ames: Iowa State University Press, 1990.

Campbell-Kelly, Martin, and William Aspray. *Computer: A History of the Information Machine*. New York: Basic Books, 1996.

Carr, William H. A. *From Three Cents a Week: The Story of the Prudential Insurance Company of America*. Englewood Cliffs, N.J.: Prentice-Hall, 1975.

Castells, Manuel. *The Rise of the Network Society*. Vol. 1 of *The Information Age: Economy, Society, and Culture*. Malden, Mass.: Blackwell Publishers, 1996.

Ceruzzi, Paul E. "Crossing the Divide: Architectural Issues and the Emergence of the Stored Program Computer, 1935–1955." *Annals of the History of Computing* 19:1 (1997): 5–12.

———. "Electronics Technology and Computer Science, 1940–1975: A Coevolution." *Annals of the History of Computing* 10:4 (1989): 257–275.

———. *A History of Modern Computing*. Cambridge: MIT Press, 1998.

Chandler, Alfred D., Jr. *Inventing the Electronic Century: The Epic Story of the Consumer Electronics and Computer Industries*. New York: Free Press, 2001.

———. *Scale and Scope: The Dynamics of Industrial Capitalism*. Cambridge: Harvard University Press, Belknap Press, 1990.

———. *The Visible Hand: The Managerial Revolution in American Business*. Cambridge: Harvard University Press, Belknap Press, 1977.

Chandler, Alfred D., Jr., and James W. Cortada, eds. *A Nation Transformed by Information: How Information Has Shaped the United States from Colonial Times to the Present*. New York: Oxford University Press, 2000.

Collier, Abram T. *A Capital Ship, New England Life: A History of America's First Chartered Mutual Life Insurance Company, 1835–1985*. Boston: New England Mutual Life Insurance Co., 1985.

Cortada, James W. *Before the Computer: IBM, NCR, Burroughs and Remington Rand and the Industry They Created, 1865–1956*. Princeton, N.J.: Princeton University Press, 1993.

———. "Commercial Applications of the Digital Computer in American Corporations." *Annals of the History of Computing* 18:2 (1996): 18–29.

———. *The Digital Hand: How Computers Changed the Work of American Manufacturing, Transportation, and Retail Industries.* New York: Oxford University Press, 2004.

David, Paul A. "Understanding the Economics of QWERTY: The Necessity of History." In William N. Parker, ed., *Economic History and the Modern Economist,* 332–337. New York: Blackwell, 1986.

Davis, Malvin E. *Industrial Life Insurance in the United States.* New York: McGraw-Hill, 1944.

Douglas, Susan. *Inventing American Broadcasting, 1899–1922.* Baltimore: Johns Hopkins University Press, 1987.

Dublin, Louis I. *A Family of Thirty Million: The Story of the Metropolitan Life Insurance Company.* New York: Metropolitan Life Insurance Co., 1943.

Eilbirt, Henry. "The Development of Personnel Management in the United States." *Business History Review* 33 (1959): 348–352.

Fischer, Claude S. *America Calling: A Social History of the Telephone to 1940.* Berkeley: University of California Press, 1992.

Fisher, Amy W., and James L. McKenney. "The Development of the ERMA Banking System: Lessons from History." *Annals of the History of Computing* 15:1 (1993): 44–57.

———. "Manufacturing the ERMA Banking System: Lessons from History." *Annals of the History of Computing* 15:4 (1993): 7–26.

Fisher, Franklin M., James W. McKie, and Richard B. Mancke. *IBM and the U.S. Data Processing Industry: An Economic History.* New York: Praeger, 1983.

Flamm, Kenneth. *Creating the Computer: Government, Industry, and High Technology.* Washington, D.C.: Brookings Institution, 1988.

Friedman, Andrew L. *Computer Systems Development: History, Organization and Implementation.* New York: John Wiley and Sons, 1989.

Giddens, Anthony. *The Constitution of Society: Outline of the Theory of Structuration.* Berkeley: University of California Press, 1984.

Gillespie, Richard. *Manufacturing Knowledge: A History of the Hawthorne Experiments.* New York: Cambridge University Press, 1991.

Goldstine, William. *The Computer from Pascal to Von Neumann.* Princeton, N.J.: Princeton University Press, 1972.

Goode, William J. "The Theoretical Limits of Professionalization." In Amitai Etzioni, ed., *The Semi-Professions and Their Organization: Teachers, Nurses, Social Workers,* 266–313. New York: Free Press, 1969.

Gray, George. "The UNIVAC Solid State Computer." *Unisys History Newsletter* 1:2 (1992; rev. 1999): 1–4. At www.cc.gatech.edu/gvu/people/randy.carpenter/folklore/v1n2.html (accessed June 15, 2001).

———. "The UNIVAC III Computer" *Unisys History Newsletter* 2:1 (1993; rev. 1999): 1–4. At www.cc.gatech.edu/gvu/people/randy.carpenter/folklore/v2n1.html (accessed June 15, 2001).

Haigh, Thomas. "The Chromium-Plated Tabulator: Institutionalizing an Electronic Revolution, 1954–1958." *Annals of the History of Computing* 23:4 (2001): 75–104.

———. "Inventing Information Systems: The Systems Men and the Computer, 1950–1968." *Business History Review* 75 (2001): 15–61.

———. "Software in the 1960s as Concept, Service, and Product." *Annals of the History of Computing* 24:1 (2002): 5–13.

Hargadon, Andrew, and Robert Sutton. "Technology Brokering and Innovation in a Product Development Firm." *Administrative Science Quarterly* 42 (1997): 716–749.

Hawley, Ellis W. *The Great War and the Search for a Modern Order: A History of the American People and Their Institutions, 1917–1933.* 2d ed. New York: St. Martin's Press, 1992.

Hooker, Richard. *Aetna Life Insurance Company: Its First Hundred Years.* Hartford, Conn.: Aetna Life Insurance Co., 1956.

Hughes, Thomas P. *Networks of Power: Electrification in Western Society, 1880–1930.* Baltimore: Johns Hopkins University Press, 1983.

Hurd, Cuthbert C. "Computer Development at IBM." Presented at the International Research Conference on the History of Computing, Los Alamos Scientific Laboratory, 1976. Reprinted in N. Metropolis, J. Howlett, and Gian-Carlo Rota, eds., *A History of Computing in the Twentieth Century*, 479–483. New York: Academic Press, 1980.

Iacono, Suzanne, and Robert Kling. "Computerization Movements: The Rise of the Internet and Distant Forms of Work." In J. Yates and John Van Maanen, eds., *IT and Organizational Transformation: History, Rhetoric, and Practice*, 93–136. Thousand Oaks, Calif.: Sage, 2001.

Jacoby, Sanford M. *Employing Bureaucracy: Managers, Unions, and the Transformation of Work in American Industry, 1900–1945.* New York: Columbia University Press, 1985.

James, Marquis. *The Metropolitan Life: A Study in Business Growth.* New York: Viking Press, 1947.

John, Richard. *Spreading the News: The American Postal System from Franklin to Morse.* Cambridge: Harvard University Press, 1995.

Jordahl, Gregory. "Software Explosion: The Choice Is Yours." *Insurance and Technology* 18:8 (August 1993): 28–32.

Keller, Morton. *The Life Insurance Enterprise, 1885–1910: A Study in the Limits of Corporate Power.* Cambridge: Harvard University Press, Belknap Press, 1963.

Kubie, Elmer C. "Reflections of the First Software Company." *Annals of the History of Computing* 16:2 (1994): 65–71.

Kwolek-Folland, Angel. *Engendering Business: Men and Women in the Corporate Office, 1870–1930.* Baltimore: Johns Hopkins University Press, 1994.

Levin, Doron P. *Irreconcilable Differences: Ross Perot versus General Motors.* Boston: Little, Brown, 1989.

Litterer, Joseph. "Alexander Hamilton Church and the Development of Modern Management." *Business History Review* 35 (1961): 211–225.

———. "Systematic Management: Design for Organizational Recoupling in American Manufacturing Firms." *Business History Review* 37 (1963): 369–391.

———. "Systematic Management: The Search for Order and Integration." *Business History Review* 35 (1961): 461–476.

Mackay, Hugh, Chris Carne, Paul Beynon-Davies, and Doug Tudhope. "Reconfiguring the User: Using Rapid Application Development." *Social Studies of Science* 30 (2000): 737–757.

Mackay, Hugh, and Gareth Gillespie. "Extending the Social Shaping of Technology Approach: Ideology and Appropriation." *Social Studies of Science* 22 (1992): 685–716.

MacLeod, Christine. "Strategies for Innovation: The Diffusion of New Technology in Nineteenth Century British Industry." *Economic History Review* 45 (1992): 285–307.

Marvin, Carolyn. *When Old Technologies Were New: Thinking about Electric Communication in the Late Nineteenth Century.* New York: Oxford University Press, 1988.

May, Earl Chapin, and Will Oursler. *The Prudential: A Story of Human Security.* Garden City, N.Y.: Doubleday, 1950.

McKenney, James L. *Waves of Change: Business Evolution through Information Technology.* Cambridge: Harvard Business School Press, 1995.

Moorhead, E. J. *Our Yesterdays: The History of the Actuarial Profession in North America, 1809–1979.* Schaumburg, Ill.: Society of Actuaries, 1989.

Moreau, R. *The Computer Comes of Age: The People, the Hardware, and the Software.* Translated by J. Howlett. 1981 [in French]; Cambridge: MIT Press, 1984.

Norberg, Arthur L. "High Technology Calculation in the Early 20th Century: Punched Card Machinery in Business and Government." *Technology and Culture* 31 (1990): 753–779.

North, Douglass. "Entrepreneurial Policy and Internal Organization in the Large Life Insurance Companies at the Time of the Armstrong Investigation of Life Insurance." *Explorations in Entrepreneurial History* 5:3 (1953): 139–161.

———. "Life Insurance and Investment Banking at the Time of the Armstong Investigation of 1905–1906." *Journal of Economic History* 14 (1954): 209–228.

Nunis, Doyce B., Jr. *Past Is Prologue: A Centennial Profile of Pacific Mutual Life Insurance Company.* Los Angeles: Pacific Mutual, 1968.

O'Brien, Francis J. *The Fabulous Franklin Story: The History of the Franklin Life Insurance Company.* Springfield, Ill.: Franklin Life Insurance Co., 1972.

Orlikowski, W. J. "The Duality of Technology: Rethinking the Concept of Technology in Organizations." *Organization Science* 3 (1992): 398–427.

———. "Using Technology and Constituting Structures: A Practice Lens for Studying Technology in Organizations." *Organization Science* 11 (2000): 404–428.

Oudshoorn, Nelly, and Trevor Pinch. *How Users Matter: The Co-construction of Users and Technology.* Cambridge: MIT Press, 2003.

Pinch, T. "Why You Go to a Piano Store to Buy a Synthesizer: Path Dependence and the Social Construction of Technology." In R. Garud and P. Karnoe, eds., *Path Dependence and Creation,* 381–399. Mahwah, N.J.: Lawrence Erlbaum, 2001.

Porter, Theodore M. *Trust in Numbers: The Pursuit of Objectivity in Science and Public Life.* Princeton, N.J.: Princeton University Press, 1995.

Pugh, Emerson W. *Building IBM: Shaping an Industry and Its Technology.* Cambridge: MIT Press, 1995.

Pugh, Emerson W., Lyle R. Johnson, and John H. Palmer. *IBM's 360 and Early 370 Systems.* Cambridge: MIT Press, 1991.

Rapone, Anita. *The Guardian Life Insurance Company, 1860–1920: A History of a German-American Enterprise.* New York: New York University Press, 1987.

Rousmaniere, John. *The Life and Times of the Equitable.* New York: Equitable Companies, 1995.

Sammet, Jean E. "Brief Summary of the Early History of COBOL." *Annals of the History of Computing* 7:4 (1985): 288–303.

Scranton, Philip. *Endless Novelty: Specialty Production and American Industrialization, 1865–1925.* Princeton, N.J.: Princeton University Press, 1997.

———. "Giddens' Structuration Theory and Research on Technical Change." Draft text for Oxford University Conference on Technological Change, 1993.

Shenhav, Yehouda. "From Chaos to Systems: The Engineering Foundations of Organization Theory, 1879–1932." *Administrative Science Quarterly* 40 (1995): 557–585.

Sobel, Robert. *IBM: Colossus in Transition.* New York: Times Books, 1981.

Stalson, J. Owen, D.C.S. *Marketing Life Insurance: Its History in America.* Cambridge: Harvard University Press, 1942.

Stern, Nancy F. *From ENIAC to UNIVAC: An Appraisal of the Eckert-Mauchly Computers.* Bedford, Mass.: Digital Press, 1981.

Truesdell, Leon E. *The Development of Punch Card Tabulation in the Bureau of the Census: 1890–1940.* Washington, D.C.: U.S. Bureau of the Census, 1965.

Turner, Frederick C., Jr. "From Counterculture to Cyberculture: How Stewart Brand and the *Whole Earth Catalog* Brought Us *Wired* Magazine." Ph.D. diss., University of California, San Diego, 2002.

Usselman, Steven W. "Fostering a Capacity for Compromise: Business, Government, and the Stages of Innovation in American Computing." *Annals of the History of Computing* 18:2 (1996): 30–39.

Van Maanen, John, and Steve R. Barley. "Occupational Communities: Culture and Control in Organizations." *Research in Organizational Behavior* 6 (1984): 287–365.

von Hippel, Eric. *The Sources of Innovation.* New York: Oxford University Press, 1988.

Ward, William Rankin, M.D. *Down the Years: A History of the Mutual Benefit Life Insurance Company, 1845–1932.* Newark, N.J.: Mutual Benefit Life Insurance Company, 1932.

Watson, Thomas J., Jr., and Peter Petrie. *Father, Son, and Co.: My Life at IBM and Beyond.* New York: Bantam Books, 1990.

Wiebe, Robert H. *Search for Order, 1877–1920.* New York: Hill and Wang, 1967.

Wren, Daniel. *The Evolution of Management Thought.* 2d ed. New York: John Wiley and Sons, 1979.

Yates, JoAnne. "Application Software for Insurance in the 1960s and Early 1970s." *Business and Economic History* 24 (1995): 123–134. Proceedings of the 1995 annual meeting of the Business History Conference, Ft. Lauderdale, Florida, March 17–19, 1995.

———. "Business Use of Information and Technology from 1880–1950." In Alfred D. Chandler Jr. and James Cortada, eds., *A Nation Transformed by Information: How Information Has Shaped the United States from Colonial Times to the Present,* 107–135. New York: Oxford University Press, 2000.

———. "Co-evolution of Information Processing Technology and Use: Interaction between the Life Insurance and Tabulating Industries." *Business History Review* 67 (1993): 1–51.

———. *Control Through Communication: The Rise of System in American Management.* Baltimore: Johns Hopkins University Press, 1989.

———. "Early Interactions between the Life Insurance and Computer Industries: The Prudential's Edmund C. Berkeley." *Annals of the History of Computing* 19:3 (1997): 60–73.

———. "Evolving Information Use in Firms, 1850–1920: Ideology and Information Techniques and Technologies." In Lisa Bud-Frierman, ed., *Information Acumen: The Understanding and Use of Knowledge in Modern Business,* 26–50. London: Routledge, 1994.

———. "The Structuring of Early Computer Use in Life Insurance." *Journal of Design History* 12:1 (1999): 5–24.

———. "Using Giddens' Structuration Theory to Inform Business History." *Business and Economic History* 26 (1997): 159–183. Proceedings of the conference "The Future of Business History," Hagley Museum and Library, Wilmington, Delaware, March 1997.

Zelizer, Viviana A. Rotman. *Morals and Markets: The Development of Life Insurance in the United States.* New York: Columbia University Press, 1979.

Zuboff, Shoshona. *In the Age of the Smart Machine: The Future of Work and Power.* New York: Basic Books, 1988.

Zunz, Olivier. *Making America Corporate: 1870–1920.* Chicago: University of Chicago Press, 1990.

# Index

Page numbers in *italics* indicate figures and tables.